THE EMERGING MONOCULTURE

Assimilation and the "Model Minority"

Edited by Eric Mark Kramer

Westport, Connecticut
London

Library of Congress Cataloging-in-Publication Data

The emerging monoculture: assimilation and the "model minority" /
    edited by Eric Mark Kramer.
        p. cm.
Includes bibliographical references and indexes.
ISBN 0–275–97312–3 (alk. paper)
    1. Assimilation (Sociology) 2. Acculturation. 3. Globalization. 4. Urbanization.
5. North and South. 6. East and West. 7. Eurocentrism. 8. Minorities. I. Kramer,
Eric Mark.
HM843.E44   2003
303.48'2—dc21   2002029757

British Library Cataloguing in Publication Data is available.

Library of Congress Catalog Card Number: 2002029757
ISBN: 0–275–97312–3

First published in 2003

Praeger Publishers, 88 Post Road West, Westport, CT 06881
An imprint of Greenwood Publishing Group, Inc.
www.praeger.com

Printed in the United States of America

The paper used in this book complies with the
Permanent Paper Standard issued by the National
Information Standards Organization (Z39.48–1984).

P

I dedicate this book to two people I know and admire for their courage to change society rather than passively "adapt" to it just for personal security and comfort, and who have generously spent many hours teaching me about the true and revolutionary essence of the ongoing American experiment: Professors George Henderson and Melvin Tolson. This is also dedicated to Ada Lois Sipuel Fisher, who sued for her right to attend the University of Oklahoma law school in 1946, a case that went all the way to the U.S. Supreme Court. It is also important to remember the white students, professors, and administrators who supported these people in the face of majority indignation. These three, who were willing to "die to make a difference," as Professor Henderson has conveyed to me, made it possible for women and people of color to attend and teach at the University of Oklahoma.

During hours of conversation with Henderson, he relayed to me many truths, some very personal. With his permission I share a few: In 1967, the Henderson family became the first black family to own a house in Norman, Oklahoma. One of their neighbors at the time asked his minister why God hated him so much that He allowed a black family to move in next door. The family's windows were broken, racial slurs were endured, and Professor Henderson suffered doubt from what he had asked his family to endure by moving to Norman. Today, he is one of the most celebrated faculty members at the University of Oklahoma, having a wall full of awards, including being named a Regent's Professor. His conviction of presence changed the state and the university.

Ms. Fisher later became a member of the board of regents to the university that once denied her admission.

Contents

Acknowledgments

I thank Alexander Jeffrey Kramer for his hours of work helping me compile the bibliography during one of his winter breaks from college. All the authors thank Chasu An for his enormous help with this large effort, including tracking down partial citations in three languages. I very much appreciate Karola's honest feedback on some chapters. Finally I say thank you to Preston Elliot Kramer for keeping my spirits up and bringing me coffee when I was in need.

Introduction: Assimilation and the Model Minority Ideology

Eric Mark Kramer

The point of this book is to bring together experts from a variety of "minority" backgrounds and from around the world to give their learned and unique perspectives on the most pervasive ideology today, which is assimilation on a global scale. The basic premise of this book is that both a developed *country* and a developed *market* are different from a developed *community*. They need not be mutually exclusive, but neither is it assumed that they are necessarily consonant. Increasingly, even the behavioral sciences are reducing all human behavior to simple material exchange, evaluations of human behavior solely in terms of utilitarian "skills," such as "flexibility" and technical expertise. Thus we have the domination of a new morality put forth by bourgeois positivism.

This book presents thirteen original chapters written specifically for this project. Each one offers answers to several questions, including what it means to become a "global citizen" and what it means to be a "model minority" in a global economy. Another issue is whether forced compliance in the name of reducing uncertainty really makes a person happier, more well adjusted, balanced, or evolved. The process of becoming a "mainstream person" involves first being marginalized with the implication that something is inadequate about one's attitude, cognitive competence, and/or behavior. The process of assimilation is manifested as various forms of enforced and/or rewarded acculturation. With the vast human migration from the agrarian world to the urban world that is currently under way, the notion of assimilation has become a global phenomenon. What is occurring is a global shift from village milieu to city lifestyle. This migration is a polycentric and global phenomenon whereby the "promised land" is nowhere in particular; instead it is a way of life and a mindset—an urban lifestyle. This process is far more than a simple change in geography. Moving from the village to the cityscape involves a mutation in worldview and self-identity. Additional issues these authors address involve the persuasive assumptions that lead the world in this direction and what might be lost in the process.

For tens of thousands of years humans organized their lives according to the pacing, obligations, and expectations of the Mesolithic hamlet. From the point of view of globalism, the village is a narrow experience functioning to retard the personal, economic, and intellectual development of its inhabitants. But we ask whether it is accurate to refer to the village lifestyle in such evaluative and impoverished terms. Does not this way of life, which has sustained the species for countless generations, have anything of value to offer the future beyond its very existence and ability to conceive (language)? Today, traditional communities and their ways of living are vanishing overnight. The benevolent claim that wealthy nations should not turn their backs on the rest and leave them poor and ignorant is not an anachronistic attitude but a driving motive in the neo-colonial justification for globalism.

It is argued by many of the authors in this volume that the urbanizing process involves an entirely new set of values, desires, and expectations from what has been known before and still is known today for millions of humans in less developed communities. Beneath the overarching appeal of becoming cosmopolitan is the threat of being left behind, having no competitive edge and, literally, no future.

Many publications couch this faith in a neopositivistic rhetoric, which erroneously conjoins cognitive learning theory with development political economics and evolution theory. The dominant ideology of cultural/economic adaptation, which reaches from global sociocultural and economic restructuring to the level of reorganizing the cognitive architecture, the very way of thinking of individuals (their mindset) presents itself as an inevitable and natural course of progress for the human species. The moral ideology of progress is widely used to justify the universal value of assimilation both within and among nations. A keystone concept in the justification of benevolent assimilationism is the notion of the model minority, which will be assessed in this collection. This is often stated in terms of being "forward looking," "flexible," and "adaptable." The model minority is basically one who willingly struggles to get in line for the operation of being cognitively, emotionally, and behaviorally reorganized, in hopes of being accepted and rewarded by the system.

Unlike many other books (referenced later) that critique globalism in highly abstract terms, such as macroeconomics, geopolitics, or cultural studies, this volume takes a close look at what it is to be a model minority at the level of personal experience.

THE GLOBAL PERSON

At the turn of the twenty-first century there are profound forces working overtly and covertly to create the so-called global village and the transcultural person, or global citizen. In the interest of global efficiencies, cultural main-streaming and convergence are self-accelerating; great efforts are under way to universalize uniform business law, management feedback and control, commu-nications interconnectivity, and so forth, to facilitate cultural and economic ho-mogenization. The Western model of infrastructure, however, is not merely a tool for expansion. It presumes a set of values, expectations, motives, and defi-nitions that are foreign to much of the rest of the world's population. In the process, thousands of linguistic communities and local cultures are becoming extinct. Rising expectations and a sense of inadequacy are proliferating across the globe. The promise of a new global world leads many to the inevitable con-clusion that their own cultures are bastions of ignorance, irrationality, and in-feriority. To move "ahead," one must abandon the ways of one's own culture and one's own personal way of thinking, escape parochial subjectivity, and be-come objective and rational. To be rational and developed, a person should be-come objective in their self-evaluation. But of course a set of criteria (values) is implied in that process of self-criticism. One's parents and grandparents—in-deed all of one's tradition—come to be seen as foolish and immature. Culture itself, insofar as it is embodied and localizable, comes under attack by cosmo-politan transcending truth and beauty. Thus many argue that progress can occur only to the extent that a less developed person abandon his or her tra-ditional self. Rising expectations and the felt need to "grow," "learn," and "evolve" work at the level of individual self-esteem, ambition, ethics, spiritual-ity, and identity.

The overarching concern taken up in this collection is the issue of the shrink-ing variety of meanings, values, expectations, motives, and ways of living. The central and shared theme of all the authors herein is the possibility that what is emerging is a monoculture, a global city. Not only is urbanization around the world increasingly driven by the same dreams and motives and manifesting the same outcomes, but the city metaphor leads to a very different set of evaluative criteria than the village metaphor. The very notion of what is a moral and suc-cessful human being is being universally urbanized. In this volume, the case is made from various perspectives that a global city (rather than a global village culture) is emerging with profoundly different consequences for human be-ings, not just systems. Although there is an overwhelming number of books celebrating the various technical, economic, political, and moral advantages of global connectivity and cosmopolitanism, this collection takes up a different side of this momentous process. We examine the loss of localism, concerns about sovereignty (including that of self-identity and self-definition), and the moral assumption that a single ideal path of progress to the right future is known and is of equal value to all. Six questions guide all the authors. They are:

1. What are "developing peoples" expected to develop into?
2. How may this global process be based on a false set of utopian assumptions?
3. How are persistent and resistant groups viewed by the dominant ideology of pos-itive assimilation?

4. How do resistant peoples endure?

5. What kinds of pressures are coming to bear on resistant peoples to encourage them to change?

6. If identity and meaning depend on difference, then is it not important for us all to protect cultural diversity?

In short, in daily life, what does it mean to be developing, to be normal, abled, fit, an in-group member? Assumptions and conceptual entanglements are explored. For instance, in much literature growth, learning, integration, adaptation, evolution, satisfaction, and progress are confused or used interchangeably without rigorous definition. Much literature harbors a strong ethnocentric bias in favor of ideological positivism in the style expressed by the St. Simonians and neo-Hegelians.

RESEARCH AGENDA

The issue of globalism and diversity spans several academic fields, including sociology, psychology, anthropology, communications, development studies, geography, international studies, and the literature of minorities. What is presented herein is a brief overview of the major themes now drawing enormous attention.

There are many books entirely dedicated to single groups. Examples include: Laotian refugees in the United States (Foot, 1990; Haines, 1988), Lithuanians in Chicago (Van Reenan, 1990), Finns in Minnesota (Jarvenpa, 1992), Chinese in Canada (Tian, 1999), whites in Hawaii (Whittaker, 1986), Senegalese in Italy (Carter, 1997), Soviet children in Israel (Horowitz, 1986), and so forth. There are also many books dedicated to single approaches and levels of analysis, such as adaptation (Ng, 1998), adjustment (Sung, 1987), postcolonialism (Hoogvelt, 1997; Juan, 2000; Narayan & Harding, 2000), resistance (Haig-Brown, 1988; Spring, 2000), accommodation (Jo, 1999; Zia, 2000), preservation (Flinn, 1992), assimilation (Axtell, 1986; Bacon, 1996; Gordon, 1964; Miller, 1984; Silverstein, 1995), the politics of tolerance (Bartolome & Macedo, 2000), multiculturalism (Aquero, 1993; Barnhill, 1999; Lester, 1995; Nieto, 2000), globalizing threats to democratic comportment (Barsamian, 1992; Bowden & Chomsky, 1998; Chomsky, 1979; Cox & Sinclair, 1996; Greider, 1997; Held, 1996; Storper, 1997; Strange, 1996), and international trade and economics (Ambrose, 1997; Dunkley, 2000; Viotti & Kauppi, 1998).

There are many books singly dedicated to specific contexts like immigrant children in schools (Gibson, 1998; Giroux, 1993; Gutek, 1996; Miyares, 1998; Tucker, 1998; Zhou & Bankston, 1998), crossing religious boundaries (Fenton, 1988 Widder, 1999), multicultural counseling (Battle, 1997; Paniagua, 1997; Parker, 1998), constructing gender across cultures (Julia, 1999), Native American experiences (Fenelon, 1998; Kroeber, 1994), cultural extermination (Dia-

mond, 1997; Gheerbrant, 1992; Margolis, 1992; O'Connor, 1998), multicultural
and cross-cultural management (Seelye et al., 1996), and so on.

In this volume we illustrate how many concepts and processes (such as multiculturalism, diversity, assimilation, globalism, aboriginal resistance, and so forth) are interrelated. This collection offers a multiplicity of views on these themes. The following essays offer actual as well as theoretical illustrations of these centralizing processes. Readers will also find a selected bibliography of the most important works about the increasingly global reach of assimilationism and the idea of being a model minority as an ideology promoting the dissolution of diversity and the consequence of self-hatred. We want to show how assimilationism has moved beyond colonial nation-building to a global phenomenon. We illustrate how quite diverse groups, such as the disabled and Ainu in Japan and Native Americans in the United States, are resisting being either defined by dominant interests or being encouraged to integrate and disappear.

In Chapter One, "*Gaiatsu* and Cultural Judo," Eric Mark Kramer draws on the rich literary voices of Meiji and post-Meiji Japan to demonstrate how assimilation and adaptation to Westernization pose a profound—and in many instances excruciating—choice to modernizing nations. The fundamental question is whether an individual or a nation must give up their tradition to modernize; if the answer is yes, then the primary issue becomes what that decision means.

Chapter Two, "The Hidden Justification for Assimilation, Multiculturalism, and the Prospects for Democracy," by John W. Murphy and Luigi Esposito, exposes the primary arguments and philosophical assumptions used to justify assimilationism. If these presuppositions are not understood, changes in governmental policy may not have much impact on how minorities are treated. Specifically, current approaches to social integration are based on a very conservative view of social order. Moreover, this imagery requires that cultural differences be sacrificed to preserve social harmony. Multiculturalists, on the other hand, have abandoned this general approach to sociological theory; thus they have set the stage for cultural differences to be appreciated and embraced. The new social imagery advanced by advocates of multiculturalism allows the proliferation of cultural differences to be viewed as compatible with order. In this regard, multiculturalists support a far-reaching strategy for democratizing culture and order. Murphy and Esposito discuss the consequences for a democratic ideal of authentic alternatives in the face of powerful and singular solutions to personal and social problems. They address the assumption that there is one best order, one rationality that demands implementation as a natural course of progress.

Chapter Three, "Adopting the Caucasian 'Look': Reorganizing the Minority Face," by Masako Isa and Eric Mark Kramer, explores the proposition that ideology is more than skin deep. They explore how the Caucasian phenotype is promoted around the globe as the ideal model of beauty. This chapter considers the process of convergent thinking about what beauty is and its value, specifically in Japan. The chapter also explores the consequence of this hegemonic force by observing that the cosmetic industry (including cosmetic reconstructive surgery) around the globe never promises to make people look more African or Asian but always (so far as this research shows) to look more white European. This dissatisfaction with one's own face as inadequate, often even ugly and/or "primitive," is presented as a manifestation of the attempt to assimilate to a singular image of beauty, an attempt that presupposes a sense of dissatisfaction and even, in some cases, self-hatred.

In Chapter Four, "The Violence of Assimilation and Psychological Well-Being," by Chi-Ah Chun and Jung Min Choi, the central argument is that equality cannot be gained as long as minorities accept and work within the framework of the assimilation perspective. Due to its dualistic philosophy, the assimilation perspective does not allow for egalitarian relations to ensue. The assimilation perspective hinders minorities from understanding properly the nature of oppression. To be sure, the assimilationist perspective is grounded on inherent hierarchy and symbolic violence. Assimilation is a promise built on a dubious foundation that presupposes cultural supremacy and domination. Assimilation is accompanied by the loss of tradition, community, and (possibly most important) self-respect. Obviously, within this framework, a person's well-being is threatened. Indeed, to organize an egalitarian society, the assimilation perspective must be dismantled. Specific research conducted with Asian American women in California regarding their effort to fit into mainstream expectations of beauty by turning to cosmetic surgery is presented in this chapter.

In "The Ainu: A Discourse on Being Japanese," by Masazumi Maruyama, the effort of the Ainu in Japan to survive ethnic and cultural extermination is discussed. Japan is a relatively homogeneous country, but its purity is often overstated by both Japanese and foreign observers of Japan. The Ainu constitute one of the minority groups in Japan, along with Korean Japanese and *Ryuku* people (those in Okinawa). Due to their relatively few numbers, minority groups in Japan have tended to be overlooked both in social reality (e.g., discrimination) and in academic attention. This chapter redresses this oversight of minorities in Japan generally and of the Ainu in particular. Several aspects of the Ainus' struggle to survive will be described to shed light on what it is like to be a minority in general and in Japan in particular. This chapter especially focuses on the interplay between national identity and ethnicity (or diversity) in the modern nation-state system. In doing so, this chapter examines (1) how the identity of the Ainu was created; (2) why the "Japanese" felt the need to incorporate or assimilate the Ainu people into Japan; (3) how the Ainu have struggled against discrimination by the Japanese and to redefine their identity in their own terms; and finally (4) how we should reconceptualize the key concepts of nation, ethnicity, and the relationship between them. Commentary about the value of preserving diversity in postmodern Japan will serve as a conclusion to this chapter.

Chapter Six, "Headache and Heartbreak: The Elusiveness of 'Model Minority' Status Attainment for African Americans," was written by Lonnie Johnson Jr. and Charlton D. McIlwain. In this chapter the authors discuss the model minority ideology, how it was manifested in the past, and how it is currently used in American society to mandate conformity among groups of people who by definition are seen as inferior to the dominant Eurocentric ideal. This ideology promotes self-hatred, the disintegration of individual identity, and the adoption of a new identity prescribed by dominant social forces. The model minority ideal is propagated through kin ideologies of assimilation and cultural adaptation. However, in this pursuit, few if any have managed to cross the finish line. Few black Americans have attained that status in which one's life and social actions are completely satisfactory to dominant white society, providing for a place of acceptability among whites and a state of psychological well-being for minority individuals. This is the case principally because there is no clear model. Those who have begun on this quest find that they are indeed chasing a ghost, a figment of the imagination. This chapter seeks to reveal the elusiveness of model minority status by demonstrating how the model contradicts itself and debunks its own definitional and ideological foundations. Finally, Johnson and McIlwain critique how the ideology of the model minority manifests itself in black culture in the notion of racial authenticity, which dictates whether or not one is really black. It only stands to reason that if dominant society defines the ideal minority, then the reactionary force is for minorities to define the real minority. Essentially, this is another type of ideal. They are the "should be's" of opposing forces attempting to maintain social dominance, whether it be inter- or intraracial dominance. In this bipolar struggle for dominance, to become more ideal is to become less real, and vice versa. Ultimately, definitional attempts toward solidifying racial identity, whether ideal (model minority) or real (racial authenticity), are centered around a game of social dominance and posturing. As such, they are often understood better not by the conceptual logic of definitional issues, but rather by the logic of social survival and dominance.

Chapter Seven, "Being Disabled in Modern Japan: A Minority Perspective," by Miho Iwakuma, presents interviews and observations about the dominant discourse that distorts transparent communication about disability in Japan. Despite the pervasiveness of disability in societies, persons with disabilities (PWDs) remain hidden minorities within most societies, including modern Japan. Communication between "abled" and "disabled" people tends to be awkward and filled with anxiety. Indeed, as with other minorities, stereotypes and prejudices against PWDs feed into this communication distortion between the nondisabled and PWDs. The core of this communication problem stems from the difficulty the disabled have in telling their stories about being disabled. Social etiquette makes the nondisabled feel uncomfortable about discussing the everyday experiences of the disabled. As a result, instead of asking questions directly of PWDs, members of the nondisabled majority rely on minority spokespersons' voices and generate perceptions about minorities from those few highly selective and managed voices. However, these minority spokespersons attain such a position by being the most successfully adapted and presentable according to nondisabled criteria. For PWDs, the most successful level of adaptation refers to the stage when one no longer feels oneself to be disabled. The issue is how one can, without conscious awareness of being disabled, speak about disability experiences on behalf of others with disabilities. Other minority groups experience a similar dilemma. There is a vicious circle of miscommunication between the majority and the minority. The majority learns from the limited voices of appropriate minority spokespersons, who share experiences more with the majority than with other PWDs. The members of the minority feel a need to change who they really are and adapt to the majority to be heard. But for many, such a change is impossible. This chapter discusses this communication dilemma. It also explores the paradoxical role of minority spokesperson by using the example of PWDs. The author is especially interested in the perspectives of PWDs, such as how PWDs perceive themselves through the eyes of the mass media and of the nondisabled. The research presented includes not only an analysis of mass media coverage of PWDs but also autobiographies of PWDs and interview data obtained in Japan.

Chapter Eight, by Philip Lujan and Karola, is titled "Successful Indians: Benevolent Assimilation and Indian Identity." This essay argues that Native Americans (Indians) have been the targets of perhaps the most concerted, lengthy assimilationist push confronting any ethnicity in the history of the United States. Yet relatively few Native Americans seem to have made it as successes in mainstream American terms (i.e., maintaining a prominent, secure, or financially rewarding job and lifestyle). Those who have may experience pressure from both the Indian and non-Indian communities, thus threatening their ability to maintain positive self-images as Indians. Unlike many studies about Indians, this chapter presents research that does not attempt to define "real" Indianness in either legal or cultural terms. Instead, it takes Indianness as an ascribed identity that is simultaneously posited (by Indians and non-Indians alike) as an achievement. Because Indian identity is posited as achieved, as such it is precarious. This situation is one of the major stresses facing successful Indians, though it is by no means the only one. For example, Indians fit into both collectivist and individualist cultural categories, which may bring pressures to bear on successful Indians trying to maintain familial and tribal ties on one hand, and to assert individuality in a conformist mainstream workplace on the other. This chapter explores the tug at identity and other issues confronting successful Indians through extensive theoretical grounding informed by ethnographic interviews. Interviewees were drawn from both reservation and nonreservation populations, from positions both within and without the Indian world.

In Chapter Nine, "Abandoned People in Japan: The First Generation of Koreans in Japan," by Richiko Ikeda, the struggle by Korean Japanese to be accepted into mainstream Japanese society is presented. It has been said that to be successful in Japanese society, Koreans in Japan must either hide their ethnic identity or be naturalized. However, Ikeda presents data that show that to become Japanese legally is not enough to be totally accepted or even to survive in Japan. The assimilation policy the Japanese government has adopted has not diminished discrimination against Koreans; instead, the policy has facilitated it. Koreans in Japan are Others who are created and maintained to make Japanese feel more Japanese. They are a model minority that has been forced to assimilate into the dominant society, but theoretically and practically they cannot assimilate. To integrate properly by the dominant plan, they must remain marginal, for that is their desired function within the larger system of relationships. Thus, to be an ideal minority means for Korean Japanese to be a scapegoat. The model minority ideal in Japan involves assimilating like a robot, not exercising free will, and accepting the normative role they are given, including the dominant expectations that follow. The need for nursing homes for Koreans reveals that older Koreans born and raised in Japan have not adapted to Japanese culture. Younger Koreans display a search for identity, which also proves that they have not assimilated. This chapter describes the present situation of Koreans in Japan and shows how major assimilation/adaptation theories in the social sciences fail to explain the real world of real minorities.

Chapter Ten, "Old and New Worlds," by Algis Mickunas, traces the ways Eastern European immigrants to the United States regard their Old Countries and their new home in terms of utopian imageries and the dystopian disruption of such imageries. The complexity of the issues includes religious, moral, and familial relationships with "outsiders" and the building of ethnic communities. It also involves the preservation of languages. Drawing on several forms of knowledge, Mickunas demonstrates how self-segregating Eastern European communities in the United States suffer from diasporic alienation whereby, despite their dreams, they cannot hang on to the identities they had had in the Old Country while simultaneously being unable to become Americans despite their abilities to thrive economically.

In "Demythologizing the 'Model Minority,'" Eungjun Min traces how the perception of Asian Americans in general has evolved in the United States from that of being a reserved and uncivilized people to the dominant model minority image. In the 1960s, the media promoted the model minority theory through stories laden with statistics (e.g., SAT scores) depicting Asian Americans as a homogeneous and exceptionally accomplished and industrious minority group. Initially, Asian Americans enjoyed the flattering image assigned to them by their white evaluators. They were extolled as a model minority who had overcome racism and had successfully integrated themselves into American society. By the late 1960s, however, a greater ethnic consciousness and political activism among the Asian community created a backlash against this image. Underlying the misinterpreted statistical evidence may be the notion of the superiority of Anglo Saxon values. Often, Asian Americans are said to succeed because of their work ethic and because their values are compatible with

Anglo Saxon values. Thus, the model minority theory ultimately serves a purpose. This theory bolsters the much-valued American dream. At a time when minority groups conducted civil unrest and mass political protests, the portrayal of Asian Americans as a successful minority served a need. The myth defended and promoted the very foundations of economic stability more than democracy and an image of egalitarianism not only domestically but internationally.

Ultimately though, as is demonstrated, the prevalence of the model minority theory would later have an immense impact on society. Widespread acceptance of the model minority success story hints at discrimination, an excuse not to undertake the difficult task of reforming U.S. schools to help students understand and value a multicultural society, which the United States has become. The attitude that there is no need to worry about Asian American children because they are doing better than everyone else is divisive and destructive. The reality is that recent immigrants and refugees from Southeast Asia, China, the Philippines, and the Pacific Islands require the same special attention that any member of a cultural minority in America requires. This essay examines: (1) the history of mythologizing Asian Americans as model minorities, (2) various models of the ideal minority, and (3) underlying ideologies of model minority discourses and advocacy. It also suggests an alternative theoretical framework for understanding Asian Americans.

"Asian Indians and the Model Minority Narrative: A Neocolonial System," by Archana J. Bhatt, explores questions of race, equality, and civil rights generally and the issue of Asian Indian attempts to fit into America specifically. Though it has been about three decades since the Civil Rights Act was passed, the underlying and lasting effects of that era and that particular piece of legislation resound throughout today's race politics. One particular element of the civil rights era that continues to attract attention is the notion of minority status, specifically model minority status as a presumed set of criteria for identifying nonwhite yet good citizens. Originally used to identify African Americans who conformed to the dominant social system, *model minority* is a phrase used to identify groups of minorities who live according to the current social guidelines. Currently, most Asian immigrants tend to fall in this category. Model minority is a classic colonial setup in that a few are utilized to control the many. By identifying Asian Americans as model minorities, the conservative right wing manages to create a rift between minority groups within the United States. In a parallel ideological construct to the house slave/field slave scenario, Asian Americans are encouraged to see their lot as one of privileged status, in comparison to the lot of other people of color. They also see themselves as better than their field counterparts. Finally, they consider their status to be a direct result of their skills, their willingness to work, and their ability to perform. They believe that their counterparts lack something that keeps them in the fields. In actuality, the status of house slave versus field slave is solely based on the whims of the master (in this case, the dominant culture/political powers that be). The status of model minority doesn't sit completely well with all Asian Americans. This chapter focuses on Asian Indian Americans, positing that one reason the Indian American community is so susceptible to the beguilements of the model minority status is because of the status these immigrants held in India. Most Indians in the United States are upper-class, upper-caste Indians who see themselves as socially equal to the members of the dominant culture. Their status in India, although not transferable to the United States, is what defines them, and they use it as a reference point for their place in the race politics of the United States. Indian Americans see themselves as members of higher society in India and thus, by correlation, as members of the high society in the United States. What is lost in the translation is the nonrefutable foreignness of Asian Americans. Unlike African Americans and Hispanic Americans, Asian Americans hold a permanent status of foreigner, regardless of length of stay in the United States. Indian Americans also do not recognize that by taking the status offered them by the dominant culture, they accept their place within the power structure, and that place is automatically subservient to those in power. This chapter examines the concept of model minority specifically within the Asian Indian American community. The chapter reviews the historical elements of Asian immigration and the history of the phrase *model minority*. An argument is made regarding the effectiveness and impact of such a system in contemporary U.S. race politics.

Chapter Thirteen, "A World of Cookie-Cutter Faces," by Rachael Rainwater-McClure, Weslynn Reed, and Eric Mark Kramer, explores global trends in cosmetic surgery as empirical evidence of the extreme efforts many thousands of individuals go to in an effort to fit into the emerging aesthetic system. This chapter critiques adaptation ideology and its impact on individuals trying desperately to conform to expectations of what counts as beautiful. It also compares and contrasts fusion theory with cultural adaptation theory, holding each up to the empirical fact of widespread cosmetic surgery as a response to a global sense of forced compliance.

Chapter Fourteen, "Cosmopoly: Occidentalism and the New World Order," by Eric Mark Kramer, presents a critique of various intellectual justifications for absolute cultural conformity on a global scale from Hegel to Spencer and beyond. This chapter empirically challenges the secure and pleasant-sounding ideology of the global village and the claim that the world is a richer and happier place because of globalism.

Chapter 1

Gaiatsu and Cultural Judo

Eric Mark Kramer

The train came out of the long tunnel into the snow country.
—Yasunari Kawabata

PRESCRIPT

Nothing is more dramatic than running out of time and uncertainty. The fear of drama can be finally overcome by embracing the permanence of death bringing to an end the disease of life. However, the attempt to eliminate all risk has its own risks.

PRESSURE FROM OUTSIDE

Because of Japan's rich literary legacy, its relationship with the West is wonderfully documented from the point of view of the culturally, economically, and (one must not forget) militarily colonized. It is an excellent case study of the confusion and suffering that colonization has on the colonized.[1]

The Japanese term *gaiatsu* means "outside pressure." It was most commonly used in the late 1980s to refer to coercion from powers outside of Japan, usually the United States. Such coercion typically referred to colonial practices, such as encouraging Japan to open domestic markets to global competition and to modify regulation on financial institutions so that they would come into line with Western practices. This is what William Greider (1997) derides as so-called harmonization. This process is what others legitimize in pseudo-scientific and inoculating rhetoric as a natural evolutionary tendency toward equilibrium manifested as wise conformity to a dominating culture.

Currently, there is a tension the world over between various forms of sovereignty (national, regional, and of the self) and global homogenization (Kramer, 1992; 1997; also see Chapter Fourteen in this volume). But *gaiatsu* is neither a new term nor a new process. Nor is it unique to Japan. According to Jared Diamond (1993) and Eric Kramer (1992), the trend toward global homogenization and cultural extinction began in massive earnest with Columbus's voyage to the New World in 1492.

In this chapter, I compare and contrast what Edmund Husserl (1913/1980) calls the natural attitude as it is evinced in Japan and the United States as projected through government and business interests. I also wish to address the quality of the contact between the two cultures, which may be characterized as *gaiatsu*, at least from the Japanese point of view or as inevitable modernization from the Western perspective. I have chosen as data the reflections of Japan's greatest writers, including Soseki, Tanizaki, Futabatei, Kawabata, and others. As makers of culture, they were and are especially cognizant of cultural pressures coming to bear from imported (nonindigenous) value systems, expectations, imaginations, and lifestyles (Smith, 1997).

According to Husserl, a natural attitude is an untested metaphysical thesis that is so completely presupposed that to the person who lives the attitude it remains fundamentally invisible and, as such, practically untestable. In short, it is not yet thematized as a contingency, as being merely hypothetical. The natural attitude is the basic sense of reality (the nature of the world), a prejudice so deeply ingrained that it rarely occurs to one to question its veracity and validity. It is the way things are.

So, then, how do we propose to talk about the hypothetical natural attitude, to liberate ourselves from dogmatic slumbers? The best and perhaps only way is through the difference of antithetical propositions. There are two ways to be exposed to difference, and the first is very easy: Leave one's life-world. When we enter a very foreign milieu, what is real, true, predictable, and innocuous becomes foregrounded for us. The second way is more difficult. To this end one must proceed in a sort of two-step fashion. The first step involves reflexively scrutinizing two or more different systems, for instance the Euro-American and Japanese senses of what is naturally given; uncritically presupposed by each. The second step—which is more basic and leads to the first way of liberation from dogma—is to compare two or more respective beliefs about knowledge, including artistic practice, for in the attempt to render reality capacities, perspectives, illuminations, and limitations are most clearly revealed. Each culture offers a unique solution to living, a style of living that embodies prejudices and presumptions about what is possible and impossible, good and bad, practical and impractical, sacred and profane.

One does not realize that one is Japanese ever so much as when one leaves Japan or finds oneself confronted with the foreign. Just as a sense like touch is not noticed until it is violated or disappears, so, too, identity is most salient when it is confronted, perhaps threatened, by difference.

But what happens if the foreign becomes ubiquitous in one's home world? What happens when Japanese find themselves, as Kenzaburo Oe put it, "up to our necks in Western culture" (as quoted in Smith, 1997, p. 234)? Can one be so overwhelmed as to lose one's indigenous identity and become the Other (meaning to come to see the world through the eyes of the Other such that one's own body and culture appear foreign, quaint, silly, or obsolete)? One can, but not entirely. This is because identity conversion can never be complete. Thus, a more or less painful (sometimes even uncannily pleasant) dissonance always manifests and this is the presence of the "Other within" (Smith, 1997). Under such conditions, the foreign may become exalted and mystically exotic, while the mundane life-world becomes drab by comparison. This is how marketing works—by hyping the always new and improved that renders the old, old as such, embarrassingly obsolete, and boring. Progress demands dissatisfaction with and the abandonment of tradition. For instance, it is no accident that the great Japanese author Jun'ichiro Tanizaki has been regarded as a tourist in his own country.

In his romantic youth, Tanizaki rejected all things Japanese and became a Jazz Age dandy. He moved to the heart of the *giajin* community at the Bluff in Yokohama, took Western-style dancing lessons, studied English, and in 1923 proclaimed the devastating earthquake marvelous because it afforded an opportunity to rebuild the capital in the image of great Western cities with: "Orderly thoroughfares, shiny new paved streets, a flood of cars, blocks of flats rising floor on floor, level on level in geometric beauty ... And the excitement at night of a great city, a city with all the amusements of Paris or New York" (quoted in Keene, 1984, pp. 750–751). Like so many other artists and intellectuals, Tanizaki was intoxicated with the initial wave of modernization, imagining a new Japan "where champagne glasses floated like jellyfish among the evening dresses, tailcoats, and tuxedos" (quoted in Keene, 1984, p. 750). But a strong hangover followed the libation of Western spirits. Tanizaki discovered that he could not and probably did not really want to become Western. More sober, he moved to the ancient capital, Kyoto, and penned his self-satire *A Fool's Love* (which was serialized in the mid-1920s and was also translated as *Naomi*) wherein a young femme fatale, who even looks half-Caucasian and half-Japanese, is totally immersed in Western culture and never escapes the chronic inferiority complex of those who accept the mantle of being an "under- and undeveloped" person/society—the buffoonery of imitation.

The appeal of being half-and-half marks the impact of cultural hegemony on developing countries. But the half-and-half look holds much less allure, let alone being elevated to a beauty ideal, in the pure centers of power. Although Japan has been widely criticized for being a homogenous, racist society (during the 1960s and 1970s especially), admiration for the half-Caucasian phenotype has been a beauty icon in Japan, at least since World War II. This is demonstrated by the use of mixed-race models by cosmetics giants, such as Shiseido (see Chapter Three). But this esteem for mixed-race beauty was not shared in the origins of colonial power where the All-American cover girls (Jennifer O'Neill, Candice Bergen, Lauren Hutton, Margaux Hemingway), and the mod British look (Twiggy, Jean Shrimpton, and Veruschka) reigned supreme, with Twiggy being the first mass-merchandised model in history. Tanizaki's character, who looks half-and-half, is not a fusion of cultures but a metaphor for the stress between modernization and tradition.

Tanizaki tore himself away from the hypnotizing vision of modernity and the fawning posture of what Nietzsche called the frog's perspective on the world he had assumed, meaning always looking up in adoration. Following his move to Kyoto, in 1928–29 Tanizaki published the autobiographical novel *Some Prefer Nettles* (1995 English), in which the main character (reminiscent of the real-life first minister of education in Japan, Arinori Mori, whose confusion can now be seen as a synecdoche to the entire post-Meiji era) is faced with a profound choice between East and West, tradition and the abandonment thereof. Like Mori, the main character in *Some Prefer Nettles* finally chooses the traditional Japanese way, divorcing his stylishly modern wife and coming to settle with "traditional ease" in an old Kyoto house.

THE PARADOXES OF ASSIMILATION

The expressions of artists reveal their states of mind. They are the canaries in the coal mines of cultural change. Many Japanese artists even today, like Yoshiro Kato, raise the issue of what W. E. B. Du Bois in another context called the malady of double consciousness (Du Bois, 1903/1995). Double consciousness involves the internalization of the Other's point of view, which, according to assimilationists, is exactly what the model minority is supposed to do. But original assimilationists like Herbert Spencer did not presume that such self-disintegration would make a person happy, just more functionally fit within the dominant economy.

Some, like William Gudykunst and Yun Young Kim (1997) equate adaptive conformity with survival so that nonconformists are presumably doomed, their existence anathema to life (especially of the system to which functionalists always give priority) (p. 352). One of their paradoxes is this: These writers argue a progressive ideology but also argue that only adaptation to an already existent system can lead to survival. How, then, does system ever change? This presumption is clearly not supported by observations of natural systems. Their problem seems to derive from a Cartesian bias whereby they see the components of the system as somehow different from the system. It is an antiquated metaphysic similar to form and content distinction, a problem rendered irrelevant in biology and other fields that have solved the part-to-whole problem through the concept of symbiosis.

Immigrants are colonizers who survive in part by changing the system into which they move. The idea that a person must "unlearn" or "deculturize" themselves flies in the face of massive evidence of diaspora experienced all over the highly mobile modern world. People do not unlearn or forget even as they succeed in an adopted home, for when they return to their original home their (sometimes painful) nostalgia is rooted in memories of things as they once were but no longer are.

Furthermore, Gudykunst and Kim (1997) naively assume that simply because one internalizes the values of the dominant group and mimics their behavior patterns, even self-consciously agreeing with the dominant values, such a person will integrate into the holistic system, will become a member of the in-group. Belonging, however, is not solely an individual psychological process or simple aping. Instead it is a sociological process. It is a symbiotic relationship between a person and others, including the environment as a whole. It is not within the sole control of the individual to say whether he or she has been accepted. Rather, it is up to the group to make that happen. An outsider can actually be rejected as a weirdo for acting and talking too much like the locals. Hence the designation *henna gaijin*, applied to strange strangers who do not seem to realize that they are not and cannot become Japanese. This sort of boundary maintenance is not unique to Japan (Kramer, 1997, 2000b).

Confusing Directions: Conforming Means Not to Conform

The logic of those who suggest aping behavior leads to a quagmire. The most harmonious path to take under such conditions is to accept the role the dominant group expects one to play. But if that role includes the expectation that the newcomer *will* not and *should* not act like locals, then conforming to group expectations means to *not* act like locals. If the dominant culture presumes that one can never become an in-group member, then conformity means not becoming an in-group member. Under such conditions, the more one conforms to the host society's expectations of sojourners, the more unlikely it is that the sojourner can ever belong. Their foreignness can never be forgotten. Thus, conforming to the mainstream's expectations prevents one from gaining inclusion. If group expectations present a status for the sojourner that is dehumanizing, then either resistance is inevitable or self-esteem is utterly destroyed.

To the extent that a minority person successfully internalizes the worldview (culture, including values, motives, and expectations) of the dominant group, that person comes to see him- or herself through the dominant group's eyes. It is a sort of split personality that can lead one, in extreme cases, to hate oneself and one's own traditional values, expectations, and ancestral ways and to fall under the seduction of foreign images and promises. In the case of powerful colonization, such a person can even come to see herself as foreign within her own land, which is the very definition of diaspora. There are many who, if they wake up (as Nietzsche would put it), may come to realize that they are suffering from diaspora because they have rejected their home culture (or it has rejected them) as inadequate to the point where they can never go home, and yet they are deluded into thinking that the locals where they live accept them as "one of us" simply on the basis of economic functionality. International immigrants often survive on the sense of the exotic in their adopted home. At the same time they fail to stay in touch with their old home, which they have either rejected or which is changing in their absence. They have failed to adapt to anywhere.

Some writers strain to rationalize such a plight by claiming that this is good, that such a state manifests "evolution" to "intercultural personhood," which is also called being a "universal person" with a "transcultural identity" (Gudykunst & Kim, 1997, p. 364). Such a meta-identity is defined as "mature," as manifesting the successful escape from the demonic "hidden forces" of culture, leaving behind the "parochialism of culture" altogether (Gudykunst & Kim, 1997, pp. 355–369; Kim, 2000). Following Adler (1987), Gudykunst and Kim refer to the experience of stress consequent of encountering cultural difference as a "disease," to be cured by adaptive development (the elimination of difference through assimilation). Such a decultured universal person will not only escape being maladjusted but "rise above the hidden forces of culture" and "overcome cultural parochialism" by "approaching the limit of many cultures and ultimately of humanity itself" (Gudykunst & Kim, 1997, p. 366).

Confused Advice

Their confusion is self-evident. On one hand, Gudykunst and Kim claim that becoming one with a culture is the goal of adaptation, thus rendering "well adjusted," "balanced" people, while on the other hand they claim that the ultimate goal is to become an absurdity—a totally deculturized human being (Gudykunst & Kim, 1997). These are two completely irreconcilable goals. On one hand, the advice is to sink as deep into a culture as possible and conform behaviorally, cognitively, and affectively; on the other hand, the advice is to abandon the notion of culture altogether in the attempt to achieve "meta-identity." If we take the latter claim seriously, that escaping culture is the goal of evolution, then what they are promoting is a transcendental global identity beyond viewpoints, which (according to all serious literatures on learning) would mean the elimination of mind and knowledge because all knowing involves a perspective (Nietzsche, 1882/1974; Gadamer, 1960/1993). This is what they are promoting.

Ultimately, Gudykunst and Kim (1997) advocate a dream of escaping the disease of culture (p. 360), with all of its "emotional defilements" by way of "psychic evolution" (p. 365) to achieve total "deculturation" (which means erasing or "unlearning" one's self-identity; p. 360). Gudykunst and Kim claim that only insofar as one unlearns one's self can one achieve the salvation of becoming "transcultural." This is a very old mysticism dressed up in pseudo-scientific terminology. It is a rehash of the ancient mystical dream of escaping the contingent world of subjects, the wheel of life, and achieving eternal and total equilibrium (death), becoming disembodied by "rising above" the contingencies of locale to a "higher level of cognitive complexity" (p. 364), which presumably correlates with greater communication competence. Gudykunst and Kim (1997) note that an individual who has evolved to the "mature," "adjusted," and "balanced" status of "intercultural personhood" is a person characterized by being able to communicate effectively and who manifests "individual traits within the communicator" such as unusual stability, a strong central organization based on cultural universals and "marked telepathic sensitivity" (p. 254). This, of course, begs several questions, including who picks the values, motives, and expectations that are to be elevated to absolute "universal" status.

The dream of escaping the here and now and rising through stages of evolution to a sort of astral realm of pure "good," "truth," and "beauty" (p. 366) that transcends the parochialism of any and all earthly cultures is an expression of neo-Hegelian idealism mixed with Spencerian social Darwinism (Kramer, 2000b). If the solution to problems in intercultural interaction is to simply eliminate cultural differences by eliminating culture as a salient dimension of life, then the solution to inefficient communication is to simply stop trying and instead transcend all differences that form the content of messages. Insofar as this disembodied meta-identity is evident among cosmopolitans today, they resemble what Pico Iyer (2000) calls homeless "global souls." They have no sense of place, no allegiance or loyalty, no obligations that come with group membership, and no identity. They are the fruition of extreme wealth and egocentrism: monads, but not exactly, for they are parasitic on the communities they live within but do not reciprocate. They are hermetic expressions of postmodern independence. They are infinitely narrow, obsessed with what Foucault (1981/1988) called the care and feeding of the self. But this is a care unlike that found in ancient Greece. Rather it is what Foucault calls "the California cult of self," by which hypertrophic egocentrism is manifested as an avoidance of all group obligations and emotional commitment (or the sin of "attachment," as Gudykunst and Kim call it).[2] Such self-segregation is achieved by a monkish lifestyle, which renders individuals out of touch with that which they claim to understand and explain. It is like claiming to be a child psychologist who has never had extended exposure to children.

What emerges is the opposite of what is promised about becoming a global citizen who communicates effectively with all whom he or she encounters. The current strain of assimilationism advises the impossible—that one lose one's mind, which is precisely Gudykunst and Kim's advice. This is ironic because their advice is simply a replay of Arthur Schopenhauer's position, a position that Nietzsche chided him for more than a century ago: the desire to make a "Buddhism for Europeans," thus promoting having no mind. What emerges from such advice is an intensely narrow, self-reinforcing worldview. So long as the global soul has adequate means to make life convenient and so long as he or she does not have any "defiling attachments" and obligations like children (or even a spouse, thus the monkish lifestyle), then the global soul can exist as such. But obligations, which the vast majority of human beings in the actual world experience, force adults to get involved in their local culture and community. Being obligated is identical, for example, with parenting, with socializing children. This is why it takes several years to raise human offspring.

The hypothetical transcultural or meta-identified global souls can survive on the surface of the life-world at a conceptual level because they have no adult responsibilities. They simply take for granted all those who raised them and make life around them convenient without reciprocity to the community. Without deep, compelling attachments, which preempt their obsession with total personal control, they are little more than tourists. They can dedicate all their efforts to themselves alone. The dream of total adaptation means not adapting to any culture but abandoning all cultural dimensions of life; at a minimum, it is bizarre advice. The meta-identity is utterly abstract. It is reductionism to functionality, but this is not the same as integration as an in-group member, for the in-group also includes the dysfunctional and those not seen as a function at all.

The motive to reduce life to a fetish and thereby avoid all emotional attachments results in the robot, which has no care for others or community-place (something other than physical convenience and beauty). It is identical with its function, defined by work implementation. This makes sense, because the model minority, the most malleable of individuals, is presumed to present no alter ego, no emotional needs, no disagreements—only silent, efficient, uncontentious labor. But for the assimilationists themselves, they do not conform but demand that their needs and way of doing things be the center toward which model minorities gravitate. *Effective communication* and *functional fit* mean that all accommodation and change are supposed to come from the model minority. Actual people live far more complex lives. They have multiple responsibilities and obligations, not just those associated with their personal careers. The assimilationists' ideal, their plan for escaping the pain of being alive, has never existed because forced (and sometimes even voluntary) assimilation involves its own problems. Without a cultured self, there could be no communication and also no perspective and therefore no knowledge base that would enable functional fit.

Double consciousness is a much more accurate description of the case than self-contradicting notions of adaptation leading to disembodied being in the pathetic attempt to escape all striving, attachment, caring, community, and life (Kramer, 2000a; Nietzsche, 1886/1972). The promise of escapist liberation is nothing more than a rehash of the contempt the great religions hold for the subject, the body, this world of contingencies, diversities, and culture. Culture falls opposite nature. To the positivist, culture is the realm of subjective nonsense while nature harbors objective universal truths; thus the desire to escape culture as a solution to intercultural communication. It is as Nietzsche (1886/1972) noted a "total collapse of the will," which seeks only to escape the "wheel of life" once and for all behind the cloister's walls, the *caput mortum* of existence, the celebration of death made possible by a "positive" weariness of living—the total failure to adapt.

SCIENCE FICTION AND DARWIN

It is important to recall just what *adaptation* means. It is not the same thing as learning through self-conscious self-modification in the service of a perceived future need, a mistaken version of evolution as learning presumed by some cognitivists and the theory of intercultural adaptation (Kramer, 2000a). Unless one believes in creationism or some other form of intelligent design hypothesis, evolution is random. Learning, however, is very often willfully directed and goal oriented. I want to learn how to fix my car, and so I set out to take a class in automotive repair. But evolution, so far as we know, has no final goal. For instance, if an insecticide is dumped on a swamp it may kill 99.9 percent of the mosquitoes there. One-tenth of 1 percent of the mosquitoes live, however, not because they change or adjust to the insecticide but because they were already resistant to it before ever encountering it. The accidentally resistant mosquitoes endure to reproduce and repopulate the swamp with resistant offspring. They do not mimic the majority population, nor do they consciously modify themselves to survive. Such an ability would require foresight, and it would also require operating on oneself to modify one's own genetic code, which is learning and proactive engineering to outrun the calamity. So far as we know, only humans can do this, and only humans go beyond adapting to the environment as given to proactively adapting it to their desires. Evolution and adaptation are reactionary postures with the exception of mutation, which is strictly blind trial and error. As for mutation, it, too, is a matter of pure accident, unless of course one believes in supernatural guidance, Hegel's invisible hand of the Absolute Logic of the system. Mutation involves random changes in genetic makeup, a small number of which prove actually survivable, not as coherent and consistent articulations of virtual logic but by means of implementing dependent testing.

Charles Darwin never postulated that evolution was going anywhere (he was not a positivistic mystic who believed in eschatological master plans), nor did he claim that evolution involved post facto adjusting to anything. There is no divine watchmaker with a preestablished flowchart of evolutionary niches. This misconception is what Kramer (2000b) calls nichism, and it involves politicizing Darwin's ideas, distorting them into a semi-mystical ideology of legitimation for forced compliance gaining and social conformity—a revival of nineteenth-century Spencerianism. It is a political rhetoric that attempts to naturalize and universalize a contingent political agenda.

COMMUNICATION AND RELATIVE IDENTITY

Under the condition of double consciousness, one can even come to hate one's own phenotype, as evinced by Tanizaki in his novel *In Praise of Shadows* where he describes how "the skin of Westerners, even those of a darker complexion, [has] a limpid glow. Thus it is that when one of us goes among a group of Westerners it is like a grimy stain on a sheet of white paper" (Tanizaki, 1933–34/1988, p. 31). When it is realized that becoming identical to the Other (adapting as Gudykunst and Kim use the word) is impossible, backlash often occurs. Here is where the real threat of violence and mental instability arise.

Identity is dependent on difference, which comes from context. Without difference, there is no identity. Both fold into one. As long as difference persists, then the nature of the difference affects the sense of identity.

Thus, Japan seems advanced and sophisticated when compared with underdeveloped societies. But when compared to a society perceived to be superior—as Western Europe and the United States were thought to be by many Japanese after the Meiji Restoration—then the sense of self-identity may not be so positive. Identity, as hermeneutics demonstrates, is an always shifting relational phenomenon realized through language and action, through what Mikhail Bakhtin (1975/1981) calls dialogue, and J. L. Austin (1961/1975) calls elocutionary force (see also Moore, 1959 and Wittgenstein, 1953/2002). As R. Buckminster Fuller (1970) put it, "I seem to be a verb" (also his book title).

For Bakhtin, dialogism is the epistemological mode of a world dominated by heteroglossia. Like Husserl, Bakhtin insists that everything means, is understood, as a part of a greater whole and that there is a constant interaction between meanings, all of which have the potential of conditioning other meanings. Not unlike Heidegger's (1927/1962) notion of the linguisticality of *Dasein* and Ferdinand de Saussure's (1916/1959) concept of language system, Bakhtin also argues that human being-in-the-world is essentially structured dialogically largely because meaning is mandated by the preexistence of the language-world relative to any of its current inhabitants. We are born into a linguistic community, and by communication (verbal and nonverbal), community and membership identity exists. Heteroglossia, or how one meaning will affect another, is determined only at the moment of contact.[3]

For Bakhtin, "A word, discourse, language or culture undergoes 'dialogization' when it becomes relativized, de-privileged, aware of competing definitions for the same things" (1975/1981, p. 427). Thus, undialogized reality is authoritatively blind, absolutely prejudiced. Comparison enables us to know the Other and also ourselves.[4] But how the comparison proceeds is always already perspectival. As a youth, Tanizaki saw the world differently than he did as a more mature person.

Once we are dialogized, put into discourse with an Other and so made relative, then who and what we are becomes both revealed and concealed. The concealment leads to the mode of being we shall call the search. It is an irony that at the moment of contact with an Other, which enables us to speak of "I," at that same instant the sense of "I" becomes as much problematic as clarified for it calls into question our response. Because the Cartesian duality has come to be seen as an obsolete metaphysic, the boundary between my private essence and my public deeds is erased. I am what I do and what I do with what is done to me. Action and reaction become indeterminate. How I talk about the world may very well reveal more about me than the world I purport to describe. How I see the world is as much a reflection of my perspective as what it is I am looking at. Indeed, the difference between the two in principle cannot be distinguished.

One can claim that my point of view yields a distorted version of reality only if one has what Nietzsche (1886/1972) calls a disembodied and disinterested immaculate perception of the *ding an sich* (the thing in itself). Other than the purported existence of omniscient divinity, so far as is known, only humans have knowledge of the world; insofar as it is knowable the world is knowable only as a perspective. Salience is integral to perception. Even a computer, insofar as it "thinks," already interprets (has a limited perspective), for thinking is a habit of grammar and experience, an activity, and every activity pertains to the one who acts (see Nietzsche, 1886/1972, part One, section seventeen). Perspectives are knowable as such only through communication with other perspectives. In the absence of any divine meta-criteria, no one perspective can be privileged absolutely. Thus, the world is dialogized, relativized, bringing about both the possibility and the crisis of identity.

DOUBLE CONSCIOUSNESS JAPANESE-STYLE: SELF-HATRED AND "ADAPTATION"

The sense of self that emerges through contact is largely dependent on the nature of the relationship with the Other. Joseph Campbell (1988) has noted the universalism of ethnocentrism. It is common for various indigenous groups to have a word in their language with which they denote themselves, and the word typically translates between languages as simply "the people." *All* other humans are typically accorded a status that is more like that of a subhuman species or as distorted humans.

This basic prejudice about the species-self is just as evident among European groups as it is elsewhere. In fact, it is arguable that such self-arrogance is most powerful among Europeans, but this would be incorrect. No such comparative measure is possible. All people tend to be very proud and prejudiced, and even though Western economic, military, and technological supremacy may seem self-evident in comparison to most other groups, this does not mean that they see the West as superior, for many judge on criteria other than material prowess, such as moral qualities. Nevertheless, the spread of Western European civilization has been most successful in terms of cultural imperialism. Thus, it should not be surprising that when Herbert Spencer taught Arinori Mori billiards at the Athenaeum Club in London, he also convinced Mori that according to his neo-Hegelian/Darwinian beliefs, the white European (especially the Englishman) was the most successful and therefore superior human among lesser "humans."

Mori was eager to improve Japan's lot in the great and positive evolutionary hierarchy. It is little wonder that Japan rushed to copy Western-style colonialism, with dire consequences for its Asian neighbors. Mori, like most modern-thinking Japanese at the time, embraced Westernization with gusto. On his return to Washington, D.C., from Japan some years later, Mori (along with Yukichi Fukuzawa) even went so far as to organize the famed Meiji Six Society, which loosely echoed the purpose of the Athenaeum Club. Like Spencer, Mori paradoxically came to equate civilization with the so-called natural forces espoused by social Darwinism. Following Spencer's logic, Mori advised young Japanese men studying in the United States to take American wives, which he himself did, to improve the gene pool of Japan, and also to abandon *nihongo* (our meager language) in favor of English.

Then, as is well known, the other side of Mori's double consciousness emerged with vehement reaction, a process that has been played out again and again by Japanese artists and intellectuals, and perhaps still is by the typical Japanese cosmopolitan today. He divorced and remarried in Japanese style and propagated a fervent form of nationalism, promoting the teaching of *kokutai* (the national essence) in the schools. Ironically, he would be assassinated by an ultra-nationalist, a fallen samurai like himself, for allegedly not following proper protocol during a visit to a sacred shrine at Ise and for generally betraying *kokutai*, including abandoning the teaching of Confucian ethics in the schools and Shinto as the official religion.

Although we may see this as a bygone problem, today writers like Gudykunst and Kim offer academic justification for willful "self-disintegration" and "deculturation" as a pragmatic solution to inefficient difference (Gudykunst & Kim, 1997, pp. 360–62). The inefficiency comes in the form of "disequilibrium" with the global system. In fact, they claim that the disintegration of the self will go far beyond improved communication between groups to nothing short of "psychic evolution" in an "upward-forward [dialectical] progression accomplishing an increased level of functional fitness (greater adaptation) and psychological health" (Gudykunst & Kim, 1997, p. 363). Development is teleologically and positivistically evolutionary. Conformity is the path to evolutionary progress, happiness, and sanity. Of course, positivistic thinking—a culture-specific ideology—proclaims itself to be the very tip of human evolution. This is typical ethnocentrism.

Here we have something also very different from the Nietzschean *übermensch*, for according to assimilationism, the new adaptive trans-human is not (and in fact by definition cannot be) a disequilibriatingly creative force making a future of "infinite experiments." Of course this is self-contradicting, for how can the trans-human be different if it is not to be disequilibriating in any way? We are left to believe that some sort of inert ultimate peace of mind and behavior will prevail. The new superadaptive meta-identity will be either an inert posthuman, beyond good and evil and the ability to communicate because parochial cultures and languages will have been left behind in the dustbin of failed human communities, or a dedicated conformist much more akin to the utopians offered by left and right Hegelians and their respective totalitarian regimes. In the latter case, the ideal model minority is to be as Mori was in his reactionary backlash, an ardent nationalist. Reeducation, reenculturation (for Mori, textbook censorship) via psychosocialization, is the ticket to adjustment and peace of mind. Feedback control works to maintain system equilibrium both in an individual's mind through self-monitoring and in society as a whole through what Irving Janis (1982) calls mind guards, which are very close to model minorities, for they have little power and yet tend to be the most fervent defenders of the faith, self-selecting snitches who adore authority, along with professional thought police. With their help everything is more predictable, redundant, and stable. But, as is well understood by experts in information systems, redundancy is uninformative and maddeningly boring (Kramer, 2000a, 2000b), and ultimately not very profitable either (as noted by Joseph Schumpeter's 1942/1984 concept of creative destruction). Being creative and original by definition means being unconventional and breaking rules, what Nietzsche called transvaluating values, which is revolutionary, not conformist. Beyond this the consistent and constant reinforcement of established rules—be it by social or artistic convention or by the KGB—squelches dissent as well as creativity. Such surveillance and centralized command and control can lead to the ultimate repression; the logical systematics of group-think (Janis, 1982; Koestler, 1960, 1967/1969; 1964/1990; 1946/1984; Lewin, 1948; Solzhenitsyn, 1973/1997). In 1960, after making a tour of Japan and other Eastern nations, in *The Lotus and the Robot*, Arthur Koestler, reluctantly came to the conclusion that the East cannot help the West escape its closing cage of strict ordination.

THIRD CULTURE AND THE *NIHON-GA* SCHOOL

A more modest claim offered by the modern social Darwinists/Spencerians is that as one becomes increasingly intercultural in one's "internal system" a person will create a "third culture perspective" (Gudykunst, Wiseman, & Hammer, 1977). But just as the theory of "cultural adaptation" is hardly original with Kim (1988), so, too, this notion of dialectical synthesis between two cultures was already proposed by Ernest Fenollosa, an American philosopher who taught in Japan beginning in 1878. Fenollosa promoted the new *nihon-ga* school of art, which attempted to combine media and themes from both Japanese and Western forms. But as Smith (1997) has noted, the "shriveled fruit of Fenollosa's synthesis" led nowhere because it offered no real innovation and also because it ran afoul of the officially sanctioned aesthetic enforced by nationalist reactionaries bent on supposedly preserving the system. Fenollosa defied assimilation.

According to social Darwinism, the solution to the Meiji ambivalence is to either blend back into the prison-house of traditional form, or conform to the Western-conceived world order of imported culture, thus ceasing to be Japanese. But the traditionally more collectivistic world confronts at least two paradoxes. Achieving *shutai-sei* (autonomous selfhood) demands that one not follow any tradition, including the one that promotes it! Furthermore, as Du Bois understood, how can one possibly conform to a dominating culture that defines you as never being worthy of inclusion? The more you become the Other and see yourself through the eyes of the Other, the more you must admit that the effort is hopeless. Mori's suggestion that Japanese intermarry to gain acceptance in the modern world promotes a quagmire. To be valuable is to be erased. This is senseless and, as Du Bois and countless others understand, hardly a path to happiness.

THE VALUE-LADEN GOAL OF *POSITIVE* SCIENCE

What is behind all these suggestions for engineering harmony, happiness, and proper fit? The goal of such positive science is to promote the universal good, and happiness. But Nietzsche notes that "Herbert Spencer espoused that the concept 'good' is essentially identical with the concept 'useful,' 'practical,' so that in the judgments 'good' and 'bad' mankind has summed up and sanctioned ... the 'valuable in itself'" (1887/1967, first essay, section three). Like all human experience, the useful and practical embodies a point of view of contingent interests. Difference is not a problem until moral judgment is imposed, which is to say, the good. At this moment the mere recognition of difference switches to judgmental ethnocentric prejudice. In this case, the good is defined by bourgeois positivism, as ever more predictable (stable) and expanding markets in the interest of uninterrupted capital expansion according to Western-style laissez-faire ideology.

Although fairly transparent (at least to innumerable observers of the emergent ideology of globalism), we must slow down to appreciate the morality of these social engineers who would help us escape what, to a Nietzschean, is best in life: the motor of change, the tragic worldview. For it is the optimism of science and its claim to universal validity that made a panacea of knowledge. What is the goal of science? In section twelve of *The Gay Science*, Nietzsche (1882/1974) answers:

The ultimate goal of science is to create for man the greatest possible amount of pleasure and the least amount of pain? But suppose pleasure and pain were so linked together that he who *wants* to have the greatest possible amount of the one must have the greatest possible amount of the other also ... ? And perhaps that is how things are! The Stoics, at any rate, thought so, and were consistent when they desired to have the least possible amount of pleasure in order to have the least possible amount of pain from life.... Today, too, you have the choice: either *as little pain as possible,* in short painlessness ... or *as much pain as possible* as the price of an abundance of subtle joys and pleasures hitherto rarely tasted!

Nietzsche points out that with the hypervaluation of a positive attitude comes the end of Attic tragedy and lyric poetry, the spirit of spontaneity and music. Yet out of the vitality of the Attic dithyramb, science was born (Nietzsche, 1872/1967, section seventeen)! But once born, the scientific perspective becomes institutionalized as an "ism." The enthusiasm of true spontaneous music gives way to recitation and replication (the timid copying of success), to rote memory and blind devotion for which we stupidly admire computers and even seek to call ourselves cognitive machines.

With the death of tragedy comes the new virtue of *stilo rappresentativo* (representational style; Nietzsche, 1872/1967, section nineteen). And what is science? It is the Apollonian defeat of suffering. "Apollo overcomes the suffering of the individual by the radiant glorification of the eternity of the phenomenon: here beauty triumphs over the suffering inherent in life: pain is obliterated by lies from the features of nature" (Nietzsche, 1872/1967, section sixteen). Thus we have the emerging opposition between status quo and its champion, transcendental certitude, on one hand (Plato), and ecstatic art, which can flourish only in the flux of "experimental life," on the other hand (Heraklitus) (Kramer, 1997).

Out of the vital power of Attic mysteries was born a spoiled child that turned against the forces of creative vitality and toward absolute predictability. One can only wonder what (if any) grandchild science will bequeath to its energetic Dark Age parents. Perhaps it is sterile. Otherwise, any accidental pregnancy and surprise culture of the future would be greeted as a wildfire terrorist, an invalid mistake disruptive of the zero-degree equilibrium.

As Nietzsche pointed out in 1887, those who flee from life and action instead place

"adaptation" in the foreground, that is to say, an activity of the second rank, a mere reactivity; indeed, life itself has been defined as a more and more efficient inner adaptation to external conditions (Herbert Spencer). Thus the essence of life, its *will to power,* is ignored; one overlooks the essential priority of the spontaneous, aggressive, expansive, form-giving forces that give new interpretations and directions, although "adaptation" follows only after this; the dominant role of the highest functionaries within the organism itself in which the will to life appears active and form-giving is denied. One should recall what Huxley reproached Spencer with—his "administrative nihilism": but it is a question of rather *more* than mere "administration." (Nietzsche, 1887/1967, second essay, section twelve)

According to the neo-Hegelian Spencerians Gudykunst and Kim (1997), what is ultimately required of strangers (if they want to be happy) in the host global society is to attain functional fit according to its criteria. Friction causes heat.

Heat disrupts equilibrium and therefore it is bad. The chill of rigor mortis is the goal. Although some assimilationists quote Marshall McLuhan, they don't seem to really understand him yet. Nichism is classic modernism that can be stated with a turn of one of McLuhan's (1967, p. 53) phrases, "a piazza [place] for everything [everyone] and everything [everyone] in its [her] piazza [place]." Perfection is a cubical for all. No one is more predictable than a dead man, and row upon row, nothing is more peaceful and orderly than a well-kept modern cemetery.

As Westernization spreads and the entire globe is culturally homogenized, indigenous cultures are suddenly reduced to being squatters in their own lands, of being parasites to the global host culture. According to Gudykunst and Kim (1997), *functional fit* means "the operational (or behavioral) capacity that enables a person to carry out behaviors externally in accordance with the host cultural patterns" (p. 342). This "operational (or behavioral) capacity which enables" a person to mimic normative "external" behavior patterns is, according to Gudykunst and Kim (1997), a mindset that is malleable, passive, flexible, mature, and advanced. This comes down to being user-friendly, easily reprogrammable, to being able and willing to "deculturize," "disintegrate," and "unlearn" one's "cognitive, affective, and operational" self (Gudykunst & Kim, 1997, pp. 335–53). For the individual, not the monolithic system, is expected to do all the accommodating. In modern dialectical parlance, people are defined as either assets or liabilities. This is Mori's initial dream come true. But there is the opposite dream.

EAST MEETS WEST

Since the Meiji Restoration, Japan has been pressured to open itself to even more outside pressure under the aegis of being cosmopolitan, sophisticated, and mature. This has called into question the very sense of what is natural and what is cultural for Japanese. Even the sense of the purpose of art has been disrupted by the Western presumption that the endeavor of art is to see oneself by challenging mundane perception, by perpetually abandoning tradition and convention.

For instance, in 1876, the Tokyo government recruited the Italian Babizon-style artist Antonio Fontenesi to come instruct Japan's first oil painters. As recounted by one of his students and an important Meiji-era artist, Chu Asai, one day Fontanesi told his students to go out into the city and sketch. The next day they all returned with blank sketchbooks claiming to have found nothing appropriate to draw—no temples, scholar's retreats, blossoming trees, or dancing cranes. Fontanesi realized that despite the city's endless vistas and scapes, they were unable to see them because they could not (via coconstitutive genesis) see themselves and comprehend where they stand (Kramer, 1993). Again, McLuhan (1967), as he proclaims the desire to suspend judgment as a Renaissance legacy, relativizes the modern truth of "the Detached Observer" and its premier value of "No Involvement!" (McLuhan, 1967, p. 53). To many Orientals, this is a curious if not suspect value, one that requires significant concessions (psychological, moral, and political) to accept, for it turns them into subhuman primates or primitivists. The great artistic traditions of the Orient were suddenly made childish, even wrong, certainly backward.

Like their contemporaries who were studying Western techniques in architecture, hygiene, education, industrial manufacture, and even government, the art students were mimicking technical aspects of form under the Meiji precept *wakon yosai* ("Japanese spirit, Western things"). But the new concept of art demanded that the artist discover something not already sedimented in the tradition, in the Japanese spirit. Thus, the critic Kojin Karatani (1993) argues two things. First, although the popular *ukiyo-e* of Utamaro, Hiroshige, and Hokusai depicted everyday life, they were part of the "little tradition," not the grand tradition. Second, Karatani argues that the *Tales of Genji*, the *Genji Monogatari*, like all *monogatari* (the telling of things) manifests a cast of many two-dimensional characters conventionally recycled (a style of writing that even Tanizaki follows as he creates new versions of old tales) rather than an in-depth plot. According to Karatani, "*Monogatari* is pattern, nothing more, nothing less," a "repetitive ritual" (Karatani, 1993, p. 164).

Many, like Karatani (1993) and Smith (1997), argue that the cultural inertia to repeat convention, "reflected no point of view, no transforming individual experience. In painterly terms, missing from the tradition was perspective" like premodern art elsewhere (Smith, 1997, p. 237). The paintings and novels of pre-Meiji did not explicitly say, "I am standing here, and this is what I see" (Smith, 1997, p. 237). However, this assessment is both true and false. The natural attitude (a sort of primordial prejudice) that constitutes identity and perspective and is expressed in the works of the early Meiji artists was what Gebser (1949/1985) calls a "two-dimensional mythic consciousness structure." But this *identification* becomes increasingly revealed as such, as artist after artist confronted the pressure to Westernize. Adaptation engineers' valorization of the mental and moral qualities of the intercultural human, barring any other trans-human criteria, is senseless because it also presumes, in positivistic fashion, that one attitude is more advanced or better than another. In fact, artists like Pablo Picasso and Tara Okamoto were inspired by the prehistoric.

This confrontation with Western techniques and values, which has pushed the Japanese spirit into relief, has had political as well as psychosocial and aesthetic consequences. *Nihon-ga* was a term coined only after the arrival of Western influences. The cultural fusion that marked the new *nihon-ga* style that combined traditional Japanese style with Western techniques presupposed forms and techniques that were distinctly Japanese as such. Only that which has been concealed, the natural attitude of Japan, can be revealed. This process, and not merely the school of thought developed by Fenollosa, is uncontrollable and continues (as we see in the *Sogetsu* school of *ikebana* and the architecture of the new internationalism). But at the same time, the pressure to Westernize has foregrounded the issue of *kokutai*, the soul of what it is to be Japanese, igniting the debate about who the modern Japanese are and what type of individualism (if any) will flourish. Recalling the coconstitutional process that characterizes the "I" in context, if a new identity emerges, then so does a new world, a new society.

In 1886, the serial novel by Shimei Futabatei, *Drifting Clouds* (1887/1990), appeared, giving its readers a sense of interiority and psychological depth in colloquial language. Hailed as Japan's first modern novel, the isolation of the main character, Bunzo, propels the reader past the dogmatic explication of democratic values into the more intimate question of the individual's place in society. A Japanese critic of the time recognized the paradigmatic shift this novel manifested: "The characters in most novels these days resemble figures in woodblock prints. The characters in *Drifting Clouds*, however, are people in oil paintings" (quoted in Smith, 1997, p. 240). Individualism articulated through naturalism and realism became the metaphysical prejudice of the late Meiji and beyond. But this was a European naturalism, which insisted that a landscape (or psychoscape) be rendered by the artist from within it, that the artist be a personal witness to what he or she represents. And as György Lukács (1958/1963) reminds us, realism is a genre of fiction.

The old Tong Chinese aesthetic criteria adopted by the Japanese, by which an artist could be acclaimed for his skill at painting a flock of geese without having ever seen one, was dismissed. The imperialistic privileging of the European version of perspective would find its resisters, however, as the tragic experience spawned fantastic creativity, just as Nietzsche predicted the unpredictable. Tanizaki (and, we must hasten to add, two born in his literary shadow: Yasunari Kawabata and Kawabata's protégé, Yukio Mishima) has already been acknowledged, but there were also resisting voices that preceded his, such as Mori Ogai and Nagai Kafu, whose characters expressed a revolution toward the new. In Kawabata's masterpiece *Snow Country* (1937/1985), written over a long period of time during the 1930s and 1940s, the protagonist is a modern dance critic who has never seen a ballet and who is utterly detached from his life in Tokyo. But then he takes a trip into the rural snow country and also into the past that still exists, where a geisha shows him the way back to a Japan of intimate peace that he had not known. Smith (1997) tells us that "in these two characters lies the discord between what the Japanese made of themselves and what they had been ... *Snow Country* derives its power from the impenetrable barrier it depicts: the inaccessibility of the past—a past that Kawabata mourned on behalf of many modern Japanese" (p. 161). But it is Soseki Natsume who remains an icon of Meiji and post-Meiji ambivalence toward modernity.

With continued Westernization, it is arguable that the sense of transformative pain, the tragic worldview, has ebbed from Japan's consciousness. Thus, the creative energies that propelled these geniuses have waned, leaving in their wake what has been called Japan Inc.'s trophy art collecting and GNPism.

Japanese art may imitate European trends more now than before when Zola and Flaubert set the standard. Today, the so-called postmodern novel constitutes cutting-edge literature by authors like Haruki Murakami and Banana Yoshimoto, who take pride in having never read the old gatekeepers like Mishima and Oe and who fear being too Japanese. But as name brands and appliances proliferate in their stories as supporting characters, what one sees are shades of Andy Warhol all over again.

CULTURE AS WOMB: THE LOST REFUGE AND SUICIDE

The gathering storm of global sameness, which many like Nietzsche, Paul Feyerbend (1987), and Hans-Georg Gadamer (1981/1983) have warned us of and which Greider (1997) documents in his book *One World, Ready or Not*, is being sold to all of us by special interests as a positive development. As many have noted, this issue is not a uniquely Japanese problem.[5] Seeking traditional cultural ways as a shelter from the onslaught of global capitalist culture continues in and among many cultures.

We turn again to Japan, for here we see some of the clearest and earliest outlines of a struggle that is increasingly global that is to be confronted with the dualism of finding one's identity in either the past or the future, which are increasingly disconnected (break with the past and leave it behind is the motto of development ideology). As noted concerning the irrelevance of the Cartesian metaphysic, the struggle pertains to everything in the life-world, from the individual's most intimate subjective desires to global financial policy.

One quality of the modern (not postmodern) world is that one can suffer the consequences of diaspora without leaving one's homeland (Kramer, 1997). Before Tanizaki, there was Soseki's ambivalence toward the modern. In Soseki, we find a person so conflicted that he chose to write Western-style fiction in the morning and poetry in the classical Japanese manner in the afternoon. After spending two years studying in England, he disliked it so much that he vowed never to return. But the more famous he became in Japan, the more he hated it, too. He found himself caught in a lonely predicament between tradition and modernity. The dualism in his mind was insurmountable. Thus, his famous dictum that the Japanese could not expect someone else to taste their liquor for them.

Neither the past nor modernity would ultimately be satisfying. Many of Soseki's characters, like Botchan (from the novel *Botchan*, 1906/1992), ape the West, rashly dismissing the old ways while at the same time depending on them. After concluding that the modern world is filled with impostors, Botchan finds solace in the person of an aging maid (his father-in-law's mistress), a literary device used again and again in modern Japanese fiction with woman representing the shelter of the past against the gales of modernity, a telling metaphor as the linear-rational West represents the aggressive masculine—line against the more content feminine mode of being (Gebser, 1949/1985; Kramer, 1997). The psychic fault line separates sentimental feeling from calculation.[6]

In the book *Kokoro* (1914/1991) Soseki once again explores Japan's confusion between selfishness and individuality, as well as the loneliness of being "swallowed by the whirlpool." Reminiscent of Plutarch's confession at being awestruck by the realization of depth space on the summit of Mt. Ventu in the south of France, the student in *Kokoro* is bedazzled by the sky and open sea, as well as intrigued by the intimate secret of the character K. The experience of sight and sensation becomes for the student the conduit to a new individuated selfhood, an experience so purely personal that only seeing for oneself, without the obligations of relationships on truth, can seem real. But as Sensei warns his student that an indefinite ocean of moral chaos characterizes the world outside the group, he also demonstrates a lack of attachment to the past. Outside the group is the modern, which harbors an amoral anarchy, a boundless sea. There live the twin dragons of relativism and unbearable solitude.

Although Soseki may have transcended the world of opposites, Tanizaki, Kawabata, and Mishima not only reiterated the oil-and-water relationship between modern technocracy and artistic tradition but also chose sides. In Kawabata one finds a sort of resignation or passive acceptance in the face of overwhelming modernization. In this sense he is similar to Thorstein Veblen and Nietzsche in the West.

To Nietzsche's consternation, he reluctantly admits that because of the hegemonic influence of Malthus and Spencer, especially among English psychologists and "for an uncouth industrious race of machinists and bridge-builders of the future, which has nothing but *course* work to get through," this poverty-stricken perspective may have become normative (Nietzsche, 1886/1972, part one, section fourteen). Only a few years later in 1899, Veblen (1899/1994) published his famous *Theory of the Leisure Class*. Like Nietzsche, Veblen reluctantly acknowledges the powerful inertia of modern mass thinking. After critiquing mass culture as barbaric, he put forth his central concept of adaptation, which meant for him the acceptance of adaptation, the adjustment to the new social Darwinism. He fell victim to the rhetoric of bourgeois positivism, with its ethnocentric self-congratulatory posture that argues that it is only natural, only Darwinian to accept Social Darwinism—the tightest hairpin turn of cybernetics. Such a collapse constitutes a pathetic surrender to the sphere of mass consumption. Culture sui generis is reduced to resource allocation. In such a world, individuals guard most selfishly the two scalar phenomena that characterize modernity: money and time.

In his novella *House of the Sleeping Beauties*, Kawabata (1933/1969) expresses *bitai*, the contradiction of a deep nostalgia for unfulfilled allure. He attempts to express the feeling of being unable to genuinely repair to a pure past or to embrace modernity. It is a poignant and very insightful articulation of true postmodern diaspora (postmodern in that it does not require physical mobility). In the story an old man frequents a brothel where the prostitutes are, paradoxically, untouchable virgins. That which makes them so tempting also frustrates, for to touch them ruins them. Thus, Kawabata articulates the frustration of the seductively unattainable, an unadulterated tradition, or a pure modernity (see Mishima's introduction to *House of the Sleeping Beauties*).

Mishima takes a different approach toward the confrontation between creativity and tradition in *The Temple of the Golden Pavilion* (1956/1994). The story was first published as *Kinkakuji* in 1956, a fictionalization of an actual torching of a Kyoto temple by a young monk in 1950. In the novel, Mizoguchi, born physically ugly, poor, and weak, is a hopeless stutterer who is bullied by his classmates. He seeks refuge as an acolyte in a temple in Kyoto. There the young monk becomes obsessed with the temple, at times caught up in his reverence for it, even identifying with the structure. But in the end he destroys the temple wherein he lives because its beauty oppresses him. In real life, Mishima's increasingly schizophrenic despair about the evils of modernity and his inability to truly escape into a characterized past led him to be seen more and more as a farcical buffoon whose public antics embarrassed many who admired his genius.

In the end both Mishima and Kawabata killed themselves, for the temple (Japan, the womb) had been destroyed by others. This is intense diasporic alienation without leaving home, for it had left them. It is no wonder that those who thrive on tradition, artists, would sense this despair more than most. The unfinished and, more important, unfinishable dream of the virgin brothel was "the regret for days lost without ever being had" (Kawabata, 1933/1969, p. 39).

PECUNIARY TRUTH, THE NEW EQUILIBRIUM?

According to Oe (quoted in Napier, 1993), Mishima's death marks the end of the public clash and churning of tradition and modernization. Now the waters have become placid as the divinity of universal market forces rule with little resistance. Traditional Japan, the beauty does not have the strength to fight the West. With the tragic worldview resolved, the creative energies that flow from such conflict have evaporated (Nietzsche 1872/1967). As Smith (1997) writes, "No one would write like them [Soseki, Tanizaki, Kawabata, and Mishima] again" (p. 248). Such a strong sense of *bitai* requires a feeling of profound loss, a regret expressed in an anthem Mishima wrote in which he says, "We must hide our great sorrow ... In our land so low fallen" (as quoted in Scott-Stokes, 1974, p. 247).

Perhaps to the ordinary person this is pure bombast. Yet what has globalization brought? A commercial culture wherein Caucasian models are used to promote elite products, even (amazingly) cosmetics for Japanese women, where Western celebrities like Leonardo Di Caprio, Harrison Ford, and Mel Gibson become pitchmen, whereas at home they restrain from such crass commercialization. Anything goes in Japan. The "liberation" of *joshi-puro* (women's pro wrestling), and hot springs faux "geisha," like the plastic cherry boughs that line city streets, signals what Oe (1993) calls a culturally infantilized Japan; the model minority that is seen but not heard. Japan must struggle to say "no."

During the Japanese Roaring Twenties, even sensuality became ambiguous as geisha became confused with prostitutes in the new capital economy, a trend that became hypertrophic after World War II, with Allied soldiers enjoying the value vacuum that many sojourners presume and exploit in their personal liberation, a sort of ersatz nostalgia for cheap "geesha [sic] girls," an offense returned in kind to the West with the reproduction of European village theme parks throughout the 1980s in Japan. For both sides, a version of the Other became commodified. Once the imitations completely displaced the originals, they became the new authentic culture, a postmodern culture of representation without referent—globalized culture without location. Although the Europeans still had their authentic towns, traditional Japan has slipped away bit by bit.

As if this weren't enough, now many are cheering the shift from the actual to the virtual. The rhetoric of global village has been exposed as the propaganda of the imperial center (Kramer, 2000b). Instead we have the aggregate of the global *city* with an emphasis on instrumental rather than organic relationships (Kramer, in press). The homogenizing world culture with its particular reality and truth appears to be just as Jules Henry suggested in 1963, a new "pecuniary truth"; truth is what sells.

When Japan came to suffer from double consciousness, it manifested not just in the ambivalence artists felt toward both their home and modernity but also as a national generation gap. Culture came to be equated with *dento* (official tradition), which became institutionalized, embalmed, and interred; in other words, museumized. Culture and tradition became that which was officially selected as worthy of preservation in a glass case and therefore as antiquated and dead (Ikeda & Kramer, 1998). The new Western mode of observation that objectifies culture itself in the peculiar viewing space of the museum had arrived in Japan. Thus, culture, being officially reduced to the antique, is that which the elderly yet value but the young disregard. As such, it came to be displaced in everyday life by the new imported culture of the West like Disney, blue jeans, and James Dean, whereas the new Japanese cultural contribution to the rest of the world became the ability to mass-produce Western inventions cheaply—electronics, cars, and cameras. Industrial products with powerful name recognition came to be the emblems of modern Japanese culture (Miyoshi & Harootunian, 1993). Culture became an industrial by-product, the fruition of Premier Hayato Ikeda's Income Doubling Plan for unfettered economic development. Thus was born the land of the ubiquitous salaryman, a vacant society, "that could neither nourish its artists nor be nourished by them" (Smith, 1997, p. 255).

With the passing of a generation of artists, including Akira Kurosawa, Oe, and Kobo Abe, Japan has few artists of stature. Rather than the coherent mutations that creative genius manifests, aimless "drifting" characterizes contemporary Japanese creative impulses. In Abe's *The Woman in the Dunes* (1962/1991) and also *The Ark Sakura* (1984/1988), human isolation, identity, the flux of continually shifting contexts, and the status of the idea of progress are masterfully illuminated.

Published in 1962 as *Suna no Onna*, *The Woman in the Dunes* is about an amateur entomologist who wanders into a seaside village, where he is taken prisoner and lowered into a sandpit, and he is forced to live with a young widow there. Typical of the bizarre plots that Japanese existential novels often have, the widow and the wandering teacher are forced to continually shovel the ever-encroaching sand dunes that threaten to bury them and the town. Over the course of the drama, Niki Jumpei, the protagonist, must come to accept his new identity. It may not be incorrect to suggest that the threatening tide of sand represents the onslaught of Western culture and the despised young widow represents tradition's continual struggle to survive. Modern Japanese are ants in the sand of the cosmopolis, the global city that is everywhere and nowhere.

In Abe's *The Box Man* (1973/2001), which is reminiscent of Dostoevsky's *Underground Man*, the entire point of the story is a man's attempt to abandon his original identity and become totally anonymous. In the story he literally decides to lose himself on the dehumanizing streets of Tokyo while wearing a box on his head. This is similar to Ozamo Dazai's *No Longer Human* (1948/1973). Dazai, like Mishima and Kawabata, was a victim of suicide. The actual title of the book literally translates "Disqualified as a Human." Like *The Box Man*, the main character of *No Longer Human* spends the entire story slowly alienating himself from everyone he knows until he is homeless and dies. In the process he attempts unsuccessfully to identify with the women in his life: his sister, his mistress, and his wife.

Differently, but still stressing the marginality of contemporary life, Oe's dedication to his son, Hitari, inspired his search for the ordinary in the margins of life. Such works are unmistakably Japanese, while at the same moment expressing universal human themes. Even the cinema of Torasan approaches this quality of art, though common it may seem by comparison. But the character Torasan (of which a series of nearly thirty movies over three decades was made), though he is always wandering and selling whatever he can to make a living, always has a bed to return to at his sister's house in Tokyo.

In contrast, the so-called postmoderns, as represented by Murakami's *A Wild Sheep Chase* (1982/1989), *Dance, Dance, Dance* (1988/1995), and *The Wind-Up Bird Chronicle* (1994/1997), strive to dislocate any hint of local meaning. In *Dance, Dance, Dance*, the sequel to *A Wild Sheep Chase*, an ordinary divorced man searches for a lover who mysteriously vanished from a dilapidated hotel. He is transformed by a disturbing encounter with another world; in this case a modern hotel in another dimension. Emotionally retarded, the protagonist is an engaged consumer of every current fad from foods to music while describing his journalistic occupation as "shoveling snow," a job nobody likes but somebody has to do. He never signs his stories. He is increasingly harassed by dreams of his former lover, who disappeared from a shabby old hotel where they had stayed together in Sapporo. An assignment takes him there again only to find the hotel replaced by a new one. When he decides to stay there, he not only finds that something of the old hotel is still supernaturally there but also finds the Sheep Man, a son of the original owner "living in hiding from the system." Each new clue to his lover's whereabouts only leads him deeper into a labyrinth of chaos. He suspects that she has been strangled.

These globalized, decultured, postmodern books exploit a technique of aggregating fragmented episodes of sex and fast food, interjected with brand-name icons, while not even offering a view from the margin via the deconstructive reversal of center with periphery. Not surprisingly, having perhaps achieved transcultural personhood, these new writers dwell on themes of boredom without any "upward-forward" progress. Comparing their lack of attachment and caring to the cultural environment with that shown by Japanese architects of the same generation Smith (1997) notes, "It seems odd that writers, the inheritors of a Soseki, an Abe, or an Oe, have so little to contribute as Japan finds its way forward" (p. 259). What seems lost is confidence and respect for that which one must assume to be what one is. But there is at the same time a sort of junior attempt to imitate Western "Zen punk" writers, like Tom Robbins from Seattle (*Another Roadside Attraction*, 1971, for instance). Yet Robbins's stories cannot work without presuming a truckload of traditional symbolism. The ability to admire past genius comes from contemporary confidence. What is found in some current Japanese arts (with the noteworthy exceptions of architecture, fashion, and animation) is what Harold Bloom (1973/1997) calls the anxiety of influence, and also an obsession with speed like Hollywood action movies, both thoroughly modern syndromes.

Even in the act of rejecting something, I must acknowledge its existence and even its power to motivate my act of rejection. The contextual position of the self relative to tradition and modernity forms not only the heteroglossia of contemporary Japan but of most of the world's developing peoples and, *by implication*, the so-called non-Japanese developed world, too. As Disney has demonstrated in the case of *The Lion King* (Allers & Minkoff, 1994), imitation is no longer unidirectional nor always the greatest form of flattery. Practically everywhere, identity is an issue.

EVEN THE DESPISED PERSISTS

Despite the tidal wave of Western cultural influence, nothing is lost. Even in the act of a failed experiment things are created and learned. One of the most interesting twists in Japan's struggle to find itself is Okamoto's (1963) treatise "What Is Tradition?" This short work offers a way past the impossible choice of being imprisoned in a static tradition or endlessly imitating Western things. Like Soseki, Okamoto neither transcends nor renders irrelevant the oppositional forces between Japanese tradition and modernity, the community and the individual; instead he integrates them. We also find this in the symbiotic philosophy and architecture of Kisho Kurokawa, who attempted in his designs "to be at once public and private. To be open and closed at the same time. To be unified even while being fragmented: the antagonism of the multiple contradictions that architecture cannot escape" (1993, as quoted in Smith, 1997, p. 261).[7]

According to Okamoto (1963), "The most urgent task of contemporary art is to synthesize the global and the particularly local; to understand the particular from a global perspective; and to achieve a global perspective that is based in the particular" (as quoted in Munroe, 1994, p. 381). Okamoto reminds us of Jean Gebser's (1949/1985) notion of the integral consciousness that neither promotes homogenization to unity nor surrenders to the structure of system, but instead continually changes in a way Gebser calls systasis, which is neither system nor chaos but the interplay of the potential of each. According to Gebser, systasis is expressed by means of the eteologeme rather than the two-valued representational philosopheme. According to Kramer (1997):

Gebser argued that, just as philosophy had replaced myth, so "eteology" would replace dualistic, two-valued conceptualiztion. The aperspectival world does not establish orders as such. The validity of the group, the individual, and their relatedness is recognized but not as the one and only viable structure ... what replaces the great logical systems that were articulated in the form of philosophemes and synchronic structures (ideological rationalisms) is a new form called the "eteologeme." (Kramer, 1997, p. 137)

Eteologeme is derived from the Greek *eteos*, which means "true, real." An eteologeme is a "verition" free of dualities, such as subject and object, permanence and flux, referent and representation. It "has nothing to do with representation; only in philosophical thought can the world be represented; according to integral perception, the world is pure statement, and thus 'verition'" (Gebser, 1949/1985, p. 309). System stresses statics, and systasis integrates time, thus manifesting a process of infinite morphogenesis (or, if one prefers, cultural churning, fusion, heteroglossia). *Systasis* means putting together or connecting phenomena (both spatial and nonspatial) so that partials merge. While system reveals static relationships (structure), systasis reveals a semantic world of synergies made both coherent but discontinuous within four-dimensional integrality (Fuller, 1975). Thus, systasis yields an (a)waring of temporalization and therefore a consciousness not of isolated (mutually excluding) self-contained systems, the monadology of Leibniz, but instead a communicative (temporal) field (for communication presumes time) that sustains community through time.

Some thirty years later Fuller would agree, coining the word *synergetics*. Fuller describes synergetics: "only one-half a century old, the science of Synergetics presents an experimentally verifiable, conceptual mathematics which faithfully accommodates all of the morphological dynamics of nature's inherently four-dimensional behaviors" (Fuller, 1970, sections 101.01–102.00). He defines *synergy* also as the "behavior of integral, aggregate, whole systems unpredicted by behaviors of any of their components or subassemblies of their components taken separately from the whole" (Fuller, 1970, sections 101.01–102.00). Similarly, we find Bohm (1980) arguing that the traditional reductionistic notion of separate empirical objects, entities, and structures around us that seem relatively autonomous, stable, and temporary (what he calls subtotalities) are actually derived from a deeper, implicate order of unbroken yet continually changing wholeness, a "holomovement." The part-to-whole relationship of integrality is maintained as unique identities are not homogenized and lost but persist and communicate, creating a complex and dynamic system with internal stresses and harmonics. Just as Husserl (1913/1980) had stressed, the relationships are the important part of the universe. Bohm gives the analogy of a flowing stream:

On this stream, one may see an ever-changing pattern of vortices, ripples, waves, splashes, etc., which evidently have no independent existence as such. Rather, they are abstracted from the flowing movement, arising and vanishing in the total process of the flow. Such transitory subsistence as may be possessed by these abstracted forms implies only a relative independence or autonomy of behaviour, rather than absolutely independent existence as ultimate substances. (Bohm, 1980, p. 48)

According to Lewis Mumford (1934/1963), Gebser, Fuller, Bohm, Kisho Kurokawa (1994), and many others, community is not comprised of uniform assimilation whereby all converge on a single language or style of behavioral, cognitive, and affective identity, but rather an integral process of communication between diverse elements. This four-dimensional dynamic, rather than the one- and two-dimensional x and y graphical fixture (which was invented around 1350 by Nicolas Oresme in his *Tractatus de Latitudeine Formarum*), is the origin of unfixed creativity that defies prediction, of life in all its delightful and awful randomness and surprise (Kramer, 2000a).

Without surprise there is no discovery and without discovery there is no science, only endless reproduction of the same, the handmaiden of enterprises that preposit goals and strategize action plans (developers) like militaries and businesses. For those who direct such institutions the future is limited by what they make of it. They do not like surprises but prefer fixed order, which enables normalization and efficiencies. This is a specific culture, the culture of empire and power politics. The fear of life with all its stresses and strains and anxieties fosters the dream of total certainty and equifinality, a fancy name for the *caput mortum* of life, otherwise known as death.

To both Gebser and Fuller, due to the realization of morphological dynamics in practically every field of scholarship, hypothetical thinking is reaching its limits. Many fields are achieving a status of art, in the ancient Greek sense, reaching beyond mere *techne* or engineering. Gebser and others are thus developing the hermeneutics of symbiotic histories and cultures exposing controlled aggregation to be something less than dynamic community (and membership). Despite their differences in emphases, these scholars exhibit a pronounced agreement on the nature of reality as a much more surprising place than the old Newtonian mechanical view would permit.

FLOWERS AND THE UNEXPECTED JAPAN

Unlike the view that tradition equals the antiquated, Okamoto argues that tradition is vital and alive in every present creation, even when that creation struggles to be different. For to be different presupposes that from which one is attempting to escape. According to Okamoto (1963) it is tradition itself, which "is the driving force that can tear down the old structure, open up the horizon for new ideas, and enable new possibilities" (as quoted in Munroe, 1994, p. 382). Okamoto has independently discovered what others have called the hermeneutic circle, which is neither closed nor vicious but limited and, as such, enables the possibility to go beyond itself. There can be no freedom without structure. Doors exist in walls. It is immature egocentrism to deny that we stand on the shoulders of giants, that the origin is ever present.

But it seems that both the excruciating interiority of the Meiji-era fictional characters and the shallow exteriority of the postmodern characters manifest the Western Cartesian dilemma. Neither seems at all indigenous to the Japanese world. This dilemma is an essentially Western construct with contingent Japanese content. What is essentially Japanese does appear, however, when the Western split between form and content, interior and exterior, is ignored. This happens, for example, in the uniquely Japanese sort of ambiguous space created by the *fusuma* sliding door (Kurokawa, 1988). A similar confidence of purpose is manifested in the work of the Sogetsu School of *ikebana* (flower arrangement), founded by Sofu Teshigahara and continued by his son Hiroshi.

CONCLUSION

Hermeneutics is about the gap, the liminal in-betweenness of a world of endless diversities. The postmodernist world must presuppose these even while it deconstructs them, creating a homogenous place of identity crisis, a holism of nothingness and boredom, a pseudo-Zen, New Age of monotony. Even traces and grafts are rejected as obstacles to efficient functioning within the emergent world system.

This chapter began with one of the most famous quotes in Japanese literature, the first line of Kawabata's classic *Snow Country*. It is about a train journey taken by a modern man who has no caring attachments for the metropolis of Tokyo. It begins at Ueno station and ends in *ura nihon*. It is a passage from the modern to the traditional, the meaningless and the meaningful, to the land and woman who give him a purpose worth living and dying for. Written in the

1950s by a man who could still recall traditional Japan, by an author who straddled the boundary between the past and the present, the traverse manifests nostalgia, alienation, wonder, reflection, and finally great art.

Smith (1997) draws an important parallel between Kawabata's train trip and the one described in the 1982 novel *A Wild Sheep Chase* by Murakami. Smith notes that the postmodern trip crosses no great boundaries culturally, psychologically, or spiritually. Murakami's train ride is noteworthy for its "utter lack of sentiment" and boredom (p. 162).

During his journey the narrator scarcely bothers to look out the window. Instead he puzzles over an obscure history of the village he is heading toward. The book he found of desultory interest. "But if the truth be known, Junitaki today was a dreadfully dull town," he observes. "The townsfolk, when they came home from work, watched an average of four hours of television before going to bed each night." (Smith, 1997, p. 162; and Murakami, 1982, p. 208)

Murakami is describing the new improved Japan, the modern Japan, a Japan Inc. dominated by work without community, an aggregate of disconnected, unattached individuals, each peering at their televisions and increasingly personal/private computer screens in an unshared yet common attempt to forget the day's alienating labor and inevitable temporal pressure. The screen world is a mass phenomenon, a common form but without shared content. The mass society shares a grammar, a flowcharted ordination, but also a commercial content, one that is not consumed together. Increasingly people eat alone, read alone, watch alone, even have sex alone (Kramer, 1994).

One of the most common themes in world literature since World War II is this sense of loss—loss of community, self, interest, belonging, curiosity, hopefulness, attachment, caring, drama, *life;* many of the qualities now espoused by handmaidens and consultants as the singular "good, true, and beautiful" (Gudykunst & Kim, 1997, p. 366). The new uniformity is robotic and insectlike, and this is the dream of the model minority ideology, with its push to include vaster numbers of us as we all become coordinated by the mechanical clock, the value of detached disinterest, abstract credit and corporate culture, with no sense of sentimental place or "spare time" but only "course work to get through" before we die (Nietzsche, 1886/1972, part one, section fourteen). Reflection dies when tragedy dies. This is the first age that has made numbing comfort of redundancy (certainty) its highest ideal, when philosophy is regarded as unproductive nonsense and value judgments pathetic subjectivism.

NOTES

1. Although it is very fashionable these days to speak of the postcolonial situation, I see this as a misconception. To me the planet is currently undergoing more intense and

accelerating colonization than ever before. In other publications, I have referred to tele-colonialism as one of the major ways colonization is occurring today (Kramer & Ikeda, 2000). Basically I see nothing "post" about global homogenization and the loss of cultural and linguistic diversity that has accelerated greatly since World War II and is happening now, at the beginning of the twenty-first century.

2. Many years ago, while studying with Detlef Ingo Lauf, one of the world's greatest authorities on Eastern religions and Buddhism specifically, I asked him what he thought of the book *Zen and the Art of Motorcycle Maintenance: An Inquiry into Values* (1984) by Robert Pirsig. Professor Lauf responded that beyond reiterating a bit of phenomenology of quality more or less well, it was typical "California consciousness" "beat-Zen." It is curious that the book would begin with "I can see by my watch." Lauf decried what had happened to his friend Allen Watts in California, where an "initially strong and serious young scholar" drifted into celebrity and alcoholism and where studying Buddhism too often meant listening to self-help cassettes while stuck on the highways.

3. Heteroglossia is evident in nonverbal communication. A wink, for instance, means different things among different people and in different contexts.

4. A point of clarification: I agree in principle with the dialogical imperative, but I do not accept the notion of holism nor that of reductionistic lingualism put forth by these earlier writers. Instead I argue, along with Gebser (1949/1985), that the world is an open horizon of potential interconnections that integrate (communicate) in various, often unpredictable ways, not a closed language system that has the potential of becoming totally homogeneous and thus nihilistic. Furthermore, I do not believe that meaning is generated only through words but also through artifactual deeds and even random acts that breach the consensual rules of language games. In this sense, I tend to agree with Roland Barthes (1982) when he argues for the universal semantization of experience, such that a sunset or a dog's smile have the same potential for meaning as a word. Therefore, the static logic of binary opposition is rendered inadequate as the sole explanation for morphology.

5. Also see David Korten's book *When Corporations Rule the World* (1995), the work of Teddy Goldsmith, the founding editor of *The Ecologist*, and Barnet and Cavanagh's *Global Dreams* (1995).

6. The first word of the first verse of the first canto of the first major work of the Western world, the *Iliad*, is *menin* (the accusative of *menis*) (Gebser, 1949/1949, pp. 70–78). The Greek word *menis* means "wrath" and "courage." *Menis* comes from the same stem as *menos*, meaning "resolve," "power," and "conviction." In turn, the Latin *mens* means "intent," "anger," "thinking," "thought," "understanding," and "deliberation" (not liberation). The masculine is manifested as directed or discursive thought, which is causal and willfully ordered. *Menos* is the root of *men(tal)*, as in the modern mental-rational mode of experiencing the world as opposed to the traditional mythological, emotional ,and narrative way. The masculine seeks to control the cyclical nature of the imagination.

7. Also see Kurokawa's *Rediscovering Japanese Space* (1988), *From Metabolism to Symbiosis* (1992), and *The Philosophy of Symbiosis* (1994).

REFERENCES

Abe, K. (1084/1988). *The ark sakura* (J. W. Carpenter, Trans.). New York: Vintage.

Abe, K. (1973/2001). *The box man* (D. Saunders, Trans.). New York: Vintage.

Abe, K. (1962/1991). *The woman in the dunes* (E. McDonald, Trans.). New York: Vintage.

Adler, P. (1987). Beyond cultural identity: Reflections on cultural and multicultural man. In L. Samovar & R. Porter (Eds.). *Intercultural communication: A reader* (4th ed.) (pp. 362–380). Belmont, CA: Wadsworth.

Allers, R., & Minkoff, R. (Directors). (1994). *The Lion King* [Motion picture]. United States: Disney.

Austin, J. L. (1961/1975). *How to do things with words.* Cambridge, MA: Harvard University Press.

Bakhtin, M. (1975/1981). *The dialogic imagination.* Austin: University of Texas Press.

Barnet, R., & Cavanagh, J. (1995). *Global dreams: Imperial corporations and the new world order.* New York: Touchstone Books.

Barthes, R. (1964/1977). *Elements of semiology* (C. Smith & A. Lavers, Trans.). New York: Hill and Wang.

Bloom, H. (1973/1997). *The anxiety of influence: A theory of poetry* (2nd ed). New York: Oxford University Press.

Bohm, B. (1980). *Wholeness and the implicate order.* London: Routledge and Kegan Paul.

Campbell, J. (1988). *The power of myth.* New York: Doubleday.

Dazai, O. (1948/1973). *No longer human.* New York: Norton.

Diamond, J. (1993). *The third chimpanzee.* New York: HarperCollins.

Du Bois, W. E. B. (1995). *The souls of Black folk.* New York: Penguin Putnam.

Feyerbend, P. (1987). *Farewell to reason.* London: Verso.

Foucault, M. (1981/1988). *Technologies of the self.* Amherst: University of Massachusetts Press.

Fuller, R. B. (1970). *I seem to be a verb.* (With J. Agel & Q. Fiore). New York: Bantam.

Fuller, R. B. (1975). *Synergetics.* (With E. J. Applewhite). New York: Macmillan.

Futabatei, S. (1887/1990). *Drifting clouds* (M. G. Ryan, Trans.). Ann Arbor: University of Michigan Center for Japanese Studies.

Gadamer, H.-G. (1960/1993). *Truth and method* (J. Weinsheimer & D. Marshall, Eds.). New York: Continuum.

Gadamer, H.-G. (1981/1983). *Reason in the age of science* (F. Lawrence, Trans.). Cambridge, MA: MIT Press.

Gebser, J. (1949/1985). *The ever-present origin* (N. Barstad & A. Mickunas, Trans.). Athens: Ohio University Press.

Greider, W. (1997). *One world ready or not: The manic logic of global capitalism.* New York: Touchstone.

Gudykunst, W., & Kim, Y. (1997). *Communicating with strangers.* New York: McGraw Hill.

Gudykunst, W., Wiseman, R., & Hammer, M. (1977). Determinants of a sojourner's attitudinal satisfaction. In B. Ruben (Ed.), *Communication yearbook 1.* New Brunswick, NJ: Transaction.

Heidegger, M. (1927/1962). *Being and time* (J. Macquarrie & E. Rodinson, Trans.). New York: Harper and Row.

Henry, J. (1963). *Culture against man.* New York: Vintage.

Husserl, E. (1913/1980). *Ideas pertaining to a pure phenomenology and to a phenome-nological philosophy* (T. Klein & W. Pohl, Trans.). Dordrecht, Germany: Marti-nus Nijhoff.

Ikeda, R., & Kramer, E. (1998). *Enola Gay:* The transformation of an airplane into an icon and the ownership of history. *Keio Communication Review, 20,* 49–73.

Iyer, P. (2000). *The global soul: Jet lag, shopping malls, and the search for home.* New York: Vintage.

Janis, I. (1982). *Groupthink: Psychological studies of policy decisions and fiascoes.* Boston: Houghton Mifflin.

Karatani K. (1993). *Origins of modern Japanese literature.* Durham, NC: Duke Univer-sity Press.

Kawabata, Y. (1933/1969). *House of the sleeping beauties and other stories.* Tokyo: Ko-dansha.

Kawabata, Y. (1937/1985). *Snow country.* Tokyo: Charles E. Tuttle.

Keene, D. (1984). *Dawn to the West: Japanese literature in the modern era.* New York: Henry Holt.

Kim, Y. (1988). *Communication and cross-cultural adaptation: An integrative theory.* Clevedon, UK: Multilingual Matters.

Kim, Y. (2000). *Becoming intercultural: An integrative theory of communication and cross-cultural adaptation.* Thousand Oaks, CA: Corwin/Sage.

Koestler, A. (1946/1984). *Darkness at noon.* New York: Bantam.

Koestler, A. (1960). *The lotus and the robot.* London. Hutchinson.

Koestler, A. (1964/1990). *The act of creation.* New York: Viking/Arkana.

Koestler, A. (1967/1969). *The ghost in the machine.* New York: Macmillan.

Korten, D. (1995). *When corporations rule the world.* West Hartford, CT: Kumarian.

Kramer, E. (1993). Understanding co-constitutional genesis. *Integrative Explorations: Journal of Culture and Consciousness, 1,* 41–47.

Kramer, E. (1994). Making love alone: Videocentrism and the case of modern pornogra-phy. In K. A. Callihan (Ed.), *Ideals of feminine beauty: Philosophical, social, and cultural dimensions* (pp. 78–98). Westport, CT: Greenwood.

Kramer, E. (1997). *Modern/postmodern: Off the beaten path of antimodernism.* West-port, CT: Praeger.

Kramer, E. (2000a). *Contemptus mundi:* Reality as disease. In V. Berdayes & J. Murphy (Eds.), *Computers, human interaction, and organization: Critical issues* (pp. 31–53). Westport, CT: Praeger.

Kramer, E. (2000b). *Ressentiment* and racism: A Nietzschean reading of African Ameri-can and Korean American conflict. In M. K. Asante & J. E. Min (Eds.), *Socio-cultural conflict between African and Korean Americans* (pp. 34–62). New York: University Press of America.

Kramer, E. (Contributing Ed.). (1992). *Consciousness and culture: An introduction to the thought of Jean Gebser.* Westport, CT: Greenwood.

Kramer, E., & Ikeda, R. (2000). The changing faces of reality. *Keio Communication Re-view, 22,* 79–109.

Kurokawa, K. (1988). *Rediscovering Japanese space.* Tokyo: Weatherhill.

Kurokawa, K. (1992). *From metabolism to symbiosis.* New York: St. Martin's.

Kurokawa, K. (1993). *Recent works: 1987–1992.* Tokyo: Weatherhill.

Kurokawa, K. (1994). *The philosophy of symbiosis.* London: Academy Editions.

Lewin, K. (1948). *Resolving social conflicts: Selected papers on group dynamics.* New York: Harper and Row.

Lukács, G. (1958/1963). *The meaning of contemporary realism.* New York: Merlin.

McLuhan, M. (1967). *The medium is the message.* New York: Bantam.

Miyoshi, M., & Harootunian, H. (Eds.) (1993). *Japan in the world.* Durham, NC: Duke University Press.

Mishima, Y. (1956/1994). *The temple of the golden pavilion* (I. Morris, Trans.). New York: Vintage.

Moore, G. E. (1959). *Philosophical Papers.* London: Allen & Unwin.

Mumford, L. (1934/1963). *Technics and civilization.* New York: Harcourt, Brace and World.

Munroe, A. (Ed.) (1994). *Japanese art after 1945: Scream against the sky.* New York: Harry N. Abrams.

Murakami, H. (1982/1989). *A wild sheep chase.* Tokyo: Kodansha.

Murakami, H. (1988/1995). *Dance, dance, dance* (A. Birnbaum, Trans.). New York: Vintage.

Murakami, H. (1994/1997). *The wind-up bird chronicle* (J. Rubin, Trans.). New York: Vintage.

Napier, S. (1993). Marginal arcadias: Oe Kenzaburo's pastoral and antipastoral. *Review of Japanese Culture and Society,* Dec. 5, 48–58.

Nietzsche, F. (1872/1967). *The birth of tragedy* (W. Kaufmann, Trans.). New York: Random House.

Nietzsche, F. (1882/1974). *The gay science.* New York: Vintage.

Nietzsche, F. (1886/1972). *Beyond good and evil.* New York: Penguin.

Nietzsche, F. (1887/1967). *On the genealogy of morals.* New York: Vintage.

Okamoto, T. (1963). *My contemporary art.* Tokyo: Shincho-sha.

Robbins, T. (1971). *Another roadside attraction.* New York: Bantam.

Saussure, F. de (1916/1959). *Course in general linguistics* (W. Baskin, Trans.). New York: McGraw Hill.

Schumpeter, J. (1942/1984). *Capitalism, socialism and democracy.* New York: Harper-Collins.

Scott-Stokes, H. (1974). *The life and death of Yukio Mishima.* New York: Farrar, Straus and Giroux.

Smith, P. (1997). *Japan: A reinterpretation.* New York: Random House.

Solzhenitsyn, A. (1973/1997). *Gulag archipelago* (Vol. 1) (W. Thomas, Trans.). Boulder, CO: Westview Press.

Soseki, N. (1906/1992). *Botchan* (A. Turney, Trans.). Tokyo: Kodansha.

Soseki, N. (1914/1991). *Kokoro* (E. McClellan, Trans.). New York: Madison.

Tanizaki, J. (1924). *A fool's love/Naomi* (A. Chambers, Trans.). New York: Vintage.

Tanizaki, J. (1933–34/1988). *In praise of shadows* (E. Seidensticker, Trans.). Stony Creek, CT: Leete's Island Books.

Tanizaki, J. (1928–29/1995). *Some prefer Nettles.* New York: Knopf.

Veblen, T. (1899/1994). *Theory of the leisure class.* New York: Penguin.

Wittgenstein, L. (1953/2002). *Philosophical investigations.* Cambridge, England: Blackwell.

Chapter 2

The Hidden Justification for Assimilation, Multiculturalism, and the Prospects for Democracy

John W. Murphy and Luigi Esposito

INTRODUCTION

With the recent emphasis placed on multiculturalism, assimilation is again under attack. In fact, integration has become a code word in some circles for intolerance and discrimination. But assimilation has seldom been viewed without a healthy skepticism. The recent criticisms raised by multiculturalists about the repressive nature of assimilation are not new but represent the most recent attempt to illustrate that this kind of conformity is not necessary for order to prevail (Murphy & Choi, 1997, pp. 16–19).

During the 1920s, for example, pluralists such as Horace Kallen and Randolph Bourne rejected the link that was made between assimilation and becoming an American.[1] Throughout the 1900s, and especially in the 1960s, Marxists and other conflict theorists argued that assimilation was based on racism and was used as a method to undermine a large segment of the working class. Even the pragmatists, including their sociological followers, recognized that maintaining order was a lot more complicated than just having persons assimilate to a cultural ideal. A host of writers, in short, has recognized that assimilation and the generation of a vibrant society are not synonymous.

Yet only recently, and to a very limited degree, has the hidden justification for assimilation been the focus of attention. Simply stated, the foundationalist character of traditional sociological theory has imposed strictures pertaining to how order has to be maintained (Fish, 1989, p. 542). In the field of race relations, assimilation was considered to be a logical extension of this theme. As a result of this trend, the political side of assimilation is overlooked; most persons tend to believe that assimilation is a rational social imperative. In terms reminiscent of Baudrillard (1983), assimilation is popular even among minorities because the politics of this process has vanished. Political will and ambition are concealed in the form of economic and social necessity. Assimilation is simply necessary for social mobility.

Because of their attack on foundationalism, however, multiculturalists have drawn attention to this underside of assimilation. They have shown that assimilation has been sustained by a particular form of metaphysics—referred to by Gilroy and Baker (1991) as the "metaphysics of Britishness"—which they claim is no longer credible. Accordingly, they have demonstrated that there is nothing natural or inevitable about assimilation. From the time when cultural ideals are established to the stage when they are enforced, assimilation represents a particular approach to understanding how order survives. Even Marxists have not taken their political critique of assimilation to this level; in many of their discussions of integration, remnants of naturalism are present.

Nonetheless, alternatives to assimilation will not be easy for the public to accept. To most people, assimilation makes sense and anything more than a moderate pluralism is perceived to pose a threat to society. Multiculturalists, on the other hand, try to decenter society and reveal how order can be predicated on the proliferation of cultural differences. As might be expected, their efforts have been viewed with suspicion and, for the most part, have been rejected. Their rationale for order strays too far from the traditional way in which society has been conceived. What is problematic, however, is that their proposals on race may hold the key to democratizing American society.

ASSIMILATION AND SOCIOLOGICAL THEORY

The cornerstone of modern sociological theory has been foundationalism (Murphy & Choi, 1997, pp. 12–16). In other words, most writers believe a reliable order can be based only on norms that are unaffected by quotidian concerns. For this reason, Niklas Luhmann (1982) argues that sociologists have had a penchant for portraying society in a centered manner (pp. 353–55). Specifically, social order must evolve around a core that has the stature necessary to control persons. In the absence of this constraint, *anomie* will likely erupt any moment.

Realism and nominalism have been the dominant approaches to conceptualizing order (Stark, 1963, pp. 2–3). Realists contend that only society is real and that order constitutes a force greater than all individuals combined. Their primary concern, as reflected in the work of Comte, Durkheim, and Parsons, is that order be understood to represent a "reality *sui generis*" or an "ultimate reality." Given this exalted position, norms are immune to the contingencies of everyday existence and appear to have universal validity. Norms are similar to Platonic forms. Order is thus substantial enough to thwart any challenge to society posed by radicals or the infirm.

Nominalists propose, at least initially, that only individuals are real and society is an illusion. The difficulty they face pertains to explaining how disparate persons are transformed into a coherent system. In the end, nominalists make a non sequitur and introduce higher-order mechanisms that are designed to control persons. The "invisible hand" proposed by Adam Smith, not to mention Spencer's use of the organismic analogy, is an example of this shift in orientation. At first persons are free to pursue their own aims, whereas later these goals are substantiated by autonomous forces that direct their behavior.

As should be noted, in each case society is provided with a foundation that is unresponsive to human praxis. In point of fact, this base has been described by using structural metaphors—web, network, and system of roles—and provided a patina of objectivity. In a typical foundationalist manner, individuals are juxtaposed to an ominous reality in such a way that they are easily controlled. Simply put, all reasonable persons are expected to abide by norms that are characterized as universal and unbiased.

In view of the way order has been traditionally described, no one should be surprised that assimilation has dominated race relations in the United States and elsewhere. The foundation that is assumed to be required to unite society is easily translated into cultural ideals, which all normal persons should strive to emulate. Furthermore, those who choose not to adhere to these standards are perceived as a threat to society. Indeed, minorities are anathema to a sane and coherent culture when they refuse to assimilate.

In terms of contemporary politics, conservatives have been straightforward about their advocacy of assimilation (Bennett, 1992, pp. 35–36). They believe that modern society will be weakened, possibly beyond repair, if any credence is given to multiculturalism. Liberals, on the other hand, mostly start out as pluralists and eventually begin to express concern about the amount of cultural difference that can be tolerated in any functional society (Schlesinger, 1992). Like conservatives, they presume that without a uniform base, order is destined to dissolve into chaos. In this regard, both of these political positions are underpinned by foundationalism and resort to using cultural mandates to ensure the integrity of society. Particular cultural ideals must be internalized by everyone, or serious social difficulties will arise.

Both conservatives and liberals have externalized the source of social order. As part of this strategy, order can never be predicated on the principle of cultural uniqueness; the universals necessary to unite society can never be forthcoming from this tactic. But what modality of culture can meet this prerequisite? Because no culture is inherently universal, the illusion must be perpetrated that one or some fulfill this criterion. The political act of elevating one culture over others, however, will not likely create the integration that foundationalists value. Animosity and resentment result typically from this process, because some people are likely to feel slighted.

THE METAPHYSICS OF DOMINATION

To avoid the turmoil that can result when one culture is given primacy capriciously over others, any distinctions that are made between them must appear to

be natural. Sartre (1948) made this observation in his discussion of the discrimination experienced by Jews. Depriving people of their freedom and possibly their
lives must be based on something other than personal whims or the vagaries of
history. But given the limited validity of every culture, Michael Zimmerman
(1996) refers to the justification of cultural supremacy as "ontological hubris"
(pp. 246–60). In this chapter, this process is called the metaphysics of domination.

The pertinent question is: How is a unique and finite culture transformed
into a universal? As suggested earlier, finitude is believed to be overcome once
a differentiation is accepted between what is objective and subjective. Around
1600 this schism came to be known as Cartesianism. Most important is that
some information is thought to be uncontaminated by interpretation, political
motives, or other kinds of biases. Subsequent to accepting this form of dualism,
some positions are by their very nature pure and more valuable than others.
Cultures are no exception!

Assimilation, therefore, is not an unfair burden placed on minorities. Without a doubt, they should relish this opportunity to enhance themselves. All
they are asked to do is jettison traits that are inimical to the cultural ideals most
persons agree represent the best of humanity. With respect to the metaphysics
of domination, minority culture embodies the flaws that contaminate these
universal measures of civility (Murphy & Choi, 1997, pp. 108–10). In this
sense, the benefits of assimilation are not a matter of opinion or perspective. Instead, assimilation signals a commitment to cultural standards that promote
the commonwealth and historical progress.

Cultural supremacy is thus justified by ahistorical principles, which are divorced from any attempts to rationalize or enforce the dominance of a particular group. Rather than a product of collusion or ideology, essential characteristics
separate minorities from the persons who are in the mainstream of society.
These differences are simply a fact of life, and the necessary adjustments should
be made without resistance. Assimilation is a product of this wisdom! What is
often difficult to accept is that some minorities are incapable of assimilating.
They are simply too far removed from the norm presupposed by assimilation.

What is significant is that a particular philosophical démarche supports assimilation and removes a particular mode of culture from the influence of any
contingencies. Likewise, the use of political muscle to expedite assimilation is
deemed acceptable because of this philosophical maneuver. What sensible person would balk at any opportunity to mimic a cultural ideal? The point is that
assimilation is necessary for order to prevail only after foundationalism, and
the accompanying dualism, has gained legitimacy.

THE DISAPPEARANCE OF POLITICS

In actuality, however, the politics of assimilation is quite nasty. One group has
the power to demand that all others abandon their cultures. As part of this process,
some are compelled to suppress their language and heritage and even alter their

physical appearance. Those who reject this process of inferiorization are ostracized from society. Clearly, assimilation can take a high toll on the soul of a culture.

Despite the efforts of multiculturalists, most minorities still strive to assimilate. The rationale given most often for this adjustment is the promise of equality and upward social mobility. But something else seems to be driving this desire. Why would persons demean themselves for a payoff that is never fully realized? Integration is not as glorious as it is initially portrayed. Because of the implied power differentials, assimilation usually begins a spiral of increasing demands and exploitation. Minorities must relinquish more and more of themselves. As this process unfolds, many minorities become increasingly alienated, resentful, and isolated. The promise of acceptance turns into self-rejection and the loss of community. According to the politics of assimilation, there are no model minorities, only those who are deluded by the prospect of equality.

Nonetheless, the question is seldom raised by those who are striving to assimilate (not to mention the remainder of most societies) about why certain persons have the right to dictate the conditions for entry into the social mainstream. Who determines why specific cultural traits constitute a liability but others are an asset? This political choice is not usually given serious scrutiny. In view of the metaphysics of domination, the reason for this omission is quite simple: The identification of inferiority has nothing to do with politics. In other words, politics disappears behind the facade of objectivity and neutrality (Murphy & Choi, 1997, pp. 103–4).

According to assimilationists, there is nothing political about comparing a particular culture to the norms that are universal. These assessments are conducted in a dispassionate and rational manner. For example, sometimes medical professionals and other experts are summoned to explain why specific traits are unacceptable. Often these explanations are couched in high-tech nomenclature and practices, thereby reinforcing the view that the claims made by the advocates of assimilation are apolitical. As a result, the required cultural universals are internalized without the displays of power often associated with politics. Essential traits are merely cataloged properly and assigned their rightful place in the social hierarchy. Logic, rather than politics, seems to be operative throughout this endeavor.

Concealing politics, obviously, should not be confused with eliminating the exercise of power. But the presence of foundationalism makes the politics of assimilation difficult to detect. After all, reason and objectivity, as opposed to ideology and manipulation, are used to coerce persons. Following the Enlightenment, rationality was thought to be liberating. In the case of assimilation, the opposite is true. Persons are cajoled into submission by the use of reason and universals. Hegemony is thus given a new and dangerous twist.

DECENTERING REALITY AND MULTICULTURALISM

Assimilationists fear multiculturalism. They contend this trend will dilute culture and subvert the norms that hold society together (Bloom, 1987, pp.

155–56). Basic values will collapse into a morass of conflicting opinions and interests. In this regard, multiculturalism is understood to advance beyond pluralism and call for the overthrow of any common standards. However, from the perspective of assimilationists, abandoning the centered image of society will have dire consequences.

Assimilationists are correct in one respect. Stated simply, multiculturalists are not interested in preserving the ultimate foundation sought by assimilationists. In fact, the cultural ideals that are associated with this exalted base are described to be the product of political decisions that have inflicted harm on most minorities. As a result of this viewpoint, multiculturalists are recognized as decentering society.

But the critique of assimilation proffered by multiculturalists is more profound than a banal appraisal of class interests. According to multiculturalists, political analysis does not usually go to the root of assimilation; politics, they contend, is thus insufficient to end the metaphysics of domination. Therefore, political changes may not bring about the demise of demands for assimilation and the accompanying repression. Politics may play an important role in enforcing domination, but the rationale for assimilation does not exist simply at this level.

Because of the influence of postmodernism, multiculturalists argue that the ideals extolled by assimilationists lack the requisite ahistorical status. Relying on the later work of Wittgenstein, multiculturalists recognize that all knowledge is mediated by "language games" (Lyotard, 1984, pp. 9–11). Therefore, cultural ideals are implicated in the process of legitimizing interpretations; these norms embody one among many modalities of language and interpretation. With this epistemological maneuver, multiculturalists have challenged the dualism at the heart of assimilation. Without dualism, the standards presupposed by assimilation cannot be said to exist sui generis.

Cultural ideals, accordingly, are "discursive formations" that are never universal because of their existential character (Foucault, 1989, pp. 31–39). Now that the norms of assimilation are exposed to be contingent, the appeal of integration is tempered. Why should minorities abandon their heritages to adjust to the expectations of another group? At this juncture politics may be relevant, for multiculturalists do not focus simply on whether persons should be made to conform to specific norms that are beyond scrutiny. Instead, they ask why conformity to particular norms should be demanded when these standards reflect commitments that are not and can never be universal. In this sense, multiculturalists have decentered reality; they have shown that political power and all other methods of installing order rest on an interpretive base that is elusive.

No wonder assimilationists loathe multiculturalism. Multiculturalists are not interested in squabbles over how much freedom should be permitted within an a priori cultural framework. Rather, they have brought to center stage the link between praxis and cultural universals, and thus they have introduced a new dimension into the process of adjusting to norms. Specifically, persons now have the latitude to determine whether cultural ideals meet their needs and have any validity. As might be expected, standards that were formerly held to be unassailable will likely be rejected. After all, subsequent to the onset of multiculturalism, assimilation does not represent the paragon of rationality. In short, assimilation no longer transcends class and other interests that served to undermine minorities.

THE VOX POPULI AND DEMOCRACY

But contrary to what assimilationists say, abandoning these faux universals does not automatically plunge society into chaos (Choi, Callaghan, & Murphy, 1995, p. 3). Instead, and consistent with true democracy, the vox populi is permitted to extend to the root of the polity. Everything is addressed that can impede the expression of personal or collective values. Furthermore, multiculturalists question why culture has been sequestered from praxis. Their answer has been unsettling to some persons: Social advantages have been concealed behind these universals. This kind of protection, declare multiculturalists, is hardly democratic. Multiculturalists illustrate the linguistically inscribed limits of all cultural imperatives. Accordingly, they maintain that the growth of cultural differences is not restricted by social a prioris; instead, normative boundaries are predicated on commitments to various discourses. In effect the only arrangement of cultures that is not purely speculative is one where linguistic praxis differentiates cultural regions. In this process, the metaphysics of domination is rendered inoperable. Simply put, any inherent hierarchy of cultures requires an autonomous justification that cannot be summoned.

All multiculturalism represents is the extension of the vox populi into a new area. Finally, someone is addressing the issue of democratizing culture. Cultures are encouraged to proliferate without threatening order. For this reason, multiculturalists compare society to a montage, jazz, rhizome, or collage, whereby cultural differences are juxtaposed and continuously added to the whole without causing disruption. What is more democratic than celebrating diversity and eliminating any obstacles to expanding the number of cultures recognized as contributing significantly to the formation and development of a society? Multiculturalists make sure that the antidemocratic theory and practice of supremacy cannot lurk any longer behind pronouncements about cultural universals.

Critics attack multiculturalism because proponents of this position question the virtue of having so-called basic values—particularly related to identity, intelligence, language, and similar issues—linked to a particular culture. If absolute authority is detrimental to democracy, why are unexamined cultural ideals acceptable? Multiculturalists argue that extolling these ideal norms represents a contradiction that imperils democracy and should not be overlooked. How can democracy be said to exist when particular cultures are thought to warrant inherent marginalization? Rather than destroying society, multiculturalists are merely confronting a type of unearned privilege. What is undemocratic or unhealthy about this activity?

NOTE

1. See for instance Kallen's books, *Structure of Lasting Peace, Culture and Democracy in the United States,* and *Freedom in the Modern World.* Also see Bourne's books, *The Radical Will* and *Towards an Enduring Peace.*

REFERENCES

Baudrillard, J. (1983). *In the shadow of the silent majorities.* New York: Semiotext(e).

Bennett, W. J. (1992). *The devaluing of America.* New York: Summit Books.

Bloom, A. (1987). *The closing of the American mind.* New York: Simon and Schuster.

Choi, J. M., Callaghan, K. A., & Murphy, J. W. (1995). *The politics of culture: Race, violence, and democracy.* Westport, CT: Praeger.

Fish, S. (1989). *Doing what comes naturally.* Durham, NC: Duke University Press.

Foucault, M. (1989). *The archaeology of knowledge.* London: Routledge.

Gilroy, P. & Baker, H. (1991). *There ain't no black in the Union Jack: The cultural politics of race and nation.* Chicago: University of Chicago Press.

Luhmann, N. (1982). *The differentiation of society.* New York: Columbia University Press.

Lyotard, J.-F. (1984) *The postmodern condition.* Minneapolis: University of Minnesota Press.

Murphy, J. W., & Choi, J. M. (1997). *Postmodernism, unraveling racism, and democratic institutions.* Westport, CT: Praeger.

Sartre, J.-P. (1948). *Anti-Semite and Jew.* New York: Schocken Books.

Schlesinger, A. M. (1992). *The disuniting of America.* New York: Norton.

Stark, W. (1963). *The fundamental forms of social thought.* New York: Fordham University Press.

Zimmerman, M. E. (1996). The death of God at Auschwitz. In A. Milchman & A. Rosenberg (Eds.), *Martin Heidegger and the Holocaust* (pp. 246–260). New Jersey: Humanities Press.

Chapter 3

Adopting the Caucasian "Look": Reorganizing the Minority Face

Masako Isa and Eric Mark Kramer

INTRODUCTION

Traditionally cultures have differed concerning ideals of beauty (Cash, 1981). These ideals, as physical characteristics, are amplified by the use of adornments, including modern cosmetics. Ideas of what is and is not beautiful are thus emphasized, exaggerated. The modern cosmetics industry and related mass marketing are acting in unison today like a cultural steamroller, eliminating traditional ideals of beauty and replacing them with a uniform global look that emerges from the fashion centers of the world. The cosmetics industry, including its mass marketing of course, plays an enormous role today in teaching young women and men what is beautiful and also the value of beauty such that it is smart and chic to conform to certain body and phenotypic standards.

As the modern saying goes, one can never be too rich or too thin. Any suggestion to the contrary is widely seen as quaint at best or more likely as patently stupid, but at least deviant (Dion & Walter, 1972). But one, especially a woman, can be too smart (Cash, Rossi, & Chapman, 1985). Chic and intelligent are not exactly the same things. Many so-called supermodels are in fact high-school dropouts. To be chic is to follow fashion, to be a sort of dumb or passive medium, infinitely adaptable to every current of fashion, willingly dressed and painted by the industry in the hope of being acceptable if not desirable. It is practically a tautology: it is fashionable to be fashionable.

But traditionally what exactly constitutes beauty has always been a locally indigenous evaluation. This fact is changing across the world. We can see the initial impact of the globalization of beauty in Japan, the first and arguably most Westernized nation in Asia.

The multibillion-dollar-per-year cosmetic industry is trans- not multinational, which means that it purviews a very narrow spectrum of what constitutes chic across national and cultural boundaries, effectively replacing local versions with the notion of a single global market selling cool.

In the past Japan was influenced by Chinese concepts of beauty, but the modern sense of beauty in Japan is an industrial product. The modern version also saturates all of Japanese culture, not just the nobility, and it constitutes a special challenge because modern beauty is based on a Caucasoid (not Mongoloid) body type and phenotype, which includes larger breasts, eye folds, round eyes, longer legs, light hair and skin, and so on. Otherwise, as in the case of Sayoko Yamaguchi, who debuted in Paris, not Tokyo, the ideal Japanese beauty is a Westernized Oriental; it is, to recall Edward Said (1979), a Western version of what the exotic Orient should be. The chic official version of beauty is generated by a tiny cadre of high-fashion power brokers who then sell it to Oriental consumers as *their* ideal beauty.

The cosmetic industry as it is now configured originated in the industrial West and remains centered in Westernized urban cosmopolitan areas, such as Paris, New York, and Tokyo. This highly lucrative industry has a very powerful influence in creating a kind of real, a new "naturalism" that is anything but natural (Cox & Glick, 1986; Williamson, 1994). The "natural-looking" beauty is difficult to challenge and even more difficult to achieve without hours of sitting under the expert hands of an artist. The hypertrophic egocentrism that has imploded to a single celebrated face or look (for that's what the worship of celebrity is) is not restricted to fashion models, as we see with the singularity of "O." The TV personality Oprah Winfrey, arguably the most visible black woman in the world, takes at least three hours every day just for her hair, as well as several more hours under the guidance of a personal trainer, dietician, and cosmetologist. By the time she goes before the cameras on her TV show she is practically a mannequin who dares not move too fast or dynamically lest her face and hair come apart. She is a model minority, doling out mainstream-sounding advice without herself having ever been married or having ever raised a child. Like most model minority exemplars, she is one who can hardly be emulated. As noted in Chapter Six of this volume about minority spokespersons, Oprah (and Martha Stewart) is a category of one. Yet she claims to be an expert and spokesperson, with a huge megaphone, for both women and blacks. She is very removed from the daily experiences of the groups she claims to not just be a member of but a prime example of success for.

However, as a heroine, she fails to demonstrate an alternate path and set of principles for her followers, for even she cannot escape the larger hegemonic forces impinging on women's self-esteem. Her success is in fitting with the mainstream culture's version of the ideal woman and ideal black woman. Even though they may bemoan the power of the beauty myth, most women still continually struggle to measure up to the increasingly mass-mediated, pervasive version of what is beautiful, desirable, and acceptable. Even models suffer from the power of the myth, many (including Oprah) struggling with weight "problems" to the point of needing psychological and psychiatric care.

As for Japan, although these standards may have originated in foreign lands, they now dominate the psyches of Japanese people through intercultural transmission, cultural borrowing, and the power of mass marketing. Via cultural fusion and integration, these values have become Japanese. Modern (visiocentric) boys and girls stand before their mirror images and compare themselves with the buffed and beautiful fantasies of digitally enhanced nobodies (literally so, as they are sometimes computer-generated virtual people) on magazine covers (Kramer, 1997; Kramer & Ikeda, 2000; Wolfe, 1991). Millions are obsessed with a relative handful of fabricated body images (Cash & Wunderle, 1987). This is the power of mass mediation with its fantastic narrowing of horizon. A single persona "speaks" to millions simultaneously. This is the concentration of will-power-drive that characterizes massified visiocentric modernity (Kramer, 1993; 1994; 1997).

Homogenization manifests the Western ideology of bourgeois positivism with its faith that life progresses by solving a series of discrete problems and that each problem has one best solution, which is discovered through the therapeutic steps of the one best way to think and believe. Experts become distant personae who never listen, who cannot hear, for the structure of the communication process is manifestly dictatorial (Lyotard, 1984). According to this Hegelian dream, insofar as people are rational, human life will converge on the one best culture or way to live, which, by coincidence, just happens to be the style of thinking, believing, and acting that originated in Western Europe. This is to be expected because the ones doing most of the communicating are Western Europeans and their former colonies. Thus, their ethnocentrism is manifested in their messages; perspectivism is inflated to global validity via the status conferred on it by virtue of being "the message" that is globalized by means of telecolonialism (Ikeda & Kramer, 2002 Kramer & Ikeda, 2000). All that is needed is mass education, all from the same book. This is what is unique about late modern cultural transfer. Modern mediation is not exchange between traders facing each other eye to eye. Rather, it is a one-way disembodied electronic message (not a conversation, exchange, or negotiation) with a single voice that is deaf, being attended to by the masses, that is, by a huge synchronized aggregate of individuals without a sense of community unless it be a cybercommunity. They are mesmerized by the rhetoric of the technological power in and of itself. People rush out to buy the means of mediation, a radio or television or personal computer (*personal* stressing the isolation of viewing by one's self, like "bowling alone"), for the technology itself is the message (McLuhan, 2001), and the message is "get with it," be modern, even futuristic (by skipping the now altogether, for the future is here today!).

The first lesson is that the positive progressive voice is new and good; one should listen to it because it is the solution, the path, (the) (ab)solution and happiness. It knows reality positively. This is self-evident, for after all, just look at the way it arrives. The gadgetry confers status onto the message, which cannot be separated from it; form and content are one. The message is the way to a satisfying future; in fact it *is* the future (Mumford, 1966). You just need to stay tuned to not fall further behind, to stay "current," like the electricity that brings the world to us.

THE GOD-MAKERS

Careful meditation on and worship of the ideal beauty images preoccupies the psyches of millions. Mass media create a collective psyche that shares a very few (if not singular) images of beauty. Primarily women editors of fashion magazines and Hollywood casting directors comb through thousands of would-be idols, selecting the right look. Tens of thousands of teenage girls and their parents invest in photo sets, cosmetic surgery, and hair work to conform to and complete the mythic circle and desperately try to become a model, even a supermodel. But first the hopeful must be selected by those with super-vision, the bosses of the image, the gatekeepers. Their power is enormous for they are the vision givers and god-makers, the teachers. Following Carl Jung's (1981) observation that myth is collective dream, we agree with Naomi Wolfe's (1991) application of this insight, that what we are discussing here is a beauty myth and the shamanic might of the media apparatus to create and propagate it, now to global audiences. The beauty myth is like a dream, which is essentially not the same as the actual. It is of the realm of virtue. As such, it can never be actualized but instead remains a constant exemplar and evaluator, an irritating taskmaster and authoritative threat to actual women.

There has never been a power or age like this one. It is the age of mass seduction, where heavily hyped nymphets tear their own clothing off before screaming preteens while strutting before cameras singing "I wanna be your lover," which, of course, is impossible. A time when children's toy makers argue over which video game babe offers the most booty, *Tomb Raider's* Lara Croft or *No One Lives Forever's* Cate Archer (*Maximum PC,* August 2001, p. 96). Through the gadget power of interactive video, you can make these "women" bounce again and again. Roland Barthes (1973), who brackets the metaphysics of realism, notes that myth is neither true nor false; rather it functions to de-historicize, to decontextualize, we say to deactualize, and thus and ironically naturalize a virtual reality that is an invention, a mere contingency masquerading as an absolute. Naturalism is an ideology, a mythic process. It is ultimately a political move, a rhetorical ploy to make the contingent seem eternal and therefore beyond criticism. Thus, we are talking here not merely of the politics of conventional colonial encroachment and overt oppression but of the politics of the self, which is the most egregious trespass for it invades the confidence people have in their own value. No assault could be more intimate. It threatens their sense of self-worth in the all-important life of desire, of a person's wish to be wanted, accepted, and even worthy of amorous pursuit. Threatening a person's sense of self-worth is to assault them below the belt as it were, to make them insecure and then manipulate those insecurities explicitly for the sake of profiteering. This is not new. What is new is the global scope and psychographic precision of the efforts now under way and the narrowness of alternatives being entertained.

As Mircea Eliade (1998) states, the important question to ask about myth is not merely if it is true or false, especially in the case of aesthetics, but rather to determine if it is alive or dead, for living myth is image that is manifested as prejudgment (prejudice) and as such lies outside the reach of reflexive reason and analysis. Either you are or are not beautiful. Research indicates that people make this judgment of others' physical characteristics within ten seconds (usually less) of first contact. Living myth is not seen as myth at all. Rather, it is simply the real. Living myth means that the myth, the evaluation, has become an integral part of perception itself.

This chapter is an effort to rehistoricize, to recontextualize the concept of beauty in Japan, and thus to demythologize (denaturalize) it, rendering it available to analytic scrutiny.

THE PATH OF BEAUTY

What characterizes modernity is an obsession with space as such and the expansion into it, the exploration of it, the fragmentation of it, and the replication of it. Modernity is not new. It first erupted into Western consciousness with the classical Greeks, reaching its ancient zenith in imperial Rome. Then it subsided as the West vacillated, becoming predominantly two-dimensional again for about twelve hundred years (Gebser, 1985; Kramer, 1992, 1997). The apogee of the second eruption of three-dimensional spatial thinking (with its attendant dissociative consequences leading to the valuation of "disinterest") occurred at the height of the cold war between the Soviet and Western industrial economies. Since about 1975, the consciousness of time (already crystallizing with Benjamin Franklin, Henri Bergson, Edmund Husserl, Albert Einstein, Pablo Picasso, Henry Ford, F. W. Taylor, the Blitz, an obsession with accelerating computation, etc.) has marked the so-called postmodern West. Although ample evidence has been amassed to demonstrate the current struggle to spatialize and control time (reified fragmented, measured existential duration), spatial thinking is still a major aspect of the Western world. This is clear in the continuing project of the age of exploration (globalization) and the domination of the philosophical ideology of empiricism. Under these conditions, the direction of transmission has almost always been from the "advanced" nations to those still "developing" (according to the hegemonic criteria deployed by the advanced countries, criteria which, when applied reflexively to the West, just happen to demonstrate its evolutionary superiority).

In the face of colonial wealth and power, developing nations have wished to be developed, too. Why? After initial resistance and attempts to protect traditional identities, military and economic sanctions launched by colonial powers have tended to bring the less developed around to accepting the criteria of advancement so generously offered. They, the backward peoples, are continuously told, in modern linear (spatialized) terms, that they are "backward," and "culturally lagging" behind the forward, most advanced leading authorities. Leading to where? A utopia, of course, which is by definition unreachable because it promises permanent progress. Insofar as they internalize this way of thinking and accept the lifeline that has been given to them—a line extending, in classically narrow-minded variable analytic style from primitive to advanced—they come to see themselves through these metaphors, this scheme of comparative/competitive human development, as indeed underdeveloped.

This neo-Hegelian notion of developmental evolution extends beyond mere technological know-how. It inevitably implicates the entire globe (physically and psychologically), applying a single scale to all societies, so that it is not merely technologies that are evaluated as comparatively inferior but the people who created the inferior technologies. Hence we have the periodic recurrence of global scaling from Buffon and Linnaeus in the early nineteenth century, to Alfred Binet's IQ testing in the early twentieth century, to Richard Herrnstein and Charles Murray's *Bell Curve* (1994). In fact, Francis Galton (a cousin to Charles Darwin) along with his follower, Karl Pearson, launched mathematical social science as eugenics. Modern materialism reduces the value of a people to the power of their technology. Such global criteria, which are applied to the entire world with such ethnocentric audacity, are imposed by the powerful onto minorities, for the very act of measuring is a one-sided conversation whereby one person defines another with categories and scales of his or her own making. The definer has power over the defined. Minorities are thus established in the very process of reckoning them and objectively (for the same scale is applied to all equally) "proving" them to be backward. Of course the calibration of the scale, and the human characteristics selected as salient and included (privileged) as the very structure of the operational process of definition, manifests the ethnocentric attitudes of the designers of the scale (despite their pretense to be unbiased). What Jim says about Bob may or may not tell me something about Bob, for it may be forever indeterminate. But it surely, manifestly, tells me something about Jim. The scale may or may not reveal something about those subjected to it. But it certainly tells me about those who designed it. Yet the rhetoric of instrumentation insists, "Look for yourself!" The unbiased expert will say, "What a pleasant surprise. When I apply my scale to myself, I come out on top! This is not a cultural bias but a disinterested observation because, after all, I applied the scale to myself just as I did to others. Never mind the fact that I generated the scale, thus reifying my own perspective, reifying and elevating my own values to the status of universal validity by virtue of the fact that I then go around applying it to everyone in the world." Thus, whole countries can be ranked from one to ten in beauty and desirability.

To be developed and advanced in part means to be modern, smart, and chic, all of which usually means Western and presumes wealth in a strictly and restrictively materialistic way, because that fits the metaphysical prejudice of quantitative methods. A case in point is Bhutan, which is presumed to be one of the least developed nations and peoples on Earth, despite having cultural practices rooted in thousands of years of tradition. When told that the United States enjoys a standard of living seventy-eight times higher than his countrymen, King Jigme Wangchuck of Bhutan retorted that he doubts very much that gross domestic product is identical with happiness; he doubts that Americans are seventy-eight times happier than Bhutanese (statement made at the 1987 South Asian Association for Regional Cooperation, hosted by Bhutan). Bhutan is a prime example of a country under great pressure to open up and develop, but the country is trying to control its own destiny. Thus, the government strictly controls tourism. The notion of development being applied to the Bhutanese according to many Western Christian missionaries includes moral development, as many Web sites run by such organizations decry the fact that the king married four women at once, all sisters, and lives with none of them (each has her own house). Yet Bhutan is famous for gender equality. It is traditional there among the Buddhists for a woman to have several husbands, too.

The criteria and definition of what counts as advanced and developed (and presumably happy, according to positivism) originates in the most advanced and developed centers so that the evaluation is biased in favor of those who see as salient such characteristics as number of televisions or telephones per thousand population. The measures come from the urbanized who are economically and technologically privileged. Yet the suicide rates among the privileged are much higher than among traditional, backward peoples. Throughout the great age of globalism (beginning in the 1400s), the seduction of wealth and power has led to comparative rankings, self-appraisals, and competition. Thus, we have the first, second, third, and, some add, fourth worlds. This very way of seeing and evaluating the world is highly restrictive and purely economic in the modern Western sense of the term.

BACKWARD AND FORWARD JAPAN

During the nineteenth century, Japan perceived itself as backward as compared with forward nations like Germany, the United States, and England. Presuming the authority of Western criteria—after all, gunpowder and a belligerent mindset willing to use it is quite convincing—the Japanese came to accept this comparative conclusion. According to Western criteria, of course, the West was advanced, progressive, and positive. Thus, with the Meiji Restoration,

Japan launched itself into an all-out effort to catch up, which included, to the detriment of the rest of Asia, the Japanese mimicking of Western-style colonial ambition. Of course, to be advanced, one must assume some final goal, and (as has been explicated elsewhere) the definers of the final solution live in the centers of the West. Colonial expansion leads logically to global conquest. This is the final solution, the completion of salvation via the domestication and cultivation of the wild, which most especially includes "dark savages." However, this program, this utopian goal (i.e., various incarnations of manifest destiny rooted in the natural superiority of some peoples and societies over others) is a figment of the Western urban imagination.

Although phenomenologically an essentially shared ambition can be discerned, each version of colonial ambition can be analyzed as historically and culturally contingent. That is, although the same logical form is evident, clearly there is a unique age of global expansion that can be traced in its origins to the rebirth of the ancient Alexandrian dream of world conquest, revisited by the Romans, and reborn with the Renaissance. The inspiration remains the same despite technological and historical differences. Each reincarnation of this world ambition gets stronger, improving on the limitations of its previous manifestation. In its current manifestation, Western globalism can be seen as what Jared Diamond (1993) calls a cultural steamroller, eliminating a myriad of languages and cultures in its path; what Friedrich Nietzsche, a hundred years before Diamond and sensing the rising tide of fascism in Europe, called the elimination of the play that enables experimentation at living. Alternative lifestyles, legal systems, religions, economic systems, value systems, belief systems, and motivations are seen from the center as merely contingent deviants that must and will (by the laws of nature no less) eventually "tend toward the mean," which means the majority with its central tendency. Hence the obsession with measures of regression and correlation that characterize Galton, Pearson, and Yule's version of Western social science.

The current Western expansion makes Roman imperial ambitions pale by comparison. To have a future, developing nations are confidently told they must get in and online. Some mainstream writers, such as the neo-Hegelians Gudykunst and Kim (1997), who interpret the world from the center, even equate such conformity with "evolution," "becoming mature," to "upward and forward" progress along an evolutionary dialectic, and being "mentally healthy!" Local diversity is labeled by them a "defilement"; a pathetic attachment to backward parochialism that must be eliminated for people to grow into healthy "transcultural identity" or "personhood" (Gudykunst & Kim, 1997, p. 364).

The success of the United States during World War II underscored the validity of its path to the future, proving that alternative ways of seeing time and the future are inferior. Not only do the victors write history, but so, too (and more important), they define the sense of the possible; the future. Those who win determine the course of future history, especially when the winners think in pseudo-religious (Hegelian) notions of destiny and fatalism; conform or fail.

THE NEW, IMPROVED MODERN BEAUTY

During Japan's self-criticism and its resultant clamor to catch up with the West, she not only embraced machine technology but also white Western/ American ideals of female physical beauty in place of her own traditional, indigenous ideals. This transmission was a part of an Othering process, at least in a Lacanian sense, whereby a false alter ego or Other is created in mass-mediated images. These images are promoted as advanced, modern, and as such desirable. Not just physical culture and technology can be advanced, cutting-edge, or obsolete. With the advent of positivism, people, too, becoming reduced to measured functions, resource base, and behavior patterns, are seen through these adjectival lenses. Thus Japanese women were taught that a certain type of beauty is what Western men want, and that so far as Japanese men are forward thinking, they also want this foreign style of beauty; therefore, in their mode of conforming to what is expected of them to be desirable, they should also desire to look Western/modern. Otherwise, they were out of date, old fashioned, and ignorant. In this process, Japanese women were also taught that style and beauty is something one does not have inherently or naturally but is something that one can buy at a store and put on (be it Western clothes, hairstyle, or cosmetics). The notion that beauty can and in fact must be bought serves the obvious interest of those who have it to sell.

Thus, beauty in Japan changed dramatically to a commodity first found in advertisements and then in products. Beauty had a price. It was an essential part of opening Japan to international trade. Thus we have the commercialized image of beauty found in many advertisements, especially those promoting the sale of Western-style cosmetics and their manifest ideal face. The ads worked as mirror imaging (Lacan, 1982; Williamson, 1994). Nothing less than self-esteem was at stake (Cash, Rossi, & Chapman, 1985; Miller & Cox, 1982). Thus, the female Japanese face was systematically devalued and then hijacked.

Nothing less than the faces of Japanese women were reevaluated in a mirror held up by a dominating Other, the Western hand. And they were found lacking. The very face of Japanese women was thus seen as a problem and Westernization as the solution. This is the essence of hucksterism. First comes the pitch, which includes the claim that there is a problem, of dissatisfaction, followed by (luckily, even coincidentally) the solution! Here we have the confluence of economics and personal imagination, the political economy of desire and self-esteem. As has happened all over the world, with Japan being one of its first and greatest successes, the Western media apparatus was imported as the beachhead for facilitating all future imports. The Western apparatus of mass media arrived with its political/economic structure servicing industrialization. First come the techniques of mass mediation, which herald modernity like nothing else except perhaps the mechanical clock, then comes the rest through its channels (Kramer & Ikeda, 2000). The simple presence of channels themselves signifies modern sophistication. For example, cities often boast how many TV and radio stations and newspapers are available to their citizens. Regardless of the content, the form itself is a measure of progress. To have a telephone (let alone a cell phone, a personal computer, or a TV) as a form of importation is cherished as progressive. So, to those striving to catch up, to progress, embracing as many channels of mass (qua commercial) media as possible is a must. Once established, the channels proceed to flood the popular imagination with imported images, which immediately pose a challenge to old dreams, expectations, motivations, beliefs, and values—in a word, *culture*, and the encultured self.

This apparatus of culture formation then acts as a matrix of channels or portholes into the new environment, transforming it into a market, for development means nothing other than developing or transforming a people into a market. The channels of desire, so aptly named by Stuart Ewen and Elizabeth Ewen (1992), are lines of persuasion and suggestion promoting the super-value of all things modern/Western. Collectively, all importation, all trade and marketing, all modernity is depicted as the ultimate, unquestionable good. All indigenous cultural components, such as religion, language, race, and gender, are subsumed. It does not matter what race or religion or nationality a person is, under the transcendental gaze of capital power, anyone can be a laborer or customer. The inescapable laws that govern in the form of Adam Smith's "invisible hand" treat all equally, as market (labor and/or consumer), the new divinity that sees all, knows all, evaluates all, and rewards and punishes with utter indifference.

Once online the structural content begins to flow, including its most essential part, advertising. But it is something of a mistake to separate the shows from the ads, for both include images of a new good life that serve to create mass dissatisfaction. A prime example is the content of the enormously popular *telenovela* phenomenon around the world, the imaginary content of which consistently purveys images of surgically altered actors playing wealthy characters and lifestyles far beyond the economic reach of the average viewer.[1] But the products that just happen to decorate the *telenovela* world can be purchased (except in Venezuela, where cosmetic surgery is paid for by government entitlements, which has led to an epidemic of such procedures).

Thus, industrialization, with its ethos of standardization and mass production, which requires mass consumption, is introduced and tirelessly promoted. In this instance, it is the face of Latinos and Latinas and also Japanese women that is mass reproduced in Western style. The new, improved modern face comes from a store-bought bottle that has also been promoted as naturally and objectively better than personal likes and contingencies. Their original faces must be critically assessed; otherwise there would be no sale. Self-satisfaction is the absolute bane of the modern profiteer. To create the matrix of desire, first their faces had to be visiocentrically demonstrated to be inadequate, in need of improvement. The media apparatus works to demonstrate empirically, visually, objectively, naturally, really, that the Japanese face just does not measure up. But fear not, for the magical powers of modern industrial alchemy can fix all. All Japanese women are ugly until they purchase the new mass-reproduced face that comes from mass-produced cosmetics, available as a blessing to them for a small compensation, of course. Industrialization is thus a savior. There is no time to lose.

The Western face in the mirror had several steps to take before arriving at the surface of Japanese (qua ugly) eyes, peering as they were out of ugly faces. First the idea of industrial scale profiteering had to be transferred. Then Japanese businessmen could take it from there. They knew the mind of the Japanese woman and man better than any Western marketer. They knew their complexes, insecurities, and fears. So they took the business model and applied it. Thus, historically we find that the Western ideal was largely imposed on Japanese women by a handful of enterprising Japanese businessmen. They exploited the model and its contents to the hilt, for their own personal gain, of course, but also for the sake of progress. What does it matter if all of Japan's women come to see themselves as inadequate? So much the better for sales!

The introduction of the new face was thus part of a period of powerful, sometimes hegemonic Western/American impact on Japan. The process worked so well that many politicians and scholars have noted a pervasive inferiority complex in Japan that may very well have fueled her attempts to mimic Western-style imperialism within Asia in an attempt to measure up, to also be a world power. The Meiji Restoration and the colonial ambitions of Japan manifest its exertions to become significant on the world stage according to Western criteria. But before Japan could be a colonizer, it first had to be colonized.

THE OTHER IMAGINARY FACE IN THE MIRROR

The imaginary Other peering out of the mirror of natural beauty in the ever-so-modern newspapers and magazines and the mirror image of the inadequate self do not match. The virtual and the actual do not match. This conflict forms the nexus where the stronger subjugates the weaker to its values. Through this mirror with a double image is projected a set of evaluative and highly correlated relationships: beauty/ugly, forward/backward, rich/poor, modern/old-fashioned, sophisticated/rustic, smart/stupid, and desirable/undesirable.

What is presented here is how physical beauty has historically been promoted through the commercialization of cosmetics, its transfer to Japan, and the resultant transformation of Japanese ideals of physical beauty. Not only physical beauty but also a more spunky, sassy, cute mental outlook and way of acting characterizes the true modern woman. This transformation inherently involves Japaneseness, and its study offers a window onto Japanese conceptions of culture and consciousness. To pursue this goal, first, we explain some pertinent characteristics of Japanese beauty and cosmetics from the ancient (sixth century) to the Edo period (1868). Second, we examine the Japanese version of beauty after the Meiji Restoration (1868 to the present). We do this by using cosmetic ads and by explaining how the cosmetic industry and related mass marketing have influenced Japanese ideals of physical beauty and female attitudes that are attractive to the modern man.

Overview of Japanese Cosmetics and a History of Japanese Beauty to the Edo Period

At this point we briefly discuss the preindustrial, premassification of the ideal face and the means to try to achieve it; after all, aesthetics existed before industrialization, including cosmetics, although in a very limited, typically elitist way. Preindustrial agrarian peoples typically did not fret a great deal about their looks.

The manufacture and use of face powder, rouge, eyebrow paint, and other cosmetics were imported in the sixth century from Korea and China. In early times cosmetics were used only by special participants in religious ceremonies and festivals. Cosmetics were not worn for mundane adornment. The practice gradually spread among the aristocracy as a means of enhancing one's beauty. In the Heian period (794–1185) men as well as women used cosmetics. In the Azuchi-Momoyama period (1568–1600), in addition to face powder, facial lotion was imported from Portugal, Spain, and Holland. During the Edo period (1600–1868) makeup styles changed along with variations in hairstyles. Kabuki actors, courtesans, and geishas set the pace. They were depicted in woodblock print media, such as *ukiyoe* prints, and popular literature. Beauticians also played an important part in setting fashions.

Among the various cosmetic compounds used, *oshiroi*, a white powder, and *beni* (rouge) contributed in constructing a woman's beauty. White powder was used to whiten the face and other parts of the body. The oldest form of face powder was made from white soil and rice flour. In the seventh century, the manufacture of *keifun* (mercury chloride) and *empaku* (white lead) was imported from China. Their use was confined to the upper classes until the seventeenth century, when it became popular among the general public. In accordance with the old saying "a fair complexion hides many defects," fair skin was the foremost quality attributing to a woman's beauty. As a result, white powder was used extensively during the Edo period, especially white lead powder. It was mixed with water and applied with a brush. In the 1870s, the toxic quality of lead was recognized, and soon after a lead-free facial powder began to be domestically produced.

Beni was first seen on *haniwa*, clay tomb figures of the third to the sixth centuries, whose faces were painted with ocher and vermilion. However, this soft-hued natural red is thought to have been a form of ritual makeup. In the early seventh century safflower (*benibana*), which had come from Egypt via India, Central Asia, China, and Korea, was introduced to Japan, and an extract was used as rouge. This rouge, bright and full-hued, was regarded as a symbol of joy and happiness. By the tenth century the safflower was cultivated in Japan, but the yield was minimal, resulting in a costly product. That is why *benibana* rouge was not widely used until the seventeenth century. At the end of the eighteenth century, *sasabeni*, an iridescent greenish rouge, applied mainly to the lower lip, came in vogue and continued to the nineteenth century. Rouge was applied mainly to the lips; its facial use was limited to special occasions.

Other cosmetics, such as *ohaguro*, used in tooth blackening, were supposed to enhance sex appeal and, in the case of *ohaguro*, help maintain healthy teeth. By about the twelfth century, the custom spread to the men of nobility and the samurai class as well. By the eighteenth century, it became limited again to only women. Later, only married women used it, and the custom continued until the end of the nineteenth century. One reason for tooth blackening in Southeast Asia even today and perhaps the origin of the fad in Japan, is linked to the belief that one way to tell the difference between a female demon and a human female was black teeth. Demons have white fangs. In the Heian era, the practice of shaving the eyebrows and tooth blackening marked the transition into adulthood for girls, as well as social status among women. *Okimayu*, shaving the eyebrows and drawing new ones, was practiced particularly among the upper classes. The reshaping of one's eyebrows gradually became a custom for the average woman to show her married status and continued through the end of the nineteenth century.

The ideal of female beauty in Japan for nearly a thousand years, from the Heian (794–1183) through the Kamakura (1184–1333) and Muromachi (1391–1660) periods, was a plump woman with a round face and cheeks, a large forehead, and eyes slanting down with a fair complexion. By the end of the Edo period (1600–1868), however, some variations began to occur (Murasawa, 1987). Comparison of early with late *ukiyoe* prints reveals that the original plump woman ideal began to give way to a tall and slender body image. A fair complexion still remained as the most important attribute of female beauty. Thus, a dark-complexioned woman from a tropical area (such as Okinawa) would find beauty unattainable because dark skin was considered a defect (Wagatsuma & Yoneyama, 1967). To maintain her beautiful complexion, the woman of the past used a *nukabukuro*, a small bag of rice bran, to wash and polish her face. For Japanese people, white skin was a necessary condition for beauty, and thus they made much use of white powder.

LOVE AND ITS MANY VARIETIES

Iki is a Japanese aesthetic concept that helps explain the Japanese ideal of beauty. *Iki* originally denoted "spirit" or "heart." Later it came to mean "high spirit" or "high heart" and referred also to the way in which a high-spirited person talked, behaved, and/or dressed. As it became expressive of the Edo commoners' ideal, its connotations were affected by the Osaka concept of *sui*. The concept of *iki* is often compared with that of *sui*. These concepts are aesthetic and moral ideals of urban commoners. The concept of *sui* was a common term used initially in the Osaka/Kyoto area during the late seventeenth century, and the term *iki* came into usage in the Kanto region, where Edo (now Tokyo) exists. Both refer to the common desire for an ideal and moral lifestyle. Initially this involved the purity of Buddhism as it related to innocent beauty. Both *iki* and *sui* have implications for male/female relationships.

Until the modern (Meiji) era in Japan, male/female relationships were expressed using the words *iro* and *koi*. *Iro* includes the sense of *iki* (or *sui*, depending on the region), which means the pleasant feelings men and women have toward each other when they are in love. It also signifies carnal desire or lust, which was frowned on by Meiji (Westernized) intellectuals as primitive or obscene. *Koi* was also used in the pre-Meiji era to signify love between men and women, but it signified not physical action so much as the feelings one has within him- or herself, which are not shared. The idea of a love marriage, a modern concept of largely Western origin, stresses the role of the individual in making the choice of mate. With the advent of Western-style romanticism and also where Christianity was most successful in Japan, a highly idealized notion of love emerged and was signified by *ai* (*Ren'ai*). At the same time *sei* (sexuality) and *sei 'yoku* (sexual desire) were yet closely associated with *ai*. The combination of the two is essential to the modern Japanese version of romantic love; like its Western progenitor, a tension also exists that is expressed by the oppression of desire, especially sexuality, ironically as an expression of love. Thus, in the middle Meiji period, virginity gains a high valuation, which is quite contrary to pre-Meiji sentiments.[2] After the Meiji Restoration, *sei* and *ai* (sex and love) become more exclusively associated with the relationship of *kekkon* (modern-style marriage), but at the same time they are differentiated. Such a differentiation is basically a modern fragmentation. As Japan modernized, this ideal was relaxed and *sei* and *ai* became dissociated, and their meanings changed to an aim for pleasure (*sei*) as different from a striving for intimacy (*ai*). And *ren'ai* faltered because it was too idealistic and the above-mentioned tension was not viable. The Christian concept of love, which contains both eros and agape, was distorted in Japanese romanticism whereby *ai* means only eros.

During the Meiji era (late 1800s) the high value placed on virginity manifested as *iki*. It had to do with flirting with the unattainable, the ache of being so close yet so far. Later, *iki* came to be translated as a sort of coy mode of interaction, which was considered chic. This may seem strange, but what it means in terms of philology is that modern Western styles and morals came to dominate Japanese aesthetics. Shuzou Kuki proposed in 1930 that the essence of *iki* refers to chic, smartness, posh, dapper, elegant, and so on (Kuki, 1930).[3] It emphasized the sexual tension of sexual repression. Kuki defined *iki* as a "sensuous radiance" through whose lively delight there breaks the glow of something "supra-sensuous" (Miller, 1978, p. 114). What is meant by *supra-sensuous* is that direct embodied sexuality is repressed in favor of an ideal.

Iki is used to mean a coquettish chat with the opposite sex, with those in whom one perceives the possibility not so much of love but rather of flirtatious dalliance (Miller, 1978). It shows the quick-witted sophistication of the chivalrous sort. It indicates the beginning of the end of the floating sensual world of premodern Japan. In this marginal world we see a tension, a mixing of carnal pursuits with high ideals, of *iro* (carnal lust) and *ai*, which involves *iki*, meaning having pleasant feelings while keeping a proper distance.

This new sort of teasing, which became the modern urban style of interaction in the common public houses, characterizes the world known as *ukiyo*, where relatively poor samurai cavorted in the "floating world," the official/unofficial pleasure quarters. The floating world (*ukiyo*), made famous in *ukiyoe* woodblock prints, was a marshy area northeast of present-day Asakusa (part of Edo), about half a mile behind the Kannon temple and within site of Shin Yoshiwara's Nightless Castle (*Fuyajo*), which lent a sort of backhanded recognition (if not legitimacy) to the area. It was known for its rushes and thus came to be called *Yoshiwara*, "Rush Field." This was the demi-monde of the Edo era, a neighborhood in the marshes at the edge of civilization (old Edo—Tokyo). Yet it became the cradle of cultural invention, of the arts, which only makes sense. Invention, by definition, is cutting edge. The new always comes from the margins. Here not only bordellos appeared but also *ageya* houses (later called *machiya*, from *chaya*, or tea house) for arranging introductions. Thus came into maturity a fabled area for artists, rogues, *ronin*, or masterless samurai who formed bands, which became the modern *zakuza*, wayward monks, kabuki actors, geishas, and prostitutes. Nicholas Bornoff's excellent description of this Edo period demi-monde merits quotation here:

Wealthy townsmen eager to circumvent the austerities of the regime did so with a characteristic step-by-step escalation towards sybaritic ostentatiousness. Despite sumptuary laws and a great many sporadic and arbitrary clampdowns, the Yoshiwara was the one place in which they could enjoy with impunity a freedom forbidden elsewhere. Surpassing even Kyoto's shimabara, the Yoshiwara became much more than just the haunt of harlotry. A splendid cultural microcosm, it was to become the home of restaurants and fancy shops, high fashion and the kabuki theater, of music and dance, of literature and the visual arts. In this unique setting, there blossomed a culture, which, for the first time, issued not from the aristocracy but from the people. (Bornoff, 1991, p. 163)

Out of this milieu was born a new style, the Genroku style, which spanned the latter half of the seventeenth to the mid-eighteenth centuries and which still affects Japanese culture. It marks the apogee of the Edo period, becoming synonymous with Edo style. At this time we see the emergence of a truly popular culture articulated in the novellas of Ihara Saikaku, most notably *Five Women*

Who Loved Love (and *Life of an Amorous Man*) being representative and Murasaki Shikibu's classic *Tale of Genji* (both published in 1682), as well as books of erotic *ukiyoe*, such as *Yosiwara Makura* (*Yoshiwara Pillow Book*, in 1660). The Genroku culture was not only contrary to the Christian and Western values that would later challenge it, but in its irreverently cheeky play with authority and rules, it threatened to erase the divide between the common people and the nobles. For instance, thinly veiled political critiques in kabuki plays irritated the Tokugawa rulers.

Finally, the floating world and its decadent yet tolerated ethos came to a crisis with a scandalous affair between a woman from the aristocratic Ejima samurai family and the great actor-playwright Ichikawa Danjuro in 1711. Despite (or perhaps because of) its illicit blending of the common and the aristocratic, epitomized by the Ichikawa affair, the Yoshiwara continued to be the birthplace of cultural styles for another century. But by the 1860s with straight-laced diplomats and exploitative merchants of the "colonialist ilk" becoming more common, Japanese were being sized up through foreign eyes with a "haughty condescension" (Bornoff, 1991, p. 205).

During the 1860's, foreigners had steadily beleaguered the Japanese with their righteous indignation, which rose in summer commensurate to the mercury in their thermometers. They were horrified by the mixed public baths and at the sight of workmen wearing only a *fundoshi* loincloth; shuddering ... at the sight of naked bathers and shapely pearl divers on the coast, they averted their delicate eyes from the dreadful sight of women dropping their kimonos to the waist and fanning themselves in the sultry heat of the theaters. (Bornoff, 1991, p. 205)

Yet the *ketto* (hairy barbarians) brought money that transformed the economics of the demi-monde, bringing to an end (practically speaking) the world of the geishas and the birth of prostitution. The *ketto*, being utterly unable to appreciate the subtle arts of the geisha, including the *iki* quality of their conversational virtuosity, diverted directly to their singular sexual intent, which nearly any woman could fulfill. Meanwhile, more upright foreigners were outraged by the very existence of licensed pleasure quarters. Japan was about to be saved from itself.

Thus, the spirit of *iki*, which Kuki (1930) had described as including the Buddhist virtue of resignation (*akirame*), was coming to an end and being replaced with Western-style materialism and straightforward pragmatic positivism. Traditional Japanese beauty had as much to do with the how as the what. Traditional Japanese beauty was demure and not simply a case of physical body structure. It could not be reduced to material physicality. One might say in the vernacular that it was classy. Thus, modern Japanese chic harmoniously conjoins coquetry, resignation, and pride along with rigorous attention to detail and a presentation of self as self-effacing. *Iki* is then to be understood as commingling the ethical idealism of Bushido with the religious idealism of Buddhism (Dale, 1986). Its demise would drive many artists, including Yukio

Mishima, practically crazy. *Iki* requires patience and time, virtues lost on the modern world. By comparison, modern style has little style; it is surface only. Compare for instance, geishas, who spend years in various art classes (kimono, music, calligraphy, tea ceremony, poetry recitation, dance, etc.) and hours daily reading the news to be great companions, to the pornographic pinups of today, who are regularly humiliated on the *Howard Stern Show* for their incredible ignorance of even the most mundane knowledge. The latter have little to hide.

According to Kuki (1930), the term *iki* as an essential aspect of Bushido articulates not a dualism but a complementary polarity in the world as follows: chic—subdued elegance; sweetness—rough, uncouthness; refinement—plainness; dandyism—vulgarity. Kuki asserts that "nothing stands in the way of our considering *iki* as one of the conspicuous forms of self-expression of the unique existential modes of Eastern culture, nay, rather of the Yamato race (Japanese people) itself" (quoted in Watanabe, 1974, p.88).

Iki is viewed in four structures: its intensive structure, extensive structure, natural expression, and artistic expression. In the natural expression of *iki*, Japanese beauty is manifested. As for the agent supporting the emotional expression, a slender woman with a willowy waist is chic because slenderness shows the weakening of the flesh and at the same time the strengthening of the spirit (Kuki, 1930). As for the face, a slender face rather than a round face is *iki*. As for the eyes, *nagashime* means chic, flowing eye. That is, the movement of the pupil seems to float coquetry-like toward the other sex. As for the facial makeup, *usugeshou*, light makeup, is the expression of *iki*. *Iki* is demure yet smart, imminently aware. It is a sort of retiring intelligence, which shows itself through grace and skill rather than words. In the case of male/female relations there is also the art of conversation, which includes knowing how to listen and appreciate the varieties of quietude, especially when doing something, as well as appreciating gaiety and mirth. The power, the charm of expression comes precisely from its proper economy. As Barthes (1973) has noted, sexual appeal comes less from total nudity as it does from a gap in clothing where just a flash of flesh invites desire. The brain (with its imagination) is the most powerful erotic organ.

In the Edo period, the women of Kyoto and Osaka used heavy makeup and were ridiculed in Edo as *yabo* (rough, uncouth). Kuki (1930) says that the material cause and the formal cause of *iki* are embodied in the expression of coquetry, through makeup and then of idealism expressed by halting the makeup at the state of suggestion, at the nape of the neck for instance. A slender woman with a slender face and light makeup was considered beautiful at that time.

Japanese Beauty after the Meiji Restoration: The Influence of the Modern Cosmetics Industry on Japanese Beauty

After the Meiji Restoration of 1868, cultural exchange with Europe and the United States led to gradual Westernization of clothing, hairstyles, and makeup techniques. Tooth blackening, considered barbaric by Western standards, gradually became obsolete. Since World War II, Western influence has been so strong that Japanese styles no longer differ markedly from those of the United States and Europe. Today, traditional makeup is used only by *maiko* (young apprentice geishas), kabuki actors in performance, and during special rituals (occasionally it may be used by a bride during her wedding). The reason Japanese physical beauty became Westernized after the Meiji period can be traced directly to the strong influence of the cosmetic industry. Cosmetic and fashion industries are concerned with the look of beauty. These industries work as signifying agents that construct the look for whole societies. It is a business. We now consider some examples of cosmetic advertisements and examine how the commercialization of beauty and cosmetics transformed Japanese aesthetic ideals.

During the Meiji period (1868–1912), the new science of chemistry was introduced to Japan from the West and promoted the development of cosmetics. The new government encouraged those who engaged the development of all modern technologies, including Western-style medicine and chemistry.

In 1872, in Tokyo's high-end Ginza shopping district, Yushin Fukuhara started Japan's first Western-style pharmacy.[4] The process of cultural transmission and fusion, which marks the Shiseido vision, is personified by the Fukuhara family. Yushin's son, Arinobu Fukuhara, founded Shiseido as we know it today; in turn, his son, Shinzo Fukuhara, traveled to Columbia University in 1908 to study pharmacology and became the first president of Shiseido. While in New York, Shinzo met Noburo Matsumoto, who received a bachelor's degree in commercial science from New York University's business school in 1912. Matsumoto would become Shiseido's first managing director, handling the business end of Shiseido.

It is vital to understand three things about Shiseido. First, the Shiseido Art House was and remains a centrally important source of modernism in Japan. Second, French art and culture formed the focus of Western influence on the Fukuhara family and therefore Shiseido's artistic vision and Japan's initial sense of Westernized aesthetic. Why France? This is tied to the third point, which is that France and Japan had a strong sense of cultural reciprocity and fusion. The Paris Fairs in 1867, 1878, and 1889 (in part) introduced Japanese art to the French artistic community, which led to the Impressionist and Postimpressionist movements there. (Similarly, the Chicago Fair of 1893 introduced Frank Lloyd Wright to Japanese architecture.) Going in the opposite direction, in 1900 Shiseido's founder, Arinobu Fukuhara, traveled to Paris and visited the Universal Exposition, which intensified his obsession with French art and culture. Then Shinzo went to France, where he immersed himself in the Paris art scene and became a skilled photographer. In 1915, Shinzo himself designed the company's camellia trademark and ran the company's design department.

In 1903, Nakamura Taiyodo started the Club Cosmetic Company to sell cosmetics, such as powder, lotion, and facial soap. Club's advertisements used photographs of two beautiful women in Western clothing wearing flower crowns, called *sou bijin*. These women represented an imagined world of graceful and elegant upper-class (modern) ladies. Notice that during and after the Meiji Restoration, the upper class and opinion leaders embraced the new, progressive, Western style of all things. Eventually this picture became the trademark of the Club Cosmetic Company. To attract upper-class women to buy cosmetics, Taiyodo's company joined hands with the Mitsukoshi Kimono Shop (later the Mitsukoshi Department Store chain), where many women of the upper classes shopped.

In 1902, another cosmetic company, Momotani Juntendou, sold a lotion for eliminating acne that was a big hit and led the company to market a successful line of facial care products. The success of their original lotion was partly due to its advertising message: "A fair complexion hides many defects, so apply our facial lotion to make your skin whiter" (Mizuo, 1998). What is obvious here is that the traditional notion of beauty was still vital.

In the late Meiji period, *teikoku gekijou* (imperial theater) opened and many Western dramas, such as *Hamlet*, were performed, providing women with an opportunity to not only go out but at the same time to show that they were cosmopolitan. Going to the theater was an opportunity to dress up, displaying status and one's progressive persona. Theater attendance was a status symbol for the women of the upper class. This activity enhanced the use of perfumes and such cosmetics as face powder and *beni*. A famous advertising message of the time sums up the influence of the theater on women's fashion: "Today is for *Teigeki* [imperial theater], tomorrow for Mitsukoshi [department store]." In other words, "Today a woman will see a new Western play at a theater, and tomorrow she will buy the latest Western fashion at Mitsukoshi."

During the Taisho period (1912–1926), Japan's early flirtation with democracy further promoted the Westernization of Japan. The Ginza, for example, Tokyo's most exclusive shopping district, boomed. Along with *teigeki*, the imperial theater, the kabuki theater reopened. Although these two theaters had been rivals, they provided opportunities for cosmetic companies to advertise their products during intermission, and in this sense they shared a common purpose. Many Western-style restaurants, bakeries, tailors, and lamp shops began in the Ginza district, which was located near Tsukiji, the foreigners' residential area. The Ginza led the swift assimilation of Western culture, spurring the adoption and consumption of all things Western, from cigarettes to phonograph records to games like billiards, tennis, golf, and poker.

Under the influence of the short-lived Taisho democracy, a scientist at Shiseido invented a new, daring cosmetic product. At that time, there was only one makeup powder (white), but Shiseido invented the technology for producing powders of seven colors. This range of hues was advertised with the motto: "Let's choose your makeup powder based on your real skin color to make you beautiful." The beauty ideal, then, began to incorporate women's individual, natural skin color. The irony here is the proposition that to be more natural looking a woman had to use cosmetics. It exploited the notion that modern women are individuals. With the variety of makeup colors available, these developments were liberating to the women of that time, for they were no longer limited to just one makeup color, a color few women could match exactly.

In 1911, Japan's first Western-style actress, Sumako Matsui, performed Western drama. She is best remembered for her 1915 portrayal of Nora in Ibsen's *A Doll's House*. At about the same time, opera at Asakusa became popular. Big news was made when the first female student was admitted to Tohoku National University. Also about this time, the Japan Women's University was established. In 1920 Fusae Ichikawa joined Hiratsuka Raicho and Oku Muneo to establish the *Shin Fuji Kyokai* (New Woman's Association), and in 1924 she helped found the *Fusen kakutoku domei* (Women's Suffrage League). Thus, the liberal, Westernized atmosphere of Taisho raised women's consciousness. Women's magazines such as *Fujinn no Tomo* (Woman's Friend), and *Fujin Kouron* (Women's Review) were published. The former magazine focused on intellectual, progressive subjects, such as equal rights for women. The latter targeted middle-class housewives and their betterment. Each issue contained Christian ideas about the proper place of women, ideas that were quite foreign to Japan. The magazine was geared toward the improvement of women's lives. In total, by mid-Taisho period, five women's magazines were published. These magazines carried many cosmetics ads, promoting the sale and use of cosmetics among women.

In 1916 Shinzo Fukuhara established Shiseido's Design Department by gathering a team of gifted young artists. They created a series of beautiful art nouveau–inspired posters and advertisements. For the products themselves they began designing elegant packages with distinctive arabesque graphics. For a country still new to the ways of the West, the message was one of novel, exotic luxury—the perfect expression of Shinzo's motto, "richness in all." Shiseido used the culture of Ginza as its corporate image and changed the company's name to Tokyo Ginza Shiseido in 1923. According to a women's magazine in 1925, there were some females with blue eye makeup walking around at Ginza, which was an unprecedented event in Japan. Thus, Ginza was a fashion center, and Shiseido became a leading cosmetics company in Japan.

In the late 1920s, many Japanese women were still hesitant to wear Western-style attire. In the January 1927 issue of the Shiseido magazine, an interesting survey was published. According to the survey, in just one hour on an afternoon in December, 1,151 males passed by the Ginza Shiseido gallery; 797 wore Western-style clothing, 349 wore kimonos, and 5 were foreigners. During the same hour, 522 female passersby were recorded; 22 wore Western-style clothing, 494 wore kimonos, and 6 were foreigners. This may indicate that not only in the cosmetic industry but in society at large men were leading the way to modernization. Women readers of this survey would hardly miss the message; Japanese men like modern Western things and, by implication, girls.

In 1927, a new fashion called *mobo* (modern boy) and *moga* (modern girl) was popular. To be a *mobo* one had to wear bell-bottom trousers, round glasses with thick plastic rims, and a hat. *Moga* wore Western clothes, short hair, a hanging-bell hat, and high-heel shoes. About the same time the number of working women increased. Women started to work as telephone operators and hostesses at milk halls, which made them change from Japanese kimonos to wearing more practical (for industrial-type work) Western clothes. The Takasimaya department store hired beautiful women to work as mannequins. They wore Western-style uniforms and carried placards. They also demonstrated how to apply makeup. This marked the beginning of public relations for cosmetics. Shiseido also used beauticians who were later called Miss Shiseido. By the mid-1930s, Shiseido advertising moved beyond simply assimilating Western influences to developing a distinct style of its own. Emerging from this striking synthesis of Western and Japanese elements was a new kind of woman: an idealized woman not only at the forefront of fashion but also aware of herself and her potential. Ads in 1936 suggested a beauty from within, reflecting a woman's own sense of identity. But still this was a Westernized identity with Western-style makeup used to announce itself.

At the beginning of the Showa period (1926–1989), Japanese movies and dramas were in their glory. A Japanese version of the Hollywood star system emerged. Cashing in on the opportunity, cosmetic companies used famous movie actresses to advertise their products. But before turning to the local stars, cosmetic companies enlisted the more powerful faces of Hollywood idols. In 1936, a Japanese cosmetic company, Momotani Juntendo, first used a foreign movie actress, Foxster. The ad campaign appeared in the Osaka Asahi newspaper to sell crinsin cream. The ad read, "9 of every 10 women from the West wash their faces with our crinsin cream." Not to be outdone, Shiseido hired Marlene Dietrich to sell white powder. These two advertisements stressed Western makeup, including eyelashes, lipstick, and eye shadow. At that time, only some women wore eye shadow, but by the mid-1960s eye shadow became popular with most Japanese women. We can say that Western women with big eyes, double-edged eyelids, straight noses, and curly hair were seen as ideals and as the standard of beauty by Japanese women living in the city.

At the time of the Sino-Japanese War (1936–1937) and World War II (1941–1945), the production and use of cosmetics decreased dramatically. Due to the war, the government prohibited cosmetics ads. Due to austerity, women applied modest amounts of makeup because excessive makeup was considered an inappropriate luxury. Domestic public service announcements used phrases such as "we don't want anything until the war is won" and "luxury is an enemy." Yet the idea that popular cosmetics constituted a tacit recognition of Western aesthetic superiority was unassailable. The assumption was so deeply held that no one questioned the ultimate value of looking more Caucasian, more beautiful.

Immediately following World War II, because daily necessities were in short supply, rebuilding the cosmetics industry was not a priority, and what cosmetic products that existed were often used as barter. This served only to make cosmetics even more valuable, giving them greater status as luxuries. Shiseido commenced advertising activities in January 1946. The first advertisements were in black-and-white layouts with the camellia logo and the words "Shiseido Cosmetics." In July 1946, the Shiseido Cosmetics Store was decorated with a red Shiseido neon light, the first such light on the Ginza. By November, Shiseido used a famous movie actress, Setsuko Hara, to create a color poster for distribution to chain stores throughout the country. The poster became a symbol of Japanese postwar aspirations, reconstruction, and hope. Setsuko Hara is a Japanese actress who used to appear in the films of Akira Kurosawa, Yasujiro Ozu, Mikio Naruse, and so on. She is called the "eternal virgin" in Japan and was a symbol of Japan's golden age of film (1950s).

Setsuko Hara's Western clothes; smiling face with big eyes, big nose, and big mouth; and posture (looking skyward) projected the message that it was time to give up the old tradition of wearing *monpe*, Japanese slacks. The picture gave the impression that a woman can stand on her own two feet in the new age of Showa (Shimamori, 1998). Her physical appearance was different from that of the traditional Japanese woman. It revealed a different type of woman: an independent woman like one from the West. Yet she was unmistakably Japanese. In this image we have a fusion of East and West, the emergence of the postwar modern nation of Japan including the new Japanese woman.

One of the most talented designers of the Showa period was Ayao Yamana, who brought life to this Shiseido ideal. His refined, stylized graphics with their delicate lines captured the very essence of the company's new approach to beauty. His depictions of what came to be known as the modern girl in 1952 served as a model for young ladies while manifesting Shiseido's image as a leader in the fashion industry.

Japan in the 1960s was in the midst of an unprecedented economic boom. Consumption had gone beyond status to become practically a duty, an ethic; advertising emerged as an expression of this celebration, a true commercial art form. Shiseido launched its first seasonal promotion campaign in 1961 on the theme "Candy Tone." One poster illustration included four young ladies wearing Western clothes with long hair, big eyes, and happy faces, projecting the message that the new beauty (Western style) was within the reach of every woman. Success personally and nationally meant the transformation of Japan into a new economic power in the Western way. Showing the latest colors of lipstick, the campaign proved to be a huge success, particularly among younger women and soon grew into an annual event. With television coverage of the marriage of the crown prince (currently the emperor) to Michiko Shoda in 1959, the sales of TV sets exploded, exceeding 2 million. TV became an important medium for the advertisement of cosmetics. Shiseido used it as a medium to sell their products to the masses, which means to control their image of beauty. The candy tone ads purposely used four models to project the idea of sameness in beauty among women. Curiously, the editor of the monthly journal *Koukoku Hihyou* (Advertising Criticism), Michiko Shimamori, called this massification of beauty and the use of the four different models in the spectacularly successful campaign "the democratization of beauty," which means that a unified image of beauty was sought at that time that would be applicable to all equally. It did not mean the tolerance or promotion of diversity, however.

During the 1960s social change was in the air, and Shiseido was no exception. What was emerging was a huge, primarily white affluent youth market in the United States, with its own music, clothing, hairstyles, cinema, and fashions. In 1966 Shiseido established its summer promotion with its second campaign featuring Bibari Maeda (of later Godzilla movie fame). This was the first time they had done overseas filming, and the art director for the shoot, Makoto Nakamura, selected Hawaii. The famous color ad featuring Maeda can be seen by going to Shiseido's Art House Web page on the Internet.[5] This second summer campaign for Shiseido featured something not seen in Japan before—a seventeen-year-old woman-child in a swimsuit with tanned skin and a Western look. This was a dramatic departure from the traditional fashion of pale skin. Maeda was a half-Caucasian/half-Japanese woman with an exotic face, big eyes, bold eyebrows, and a big nose.

The picture projected the message of a liberated, fun-loving American-type girl with a healthy, outdoorsy body and carefree life. With this ad, Shiseido sold face foundation, "beauty cake," by using the phrase *Taiyou ni aisreyou* ("I want to be loved by the sun"). Maeda's tan skin and public exposure of lots of it was a clear and bold shift toward the very American surfer and beach culture then prominent. It also was a pronounced mimicking of American advertising trends, which were tapping into the emerging American youth–oriented market.

One critic has offered a different interpretation, however. Shimamori (1998), writing about the Maeda layouts, makes a very dubious attempt to link her suntan to the civil rights motto in the United States, "black is beautiful." The image, it seems to us, has much more to do with Hawaii's romance than any political consciousness about race relations. It is highly doubtful that Shiseido had any desire to associate its products with a foreign civil rights movement three thousand miles away, especially because Japan had very few black residents in 1965 (or even now). But Japan does have many young women and many beaches, and Hawaii is a favorite honeymoon spot for young Japanese newlyweds. Cosmetics appeal to the modern Western sense of romance. Shimamori's hypothesis seems unreasonable.

Besides the fact that blacks don't (noticeably) tan, during the 1960s they did not partake in the surfer mystique that dominated the American, and to some extent world, popular culture featuring the Beach Boys sound along with suntanned Caucasian boys and girls like Annette Funicello, Frankie Avalon, Fabian, and "Mr. American," the "Blond Bomber" bodybuilder Dave Draper (who helped launch Santa Monica's muscle beach into international fame that allured young Europeans like the "Teutonic Giant," Arnold Schwarzenegger). Simply put, it is impossible to comprehend a claim that Shiseido wanted to associate its products with the black racial strife that was erupting in the United States (the Black Panther slogans of "black power" and "black is beautiful";

Martin Luther King Jr.'s march on Selma, Alabama; race riots, etc.), not to mention the daily international news throughout the 1960s about apartheid conflict in South Africa, rather than the romantic and idyllic white youth culture in the early 1960s.

With Maeda's youthful, fresh, sunny portrait, Shiseido shifted its image strongly away from the traditional demure Japanese beauty to embrace and promote an Americanized image that included the cult of the beach baby teen beauty made internationally famous by movies created by American International Pictures (AIP). AIP created the beach party genre beginning with the 1963 release of *Beach Party*, followed by six more such films, including *Muscle Beach Party* (1964), *Bikini Beach* (1964), and *How to Stuff a Wild Bikini* (1965). Shiseido, like advertisers all over the world, was clearly cashing in on the new fad of sun, fun, and (literally) thinly veiled adolescent sexual exploration.

Here was an advertisement that presented not just a pretty face but also a true sense of modern chic risqué. This was a pseudo-rebel with a cause (to sell Shiseido). Shiseido once again broke with convention, firmly renewing its avant-garde reputation in Japan by conforming to current international advertising trends. This was the birth of the supermodel who had a name and celebrity. From the plastic miniskirt and op art clad mod stick girls Twiggy and Jean Shrimpton (the face of Yardley) from fab Carnaby Street to the wind-in-the-hair freshness of Lauren Hutton, Jennifer O'Neill (the face of Cover Girl Clean Make-up), and Cheryl Tiegs (the face of Revlon), and the sunbathing Maeda, youth was in, skin was in, audacity was in, and unabashed fun was in. Maeda's poster became famous in Japan; with it a deep suntanned face became the new fashion. It worked famously. For the first time ever in Japan, girls and young women came to see a suntan as beautiful, and sales of suntan oil soared.

But something more important was happening with the Shiseido look: fusion. Maeda was half-Caucasian and half-Japanese. Shiseido continued this look with other mixed-race Eurasian models. Shiseido art director and designer M. Nakamura used American sisters Tina and Bonnie Lutz, who had a Japanese mother and an American father and whose features, like those of Maeda, were neither fully Japanese nor Western but rather a combination thereof. They promoted the Love in Color line of lipstick, which featured pinks and pastels instead of reds, the color that had been dominant in Japan for many years.[6] There are other Eurasian models featured by Shiseido, including Tina Chow (who was also a designer) and her daughter, China Chow. Of course, the fusion face is even more impossible for the average women to achieve than the traditional beauty.

Always seeking to stay fresh in its image, in 1973 Shiseido seized on another foreign triumph and made it its own. This one was traditional but not much more actual than a doe-eyed mixed-race beauty with only one ear (see note six about Bonnie Lutz). In 1972, an unknown Japanese model named Sayoko Yamaguchi made her international modeling debut in Paris. She was a sensation. To Western eyes, she was quintessentially Oriental. On her return to Japan, Shiseido, realizing that the time had arrived for a pure, true Japanese face, signed her to be the persona of Japanese beauty. She was featured in their 1973 autumn makeup campaign. Tacitly, if you can make it in the West (namely Paris), you must be great. Shiseido seized on Yamaguchi's success, making it their own, and promoted her as Japan's "greatest supermodel" who also happens to use Shiseido products (at least in the ads). It was a good wedding for both parties—both Shiseido and Yamaguchi enjoyed great success together. The focus of the campaign was eye makeup, which is significant because Yamaguchi is famous for having very narrow eyes, which makeup artists and photographers further accentuated.

Though Eurasian models with Western looks were very popular in Japan at the time, Shiseido went against the trend that it had helped create with Maeda. Yamaguchi's trademark *okappa* short-bob hairstyle made her look like a traditional Japanese doll. She was hyped as the personification of Japanese beauty par excellence. She was often featured in a kimono, with white face powder and rouge. She was featured in *Shiseido Chiffonette*, which promoted eye makeup suitable for Asian eyes.[7] With her debut at the 1972 Paris collections, her charm was dubbed mysterious. She was a sensation in Paris and London, winning international fame as a classical Japanese beauty with bobbed hair and not-round eyes. In the Shiseido ads, she wore a red dress and had black hair, slit eyes, and a small red lip (traditionally, girls including *maiko*, or young geisha apprentices, put red lip color only on their upper lip to minimize the apparent size of their mouth). Yamaguchi was posed and directed into demure positions. The photos that were published did not show her smile, as was the trend. In these ads her face looks expressionless, like a *noh* mask. Yamaguchi's image embodied the Western version of idealized Japanese style, which ironically, because the West loved her, was enthusiastically adopted by the Japanese market. It seems that Japan itself had become so Westernized that the new (starting in the 1970s) Shiseido campaign was exotic even to the domestic audience.

With this campaign Shiseido reintroduced the "true" Japanese beauty. It worked. The mystique created with Yamaguchi now existed for the Japanese consumer just as it did for Parisians and New Yorkers. In other words, mimicking Western beauty had become passé, therefore Shiseido, needing a fresh angle as always, promoted the "essence" of Japanese beauty, but only after it had been so identified in the West. Although the look changed, the Western form of commercial art remained beyond question. Japan had changed forever, and just as with Western corporate culture, its commercial needs were quick to exploit any cultural form that would work. In this instance it was the creation and promotion of a myth of the true, essential Japanese beauty. It worked because the commercial landscape in Japan had become so uniform that such a break with conventional content seemed nothing short of revolutionary.

The mystique of *iki* had been rediscovered in Japanese commercial art. It can be seen in many ads, especially ones for eye shadow, for commercial art always rushes to imitate success. In 1976, a movie actress, Kimie Singyouji, was used in Shiseido ads. Similar to Yamaguchi, Singyouji has a plain, mask-like face with slit eyes. The operant phrase in the Singyouji ads was *yureru, manazasi* (swaying look), which emphasized the *iki* of chic, subtle flirtation with the eyes. Already in the 1970s Shiseido was driving to expand its market into foreign countries. It continued this effort by stressing its identity as a distinctly Japanese company to find a unique niche among all the competition. Thus, Shiseido associated its corporate image and products with an idealized Euro version of Japanese physical beauty that appealed most to foreign consumers.

During the 1980s and 1990s, some leading Japanese cosmetic companies, such as Shiseido, Kanebo, and Kose, actively engaged in global markets to boost stagnant domestic profits. To this end they established offices in Europe, the United States, and throughout Asia. Shiseido started to create many faces of beauty. To execute its global marketing strategy, Shiseido created an in-house ad department in Tokyo, which closely works with local companies to translate and tailor the basic message of their ads to each market. Their UV-White skin care and cosmetics line is a good example of how this philosophy works in practice (Herskovitz, 1997). In Japan, where UV-White is Shiseido's second most popular product line, ads feature a Japanese model demonstrating how the product prevents skin from darkening. The underlying theme is that skin protection yields whiter skin, which has come back into vogue throughout Southeast Asia. The message remains the same in other Asian markets, but local models are used. However, in Europe and the United States, the whitening emphasis is supplemented by a focus on UV protection, with local models demonstrating the product. Thus, one product is given two distinctly different identities and use values depending on the target audience, one mainly aesthetic and the other pseudo-medicinal.

The face of Shiseido varies from models to movie stars, and the age range stretches from teens to late forties. The company has always associated itself with the Miss Shiseido image. In the early twentieth century, there were perhaps twenty Miss Shiseidos at any one time.[8] There were more than one so that they could travel throughout Japan, giving sales and promotional pitches. But after World War II, with the development of much more powerful mass media and the advent of the supermodel, Shiseido began to have one flagship face, as we have seen with Maeda and then Yamaguchi. Thus, the ideal of beauty, like any absolute, became perspectively narrowed to just one set of parameters, one face.

Since the 1980s, when the company sought a new global image for itself, it employed French artist Serge Lutens as its image creator. According to Shiseido's description, he is dedicated "to creating a new concept of beauty derived from the meeting of Oriental, and Western (European and American) cultures, and to creating the colors and images of Shiseido makeup." This is essentially the engineering of a fusional face that belongs to practically no one (Kramer, 2000). His imagination roams freely from classical Greek motifs featured in his 1989 collection to the Russian supremacist influences in the 1991 collection *Les Suprematistes.*

Recent trends stress natural beauty. In the 1990s, in addition to preventing skin from aging, whitening (hardly a natural process) became an important theme. Medicated or nonmedicated cosmetics, effective for whitening (*bihaku*) such as UV-White (Shiseido), Faircrea (Kanebo), Antellige (Kosei), and Lumiera Whitissimo (Pola), are promoted for their ability to prevent freckles. Following first the West's obsession with the sun and then its awareness of the skin damage that prolonged exposure causes, Japanese companies are following this trend. Ironically these products are sold to preserve natural skin color, when, of course, it is natural to tan in the sunlight. According to Shiseido's promotional materials for 1999, that season's makeup featured a translucent yet matte-textured complexion. The enhancement of the radiance of the cheeks was supposed to generate a look of "natural elegance." Eye makeup became less pronounced with a more natural look. The new eye was one that had an artificial eye line and little else. The 1999 season's lips featured a "healthy translucent radiance," along with the striking use of red lipstick.

As Williamson (1994) notes, such products are pitched as magical potions that absurdly promise that as scientific cultural artifacts, only they can evoke nature. Nature becomes, through the incantatory power of cosmetic advertising, an industrial product. The "natural look" can be had, but only at the price of some cosmetics. And by the means of this idolic form of communication, the self as face becomes identical with the "look," which is identical with the powers of the cosmetic alchemy (Kramer, 1997). All are one, *pars pro toto*. The model in the ad is the look, she is Shiseido, and you can be the look ,too, you can become her, your face can become a Shiseido face, a beauty, but only if you buy the magic potion.

FOREIGN MANUFACTURERS IN JAPAN

According to Root and Root (1993), in order of market size and share, the top cosmetic manufacturers in Japan are Shiseido, Kao, Kanebo, Pola, and Kobayashi Kose, respectively. Though not in the top five, French and U.S. cosmetic companies are also successful in exporting their products to Japan. American cosmetics that enjoy popularity include Max Factor, Hélène Curtis, Estée Lauder, and Clinique. Historically speaking, of the American marketers Max Factor has had the greatest impact on Japanese beauty. Max Factor established his cosmetic company in 1953. In 1987, the company was replaced by the new Max Factor KK in Tokyo. In 1991, Procter and Gamble, who had started business in Japan in 1972 as a joint venture with Nippon Sunhome, acquired Max Factor.

Throughout the development of the motion picture industry in the early 1900s, Max Factor (the man) was instrumental in providing makeup consultation and expertise to American movie stars, including Elizabeth Taylor, Greta Garbo, Bette Davis, and Judy Garland. The innovations of various foundation lines, lipstick shades, and eye shadows later formed what was known as the system of color harmony. The most well-known creations include the Max Factor Lip Gloss, which appeared in 1930, the Beauty Calibrator in 1932, Pan-Cake Make-up in 1937, Pan-Stick Make-up in 1948, Erace (cover-up stick) in 1954, and waterproof makeup in 1971. In 1959, Max Factor introduced the idea of marketing to Japan and launched a sales campaign for Roman Pink lipstick.

Not accidentally, during the 1950s and early 1960s a spate of Hollywood and Italian films that were enormously popular worldwide, including in Japan, featured Rome as their romantic setting. The rage began in 1953 with Audrey Hepburn, who had started modeling at age twenty-two. She made her American film debut in *Roman Holiday* (1953) playing opposite Gregory Peck. Hepburn, who was hugely popular in Japan, won the Academy Award for Best Actress for her work in this film. That was followed by *Charade* (1963), in which she starred with Cary Grant. In 1955, *To Catch a Thief* featured Cary Grant and Grace Kelly. Alfred Hitchcock won an Academy Award for best cinematography for this film. In 1954, the Trevi Fountain became a mainstay in romantic American films, beginning with *Three Coins in the Fountain*, for which Sammy Cahn and Jule Styne won the Academy Award for best song (of the same name). In 1956 and 1957 Federico Fellini won back-to-back Academy Awards for best foreign film (*La Strada* and *Nights of Cabiria*). Again in 1960, Fellini gained international acclaim for his hit *La Dolce Vita*, and in 1962 *Marriage Italian Style* was released, featuring Sofia Loren and Marcello Mastroianni, who was nominated for an Academy Award for his work on this film. *Marriage Italian Style* won the Golden Globe Award for best foreign language film.

Our point is that during the 1950s and extending into the 1960s romantic exoticism was portrayed by two European capitals, Rome and Paris (notably *The Last Time I Saw Paris*, 1954, featuring Elizabeth Taylor, and the film *An American in Paris*, 1951). Rome had cachet, and stars like Audrey Hepburn, Grace Kelly, and Sofia Loren set the fashion pace. In films like *Funny Face* (1957), staring Hepburn and Fred Astaire, and *Cover Girl* (1944), starring Gene Kelly and Rita Hayworth, Hollywood presented a synergy of intertextual semiosis by combining high fashion with the debonair romance of classical musical stars, such as Kelly and Astaire, with Rome and Paris. Each component—the stars, the settings, and the look (the fashion)—became integral, one with the others. Max Factor the man created their look, and Max Factor the cosmetic company mass-marketed the look.

The 1959 Max Factor lipstick campaign made extensive use of the mass media. The hook phrase was "even statues in Rome can be revitalized by our Roman Pink." It was a very sensational campaign, influencing the way the Japanese cosmetics industry sold their products domestically. In 1965, Max Factor introduced a new eye shadow, called fascinated eyes, and makeup foundation. These products changed Japanese traditional makeup usage from white powder to makeup foundation, which can be applied under any condition, for example, during the summer or on rainy days. In the Japanese movie *Karumen kokyou ni kaeru* (*Carmen Comes Home*, 1951), directed by Keisuke Kinosita, Max Factor Pan-Cake foundation was used so that the actor's makeup would not come off easily. It was new to the Japanese cinema industry. Because the cinema is a powerful motor of cultural innovation, especially in the areas of fashion and beauty, pancake-type foundation gained popular acceptance. To add to the already formidable inertia of this cinematic influence, in 1959 Akiko Kojima became the first Japanese woman to win the Miss Universe beauty contest, and Max Factor, a sponsor of the contest, quickly capitalized on her victory, producing Akiko Lipstick for the Japanese market. It was very popular. Thus, Max Factor contributed to creating the beauty culture of eye makeup in Japan and introduced marketing techniques for cosmetics sales there.

CONCLUSION

Japanese ideals of beauty have gone through two fundamental changes, both caused by foreign influences, first Chinese and then Western. Because people judge and are judged on the basis of their physical appearance, beauty plays an important role in society. In practice, societies treat beauty as absolute values, but the fact is that beauty is culturally determined and societies differ radically in their definitions of what constitutes beauty. However, in recent decades a tremendous reduction and narrowing of what constitutes beauty has been occurring. This is largely due to the power of mass marketing on a global scale.

This chapter describes how physical beauty has become commercialized through the mass marketing of cosmetics. Most recently, the cross-cultural influence of Western standards of beauty has been dominant in Japan. Historically the ideal of physical beauty and cosmetics usage in Japan can be divided into three main periods: (1) the pre-Meiji period (before 1868), (2) the Meiji and Taisho periods (1868–1926), and (3) the Showa and Heisei periods (1926 to the present). In each of these periods the Japanese ideal of physical beauty went through major transformations. During the pre-Meiji period, a round face with round cheeks, a large forehead, and downward-slanting eyes characterized the ideal of physical beauty. The most common makeup was *oshiroi* (white powder) and *beni* (rouge). Fair skin was the most important characteristic of female physical beauty. A *nukabukuro* (a small bag of rice bran) was widely used for washing one's face to achieve this effect. This version of beauty most probably originated with Chinese influence during the eighth century.

However, during modernization/Westernization (the Meiji and the Taisho periods), this ideal of physical beauty was gradually Westernized, and a standardization of ideal physical beauty based on new hair and clothing styles emerged. The pre-Meiji value on white skin dovetailed easily with the new Western stress on Caucasoid characteristics. In the 1960s the value of an outdoorsy, less demure, more dynamic or spunky beauty in the fashion of Brigitte Bardot and Audrey Hepburn emerged. With it, a tanned skin became fashionable. Other physical features changed. Thus, big eyes, double-edged eyelids, curly hair, a pronounced bust line, and a straight nose became the new standard of beauty. During this period all cosmetics and fashion styles were geared toward achieving a uniquely Western look that was promulgated by mass marketing. Caucasian models were used in Japan to promote elite products (Kramer, 1999). Therefore, during the 1950s and early 1960s cosmetics that promised whiter skin and "improved" Westernized features were in greater demand and usage than the traditional style.

Dark skin (including a tanned complexion) was considered a defect. But during the mid- to late 1960s Japan followed the Western trend of the youthful, sun-and-fun beach beauty. The once negative connotation of tanned skin, which indicated that a woman worked outdoors, was replaced by the woman who played outdoors. The earlier stress on white skin in Japan had been a class marker, for elite women did not have to work in the fields. As noted, this was a concept of beauty introduced from China during the T'ang dynasty (eighth century), when Japan was heavily influenced by all things Chinese (i.e., language, religion, education, artistic styles, clothing, forms of government, etc.). This prejudice toward whiter, fairer skin would be challenged for a short time in the 1960s and early 1970s, when the influence of the American youth culture was powerful in Japan. The older standard of fair skin and demure iki-style expression, as opposed to the Western style of frank emotional expression and ostentatious display of sexuality, staged a comeback later in the 1970s. The old standard of white skin and the new version dovetailed in the persona of supermodel Yamaguchi. The theme of this ideal of physical beauty was that a whiter complexion hides many defects.

However, for Japanese women, in the long run achieving this ideal of beauty has proven to be unattainable. Few actual Japanese women can look like a virtual, kimono-clad, bob-haired supermodel. Neither the Western ideal nor the Western ideal of Oriental beauty embodied by Yamaguchi makes much sense to a typical Japanese woman. But this is part of the marketing plan. For if the ideal were easily attained, two things would result that would be bad for the cosmetics industry. First, sales would drop because once achieved, women would quit buying in an endless effort to attain the ideal. Second, it would be difficult to keep "the look" fresh by unilaterally reinventing the beauty myth periodically. This is why the new face of beauty being created by Shiseido makes perfect sense. It is a fusion face that combines Western with Japanese features that is practically unattainable except in mixed-blood persons like one of their supermodels, Maeda. All of this indicates the power of cultural imperialism as it has impacted the very self-esteem of Japanese women. But also, with Shiseido's ambition to appeal to a global market, this chapter demonstrates why that company would be moving aggressively to invent a postmodern face that fuses racial characteristics, transcending market and racial boundaries.

The overall goal is to make women feel inadequate and to keep them feeling that way. The emergence of the new virtual mixed-race global face will do just that. Its exoticism is unmatched in actuality. This is a marketing ploy that is now deeply entrenched in Japan as its culture has industrialized and commercialized. Thus the very psyche of Japanese men, women, and children is being systematically manipulated, effecting the self-esteem of millions, encouraging them to work harder to achieve a goal that is impossible because (1) it cannot be actualized and (2) it is periodically reengineered with the attendant introduction of new lines of cosmetics, clothing, and hair fashions that make the things one already owns obsolete. The modern fashion industry thrives on the passing seasons, which constitute the passing of fashions. One is always on the verge of being out of fashion, thus keeping the circle of production/consumption moving. This includes the face. Faces, phenotypic "looks," go out of fashion now just like clothes, keeping woman anxious to not fall out of favor, to become ugly. The old value of harmony has been replaced across the board, including with one's own body, with self-dissatisfaction and continual striving.

NOTES

1. The *telenovela* form of soap opera, now enjoying enormous popularity throughout the third world, originally was (and still is) designed specifically to be a vehicle for showcasing commercial products and lifestyles. The original writers and producers worked in pre-Castro Cuba. When the revolution occurred, they took their efforts to other Latin American audiences. Today, this form (which ultimately originated in the United States as daytime serial melodramas, first on radio and then TV, well before Latin American countries even had television systems) is now a very powerful motor of cultural production.

2. This stress on the value of virginity is evident in the era's literature. For instance in Futabatei Shimei's *Heibon* (About mediocrity), published in 1907, and Mori Ougai's *Vita Sexualis* (1909).

3. In 1994, Sakuko Matsui of Sydney University set out to revise John Clark's original English translation of Kuki's 1930 work on the "structure" (a curious choice of terminology itself in relation to *iki*) of *iki*. To this end he visited the Kuki archives at Konan University in Kobe to double-check the original notes and quotations. Matsui attempts to illustrate the great difficulty one encounters in trying to translate the terms *sui* and *iki*. He cites a passage as an example of how vastly different two translators can be. The first is from a recent publication on Kuki, and the second is his and Clark's more recent version. Version A: "She who wears her kimono in the style of *iki*, having attained by necessity a state of Buddhist deliverance, gathers uncommon grasses in a rarefied atmosphere redolent of *amour-gožt*." Version B: "People who live for *iki* must reach emancipation where they live in the thin air of *amour-gožt* by picking bracken." Here, with the help of one of Kuki's translators, we see the difficulty we face when discussing the meaning of *iki* (and *sui*).

4. Established in the Ginza district in Tokyo in 1872, Shiseido is today a global manufacturing and sales corporation in the fields of cosmetics, salons, pharmaceuticals, toiletries,

and nutrition products. After inaugurating its global business with sales to Taiwan in 1957, Shiseido began marketing to Europe in 1963 and to the United States in 1965. In Japan, Shiseido has long been considered an important force in the arts through its product designs and advertisements—which were originally overseen by the company's first president, Shinzo Fukuhara. Shiseido currently organizes exhibitions of contemporary art in two public galleries in Tokyo and mounts permanent installations in the Shiseido Art House and the Shiseido Corporate Museum in Kategawa. It also publishes a monthly magazine of culture and fashion, called *Hanatsubaki*.

5. The ad is featured with a brief explanation in several languages. The English-language page is at http://www.shiseido.co.jp/h/h0012arh/html/artp0007.

6. You can see one of Shiseido's promotional ads using the Lutz sisters at http://www.nyu.edu/greyart/exhibits/shiseido/pop12.htm. Also interesting is how Nakamura touched up the photo, removing Bonnie Lutz's left ear to enhance the silhouette of the two faces.

7. You can see some of her photographs at a Shiseido Web site dedicated to her, http://www.a2galler.com/html/SMITH/jp04.

8. A group picture of all the Miss Shiseidos taken in 1934 can be seen on the Web at http://www.nyu.edu/greyart/exhibits/shiseido/5wom2.

REFERENCES

Barthes, R. (1973). *Mythologies.* New York: Noonday Press.

Bornoff, N. (1991). *The pink samurai: Love, marriage, and sex in contemporary Japan.* New York: Pocket Books.

Cash, T. F. (1981). Physical attractiveness: An annotated bibliography of theory and research in the behavioral sciences. JSAS Catalogue of Selected *Documents in Psychology, 11,* 85.

Cash, T. F., & Wunderle, J. M. (1987). Self-monitoring and cosmetics use among college women. *The Journal of Social Psychology, 129,* 349–355.

Cash, T. F., & Rossi, J., & Chapman, R. (1985). Not just another pretty face: Sex roles, locus of control, and cosmetics use. *Personality and Social Psychology Bulletin, 11,* 246–257.

Cox, C. L., & Glick, W. H. (1986). Resume evaluations and cosmetics use: When more is not better. *Sex Roles, 14,* 51–58.

Dale, P. (1986). *The myth of Japanese uniqueness.* New York: St. Martin's Press.

Diamond, J. (1993). *The third chimpanzee.* New York: HarperCollins.

Dion, K., Berscheid, E., & Walter, E. (1972). What is beautiful is good. *Journal of Personality and Social Psychology, 24,* 285–290.

Eliade, M. (1998). *Myth and reality.* Prospect Heights, IL: Waveland Press.

Ewen S., & Ewen, E. (1992). *Channels of desire: Mass images and the shaping of American consciousness.* Minneapolis: University of Minnesota Press.

Gebser, J. (1949/1985). *The ever-present origin* (N. Barstad & A. Mickunas, Trans.). Athens: Ohio University Press.

Gudykunst, W., & Kim, Y. (1997). *Communicating with strangers: An approach to intercultural communication* (3rd ed.). New York: McGraw Hill.

Herrnstein, R., & Murray, C. (1994). *The bell curve: Intelligence and class structure in American life*. New York: Free Press.

Herskovitz, J. (1997). Shiseido makes over the way it sees international markets. *Advertising Age, 68* (October 27), 3.

Ikeda, R., & Kramer, E. (2002). *Ibunka komyunikeshon nyumon* (2nd ed.) [Introduction to intercultural communication]. Tokyo: Yuhikaku Press.

Jung, C. (1981). *The archetypes and the collective unconscious* (collected works of C. G. Jung vol. 9, part 1) (H. Read, Ed.). Princeton, NJ: Princeton University Press.

Kramer, E. (1992). *Consciousness and culture: An introduction to the thought of Jean Gebser*. Westport, CT: Greenwood.

Kramer, E. (1993). The origin of television as civilizational expression. In K. Haworth, J. Deely, & T. Prewitt (Eds.), *Semiotics 1990: Vol. 6, Sources in Semiotics* (pp. 28–37). New York: University Press of America.

Kramer, E. (1994). Making love alone: Videocentrism and the case of modern pornography. In K. A. Callihan (Ed.), *Ideals of feminine beauty: Philosophical, social, and cultural dimensions* (pp. 78–98). Westport, CT: Greenwood.

Kramer, E. (1997). *Modern/postmodern: Off the beaten path of antimodernism*. Westport, CT: Praeger.

Kramer, E. (1999). *Gaiatsu* and cultural judo. Paper presented at the annual conference of the International Jean Gebser Society. Matteson, IL.

Kramer, E. (2000). Cultural fusion and the defense of difference. In M. Asante & J. Min (Eds.), *Sociocultural Conflict between African and Korean Americans* (pp. 183–230). New York: University Press of America.

Kramer, E., & Ikeda, R. (2000). The changing faces of reality. *Keio Communication Review, 22*, 79–109.

Kuki, S. (1930). *The structure of Iki*. (M. Otake, Trans.). Unpublished doctoral dissertation, Syracuse University, Syracuse, NY.

Lacan, J. (1982). *Ecrits*. (A. Sheridan, Trans.). New York: Norton.

Lyotard, J.-F. (1984). *The postmodern condition: A report on knowledge*. Minneapolis: University of Minnesota Press.

McLuhan, M. (2001). *The medium is the massage*. Corte Madera, CA: Gingko Press.

Miller, R. A. (1978). The spirit of the Japanese language. *Journal of Japanese Studies, 3*, 251–298.

Miller, L. C. & Cox, C. L. (1982). For appearances' sake: Public self-consciousness and makeup use. *Personal and Social Psychology Bulletin, 8*, 748–751.

Mizuo, J. (1998). *Keshouhin no brando shi* [A history of brands of cosmetics]. Tokyo: Chuo-kouronsha.

Mumford, L. (1966). *The myth of the machine: Technics and human development*. New York: Harcourt, Brace and World.

Murasawa, H. (1987). *Bijin shinkaron* [The theory of evolution of beautiful woman]. Tokyo: Tokyo-Shoseki.

Root, D. L., & L. M. Root. (1993). New perspective on the Asian cosmetic market. *Drug and Cosmetic Industry, 153* (November), 28–35.

Said, E. (1979). *Orientalism*. New York: Random House.

Shimamori, M. (1998). *Koukoku no hirointachi* [Heroines of advertisements]. Tokyo: Iwanami.

Wagatsuma, H., & Yoneyama, T. (1967). *Henkenn no kouzou* [Structures of prejudice]. Tokyo: Nihon Housou Kyoukai.

Watanabe, S. (1974). *Bunka no jidai* [Age of culture]. Tokyo: Bunshun Bunko.

Williamson, J. (1994). *Decoding advertisements: Ideology and meaning in advertise-ments.* New York: Marion Boyars.

Wolfe, N. (1991). *The beauty myth: How images are used against women.* New York: William Morrow.

Chapter 4

The Violence of Assimilation and Psychological Well-Being

Chi-Ah Chun and Jung Min Choi

RACE RELATIONS AND ASSIMILATION

The history of race relations in the United States, in addition to almost everywhere else, has been dominated by the order perspective (Choi, Callaghan, & Murphy, 1995, pp. 154–57). According to this outlook, norms, laws, and other institutional forms are presumed to be objective and powerful enough to control persons. In fact, unless order represents a widespread system of institutional controls, the belief is that society will not survive. As Durkheim argues, in the absence of a "reality *sui generis*"—an autonomous and inviolable foundation—order will be unstable and inevitably collapse.

With regard to race relations in general and gender issues in particular, culture has assumed the role of this fundamental reality. Certain timeless standards, as Matthew Arnold contends, are available to provide the cement that is essential for uniting societies. Because these criteria transcend the limitations associated with any particular society, they are touted to be cultural ideals. These collective characteristics, moreover, are expected to be universally recognized, because they are untainted by ideological biases. They are truly cultural imperatives. According to this argument, these standards represent the best that humans are capable of creating.

Assimilationists are straightforward about their desire to have everyone adopt these principles. They make no excuses or apologies about having every ethnic group conform to a single set of cultural and behavioral expectations (Bennett, 1992, pp. 17–38). Without this type of conformity, produced by what is often called the melting pot, balkanization is guaranteed. Assimilationists maintain that no society can survive for long without a culture that is recognized universally as valid and inculcated.

The fervor of this belief has been witnessed recently in several politically motivated events. For example, immigrants are currently under attack for failing to abandon their ethnic heritage rapidly enough. As part of this trend, nobody in the United States is supposed to be bilingual, and schools especially are not expected to acknowledge cultural diversity. Society should be recognized by everyone as relatively homogeneous, although pockets of resistance are present that will be gradually eliminated (Schlesinger, 1993). There is no utility to tolerating the existence of various languages, interpretations of history, customs, or practices. In this sense, Richard Rodrigues (2001) remarks that assimilation is inevitable and beneficial to everyone. Most important is that assimilation is not thought to be harmful by most persons. After all, the cultures of immigrants are not thought to have the same stature as the ideals that are at the base of mainstream society. Simply put, these ethnic traditions are believed to be deficient in a host of ways and thus inhibit social adjustment and mobility. Any rational person, therefore, should welcome the opportunity to assimilate and acquire a proper identity. Indeed, the degree of assimilation is often touted to be a measure of a person's worth and desire to succeed. According to this outlook, both immigrants and society are understood to be improved only by the assimilation experience.

PIGMENTOCRACY

There has always been a pigmentocracy in the United States. That is, persons and groups have been arranged on the basis of color. In general forms, a continuum exists that extends from dark to light. Additionally, as noted by bell hooks (1995, p. 120), this color dimension has been linked to morality. Persons who are at the dark end of this scale are thought to have a dubious character, whereas those who have whiter skin and more European features are presumed to have fewer flaws. A moral hierarchy exists, in other words, that is predicated on skin color and related physiological traits.

Most persons are socialized to recognize and internalize this arrangement. Minorities are thus placed in a serious predicament. They must have profound justification for rejecting this hierarchy, or they must find ways to adjust to this moral order. Because marginalization is difficult to accept, many have chosen to alter their appearance. For example, they straighten their hair, have cosmetic surgery, or attempt to lighten their skin. Nonetheless, in the end, those who most closely resemble Europeans initially have the best chance of avoiding any stigma. The remainder suffers in a myriad of ways.

But there is a less destructive way out of this situation. bell hooks describes the 1960s as a time when people began to take pride in their ethnic and racial heritage. A variety of non-European hairstyles, jewelry, and dress became quite popular. What was most important about these changes, notes hooks, was the accompanying critique of the cultural ideals—"white supremacist aesthetic values"—that earlier supported the inferiorization of these modes of statement (1995, p. 121). What might be called the ontological justification of these ideals was under attack. The point was clearly illustrated that European standards were not necessarily universal or in a position to claim moral superiority. These norms were demonstrated to represent one perspective among many, one that in many cases was enforced throughout the exercise of illegitimate power.

As hooks also recognizes, this type of critique is mostly absent today. Although talk about difference abounds, the justification for cultural expansion is flimsy. In many instances persons merely demand to be recognized and base their claims on vague notions of democracy. But because this strategy does not contain a penetrating analysis of the philosophical justification of marginalization, inclusion is easily transformed into assimilation. After all, according to the usual argument, only so much diversity can be tolerated in a functioning society. As should be noted, this response presupposes the need for a privileged position that represents normalcy. Acceptability, accordingly, requires adjustment to the so-called mainstream.

Absent the critique mentioned by hooks, difference will not likely come to mean anything more than opposition to what is considered normal. In this sense, difference is still marginal. For cultural difference to be truly appreciated, the asymmetry between difference and normalcy must be dissolved. In other words, the situation must be created where difference and the norm are both viewed as differences that must compete for recognition. In this way, cultural hegemony is much more difficult to achieve. But as should be understood, this sort of critique is profound and intricate.

DEMOCRACY AND ASSIMILATION

If a society claims to be democratic, as does the United States, what justifies the compression of culture that is required by assimilation? In most portrayals, certain values that are related to toleration and pluralism are assumed to be essential to democracy. Allowing one culture to dominate others, thereby encouraging the ideology of cultural supremacy, should create dissonance. But advocates of assimilation do not seem to be especially bothered by this contradiction. Proposing a cultural litmus test apparently does not violate democracy. Proponents of assimilation have made a particular theoretical démarche that seems to soften the impact of cultural supremacy. Assimilationists, in short, are committed to foundationalism. Therefore, the cultural reductionism linked to assimilation is not viewed as malevolent. Following the acceptance of foundationalism, cultural ideals can be advanced in a manner that does not unfairly implode society and cause discomfort (Gilroy, 1993, p. 190).

Foundationalists believe that a universal base, untrammeled by personal motives and political interests, is necessary and available to unite society (Fish, 1989, pp. 344–54). This idea is not new but pervades the entire Western philosophical tradition. Truth and morality, for example, have to be established on this eternal foundation, or they will not have the stature required to suppress error and evil. Most important, the resulting standards are not contaminated by cultural idiosyncrasies but prescribe modes of behavior and other traits that are rational and that all civilized persons are expected to covet. Whatever is identified with this base is presumed to be unbiased and unintrusive.

These exalted standards are easily translated into cultural imperatives that demand universal recognition. Because these seigniorial norms are inherently superior to all others, the enforcement of these select standards should not be viewed as repressive. Asking minorities to improve themselves is not antagonistic to democracy. There is nothing sinister about the assimilation process, whereby persons abandon traits that will only impede their development. The refinement of culture is not believed to be the same as cultural supremacy. How can cultural uplift be treated as reductionistic and harmful?

Despite the illusion perpetrated by foundationalism, assimilation is not innocent. Erich Fromm (1958, pp. 13–14), for example, made this point some time ago. He recognized that as cultural ideals become larger, persons become smaller. In other words, the mores that are legitimized by these rarefied foundations are able to cast a negative shadow over all other options. By implication, these less fortunate values, beliefs, and commitments are inferiorized and undermined. Without attacking directly these alternatives, the superiority and desirability of specific traits is announced. A hierarchy of cultures is revealed, without the influence of political machinations that are anathema to democracy.

As a result, assimilation generates regularly the opposite of what this process is advertised to produce. Instead of universal well-being, bias and conflict are spawned. Culture is unfairly compressed, as minorities internalize norms that undermine their identities and histories. These persons often try to avoid stigmatization through self-denial. In many ways, they strive to embody the dominant culture. Hence, assimilation is very violent, although the attacks on minorities are mostly indirect (Derrida, 1978, p. 34ff). Social acceptance, stated simply, is predicated on minorities demeaning themselves and adopting traits they often find offensive. In a manner of speaking, their history is written by the dominant group in accordance with irrelevant criteria.

As minorities flee from themselves, a lot of anguish may be experienced. After all, both physical and emotional pain are often a part of this alteration process. To gain acceptance, many persons engage in both physical mutilation and cultural evisceration to hide their ethnicity. Contrary to what Rodrigues (2001) argues, assimilation does not "just happen." Cultural homogeneity is achieved at a very high cost and through much sacrifice. As a result of pressure to assimilate, minorities are placed in very difficult political, economic, and cultural positions. But what is the actual psychological effect of this process?

A CASE STUDY

The psychological status of minorities has been of interest to mental health researchers for quite some time. In general, many studies have found that ethnic minorities have poorer psychological adjustment than Euro-Americans. In a community sample, for example, Asian Americans were found to be more depressed than their Euro-American counterparts (Kuo, 1984, pp. 449–57). Even Asian American college students, extolled as a key example of a model minority, are more anxious than Euro-American students (Onoda, 1973, pp. 180–85; Sue & Kirk, 1973, pp. 142–48).

But what accounts for this poor psychological adjustment? Maladjustment has been attributed to the hardship of settling in a society made up of a foreign language and culture. Furthermore, the experience of prejudice and discrimination can be very unsettling. The claim could easily be made, therefore, that psychological well-being is related to how tightly persons are integrated into society. Improved psychological functioning might be expected among Asian Americans and other minorities who share mainstream American values and customs. Thorough assimilation, in other words, might be expected to culminate in fewer personal problems. Certainly this outcome is presumed by those who push for the rapid and unqualified assimilation of all minorities.

But the empirical findings do not consistently support this argument. Burnam and her colleagues (1987, pp. 89–102) found that depression and acculturation are linked. Others have discovered that those who are bicultural and embrace both their culture of origin and mainstream mores have the best adjustment (Lang, Munoz, Bernal, & Sorenson, 1982, pp. 433–50; Ortiz & Arce, 1984, pp. 127–43). Additionally, Ying's (1995, pp. 893–911) research revealed that "integrationists," those who are bicultural, are more satisfied with their lives than those who are fully assimilated. These findings contradict the charges made by assimilationists. In short, assimilation is not a panacea. As Phinney and Chavira (1995, pp. 31–53) conclude, when persons attempt to suppress their ethnic identity, their level of self-esteem falls rapidly. Low self-esteem, as many experts agree, leads to a plethora of problems.

Clearly, the pressure to assimilate can be overwhelming. Minorities are confronted by a culture they are told is superior to their own and that must be internalized completely if they are to have a modicum of success in society. What a dilemma! They must either assimilate or have no chance to develop their skills and abilities. Engage in self-denial, or experience failure and exclusion. There is no doubt that such a quandary will produce anxiety and depression. The following case study clearly illustrates this point:

Ms. C., a twenty-six-year-old woman of Asian and European descent, came to the psychological service center for anxiety and depression. She suffered from intense shyness since she was a young child and would become particularly anxious and self-conscious when in a group setting. Ms. C. noticed that her anxiety interfered with her activities at work, and she began to avoid group meetings and social gatherings after work. She stated that she accepted her shyness as part of her personality, but she wanted to acquire some coping skills to address her anxiety, so she could function better at her work place.

Ms. C. also complained that she has been obsessed for many years with the idea of getting plastic surgery. She believed that having a perfect smile will help her overcome her shyness. She believed her smile was not bright enough. In fact, her smile made her feel very unattractive and self-conscious when she was with others. She even sought several medical consultations and even scheduled two surgeries, both of which she eventually canceled.

Ms. C. explained that she grew up feeling all-American and "normal" inside, but was often told by her friends that she looked "exotic." People mistook her often for an Italian. She observed that girls who had the all-American look, particularly a big, bright smile, were most popular in school. Ms. C. came to believe that she was "inferior" to these girls because she did not look like them, and that having a perfect smile would make her one of them.

When pressed to explain why she felt inferior, Ms. C. suddenly realized that all along her self-consciousness over her physical appearance had to do with her deep-rooted shame of her Asian heritage. She had her Asian mother's smile and dark hair. All her life she wanted to be white. In high school, Ms. C. watched British movies to adopt a British accent. She confessed that she never considered herself to be Asian, and that she knew little about her mother's background. In fact, her mother never talked to her about herself and her family, and never tried to pass down any information about her Asian heritage. Ms. C's white father dominated completely the family, and the children associated mostly with his relatives.

Ms. C. began to feel profound sadness about her mother, who suppressed herself and her culture to raise the children as if they were white. At the same time she was overcome with tremendous anger toward her father, whose prejudice against other cultures did not allow room for any other ways of life at home, even the culture of the woman he married. Ms. C. now understood the symbolic meaning of her obsession with plastic surgery. Ms. C. also saw that she was unable to go through with the surgery because these operations would result in her denying her mother's culture, which Ms. C. began to recognize as a key component of her self-concept. With this newly gained insight, Ms. C. was finally able to appreciate the two different cultural aspects of her identity.

This case demonstrates the complex nature and tremendous cost of striving for complete assimilation. Ms. C. strove to become increasingly "white" linguistically, socially, and physically by mimicking a British accent, associating only with Euro-American friends, and planning to modify her physical appearance. She aimed to eliminate any element that threatened her desire to appear white. The message she accepted is that whiteness is normal and preferable to being viewed as exotic.

Ms. C. discovered what Frantz Fanon (1991) learned and described some time ago. That is, assimilation is violent, and a terrible stigma is attached to those who cannot or refuse to be entirely assimilated. To use Fanon's words, minorities represent "not only the absence of value, but also the negation of values" (1991, p. 41). Without their submission to the so-called dominant culture, minorities are a threat to themselves and society. In a manner of speaking, they must be pacified; assimilation, an ostensibly apolitical process, is the vehicle for this activity.

Ms. C. revealed that identities consist of multiple discourses, but all of these are not treated equally. As people struggle with issues related to their authentic identities, histories, and cultures, these elements are often overrun by a set of dominant ideals. Their efforts are often undercut by a view of normalcy that cannot be challenged without the threat of marginalization. For these alternative discourses to thrive, they need a safe and open space in which to reside and develop. bell hooks (1990, pp. 148–49), for example, argues that these comfortable regions are on the margins of society. But these places are not very secure! After all, they are on the periphery of society. True alternatives can be hardly expected to flourish in such an obscure site.

As Marx suggests, this sort of flight represents utopianism. Indeed, the demands of assimilation will not relent in the face of such escapism. For cultural alternatives to gain legitimacy and grow, the source of the power of assimilation must be challenged. The critique of foundationalism proffered by many contemporary philosophies attacks assimilation at this vital point. In fact, cultural difference is illustrated to be at the core of society. The ideals that are linked to assimilation are exposed to be simply one mode of culture among others. The objectivity offered by assimilationists to justify the dominance of particular ideals is revealed to be "hasard objectif." According to surrealists such as Dalí, the point is that these ideals are a product of particular circumstances and interests and thus are not necessary or natural. They are a product of chance, or, in other words, the result of praxis that has no a priori purpose or destiny. Most important is that this critique does not reveal merely the margin to be amenable to change and innovation. Instead, the core of society is shown to be an outgrowth of human action, optional and easily amended.

THE ESCAPE FROM ASSIMILATION

R. D. Laing (1967, pp. 82–90) claims that clients would be better served by consulting an epistemologist instead of a psychologist or a psychiatrist. His point is that a critique of knowledge is necessary to liberate persons from their maladies. Laing believes that most psychological and social problems result from persons rejecting themselves because of factors such as social pressure and coercion or the result of exposure to culturally insensitive diagnostic schemes. As he says, persons falsify themselves and begin to engage in bizarre behavior; they abandon authentic modes of culture and action. Due to the authority often attributed to these factors, persons begin to self-destruct. As illustrated by Ms. C., many so-called pathologies have an existential origin. As persons begin to deny their identities, histories, and cultures of origin, for example, their lives begin to lose meaning and deteriorate.

Simply ignoring or rejecting the judgments of experts or societal pressures is not a viable alternative for resolving these existential predicaments. With regard to the demands of assimilation, attempting to exhibit pride in one's culture by joining a support group is not likely to boost self-esteem for very long. After all, this strategy presupposes the legitimacy of the dominant culture, and thus consists of merely fleeing from the forces that are trying to enlist conformity. A return to this destructive condition is likely to occur unless a total escape from society is pursued. If the latter is the case, increasing marginalization will be the result. Clearly this sort of coping mechanism is not very functional.

So what is the solution to this dilemma? Laing supplies a hint with his reference to epistemology. The pressure to assimilate, in short, can be avoided only by undermining the raison d'être of this process. Specifically, the autonomous base of mores associated with foundationalism must be shown to be an illusion. Most important is to reveal the contingent nature of all cultural standards, even those touted traditionally to be ideal and universal. Every aspect of culture is thus demonstrated to be a product of a host of forces, including both personal proclivities and institutionalized commitments. No ideal escapes from the influence of human praxis; cultural ideals embody nothing more than different perspectives.

According to this approach, those who question assimilation do not have to confront or flee from social reality. Neither choice allows persons to become disentangled from assimilation. True freedom from assimilation is achieved instead by revealing that the norms linked to this process are optional rather than necessary. This maneuver, notes Max Ernst, "disrupts the relationship of realities" (Ernst et al., 1997, p. 7). The hierarchy of realities presupposed by assimilation accordingly can no longer retain the status of a natural system. Hence not pursuing assimilation does not indicate the presence of irrational or malevolent motives. Avoiding assimilation is simply compatible with a person's life project.

Recent trends in social philosophy and race relations specifically related to Afrocentrism can promote this sort of liberation. Most noteworthy is that at the heart of these approaches is the linguistic turn. They borrow from the later work of Wittgenstein, particularly his idea of the "language game" (Lyotard, 1984, pp. 9–11). The point to remember is that all knowledge, even cultural ideals, is mediated completely by language use. No knowledge is devoid of interpretation and thus is able to be treated legitimately as inherently universal. In this regard, the linguistic turn can be very liberating. Like all interpretations, the cultural ideals presupposed by assimilation can be reinterpreted and abandoned. People can make their own ideals. Instead of being tethered to a reality that at best can be ignored, persons are able to make themselves in any number of ways.

Persons are able to act affirmatively. Their choices are not controlled by an imposing reality. They are therefore not condemned to merely react to social conditions. Instead, a proactive stance can be taken. Persons can invent realities with which they are comfortable, without having to feel like failures or outcasts. As described by Marcuse (1964), persons are no longer ensnared in a one-dimensional reality, trapped between assimilation and a flight from social imperatives. In the manner envisioned by Kant, persons can be critical and autonomous, thereby exhibiting the maturity required to be considered self-directed.

Subsequent to making the linguistic turn, no version of reality is heteronomous. Each cultural ideal is provided with legitimacy by the people. Given this new image of existence, no one has the authority to impose norms in the manner required by assimilation. In this sense, the linguistic turn prepares the social world for democracy, whereby ideals are subject to constant negotiation and ratification. Because there is nothing that transcends human action, nothing has the inherent latitude to dominate persons. Persons are thus free and expected to prescribe their own ends.

REFERENCES AND SUGGESTED READING

Abe, J., & Zane, N. (1990). Psychological maladjustment among Asian and white American college students. *Journal of Counseling Psychology, 37*, 437–444.

Bennett, W. (1992). *The devaluing of America.* New York: Summit Books.

Berry, J. W., & Kim, U. (1988). Acculturation and mental health. In P. R. Dasen, J. W. Berry, and N. Sartorius (Eds.), *Health and cross-cultural psychology: Toward applications* (pp. 207–236). Newbury Park, CA: Sage.

Burnam, M. A., Hough, R., Karno, M., Escobar, J., & Telles, C. (1987). Acculturation and lifetime prevalence of psychiatric disorders among Mexican Americans in Los Angeles. *Journal of Health and Social Behavior, 28*, 89–102.

Choi, J. M., Callaghan, K. A., & Murphy, J. W. (1995). *The politics of culture.* Westport, CT: Praeger.

Derrida, J. (1978). *Writing and difference.* Chicago: University of Chicago Press.

Ernst, M. (1997). *Ernst* (J. Faierna, Ed.) (A. Curotto, Trans.). New York: Abradale, Abrams.

Fabriga, H., & Wallace, C. A. (1971). Acculturation and psychiatric treatment: A study involving Mexican Americans. *British Journal of Social Psychiatry and Community Health, 4*, 124–136.

Fanon, F. (1991). *The wretched of the earth.* New York: Grove Weidenfeld.

Fish, S. (1989). *Doing what comes naturally.* Durham, NC: Duke University Press.

Flaskerud, J., & Hu, L. (1992). Relationship of ethnicity to psychiatric diagnosis. *Journal of Nervous and Mental Disease, 180*, 296–303.

Fromm, E. (1958). *Man for himself.* New York: Rinehart.

Gilroy, P. (1993). *The black Atlantic.* London: Verso.

hooks, b. (1990). *Yearning.* Boston, MA: South End Press.

hooks, b. (1995). *Killing rage.* New York: Henry Holt.

Kuo, W. (1984). Prevalence of depression among Asian Americans. *Journal of Nervous and Mental Disease, 172*, 449–457.

Laing, R. D. (1967). *The politics of experience.* New York: Pantheon.

Lang, J. G., Munoz, R. F., Bernal, G., & Sorenson, J. L. (1982). Quality of life and psychological well-being in a bi-cultural Latino community. *Hispanic Journal of Behavioral Sciences, 4*, 433–450.

Lee, E. & Lu, F. (1989). Assessment and treatment of Asian-American survivors of mass violence. *Journal of Traumatic Stress, 2*, 93–120.

Lin, K. (1986). Psychopathology and social disruption in refugees. In C. Williams and J. Westermeyers (Eds.), *Refugee mental health in resettlement countries* (pp. 610–673). Washington, DC: Hemisphere Publishing.

Lyotard, J.-F. (1984). *The postmodern condition.* Minneapolis: University of Minnesota Press.

Marcuse, H. (1964). *One-dimensional man*. Boston: Beacon.

Munoz, F. U. (1979). Pacific islanders: An overview. In U.S. Commission on Civil Rights Conference (Ed.), *Civil rights issues of Asian and Pacific Americans: Myths and realities* (pp. 342–348). Washington, DC: U.S. Government Printing Office.

Onoda, L. (1973). Neurotic-stable tendencies among Japanese American senseis and Caucasian students. *Journal of Non-White Concerns, 5*, 180–185.

Ortiz, V. & Arce, C. (1984). Language orientation and mental health status among persons of Mexican descent. *Hispanic Journal of Behavioral Sciences, 6*, 127–143.

Phinney, J. S. (1996). When we talk about American ethnic groups, what do we mean? *American Psychologist, 51*, 918–927.

Phinney, J. S., & Chavira, V. (1995). Parental ethnic socialization and adolescent coping with problems related to ethnicity. *Journal of Research on Adolescence, 5*, 31–53.

Rodrigues, R. (2001). *Introducing modernism*. New York: Totem Books.

Schlesinger, A. (1993). *The disuniting of America*. New York: Norton.

Smith, E. M. (1985). Ethnic minorities: Life stress, social support, and mental health issues. *Counseling Psychologist, 13*, 537–579.

Sue, D. W., & Kirk, B. (1973). Differential characteristics of Japanese-American and Chinese-American college students. *Journal of Counseling Psychology, 20*, 142–148.

Sue, S. (1977). Community mental health services to minority groups: Some optimism, some pessimism. *American Psychologist, 32*, 616–624.

Sue, S., & Chin, R. (1983). The mental health of Chinese-American children: Stressors and resources. In G. Powell (Ed.), *The psychosocial development of minority group children* (pp. 385–397). New York: Brunner/Mazel.

Sue, S., Fujino, D., Hu, L., Takeuchi, D., & Zane, N. (1991). Community mental health services for ethnic minority groups: A test of the cultural responsiveness hypothesis. *Journal of Consulting and Clinical Psychology, 59*, 533–540.

Tajfel, H. (1978). Intergroup behaviour: Group perspectives. In H. Tajfel and C. Fraser (Eds.), *Introducing social psychology: An analysis of individual reaction and response* (pp. 423–446). Middlesex, England: Penguin Books.

Vega, W. A., Warheit, G., & Meinhardt, K. (1984). Marital disruption and the prevalence of depressive symptomatology among Anglos and Mexican Americans. *Journal of Marriage and Family, 46*, 817–824.

Ying, Y. (1995). Cultural orientation and psychological well-being in Chinese Americans. *American Journal of Community Psychology, 23*, 893–911.

Yu, K., & Kim, L. (1983). The growth and development of Korean-American children. In G. Powell (Ed.), *The psychosocial development of minority group children* (pp. 147–158). New York: Brunner/Mazel.

Chapter 5

The Ainu: A Discourse on Being Japanese

Masazumi Maruyama

INTRODUCTION: THE ETHNIC COMPOSITION OF JAPAN

Japan tends to be called a relatively homogeneous nation regarding ethnic composition. According to the Management and Coordination Agency (cited in Asahi Shimbun, 1999, p. 63), although there are over 125 million Japanese living in Japan, there are just over 1 million registered foreigners living in Japan (as of October 1, 1998), consisting of slightly less than 1 percent of the total population (this number has increased recently due to such factors as international labor mobility). Among these foreigners, Koreans make up 638,828 or 42.2 percent of the registered foreigners in Japan. Most of these Koreans are Korean Japanese, who are second or third generation (born and raised in Japan) but not naturalized.[1] Chinese (18 percent) comprise the second largest group among registered foreigners, followed by Brazilians (14.7 percent). Brazilians include Japanese descendents (Japanese Brazilian), whose ancestors immigrated to Brazil during and after the Meiji era.

Besides these foreigners (in terms of nationality), however, there are invisible, uncounted numbers of hidden and ethnically diverse people in Japan.[2] The first uncounted or invisible group is those who are naturalized. In Japan, no national survey concerning ethnic composition is conducted. Therefore, there are no hard data about the ethnic makeup of the foreign population. According to the Ministry of Justice, as of December 1998, there were 301,828 naturalized foreigners, cumulatively speaking. In 1952, there were more than 200,000 (those who died after naturalization are included). This means that the number of children and grandchildren of those naturalized has steadily increased. The second group is made up of children who come from multinational parentage.

Due to the change in the Nationality Act in 1985, if either the father or the mother of a child possesses Japanese nationality, the child is automatically granted Japanese nationality. Until 1985, the nationality of a child depended on his or her father's nationality. More than 80 percent of Korean Japanese marry Japanese. Consequently, since 1985, the offspring of such unions are granted Japanese nationality.

The third and final group under the rubric of foreign residents is comprised of those considered aboriginal or indigenous peoples in Japan: the Ainu (in Hokkaido) and the *Ryukyu* (in Okinawa), among others. If they appear in histories of Japan at all, it is in a negative context. Otherwise, they are typically ignored, thus leaving the "Japanese proper" innocent of conflict, maltreatment, or neglect of them.

Japan is, in fact, culturally and ethnically very diverse. Japan consists not only of new immigrants (partially as an inevitable consequence of modernization and globalization) but also of old but neglected and forgotten peoples in the archipelago (such as Korean Japanese, Ainu, and *Ryukyu*). Although the three categories of resident foreigners discussed are all defined as Japanese, they possess culturally and ethnically different qualities. Despite this diversity, ethnic minority groups in Japan have tended to be underappreciated both in terms of social reality (e.g., discrimination) and in academic elucidation. This is partly due to the strong myth of homogeneity that is widely held in Japan.

This chapter focuses on the Ainu people, who are part of the third category of residents. The Ainu comprise one of the smallest aboriginal groups enduring in any developed capitalist country (Burger, 1987). The Ainu are considered "native," "aborigine," or "indigenous" people of Hokkaido, although the government has not officially acknowledged them as such.[3]

Only since 1994, when the Ainu Shinpo (which literally means the New Ainu Act) was passed, have the Ainu been officially recognized as having a legitimate cultural identity of their own. Prior to this date, they were regulated by the Hokkaido Former Aborigines Protection Act (Hokkaido Kyu Dojin Hogo Ho) that was promulgated in 1899. This nineteenth-century law was very similar to the Native Americans' Dawes Act or General Allotment Act in the United States (1887). Thus, until 1994, the official position of the Japanese government was that the Ainu were savages or barbarians (the term *Dojin* literally means "savage" or "barbarian").[4] The goal of the 1899 act was basically aimed at assimilating or adapting the Ainu to *Wajin*, or Japanese, society.[5] The prescribed means for achieving this was by encouraging the Ainu to abandon their unique culture and acquire some of *Wajin* cultural systems (e.g., learning the Japanese written system). More details of the act are described later.

The Ainu are Japanese by law. Historically speaking, however, they were consistently considered different from, or Other than, true Japanese or *Wajin*. As early as the eighth century, there was a description of the Ainu as being culturally and ethnically (racially) distinct from the Japanese. Because the Ainu were fairly isolated, living mostly in Hokkaido, the Kurile Islands, and Sakhalin, they did not disturb the life of the *Wajin*.

Even though the Ainu did not directly disturb, interact with, or influence the *Wajin* on a large scale, they did participate in commerce with the *Wajin*. Since the Kamakura era (1185–1333), the Ainu regularly traded with the *Wajin*, bringing several types of goods to market. Why, then, were the Ainu considered Japanese by the government of the time and incorporated into Japan? What kind of discourses articulated this identity for the Ainu (without their participation), who had long been viewed as the Other? The major purpose of this chapter is to examine how the discourse of the Ainu-as-Japanese was historically created. In doing so, this chapter also introduces the reality of Ainu history, what they have faced. This chapter also seeks to explicate similarities between the experiences of the Ainu and those of other aboriginal groups in the modern world, such as Native American.

This chapter first describes who the Ainu are. In this section, demographic characteristics, cultural and life experiences, and some of the social difficulties with which the Ainu have struggled are briefly introduced. The second section historically examines how the Ainu were incorporated into Japan and what kind of discourse was instrumental in this process. This section particularly pays attention to the history of the late Edo era (1603–1867) and after, because the push to assimilate them started during that time. Some references are also made to Native Americans because some of the experiences the Ainu have had are similar to those of Native Americans.

WHO ARE THE AINU? A BRIEF PROFILE

This section offers a profile of the Ainu. First, they are described in terms of population. A description of Hokkaido, the homeland of the Ainu, follows. The culture and life of the Ainu are briefly introduced. Finally, I describe how the concept of the Ainu was created and maintained.

Population

Currently, the Ainu people mostly live in Hokkaido, which is the northernmost main island of Japan. They used to live widely throughout Hokkaido, Tohoku, the Kurile Islands, and Sakhalin. Subgroups of Ainu were designated by where they lived, such as Hokkaido Ainu, Tohoku Ainu, Kurile Ainu, and Sakhalin Ainu, respectively. After World War II, they mostly lived in Hokkaido.[6] According to a survey conducted by the Hokkaido Ainu Association, there are a total of 23,830 Ainu people in Japan (0.02 percent of the Japanese).[7] It is said, however, that there are more than 50,000 Ainu people because some of them try to hide their Ainu ethnicity to avoid social discrimination and stigmatization (Kosarev, 1990; Taksami, 1998).

Hokkaido: Homeland of the Ainu

The Ainu call Hokkaido *Ainu mosir*, meaning "a quiet land of humans" (Ainu = "human" or "man"; *mo* = "quiet"; and *sir* = "land," "world," "island," or "country"). *Ainu mosir* refers to the world of humans, in contrast to *Kamui mosir*, which means the "world of God" or "heaven." Hokkaido island was called *Yezochi* by *Wajin*; this name means "the land of the Ainu." In 1869, the Meiji government renamed the island Hokkaido. Similar to the situation of place names in North America, in Hokkaido, many place names are actually transliterations into Japanese characters of original Ainu place names based on imitating Ainu phonetics (the Ainu did not have a written system of their language; a written system has been developed only recently). Kayano (1999), the first Ainu member of the House of Councilors, estimates that there are at least 45,000 place names of Ainu origin in Hokkaido. Sapporo, the largest city on the island, derives from the old Ainu name, *sat-por-(pet)*, meaning "dry-big-(river)" (*pet* is assumed)" (Tamura, 1999). The author's hometown, Obihiro, also comes from the Ainu word *Oberiberi*, meaning "a river divided into many estuaries." The names of several surrounding cities are also filled with Ainu traditional meanings. Kayano (1999) attributes the fact that the Ainu have many place names partly to their hunting culture. Because it was typical that the hunters could not carry all of the heavy animals they had killed home from the mountains by themselves, they needed to inform other Ainu of the location where game was left. This fact is also very similar to the common Native American practice of naming rivers, mountains, and even states based on territorial hunting grounds (e.g., Oklahoma = red people) (Nishide, 1986).

Culture and Life of the Ainu

Posey (1999) identifies six general (but not universal) values and behaviors characteristic of indigenous peoples:

A. Cooperation

B. Family bonding and cross-generational communication, including links with ancestors

C. Concern for the well-being of future generations

D. Local-scale self-sufficiency and reliance on locally available natural resources

E. Rights to lands, territories, and resources, which tend to be collective and inalienable rather than individual and alienable

F. Restraint in resource exploitation and respect for nature, especially for sacred sites (Posey, 1999, p. 4)

The culture and life of the Ainu have very much in common with that of other indigenous peoples.

Traditionally, the Ainu lived in villages called *Kotan*, with up to a dozen huts.[8] They typically engaged in hunting and fishing, utilizing locally available natural resources. The flora and fauna they relied on for sustenance included bear, deer, fox, salmon, codfish, seal, sea otters, whales, and seaweed, to name a few. Just like many indigenous peoples, they did not have the notion of individual ownership of property. For the Ainu, ownership and property were collective. According to Takakura (1939): "If a land is not used by anybody and is in the right of the group to which he belongs, it is allowed to be used on a voluntary basis. When the person ends his or her use, however, the land is returned ownerless again" (p. 7).

The lack of a notion of ownership and property, along with the absence of a written system of language,[9] as in the case of other indigenous peoples, proved to be disadvantages for the Ainu in their historical struggle with the encroaching *Wajin*. As will be described, the Ainu engaged in trading with the *Wajin*. But such technical inabilities within Western, or *Wajin*, context (those who claim themselves as civilized) made the Ainu especially vulnerable to exploitation. *Wajin* often cheated the Ainu by means of corrupted contractual recording and counting. Ogasawara (1997) explains what he has named Ainu counting. This counting was used in business trading by the *Wajin* to cheat the Ainu, most of whom were not proficient at counting and calculating in the *Wajin* way.

As is obvious from their lack of individual ownership or property, the Ainu did not have a clear distinction between human (culture) and nature. They lived in the wholeness prior to the dissociation of the two in what Gebser (1949/1985) calls magic and mythic consciousness. Everything and every event (such as an earthquake or forest fire) surrounding the Ainu has spirit in it— each spirit comes down to the earth with a certain mission and lives there, changing its appearance into such forms as animals and plants (Ainu Museum, 1993). Thus, they pray to their gods before they hunt and regard their surrounding nature (e.g., river, sea, mountain) as a warehouse for food (Kayano, 1999). The bear-sending ceremony (*Iomante*) of the Ainu is one such ceremonial event. Bear is considered a god sent from the world of the gods. The spirit appears to the Ainu in the form of a bear on the ground. The bear god gives to the Ainu fur, liver, and meat in the form of itself. *Iomante* literary means "sending the god (spirit)" to the place where the god originally came from— the world of the gods. Salmon, which is the main source of food in the traditional Ainu diet, is considered a god as well. In Ainu language, salmon means "real food," "real fish," and "fish of fishes" (*Shiepe*) or "god fish" (*Kamuichep*). Given the worldview of the Ainu, they catch only enough salmon necessary for a day in summer. They also catch what is necessary of spawning salmon for long-term food stocks, which they dry for the long winter (Kayano, 1999). In their view, it is not appropriate (indeed a sort of sin) to waste the self-sacrificial gift of the salmon god.

Besides hunting and fishing, trade between Japan and surrounding countries or areas was important because it served to bring to Japan many goods and products from distant lands like China, as well as items of Ainu origin. There were three main trade routes the Ainu used. They were the Northern Trade Route (via Sakhalin by the Sakhalin Ainu), the Eastern Trade Route (via Kurile Island by the Kurile Ainu), and the Southern Trade Route (via Tohoku by the Hokkaido Ainu). The Northern Trade Route was based on taking tribute to and then receiving items from China. This was called the *Choukou* system (based on Sinocentrism). The items used for tribute included hides and furs. The Chinese items brought back to Japan were mostly clothes. The Ainu also traded with other tribute groups. Ainu trade items from China also found their way into Japanese cities, such as Tokyo, Osaka, and Kyoto.

The Kurile Ainu mainly controlled the eastern trade. From Hokkaido, mainland products, such as cotton and silk goods, pots and pans, swords, and lacquerware, were exported, whereas from northern Kurile Island were imported furs of sea otters and foxes and feathers of eagles. Products from mainland Japan were further traded to people in the Kamchatka Peninsula. Sea otters, or *Rakko* (an Ainu word adopted in Japanese), were used as tribute to China from Japan. Finally, the southern trade played an important role in modifying Japanese cuisine and agriculture in the mainland. From the Hokkaido Ainu, a lot of fish were traded, including salmon, codfish, herring (used as fertilizer), and other dietary products of the sea as well. From the mainland, rice, alcohol, and cigarettes were the major items brought to Hokkaido. Besides, salt had to be imported to use as a preservative for fish. Abalone, sea cucumber, and seaweed were especially in demand and were exported to Nagasaki and further on to China as tribute.

THE INVENTION OF THE AINU AS AN ETHNIC GROUP

It is well argued that the concept of ethnicity is a modern idea. There are at least two views as to the origin of ethnicity. The first view is that ethnicity is created or invented in the modern era (e.g., Anderson, 1983; Gellner, 1983; Hobsbawm & Ranger, 1983), and the second view argues that there is a primitive form of ethnicity called *ethnie* that existed prior to the modern era (after the Meiji Restoration in 1868) and that ethnicity is invented based on this earlier concept of *ethnie* (e.g., Smith, 1986).[10] Both views, however, agree that ethnicity became salient in the modern era.

Although the Ainu are widely believed to have a single language and culture (i.e., ethnic group), as an ethnic group or ethnicity they are also a modern phenomenon. In other words, there was no collective consciousness or identity among the so-called Ainu prior to the modern era in Japan. As mentioned, retrospectively there were various Ainu groups, each of which was categorized based on their living locations (i.e., Hokkaido, Tohoku, the Kurile Islands, and Sakhalin). They are different in ecological habitats, adaptations, and linguistic dialects (Fitzhugh, 1999). Even within each location, there was no collective or unified identity as the Ainu. There were, for example, several Ainu groups within Hokkaido: the Shumuk, Sarunk, Menashik, Peniunku, Abashiri Ainu,

Tokachi Ainu, Ishikari Ainu, Yoichi Ainu, and Uchiura Ainu (Kono, 1998). These groups are identified through differences in the headstones of their graves. Furthermore, these groups differed in their ways of life. The Kurile Ainu, for example, engaged in fishing for their living (i.e., catching fish and sea mammals, such as seals, sea lions). They also had higher mobility than other groups of the Ainu. There exists folklore (or oral history) that describes confrontations among the different groups of Ainu.

A collective consciousness of a unified Ainu ethnicity among the Ainu did not exist until the modern era, and the *Wajin* imposed it on these various groups. Ainu identity was thus formed, created, and invented, especially for political reasons of and by the Japanese. This new form of identity was particularly salient after the Tokugawa shogunate began to directly govern Hokkaido in 1855. At this time identifying all the various groups as a single category served the purposes of mainland Japanese defense against the threat of the Russian empire.

THE DISCOURSE OF BEING JAPANESE: HISTORICAL PERSPECTIVE

What follows is a brief history of the Ainu, paying particular attention to the Japanese government's policies regarding the Ainu in Hokkaido. The political rhetoric developed to legitimize the governance of the Ainu and to justify the claim of Hokkaido island as Japanese territory is also described. Finally, the actual policies and their consequences are described. In this section, a brief history of the so-called Ainu was delineated. Particular attention is paid to the history of Ainu–*Wajin* relations.

Sinocentrism, Japan, and the Ainu

Japan has traditionally perceived the world in a Sinocentric way. Sinocentrism indicates a mode of awareness whereby China perceived itself as the center of the world and as the most (if not only) civilized people on Earth. This notion, most often associated with China, marks a clear distinction between in-group civilized people and out-group barbarians. However, out-group members may also come to view a dominant power as the center of the world, as in the case of China for many Asian peoples at different periods of history. According to the Sinocentric view surrounding out-group people are typically regarded by in-group members as savages. Consistent with this view, surrounding Others were typically designated and named by the Chinese in terms of their respective directional prefixes relative to the center. Also, several different words (in Chinese characters) that mean "barbarian" in English, were used: Eastern, Western, Southern, and Northern barbarians.[11] Under the Sinocentric worldview, China is the center of the world and the rest are barbarians. As subjects of

Chinese hegemony (*Kifuku*, or surrender), barbarians were compelled to send tribute to China (the *Chokou* system). Japan was one such country, especially during the Tang dynasty. The Ainu also sent tribute to China.

Japan was strongly conscious of this Sinocentrism. Consequently, Japan emphasized its independence from China. Ironically, and to this end, Japan defensively constructed itself as an independent state in the image of China. Japan also assumed a similar outlook, developing its own Sinocentric mentality and system. In this way, that is, in imitation of the Chinese system, Japanese began to refer to people in the northeastern area of Japan, as *Yemishi*, which means marginal "barbarian" (vis-à-vis Japan). *Yemishi* means "barbarian," which includes all those who are outside of Japan and who do not follow the Japanese law (government). Those called *Yemishi* did not exactly correspond to the so-called Ainu, but the Ainu were one of the groups so designated.

This Japanese Sinocentrism, or pseudo-Sinocentrism (or as some have put it, "mini-Sinocentrism") became in a sense a rival to China in the region. It is a device for defining Others to identify oneself. The criteria used in this process of coconstitutional identity (Kramer, 1993; 1995) stress physical, cultural, spiritual, geographical, and linguistic differences, denigrating the Other as not only different but inferior. This Japanese version of Sinocentrism articulates the Ainu as the Other for the Japanese. For over a century, this defining process was the guiding principle of the relationship between the Ainu and the *Wajin*. Kikuchi (1994) describes Japan's recognition of Others including foreigners in the Edo era. In the Edo era, foreigners were perceived of in two ways: Others who understand Chinese characters (Chinese character area), and Others who use Latin characters and who do not understand Chinese characters (non-Chinese character area). The former includes *Ryukyu*, *Yemishi* (Ainu), and Koreans in Japan. The latter include the Dutch, Asian Indians, the Spanish, and others.[12]

Kikuchi (1994) further argues that *Ryukyu*, Ainu, and Koreans were specifically distinguished from other out-groups who used Chinese characters, who fit into the Chinese character category, based on Ryoan Terashima's emphasis on the "three in descriptions." This recognition reflects that Japan was strongly conscious of Chinese notions of civilization and barbarism (Sinocentrism) and that Japan tried to maintain its own independence from China by imitating the Chinese and creating similar policies toward the surrounding barbarian ethnic groups.

The Chinese notions of civilization and barbarism were thus jeopardized, along with other factors, when Russia approached the Ainu around Hokkaido. In the face of the such a threat from a Western power, the Sinocentric system had to be abandoned in favor of the modern nation-state system. The Western view of civilizations (and barbarisms) replaced the old view. In this context, the Ainu were suddenly considered insiders, belonging to Japan.

To understand official Japanese policies concerning the Ainu, Russia's influence on Japan must be taken into account. Oguma (1998) argues that Japan's colonization process should be framed trilaterally: Japan, the colonized, and the

West. When it comes to Japan's (or any other) colonial ambitions, it tends to be viewed as a bilateral process, which includes only Japan (the colonizing) and the colonized, the Ainu in this instance. In the case of the Japanese colonization of the Ainu, a trilateral framework of analysis is necessary. Kikuchi (1994) argues that the case of the Ainu for Japan is the first case in which Japan or East Asia directly clashed with a Western power (see the later discussion for details). Official Japanese policies regarding the Ainu, in fact, became the model case for all of Japan's subsequent colonial efforts in such areas as Taiwan. In each case, Japan saw itself as being in direct competition with Western empires (Takagi, 1994).

The Meiji era tends to be considered the beginning of assimilation policies targeting the Ainu. This assumption is based on the fact that the Meiji government instituted several modernization policies. However, the foundation of assimilation policies was already framed at the end of the Edo era (Kikuchi, 1994; Oguma, 1998). The following historical sketch thus focuses on that period as well.

Premodern Era

The first and critical historical event for the Ainu–*Wajin* history is Morisue Ando's escape to Yezo Island (current Hokkaido) in 1443. The Ando clan in Tohoku (in the northern part of the mainland) was defeated by another Tohoku clan, the Nanbu. The result was that the Ando clan was pushed out. They retreated to Yezo Island. Since then many Japanese (*Wajin*) immigrants, including Ando clan members, moved to the southern part of Yezo Island. With this migration of refugees, business and trade began to flourish on Yezo. Conflict between the *Wajin* and the Ainu started almost immediately. One of the most memorable expressions of this conflict was the Battle of Koshamain in 1457.

After a century-long conflict, in an effort to foster a more peaceful relationship, *Wajin* and Ainu territory was clearly demarcated: The former occupied the southern part of Yezo (later called *Wajin-Chi*) and the latter was assigned the rest. Thus Yezo was divided into East Yezo and West Yezo.

In 1593, Hideyoshi Toyotomi issued a red-seal letter to Yoshihiro Kakizaki (later Matsumae) to authorize control of Yezo and collection of tariff from ships visiting the island. In 1604, Ieyasu Tokugawa issued a black-seal letter to Yoshihiro Matsumae authorizing the right to trade with the Ainu. What is significant about these official sanctions is that they limited trading partners for the Ainu to only the Matsumae clan, excluding all other Japanese (Kikuchi, 1994). During this period, given these authorizations, many trading posts, called *Akinaiba*, were established in Ainu territory. In these places, all trade between the *Wajin* and the Ainu took place, and the former sold Ainu products to businesspersons in the mainland. Direct sales from Ainu to mainland *Wajin* were prohibited. Thus, an inherently unfair set of trade relations were imposed on the Ainu. The trading rate was determined by the *Wajin* (the right of the Matsumae clan to determine prices was authorized by the shogunate). An example is sixty-six pounds of *Wajin* rice would trade for a hundred dried Ainu salmon. Over time the exchange became more unfair for the Ainu initially. Soon a hundred salmon would buy only twenty-two pounds of rice (Kikuchi, 1994).

The monopoly the Matsumae clan exercised on Ainu trade reduced the relationship to one of a classic colonial structure, whereby the Ainu were heavily exploited. In other words, the mainlanders needed to buy Ainu products through the Matsumae clan, which severely limited the role of the Ainu as traders. Besides this unfair system, environmental damages to Ainu fishing and hunting territories by a *Wajin* gold rush on Yezo led to the Battle of Sakhalin in 1669. After being defeated, the Ainu were made to swear to the following oath: The Ainu must (1) accept eternal unconditional submission to the Matsumae clan throughout the coming generations; (2) accept the duty to inform on those who would betray the Matsumae clan; (3) guarantee free and safe passage of Yezo Island to *Wajin* and to feed *Wajin* sojourners; (4) refrain from all violence against hawk hunters and gold miners; (5) refrain from all violence against trade ships and traders from other clans; (6) accept price determination of trade goods by the *Wajin* (prohibition of price negotiation); and (7) guarantee the safe passage of the postal mail, of postal persons, postal horses, and also hunters.

In eighteenth century, the zone commissioning system (*Basho Ukeoi Sei*) became common. This system dictated that only the Matsumae clan had exclusive rights to trade with the Ainu, and only the Matsumae clan could commission businesspersons from the mainland to trade. In return for such commissions the clan received money (*Unjokin*). Because the Matsumae clan was in financial crisis, it sold some commissions outright and mortgaged others. The businesspersons not only had trading rights but also received the right to fish for salmon from the Matsumae clan.

Thus, the Ainu became involved in a marketing system structured according to this zone commissioning system, which led to exploitation by mainlanders. Not only did this system destroy fishing and hunting places for the Ainu, it also made the *Wajin* treat the Ainu as a mere labor force or even as slaves instead of business partners (autonomous traders). This severe exploitation, along with diseases brought by the *Wajin*, led to a dramatic decrease in the Ainu population. Their numbers dropped by half in less than fifty years.

The End of Pseudo-Sinocentrism and Emergent Modern Nation System

The Battle of Kunashiri-Menashi in 1789 nearly wiped out the Ainu entirely.[13] It occurred during a particularly critical period. During the battle a rumor spread among the *Wajin* that Russia was agitating the Ainu. This rumor, along with the facts of Russia's southward policy, so threatened the shogunate that he decided to take direct control of Yezo for defensive purposes. In 1799, East Yezo was in direct control of the shogunate, and West Yezo followed in

1807. Control of Yezo was not returned to the Matsumae clan until 1822, when the perceived threat from Russia subsided. In 1854, the Japan-Russia Treaty of Amity was concluded, in which the shared national boundary between the countries was fixed by designating the Uruppu Channel the border in the Kuriles and Sakhalin as a place of cohabitation for both Russians and Japanese. In 1855, on opening Hakodate Port to Russia, the shogunate decided again to take direct control of Yezo.

Feeling threatened by the West, particularly Russia in the case of Hokkaido, the shogunate promoted Japanization of the Ainu, changing the policy of the Matsumae Clan that prohibited Ainu from using Japanese language. Under the shogunate, the Ainu were encouraged to adopt *Wajin* customs including the use of woven hats, straw rain-capes, and straw sandals. Such trappings tended to make the Ainu appear like some sort of beast or bird.[14] The Japanization of the Ainu included encouraging Buddhism by founding temples while prohibiting Christianity (for fear of Western missionary influences); using Japanese language; wearing Japanese-style clothes; eating Japanese rice while prohibiting the traditional meat diet (arguing that meat-eating is savage and rice-eating is civil); changing names to Japanese style; and prohibiting mustaches, the *Iomante* (bear-sending ceremony), and tattoos, which were all essential to traditional Ainu identity. After the Japan-Russia Treaty of Amity, Japan further strengthened the assimilation policies over the Ainu. They allowed the Ainu to use Japanese language, changed their lifestyles to fit Japanese expectations, improved labor conditions, vaccinated the population, and educated the children in Japanese (Oguma, 1998).

DISCOURSES OF JUSTIFICATION

National defense was certainly the major factor for the imposition of the assimilation policy. Oguma (1998) describes the basic attitudes of the shogunate toward the Ainu during this period:

The policy toward the Ainu was closely interconnected to diplomatic relationships [i.e., Japan's perceived threat of Russia]. It is impossible that without diplomatic concerns the Ainu would have gained the attention of the central government. Already the Ainu were easily exploited and did not serve as an armed threat to the *Yezochi*. Economically, the Ainu were too few to be highly profitable for the *Wajin*. The only concern was, at a workplace level, how to use the Ainu as labor. That is to say, for the shogunate, the Ainu were neither a serious armed threat nor a significant business asset. There were only a few tens of thousands of frontier people. The reason that such a small minority could become a salient political issue is because of their diplomatic value. (p. 53, translation mine).

Given this singular reason for the change in status for the Ainu, to include them as Japanese, a discourse developed to justify the Japanization of the Ainu. As explained by Kikuchi:

If the Russians succeeded in coopting the Ainu, and they were to become attached to Russia, then Yezo Island could be claimed by Russia, making it impossible for Japan to exist as a nation. If the shogunate relied solely on the small Matsumae clan, the Ainu might be attracted to Russia because of discontent owing to the vicious profit-oriented *Wajin*, who controlled the business concessions. To prevent this, the shogunate decided to manage Yezo Island directly, putting an emphasis on nursing and education for the Ainu, and developing Yezo Island. Then defense of Yezo Island would be made adamantine [formidable/impenetrable]. (1994, p. 236, translation mine)

Thus, the discourse developed that to defend the nation required that the Ainu become Japanese and thereby the land in which the Ainu live become Japanese territory. The emergence of modern nation-statehood altered the status of the Ainu. Hokkaido was considered the northern gate of Japan. To insist that Hokkaido island is Japanese territory, the Ainu had to be claimed as Japanese. This tactic was used in an actual diplomatic negotiation. The following negotiation took place over the territorial boundary between Japan and Russia in 1854 (cited in Uemura, 1992; translation mine):

Russian Diplomat: The Etorofu Island [one of the Kurile Islands] is the place in which Russians originally lived.

Toshiakira Kawaji: It is not true. Ezo-Chishima [the Kurile] exists in an old record of my country and thus certainly it is my country that possessed the Etorofu Island at that time.

Russian Diplomat: At that time, only Ainu lived there and there were no Japanese.

Kawaji: "Ainu" is *Yezo* people. *Yezo* (*Yemishi*) are people who belong to Japan. The fact that "the Ainu" lived there evidences, therefore, that the Etorofu Island is a Japanese territory.

It is obvious that the official government doctrine on this issue was that the Ainu are primordial Japanese nationals and the land they occupy is Japanese territory. The next year at which this negotiation took place, the 1855 Treaty of Commerce, Navigation, and Delimitation (the Shimoda Treaty) (*Nichi-Ro Tsuko Joyaku*) was concluded between Japan and Russia, and the Etorofu Island and southward was defined as being Japanese territory.

To claim that the Ainu are Japanese, are Japanese insiders, was thus a rather cynical political ploy and ambivalent at that. This is so because the Ainu were considered and treated historically as the Other, as outsiders. Due to the perceived threat of Russia and the West in general, along with this ambivalence, the Ainu had to be refashioned into Japanese identity by means of assimilation policies.

THE FAILURE OF ASSIMILATION

The aggressive attempt to assimilate the Ainu, however, was not really successful. This was due in part to the strong resistance of the Ainu and the shogunate's financial weaknesses. According to Matsuura's description (cited in Kikuchi, 1994), in Kushiro, a total of 483 out of 1,326 Ainu were captured, detained, and forced to shave off their mustaches (i.e., Japanized). However, due a staunch refusal to cooperate, only thirteen Ainu people ended up with Japanese styles. As a consequence of this failure, the shogunate could not accomplish further assimilation of the Ainu, which had intended to force them into an agrarian rather than hunting lifestyle. The Ainu refused to become farmers in the Japanese fashion. In addition, due to a lack of financial power, no school was founded, nor was any supervisor of the assimilation policy enforcement assigned.

MEIJI AND AFTER

In the face of Western encroachment, Japan needed to reconstruct the country based on the Western modern nation-state system, which was a new model of civilization for the Japanese. This was deemed necessary so that Japan could maintain its autonomy as a people, instead of being viewed as backward barbarians and ripe for the plucking by Western powers. First, to defend Hokkaido from Russia, the assimilation of the Ainu had to be facilitated. Second, to appear civilized, Japan had to implement some measures demonstrating tolerance of the Ainu, curtailing abject discriminatory exploitation of them. Furthermore, Russian contacts and Christian missionaries in Japan had internally influenced the Ainu during this era. John Batchelor, a British missionary, was one of the most influential figures. He came to Hakodate in 1877, and when he witnessed how the *Wajin* discriminated against the Ainu, he decided to try to save the Ainu. He taught the Bible in their language. In 1888, Batchelor founded the Airin School to educate Ainu children. According to Batchelor,

I really feel disgusted to hear that Japanese people are discriminated against in the United States and other places. Japan should blame the misconduct and claim racial egalitarianism toward the world. I hope that Japan will pay more attention to the fact that the Ainu, who are fellow nationals, have been robbed of the right to live, have been kicked out of one mountain locale after another, and have been on the verge of extinction from the Earth due to preventable diseases, and that Japan will make a sincere effort to improve the life of the Ainu. (cited in Oguma, 1998, p. 60; translation mine)

Accordingly, Japanese authorities believed that the Ainu had to be further assimilated into Japanese society by the enactment of several laws. Though the Meiji government policy regarding the Ainu was basically the same as that of the Edo shogunate, differences existed. One crucial change during the new era was that the Ainu were incorporated into the status of commoners, even while social discrimination was still prevalent (Oguma, 1998). Many laws were imposed on them—these laws worked unfairly against the Ainu in that they neither had a writing system nor a notion of law/contract. Furthermore, during the early Meiji era, Hokkaido was redefined by policies that lay claim to the island as Japanese territory. This annexation was accomplished in mainly two ways: (1) by Japanizing the Ainu themselves, and (2) by promoting the immigration of a large number of mainland Japanese to Hokkaido as "reclaimants." In the case of the Ainu, the latter approach was most prevalent, whereas in the case of the *Ryukyu* the former approach, of overwhelming the indigenous population with mainland immigration, was most pronounced (Oguma, 1998).

The following historical descriptions will pay special attention to the approach of Japanization used toward the Ainu. The laws, policies, and regulations that articulate the intent and manner of Japanization are examined.[15] Japanization policy was implemented to (1) change the lifestyle of the target population to conform to the Japanese way and to educate the Ainu, including Japanese language instruction. The latter approach, although pursued, was not critical because Hokkaido could be claimed anyway as long as the majority of dwellers in there were mainland immigrations; and (2) transform Ainu culture from a hunting-based subsistence to becoming farmers.

Yezochi (meaning "the land for barbarians"—the Ainu) was renamed Hokkaido, and the Colonization Commission (*Kaitakushi*) was established in 1869. The zone commissioning system was abolished in the same year. In 1871, the Family Registration Act was established; it was a legal instrument enabling the Japanese authorities to categorize the Ainu as commoners. The immigration came in waves. First farmer-soldiers (*Tondenhei*) settled in Sapporo in 1875. *Tondenhei* were strategically located to open up and cultivate lands in Hokkaido during peacetime and to constitute a local defense force anytime Hokkaido was threatened by foreign countries (mostly Russia). The role played by these farmer-soldiers demonstrates that Japan was highly conscious of Russian threats. In 1878, the Colonization Commission uniformly designated the Ainu former aborigines (*Kyudojin*).

Imposing a New Culture: Japanese Lifestyle

The Ainu were encouraged to adopt the Japanese culture and lifestyle and thus were forced to abandon their own culture and lifestyle. There are several historical moments to illustrate how this assimilation process worked. In 1871, Ainu settlers were given houses and farming tools, while also being banned from practicing their original customs. They were forced to speak Japanese. The Ainu were also prohibited from using arrows for hunting; they were provided instead with hunting rifles in 1876. Sapporo Prefecture banned salmon fishing in the upper reaches of the Tokachi River in 1883.[16] Furthermore, deer hunting, which the Ainu had previously been permitted to do because deer was a major food source, was banned in 1889. As to salmon fishing, Kayano (1999) argues that the Ainu were placed in an unfair situation, which prevails even to the time of this writing:[17]

As of 1993, the amount the Ainu can catch is only twenty-five salmon, while the Japanese Fishery Cooperative can catch 37.5 million salmon in Hokkaido. The Ainu are allowed to catch salmon but not for their own food needs, only for the preservation and of their culture (and even in this case they are required to submit several documents to administrators to be allowed catch these salmon). (p. 41; translation and summarization mine)

Thus, the salmon catch is more symbolic than an authentic preservation of a fundamental cultural practice or an economically viable activity.

In terms of the education of the Ainu, schools for Ainu children were first founded in the villages in 1880. In 1901, a curriculum for former aborigine children was established, which was, however, a simplified and separate curriculum from that for real Japanese children. The Ainu schools lasted four years as compared to six years for the Japanese (*Wajin*). Because the Ainu could not initially attend school, Western missionaries had an influential opening, and thus they played an important role in educating the Ainu (around 1886, only 9.2 percent of the Ainu children attended school; Oguma, 1998). As mentioned, Batchelor founded Airin School to educate Ainu children in 1888. Several other schools were also founded by missionaries.

COMPARING LAND DISTRIBUTION LAWS: JAPAN AND THE UNITED STATES

As mentioned, during the Meiji era, the Ainu were targeted in an effort to change their way of life from hunting to a settled agrarian lifestyle. This effort to deculturize and resocialize the Ainu required that they be exposed to the concepts of individual ownership and private property. Due to their levels of illiteracy in Japanese, they could not cope with all the legal rhetoric. Also, they fundamentally did not understand the idea of private property. As a consequence, the traditional Ainu lands were taken away from them under the pretense that they were lands without owners. They were then assigned unfertile lands that tended to be inappropriate not only for their traditional habits of existence but also for agriculture.

In 1877, regulations for issuing land certificates were promulgated in Hokkaido. In the regulations, although Ainu residential areas came under the auspices of these laws, these areas were nevertheless designated as nationally owned land, as lands without owners. Hokkaido Regulations for Land Disposal were enacted in 1886. In the regulations, land of thirty-three hectares (330,000 m^2) per individual was disposed of or granted to the *Wajin*. In 1899, the Hokkaido Former Aborigines Protection Act was enacted. This act determined the current status of the Ainu as the act lasted until the New Ainu Act replaced it only recently in 1994. The act aims at assimilating the Ainu into Japanese culture by distributing lands for agricultural use and by providing education, livelihood assistance, and medical service. The act was intended to authorize the distribution of up to 15,000 *tsubo* (49,590 m^2) of land per family or household for agricultural purposes, and specifically not for hunting. *Wajin* received larger parcels of land than Ainu. The land earmarked for distribution to Ainu was often wasteland inappropriate for agriculture, whereas the disposed land for *Wajin* was fertile.

The Hokkaido Former Aborigines Protection Act requires further description. The act manifests significant influences of social Darwinism and several similarities to the Dawes Act or General Allotment Act of the Native Americans of 1887. To begin with, both acts were aimed at distributing a certain quantity of land to indigenous peoples for agricultural purposes. Article one of the Hokkaido Former Aborigines Protection Act states: "Those former aborigines of Hokkaido who engage or wish to engage in agriculture shall be granted free of charge no more than 15,000 tsubo [49,590 m^2] per household." Similar wording can be found in section one of the Dawes Act:[18]

Be it enacted by the Senate and House of Representatives of the United States of America in Congress assembled, That in all cases where any tribe or band of Indians has been, or shall hereafter be, located upon any reservation created for their use, either by treaty stipulation or by virtue of an act of Congress or executive order setting apart the same for their use, the President of the United States be, and he hereby is, authorized, whenever in his opinion any reservation or any part thereof of such Indians is advantageous for agricultural and grazing purposes, to cause said reservation, or any part thereof, to be surveyed, or resurveyed if necessary, and to allot the lands in said reservation in severalty to any Indian located thereon in quantities as follows....

Only slight differences are observed in quantity and measures for distributed lands. However, it is obvious that both acts are similar.

A second point of obvious comparison involves the status of the majority. For instance, both acts prohibited *Wajin* and whites (respectively) from acquiring the lands distributed to the indigenous populations. Article two of the Hokkaido Former Aborigines Protection Act specifically says:

The land granted according to Article 1 is subject to the following conditions:

1. It must not be transferred except by inheritance.
2. No right of pledge, mortgage, superfices, of perpetual lease can be established.
3. No servitude can be established without the approval of the Governor of the Hokkaido Local Government.
4. The land cannot be subject to a lien / a preferential right.

Similarly, the Dawes Act states in section five:

That no patents shall issue therefore except to the person so taking the same as and for a homestead, or his heirs, and after the expiration of five years occupancy thereof as such homestead; and any conveyance of said lands so taken as a homestead, or any contract touching the same, or lien thereon, created prior to the date of such patent, shall be null and void.

Finally, both acts provided several supportive measures to facilitate indigenous peoples' engagement in agriculture. In the Hokkaido Former Aborigines Protection Act, articles four through seven, which were later deleted, provided for

Ainu in poverty with farming equipment and/or seeds, affording medical expenses to those who are sick but cannot afford such expenses, supporting those who cannot earn their living due to sickness, and providing school tuition for Ainu children in destitution. Article eight establishes payment of costs incurred thus: "The expenses necessitated by the preceding article shall be appropriated from the proceeds of the Hokkaido Aborigines Community Funds, and if any shortage occurs, it shall be appropriated by the National Treasury."

Furthermore, article nine, which was also later deleted, authorized the establishment of an elementary school paid for by funds from the National Treasury. Article ten, concerning the management of common properties, specified that the governor of the Hokkaido local government shall manage common properties of the Hokkaido former aborigines. The Dawes Act similarly offered support to facilitate Native Americans engaged in agriculture:

The sums agreed to be paid by the United States as purchase money for any portion of any such reservation shall be held in the Treasury of the United States for the sole use of the tribe or tribes of Indians to whom such reservations belonged; and the same, with interest thereon at three per cent per annum, shall be at all times subject to appropriation by Congress for the education and civilization of such tribe or tribes of Indians or the members thereof. (section five)

Consequences of the Hokkaido Former Aborigines Protection Act

Not only were the lands distributed to the Ainu inappropriate for agricultural uses, they had to go through a bureaucratic process to get them. The allotment of lands for Native Americans was compulsory, but land for the Ainu was structured on an application basis—they had to apply for land. Given their lack of literacy, such an application system proved very difficult to negotiate. Experts have critically evaluated the consequences of the Hokkaido Former Aborigines Protection Act. According to a survey conducted eleven years after the promulgation of the act, very little land allotted for was actually in production. Furthermore, there were many Ainu men shunned farming for fishing, leaving the burdens of cultivation to the Ainu women (Tomita, 1989). Income from fishing amounted to twice that gained by means of agriculture. In 1918, eighteen years after the promulgation of the act, a survey conducted by the Hokkaido government was published. It included a 1917 survey conducted by the Hokkaido government that showed 69 percent of all the lands under active cultivation were lands not allotted by the government system. Of the government lands 31 percent remained uncultivated. A total of 62 percent of the land cultivated by Ainu were on owner-cultivated ("independent") farms. These numbers are misleading, however.

Another survey indicates that the claim that most of the production to have occurred was from owner-farmers' lands is misleading. The actual owners were very often *Wajin*. Ainu only cultivated a part of the lands under question, whereas the rest were rented to *Wajin*; and in some cases, *Wajin* cheated the Ainu into renting the lands to them under very disadvantageous conditions. Although the act prohibited the transferal of allotted lands to *Wajin* due to financial difficulties and deceitful negotiations, many Ainu rented their lands for lengthy ten- to twenty-year terms. It was not uncommon for the rent to be canceled out by the reputed debt owed by the Ainu to their *Wajin* renters. Often ownership ended up being transferred to the *Wajin*. Furthermore, Ainu tended to borrow money for alcohol, which was originally brought to Ainu society by the *Wajin*.

Furthermore, because of reforms after World War II, many Ainu had their lands taken away. The Ainu were formally considered absent landlords. A survey conducted during the 1970s by the Hokkaido government indicated that only 17 percent of all the originally distributed lands still remained owned by Ainu (Uemura, 1992). Today, a total of 33,000 km^2 or 40 percent of Hokkaido Island is nationally owned.

National Boundaries and the Ainu

In 1875 and 1884, respectively, while several assimilation measures were being implemented, the Sakhalin and Kurile Ainu were forced to immigrate and resettle in Hokkaido and the southern Kurile Islands (both of which had been claimed by Japan). This was consistent with the discourse that the Ainu were Japanese. After Sakhalin island became a Japanese territory as a consequence of the Russo-Japanese War in 1904, in 1906 the Sakhalin Ainu returned to Sakhalin. The so-called Hokkaido Ainu were forced to be involved in assimilation process, and the other Ainu groups lost their familiar homelands due to an official discourse that spoke of the Ainu as an ethnic group. The idea of ethnic grouping had only been required and formulated in the modern era. Hugely influenced by this discourse, the Sakhalin Ainu were relocated back and forth. In the process of Japan's struggle to modernize rapidly, the Ainu were always at Japan's beck and call.

Gradual Assimilation, or *Zenka*

The Japanization policy that was applied to the Ainu was not effective. Insofar as it succeeded at all, it was accomplished by the *Wajin* immigration to Hokkaido. When it comes to colonization, the process is usually framed in terms of those colonizing and those colonized. Oguma (1998) argues, however, that this bilateral framework does not constitute a sufficient explanation of the case of the Ainu in Japan. Rather, Oguma argues that the West must be included in the explanation. The perceived threat of the West was salient in the case of the Ainu. As mentioned, they had been consistently considered as the Other. They remained that way, for all practical purposes, even after the Meiji

Restoration. However, it became advantageous for the central authority to claim the Ainu as Japanese in the face of Western encroachment on lands that the Japanese government considered its sovereign dominion. Thus, it was that insofar as the Ainu were incorporated into Japan at all, it was on the basis of political expediency. It was the perceived threat of the West that led to the incorporation of the Ainu as Japanese nationals. The Ainu were pawns between colonial influences.

This trilateral power relationship included Japan and its ambitions for the Ainu homelands. Being forced (to some extent) to acknowledge the Ainu put Japan in ambivalent position. If the struggle over who would secure the resources of the Ainu homelands had been limited to a bilateral conflict, then Japan would have emphasized the difference between the two groups generally, and the inferiority of the Ainu in particular. This was not the case, however. Japan chose to use the identity of the Ainu as political rhetoric. Central Japanese power used a discourse of inclusion with regard to the identity of the Ainu when discussing the contested territories with Western officials. To claim sovereignty over the Ainu homelands, the Ainu had to be claimed as Japanese nationals so that the territory in which they lived could be said to belong to Japan. However, as noted, the actual bilateral dealings between the *Wajin* and the Ainu were often unfair. In bilateral dealings the Ainu remained the Other.

The essence of the difference between minority and majority status is this: The majority has the power to define itself, to define the minority, and to define the relationship between the two. In the case of Japan and the Ainu, because the Ainu culturally did not participate in such legal processes as official definitions and also because they were illiterate, they were (and to a large extent remain) largely defined rather than defining. They did not participate as equals in the defining conversation. Instead they were subjected to the defining negotiations that occurred between colonial powers, without even being at the table. Thus, the Ainu experience is typical with indigenous people everywhere. Meanwhile, this struggle over the identity of the Ainu further marginalized them. This is so because while different diplomatic discourses were defining them, they never had a right to define themselves. It is highly unlikely that they ever believed themselves to be equal with, let alone the same as, the *Wajin*. But their voice was completely silenced.

Japanese officials found themselves to be in a hypocritical position because, on one hand, they were arguing that the Ainu were Japanese, yet the Ainu could not participate in the discourse that was defining them because they were not really Japanese. Even though the logic of political expediency compelled the central government to legally define the Ainu as the same as other fellow Japanese, the reality was different. So the government adopted a logic of compromise and moderation. The discourse developed in this ambivalent situation manifested a logic of *Zenka*, or "gradual assimilation." Discourse designed for external consumption was somewhat different from official proclamations made for internal consumption. Externally (diplomatically), the Ainu were claimed to be Japanese nationals. Internally (domestically), on the other hand, they were deliberately distinguished from the Japanese.

Japan felt compelled to defend its interests in and ambitions for the Ainu homelands and resources from a perceived Russian threat. Later, the same rhetoric vis-à-vis the Ainu was exercised, only with Western Christian missionaries, such as Batchelor, taking the place of Russian competition. Throughout, Japanese central authority assumed that they had a privileged right to the contested lands even though they were actually and traditionally Ainu lands. The discourse developed during this period was well reflected in Eitaro Iwatani's notion of Zenka, or gradual assimilation (Oguma, 1998). Iwatani was vice-president of the Hokkaido Normal School and was one of the educational leaders in Hokkaido. His view of the Ainu was strongly influenced by social Darwinism. Consequently, he regarded the Ainu as a homeless race or barbaric people:

The Ainu are really an inferior race. First, Ainu do not have any hope for the future. Second, the Ainu do not have any saving graces or habits. Third, the Ainu have a bad habit of drinking alcohol and it is the only pleasure the Ainu know. Fourth, Ainu do not have any sense of hygiene or knowledge about being sanitary. Fifth, the Ainu display no discipline in their daily lives. Sixth, Ainu have many decadent habits of misconduct including being lazy, gambling, lying, and deceiving. Seventh and finally, the Ainu have inherited bad blood from their ancestors to the present. These seven qualities of the Ainu threaten to the ruin the nation. (cited in Oguma, 1998, pp. 62–63; translation mine)

Iwatani believed that the fate of the Ainu, as an inherently inferior species, was to become extinct. Iwatani based his prediction on the then-popular social Darwinian principle of survival of the fittest, a convenient scientific justification for unfair treatment used against aboriginal peoples around the globe, including Native Americans. Yet Iwatani's paternalism took the form of an argument for the protection, conservation, and education of the Ainu, saying that as a father, there is nothing so lovable as a stupid child.

Iwatani examined five possible ways to deal with the Ainu: extermination, race-changing, Westernization (radicalism), preservation (separatism), and (gradual) assimilation (Zenka). Iwatani insisted that the last policy, assimilation, be adopted for the Ainu. Extermination was considered because the Ainu were regarded as an ugly and shameful race. Race-changing policy meant to blend the Ainu away through breeding. It was a form of eugenics that was to be facilitated through intermarriage between Ainu and Japanese, creating a hybrid that would be an improvement over the Ainu and could be more readily assimilated. Iwatani rejected these two solutions, arguing that the former would damage the reputation of the nation, and the latter was unrealistic because of discrimination against the Ainu. It was believed that preservationism, or separatism, would preserve the Ainu customs and culture even while they would become educated in basic reading and arithmetic on segregated reservations. However, by the very nature of segregation, this policy would have left the Ainu uneducated in the ways of a modern education, and therefore Iwatani rejected this alternative. It would have left a nation within a nation. Westernizing the Ainu, which had already been done to some extent by missionaries, involved teaching them Western-style civilization, the Latin alphabet, and Christian values of good and evil and citizenship. This alternative was rejected because the whole point was to convert the Ainu into Japanese nationals, at least for external, political reasons. It was hoped that the Ainu could be convinced to not only not become Westernized but to defend Japan against Western incursions.

The compromise logic of gradual assimilation, or *Zenka*, is a kind of combination of preservation and assimilation. It is not truly assimilation in that both the Ainu and the Japanese are not necessarily equal. It shows Japan's ambivalence, for Japan also rejected physical extermination outright. Yet central Japan does not hope that the Ainu will become prosperous, either. In essence, the plan is to increase the power of the central Japanese authority by increasing the number of people who identify themselves as Japanese nationals by, in this case, destroying the Ainu through *gradual* assimilation, which is to say, cultural extermination. The means to achieve this transformation is through educating them as to what counts as appropriate thinking, reading, writing, and behaving in the Japanese style. For diplomatic reasons, Japan insists that the Ainu belong to the Japanese nation, and therefore Hokkaido is neither an Ainu nor a Russian territory but rather a *Japanese* territory. It does not mean, however, that the Ainu and the Japanese are equal.

CONCLUDING REMARKS: NATION-STATE AND CULTURAL DIVERSITY

While I was writing this chapter, the United Nations released a report on globalization and local cultures, warning of a rapid decrease in biological, ethnic, cultural, and linguistic diversities as a consequence of globalization across the world.[19] More than twenty-five hundred indigenous languages out of five to seven thousand world languages (four to five thousand of which are considered indigenous) are now in immediate danger of extinction. It is also estimated that over next hundred years, 90 percent of the world's languages will have been exterminated or become practically extinct. The language of the Ainu is categorized as endangered. Cultural diversity is shrinking at an alarming rate in the face of a globalizing unisystem.

As described, the life and culture of the Ainu were profoundly disturbed and practically destroyed as Japan (*Wajin*) sought to become a modern nation-state in competition with Western powers. The basic logic of the modern national system involves a close linkage between nationhood, culture, and (in the case of Japan) ethnic identity and language. That is, a nation, as it is conceived of by Japan and many European powers at the turn of the nineteenth century, consists of a single culture (and national language) expressed by the actions of a single ethnic group. To maintain its autonomy, the so-called culture (and ethnicity or ethnic group) is ideologically enforced among peoples considered to be sharing the same tradition and history (ethnicity) (in fact, such tradition is even often invented for this purpose, as Hobsbawm and Ranger [1983] reveal). The Ainu were used to defend and maintain Hokkaido as a Japanese territory. In so doing, the Ainu were conveniently defined as Japanese nationals, which in turn required that they acquire Japanese culture and language. Even the Ainu as an ethnic group is a political invention.

The Ainu Sinpo (the Ainu New Act) was promulgated in 1997 to preserve the culture of the Ainu. In fact, the New Act is formally named Act on Promotion of Ainu Culture and the Facilitation of Popular Understanding of the Ainu Tradition. Although there are many issues incorporated into it, Japan has started to acknowledge multiculturalism. As an increasing awareness of indigenous peoples emerges, Japanese authorities are reconsidering the myths of monoculture and its link to the ideology of mono-ethnicity within a nation. The emerging awareness, motivated by the realities of globalism and mobility, is that cohabitation rather than extermination must be learned.

NOTES

1. See The Ministry of Justice, as of December 31, 1998. These statistics do not reflect Korean Japanese who are naturalized. There are thus more Koreans in reality than the numbers appearing in statistics.

2. Here, I use the term *ethnic* in a commonsense way or without any question. What constitutes ethnicity, however, is a difficult question. I will elaborate on the term later.

3. In developing new Ainu policies, this issue of their indigenous nature has been discussed by expert panels formed by then–Prime Minister Murayama. The judgment was avoided on this issue. The government of Japan has never officially acknowledged the Ainu as indigenous people, though it has recognized the Ainu as a minority group in Japan. The reason for this was that "such rights have not yet been defined internationally" (Tsunemoto, 1999, p. 366).

4. The term *Dojin* was originally used to refer to native, aboriginal, and indigenous people or those who were living in a place during medieval Japan without discriminative connotations, such as *Matsumae Dojin* (those who live in Matsumae) (Kikuchi, 1994). The term came to be mean "retarded and uncivilized savage." This semantic shift combined with social Darwinist and Marxist thinking, which were schools of thought dominant at that time. Currently the term is no longer used due to its discriminating stigma.

5. The term *Wajin* refers to Japanese especially in relation to the Ainu.

6. Even though there were many Ainu tribes, in the early modern period, when Japan was constructing itself into a so-called modern nation, the Ainu were divided or separated by national boundaries between Japan and Russia. Due to boundary changes, some were thus forced to migrate from Sakhalin and settle in Hokkaido. Currently, most Ainu live in Hokkaido.

7. See Center for Human Rights Affairs (online at http://www.jinken.or.jp/jstj0102houkoku.htm). In this survey, *Ainu* is defined as those who are considered to have Ainu lineage or those who have become Ainu by marriage or adoption. This number does not include those who refuse to be considered Ainu in spite of their Ainu lineage. There were 18,298 in 1972, 24,160 in 1979, and 24,381 in 1986.

8. Here the term *Ainu* is used to describe general characteristics of the so-called Ainu. There are, however, diverse variations within the Ainu. This aspect will be elaborated later in this chapter.

9. Another aspect of illiteracy among the Ainu is a consequence of the literacy culture in Japan. The literacy rate among Japanese was already quite high even in the late Edo era (approximately 1700). Literacy was enhanced by means of private elementary schools called *Terakoya*. This high literacy rate or literacy culture caused many to view literacy as an absolute good and to look down on those who did not write and read (i.e., Ainu) (Kikuchi, 1994).

10. For reviews on the two views, refer to Yoshino (1992, 1997).

11. Each of the four refers roughly to the following: The Eastern Barbarian refers to Japan, Korea, Manchuria, and so forth. The Western Barbarian refers to Tibetan and Turkish ethnic groups. The Southern Barbarian refers to Indochina. The Northern Barbarian refers to Mongolia.

12. In medieval Japan, the recognition was Japan, China, and India. Due to the influence of the West, such recognition has changed.

13. See Kikuchi (1994), p. 125.

14. Based on the strict status or caste system during the Edo era, to acquire a language or culture beyond one's status or caste was considered shameful (Oguma, 1998).

15. Historical descriptions and English translations of laws, regulations, acts, and treaties heavily rely on the Foundation for Research and Promotion of Ainu Culture (2000).

16. Hokkaido was divided into three prefectures—Sapporo, Hakodate, and Nemuro. This remained the situation until the unifying Hokkaido government was established in 1886.

17. Kayano also introduces the episode of his father being arrested for catching banned salmon sixty some years ago.

18. The Dawes Act of 1887 (available online at http://www.udayton.edu/~race/02rights/native09.htm).

19. Press Release of the United Nations Environment Programme (UNEP), February 2001. The title is "Globalization: A Threat to the World's Cultural, Linguistic, and Biological Diversity." The content is available online at http://www.unep.org/Documents/Default.asp?DocumentID=192&ArticleID=2765.

REFERENCES AND SUGGESTED READING

Ainu Museum. (1993). *Ainu bunka no kiso chishiki* [Basic knowledge of Ainu culture]. Tokyo: Sofukan.

Anderson, B. (1983). *Imagined communities: Reflections on the origins and spread of nationalism*. London: Verso.

Asahi Shimbun. (1999). *Japan almanac 2000*. Tokyo: Asahi Shimbun.

Burger, J. (1987). *Report from the frontier: The state of the world's indigenous peoples*. N.J.: Zed Book.

Fitzhugh, W. (1999). Ainu ethnicity: A history. In W. W. Fitzhugh & C. O. Dubreuil (Eds.), *Ainu: Spirit of a northern people* (pp. 9–27). Seattle: University of Washington Press.

Foundation for Research and Promotion of Ainu Culture. (2000). *To understand the Ainu*. Sapporo, Japan: Foundation for Research and Promotion of Ainu Culture.

Imanishi, H. (2000). *Kokuminkokka to mainoritei* [Nation state and minority]. Tokyo: Nihon Keizai Hyoronsha.

Gebser, J. (1949/1985). *The ever-present origin* (N. Barstad & A. Mickunas, Trans.). Athens: Ohio University Press.

Gellner, E. (1983). *Nations and nationalism*. Oxford, New York: Basil Blackwell.

Hobsbawm, E., & Ranger, T. (Eds.). (1983). *The invention of tradition*. Cambridge: Cambridge University Press.

Kayano, S. (1999). The weight of word: History and culture of the Ainu. In Y. Ishii & M. Yamauchi (Eds.), *Nihonjin to tabunkashugi* [Japanese and multiculturalism] (pp. 36–50). Tokyo: Yamakawa.

Kida, S. (1926). Tohoku minzoku kenkyu joron [An introduction to research on ethnic group in Tohoku]. In S. Kida & S. Kida (Eds.), *Chosakushu 9* [Collected papers of Sadakichi Kida 9]. Tokyo: Heibonsha.

Kikuchi, I. (1994). *Ainu minzoku to nihonjin* [The Ainu and the Japanese]. Tokyo: Asahi Shimbunsha.

Kono, M. (1998). Ainu. In H. Harajiri (Ed.), *Sekai no minzoku* [Ethnic groups in a world] (pp. 33–53). Tokyo: Hoso Daigaku.

Kosarev, M. (1990). *Drevneiiaeiia istorieiia zapadnoaei sibiri*. Moscow: Nauka.

Kramer, E. (1993). Understanding co-constitutional genesis. *Integrative Explorations: Journal of Culture and Consciousness, 1*, 41–47.

Kramer, E. (1995). A brief hermeneutic of the co-constitution of nature and culture in the West including some contemporary consequences. *History of European Ideas, 20*, 649–659.

Nishide, K. (1986). Amerika gasshukokushi to senju minzoku [History of the United States of America and indigenous people]. In the Department of Human Sciences, Sapporo Gakuin University (Ed.), *Hokkaido to shosu minzoku: Hokkaido bunkaron* [Hokkaido and minority ethnic groups: Culture of Hokkaido] (pp. 1–59). Sapporo, Japan: Sapporo Gakuin University Cooperation.

Ogasawara, N. (1997). *Ainu sabetsu mondai dokuhon* [Readings in Ainu discrimination problems]. Tokyo: Ryokufu.

Oguma, E. (1998). *Nihonjin no kyokai* [The boundaries of the Japanese]. Tokyo: Shinyosha.

Posey, D. (1999). Introduction: Culture and nature—the inextricable link. In United Nations Environment Programme (UNEP) (D. A. Posey, Ed.), *Cultural and spiritual values of biodiversity*. London: Intermediate Technology.

Siddle, R. (1999). Ainu history: An overview. In W. W. Fitzhugh & C. O. Dubreuil (Eds.), *Ainu: Spirit of a northern people* (pp. 67–73). Seattle: University of Washington Press.

Smith, A. (1986). *The ethnic origin of nations.* Oxford: Basil Blackwell.

Takakura, S. (1939). *Ainu no tochi mondai* [Land issues of the Ainu]. Shakai seisaku jihou 230. Tokyo: Kyouhoukai.

Takagi, H. (1994). Ainu minzoku he no dokaseisaku no seiritsu [Formation of assimilation policy onto the Ainu]. In R. Kenkyukai (Ed.), *Kokumin kokka wo tou* [Questioning nation state] (pp. 166–183). Tokyo: Aoki Shoten.

Taksami, C. (1998). *Kto vy, aeiny: Ocherk istorii kultury.* Moscow: Mysl.

Tamura, S. (1999). Ainu language: Features and relationships. In W. W. Fitzhugh & C. O. Dubreuil (Eds.), *Ainu: Spirit of a northern people* (pp. 57–65). Seattle: University of Washington Press.

Tomita, T. (1989). *Hokkaido kyudojin ho to dozu ho: Hikakushiteki kokoromi* [The Hokkaido Former Aborigines Protection Act and the Dawes Act: A comparative historical perspective]. *Sapporo Gakuin Daigaku Jinbun Gakkai Kiyou, 45,* 5–21.

Tsunemoto, T. (1999). The Ainu sinpo: A new beginning. In W. W. Fitzhugh & C. O. Dubreuil (Eds.), *Ainu: Spirit of a northern people* (pp. 366–368). Seattle: University of Washington Press.

Uemura, H. (1992). *Sekai to Nippon no senjuminzoku* [World and Japanese indigenous people] (Iwanami Booklet 281). Tokyo: Iwanami.

Yoshino, K. (1992). *Cultural nationalism in contemporary Japan: A sociological enquiry.* London: Routledge.

Yoshino, K. (1997). *Bunka nashinarizumu no shakaigaku: gendai nihon no aidentetei no yukue* [A sociology of cultural nationalism: Where modern Japanese identity goes]. Nagoya, Japan: Nagoya University Press.

Chapter 6

Headache and Heartbreak: The Elusiveness of "Model Minority" Status Attainment for African Americans

Charlton D. McIlwain and Lonnie Johnson Jr.

What do you call a black man with a Ph.D.?—A nigger.

—Malcolm X

INTRODUCTION

Model minority ideology was and continues to be used in American society to mandate conformity among groups of people who, from the dominant Eurocentric perspective, are seen as being inferior. Often their status is tied to the nature of the pigmentation of their skin. This ideology promotes self-hatred among those who do not measure up, the disintegration of individual identity, and the adoption of a new identity prescribed by dominant social forces. The stress on conformity is propagated through the kindred ideologies of assimilation and cultural adaptation.

Many African Americans, from the period of slavery to the present, suffer from what W. E. B. Du Bois called double consciousness, the phenomenon of viewing the self through the eyes of the other. Those who suffer from double consciousness do so as a consequence of seeking to attain the status of being a so-called model minority. That is, many African Americans believe they are what others tell them they are and thus seek to be what and who those individuals say they *should* be.

However, in this pursuit, few if any have managed to cross the finish line—to attain that fabled status according to which one's life and social actions are completely satisfying to the dominant white society. Fundamentally, modern American society still does not accept African Americans for who they are, allowing them a place of acceptability among whites generally, and psychological health for the individual black. This is the case primarily because there is no model.

Since the time of slavery, there has existed the constant struggle between modes of attaining model minority status—a struggle between racial isolation and assimilation. During the period of slavery, most African Americans did not have much choice regarding the direction of their lives. Their lack of power kept them in "their place," leaving them little room to move. However, a few did gain some small opportunities that enabled them to decide for themselves whether they would be better served emulating whites or isolating themselves among other African Americans (self-segregation). Those who seized such opportunities ironically opened the door for black Americans to a set of competing, often confounding ideas about their own identities and their "proper place" within society, dominated as it was (and is) by white values, beliefs, motives, expectations, and behavior patterns.

The tensions grew with the coming of revolutionary changes in both the legal and political arenas, as well as changes in the American economic system. With a great surge in opportunities coming in the late 1960s and 1970s, more African Americans began seeking what they thought would fully integrate them into the fabric of American society. However, those who have begun this quest find that they are indeed chasing a ghost, a figment of their collective imaginations and aspirations. Many have given up trying to satisfy the dominant culture and are forging a multicultural society with parallel and alternate versions of success and ways of achieving. Thus, the definition of *model* is less defined from the singular perspective of Euro-Americanism. Why is this so?

First, the elusiveness of the model minority status debunks its very definition and ideological foundation. For African Americans, the definition of the model minority makes such a status unattainable because it does not occupy a fixed position in either time or space but is subject to constant change and flux.

Second, important social and political ramifications have negatively impacted African Americans in their attempts to attain some form of model minority status. The nature of model minority status suggests conformity. However, many African Americans refuse to internalize the self-hatred that underlies ideologies that suggest conformity. As a result, those who seek to conform in various ways and to differing degrees to the dominant society's dictates face opposition and possible exclusion by and from whites. This situation has ironically led to a renewed call for black isolation.

In addition, the ostracizing and opposing of blacks and black styles in the course of seeking model minority acceptance is also evident within the African American community itself. It typically reveals itself in the rhetoric of racial authenticity, which dictates the very definition of black, determining the individual's racial/cultural status vis-à-vis being "really black." This poses a straightjacket of its own such that black reality is posited as something inflexibly sui generis.

This chapter begins by providing evidence and an illustrative case for the claim that emerging tensions between assimilation and isolation exist today (to be sure) but that such a tension is essential to the black American experience, existing already during the times of slavery and immediately thereafter. Next, we follow the path of assimilation sought by many African Americans given their newfound opportunities. Finally, we look at some of the resulting tensions sparked by this effort exerted as it is by both blacks and whites.

ASSIMILATION VERSUS ISOLATION: EMERGING TENSIONS DURING AMERICAN SLAVERY AND EMANCIPATION

In many ways, the life of the former slave and freed man Frederick Douglass chronicles a set of racial tensions that became undeniably apparent during American slavery and that still persist today. Thus the institution of slavery as practiced in colonial America provides some initial considerations for understanding the dynamics of economic power and social identity.

As with most slaves, Douglass knew little of his own birth. He was born in Talbot County, Maryland, in a town called Tuckahoe, which was near Hillsborough. Although he was never sure about the date of his birth (as was common among slaves), he overheard his master say in 1835 that Douglass was about seventeen years old. Based on that information, he speculated that he was born in 1818. Still, he could never venture a guess as to the season of his birth.

Douglass also knew little of his parents. His mother was Harriet Bailey, the daughter of Isaac and Betsey Bailey. Both were "colored," of a dark complexion. He only saw his mother a few times before she died because she lived several miles away. It was a common practice to separate the mothers from their children within twelve months of birth. The few times it was possible for them to visit, she managed to either get permission from her master or sneak away to visit her son, mostly at night, only to leave by morning. He knew nothing of his father except that he was a white man. It was rumored that his own master was his father, but he never knew this for certain.

Douglass grew up initially on a plantation that was owned by Colonel Edward Lloyd, the overseer of the overseers. It was located about twelve miles from Easton, Maryland, on the banks of the Miles River. The plantation primarily produced tobacco, corn, and wheat. Not only did Lloyd own three to four hundred slaves who resided at his plantation, but he also owned several more on surrounding farms that also belonged to him.

This plantation, the Great House Farm (as the slaves referred to it) provided the stage for Douglass's encounters with slavery. He recalled one interaction between a slave named Demby and his overseer, Gore. Gore was notorious for being one of the more savage overseers. After being whipped, Demby ran and jumped into a creek and stood in it at shoulder's depth to relieve some of the pain. Gore warned Demby that if he did not leave the creek within three calls, he would shoot him. He called once; Demby said he would not leave. He called a second and third time; the slave still refused to leave the creek. With no additional calls, Gore proceeded to raise his gun, take aim, and shoot him. His justification to his boss was that Demby had been unmanageable for quite some time and needed to be set as an example for the others.

On another occasion, Douglass remembered how many slaves would often spend their spare time (nights and Sundays) fishing for oysters. This provided them with extra food to compensate for their meager rations. One day Beal Bondly, from a neighboring farm, noticed that one of Lloyd's slaves had trespassed onto his property. Without hesitation, Bondly grabbed his musket, walked down to the shore, and shot the offending slave. On the following day, Bondly explained the situation to Lloyd. After that, very little was ever said about the ordeal; certainly nothing was done about it.

On yet another occasion, Douglass described endless incidents concerning the fruit garden. During the summer months, Lloyd had a garden that would produce several different types of fruit. In fact, the garden was so big that people from miles away (all throughout Maryland) would come to see it. Many slaves would break into the fruit garden to steal fruit to subsidize their food allowances. To keep the slaves out, the overseers would line the fence with tar. If anyone was caught with tar on him or her, they would suffer lashes.

Many times, Douglass was awakened by the screaming of his aunt Hester. Plummer, also one of the more savage overseers, would whip her until she yelled and then whip her until she stopped yelling. On one occasion, Douglass hid himself in a closet, only to see her stripped from her neck to her waist, tied with her arms stretched far above her head, leaving only her toes to touch the ground. The sight of the blood itself was not enough to stop the lashes. In fact, often the only thing that could stop the overseer was his own fatigue.

These are only a few of the many incidents that Douglas recalled in his autobiography, *Narrative of the Life of Frederick Douglass: An American Slave*, first published in 1845 (Douglass, 1845/1968). For every incidence of brutality recalled and described, there were surely dozens no longer remembered. Such are the traumatizing events that marked his daily encounters with slavery as a child.

However, Douglass's personal experiences were somewhat different. In many ways, he was raised like the other slave children. Because he was too young for hard labor, he was assigned chores, such as cleaning the yard, chasing the fowl away from the garden, and running errands for his master's daughter. Just like other slave children, he only had a coarse linen shirt as his allowance of clothing. This made the nights very cold because he had no bedding, apart from the ground.

On the other hand, Douglass was also set apart from the other slave children in some ways. He spent much of his spare time with his master (at the time), Daniel Lloyd. Lloyd would have Douglass find and retrieve his birds after he shot them. During this time, Lloyd and Douglass developed a close relationship, and Lloyd became very protective of Douglass. In fact, in their competition for food, the bigger and stronger kids normally got more. However, Lloyd would always watch out for Douglass when he was present. In addition, Douglass was seldom whipped as a child.

When he was about seven or eight years old, he moved to Baltimore to live with Mr. and Mrs. Auld, relatives of his previous master. He was always amazed that out of all of the other slave children he was the only one who was chosen to go on trips to the big city. His primary job was to help care for Thomas Auld, their son. For many slaves, this was an enviable position. A city slave was considered to be one step away from a freed man. Now he was able to walk around town running errands, wear trousers, and live inside a house.

Sophia, his new mistress, was also eager to teach him to read. He was initially like another son to her. Mr. Auld quickly recognized her eagerness and immediately explained to her that slaves should be kept ignorant because knowledge would only give them the power to create problems. Eventually, he forbade his wife from teaching Douglass. Regardless, her kindheartedness compelled her to continue teaching him for a while. However, she gradually adopted the views and sentiments of her husband and stopped the lessons. Furthermore, she told him that he could no longer study.

This antagonism fueled Douglass's desire to read and write. He had not yet learned much, but he had learned enough to begin teaching himself. In his spare time, he looked for writing wherever he could find it, making the world his textbook. In addition, he made friends with many white children and sometimes traded bread for instruction with them. Eventually, Douglass learned to read and write.

After being a city slave for some time, circumstances during his teenage years led him back to the plantation where, for the first time in his life, he was put to work as a field hand (for a new master). This proved to be a shocking experience. Now he himself became the target of the sort of brutality he had witnessed as a young child. Due to his lack of physical agility, many of the tasks assigned to him were too difficult. On many occasions he was whipped simply because he was unable to complete the task in an acceptable manner.

After being a city slave for so long, being a field hand was a shocking experience that enabled him to realize that there was no possible way that he could remain a slave for long. This newfound sense of urgency prompted him to begin teaching other slaves how to read and write. Eventually, he developed an informed following that shared his desire for freedom.

However, the spark for freedom that Douglass's militant spirit provided for many of the slaves made him a threat to his master. Douglass became so resistant that he started refusing his beatings. The last time his master tried to beat him, he vehemently fought back. Even the master's helpers refused to help stop Douglass, claiming that they were only hired to help, not to do any beating. So the master finally stopped fighting out of disgust and warned Douglass to never cause trouble again. Of course, after that scuffle, the master never attempted to beat him again.

During the entire time he was a field hand, Douglass constantly dreamed of and planned for his own freedom. He decided that the best route for his freedom would be to go north to New York and eventually to Canada. Finally, after much planning, he began his journey to freedom. Along the way, he knew he would need documents from his master explaining the reason for his travel. He was able to write these for himself. In addition, his experiences as a city slave gave him the ability to talk his way out of many potentially difficult situations that he encountered along the way.

All throughout Douglass's life, he had been exposed to the "model identity" in several ways. Even at his birth, he looked more like his master than like most of the other slaves. Eventually, this relationship placed him in a situation where he could learn to read and write. As he learned to read and write, he became reacquainted with the world in a different way. He eventually learned how to talk, act like, and be like the dominant class (or at least, more so than most slaves), so much so that he was not able to return to the plantation lifestyle.

These experiences formed the foundation for him to resist the dominant order of the Southern world. His skills and experiences as a city slave brought him closer to the white world, but they also heightened his sense of despair about not being accepted. This made his experience of being a field slave unbearable. His experiences bore in him an insatiable sense of urgency to be free. The skills he had acquired provided him with the ability and the resources he needed to resist and escape the slave system, not adapt to it.

However, for Douglass and many other freed slaves, freedom quickly revealed itself to be not only the end of one form of tribulation but also the beginning of a new set of difficulties.

After obtaining freedom, blacks still faced a number of ordeals, including legal, political, and economic barriers (Frazier, 1957). Not being able to vote made it next to impossible to have a voice in the workings of their communities. In addition, they were not able to send their children to public schools. Nor did freed slaves have opportunities to move and find better jobs. Most blacks did not have very many resources after obtaining freedom. Therefore, they had to move where they could find others who were willing to help them until they found work. So they were limited to areas where there were already concentrations of freedmen. Blacks were also still in fear because they could be kidnapped from the North, taken to the South, and sold back into slavery.

So the economy of the North perhaps was not as promising as many had originally suspected (Frazier, 1965). In fact, in 1829, David Walker of Boston, a Northern black leader, claimed that the Northern system of economics was no better (or not much better) than that of the slavery economics of the South. A slave of the South had no "human" rights, thus stripping them of their humanity. Their Northern counterparts were still reduced to the point of giving thanks for the opportunity of shining the boots and washing the dirty clothes of the whites. In Walker's mind, this was barely an improvement.

Likewise, Douglass condemned many white Northern merchants. He claimed that they were quick to support the rhetoric of abolition. However, they did not follow up in their actions. Rarely would they hire blacks into decent jobs, such as clerks and bookkeepers.

Another with similar convictions and observations was Robert Morris Sr. On being admitted to the Massachusetts bar in 1847, Morris joined these initial stages of civil rights activism by challenging segregation in the Boston public school system. He also fought against the Fugitive Slave Law of 1850, which was enacted as a compromise to Southern states in an attempt to appease them and avoid civil war. The act stated that runaway slaves found anywhere in the United States, including in the free North, should be captured and returned to their owners in the South. The law mandated that all citizens should aid federal marshals in tracking down and capturing such fugitive slaves.

Technological changes also impacted the condition of blacks in America, both free and slave. The demand for efficiency in a competitive economy gave rise to technological advances. This also made it difficult for blacks to compete in the struggle for economic survival. Labor-saving mechanical devices began to change the landscape of the Northern economy. With industrialization, both unskilled and highly skilled workers were needed. Although machinery normally replaced workers in lower-skilled jobs, there was still a need for them. However, the supply of unskilled labor outpaced demand. A huge supply of women and children (and after the 1840s, Irish immigrants) easily surpassed the diminishing demand for unskilled workers. In addition, machinery required a type of skill training that Negroes often could not obtain due to their lack of educational opportunities.

Meanwhile, increasing racial tensions swept through the workplace. Many whites believed that supporting the abolition of slavery promoted a massive migration of blacks from the South into Northern cities. After being enslaved, many blacks were willing to work for far less than many of their white counterparts. Thus, whites felt that any success that blacks experienced in the workplace was at their expense. This was primarily in reference to low-skilled positions. Most factory owners would not hire blacks to work the high-skilled jobs, which involved machinery. Blacks were limited primarily to menial jobs. In some cases, they were encouraged to return to their former masters to work in the fields.

Even after the Civil War, blacks remained primarily dependent on agricultural jobs. The biggest transformation was in terms of communal life. Freedom brought about a need to establish an infrastructure for black communities so they could function cohesively. Not only did freed slaves still have to work to sustain their livelihoods, they also had to organize and run their own churches, schools, support groups, and political organizations, based on their already limited resources.

The Negro that had in some cases just risked his life for freedom had found himself faced by a set of political, economic, and social circumstances that still held him captive. Black Americans had escaped slavery, but they were still locked out of many of the privileges and rights of mainstream society. The struggle for an identity in American society continued.

ATTAINING THE NEW MODEL

With the advent of legislation and court challenges thereto, many African Americans were eager to seize on their newfound freedoms and opportunities to attain the American dream. Preeminent examples include the case of *Brown v. the Board of Education of Topeka* (1954); the executive order issued in 1961 by President Kennedy declaring that contractors doing work for the federal government should take "affirmative action" to ensure fair treatment of employees and job applicants regardless of race, religion, or national origin; and legislation such as the Civil Rights Act of 1964 and the Voting Rights Act of 1965. Until the passage of such laws, the American dream had been denied to blacks. Now, many began to take steps that would, in their minds, diminish the blight of racial identification through educational and professional attainment. The new model of black America was that of integration and assimilation into white society. Indeed, this is what many early black intellectuals such as Du Bois saw as the only hope for blacks to rise above their stagnate, inferior condition in America (although Du Bois's position later changed).

Other assimilationists, such as Gudykunst and Kim (1997), assert that cultural and individual success and satisfaction is predicated on one's communication and interaction with the dominant society. In their view, the more a minority person interacts with those of the majority, the more he or she adopts their modes of communication, lifestyle, and values, the more he or she is prone to achieve psychological health, as well as material success. The early years of African Americans' approach to attaining the new model seem to bear this out.

The largest period of professional accomplishment for blacks was the period from 1967 to 1977, when the per capita income for blacks increased by 88 percent (U.S. Census, 1998).[1] With housing discrimination outlawed in the late 1960s, during the 1970s and 1980s blacks began to occupy homes in largely white neighborhoods (Farley, 1999, pp. 327–330). From 1970 to 1980, 11.6 percent of African Americans had attended four or more years of college, which was a marked increase over both the previous and succeeding decade (U.S. Census, 2000).[2]

Not only did this attempt at assimilation occur within the economic sector, but legitimate romantic unions between blacks and whites also contributed to this process. The rise of a black middle class during the 1970s, 1980s, and 1990s seems to have some connection to the rise in black–white marriages during those periods. A recent study has found that in 1993, 12.1 percent of all new marriages involving an African American were interracial, up from 6.6 percent in 1980 and 2.6 percent in 1970 (*Newsweek*, 1996, p. 51). These marriages, as might be expected, resulted in the most magical form of communication, the sharing of blood through sexual intercourse, resulting in a growing population of children of mixed race.

Despite the growing social interaction between blacks and whites in the job market, college classroom, and bedrooms, many African Americans found that indeed what they were told they would gain was not completely realized. They found that even though the new criteria for attaining model minority status, promoted by the motto "be like us [whites]," seemed easy to follow; in fact, many whites rejected their advances. Furthermore, blacks had to endure the resulting rejection not only by whites but also from members of their own in-group.

What is evidenced by African American attempts to adapt is precisely what Kim and other assimilationists fail to explain. They assert that the onus to adapt is solely on the minority. But what happens when the "stranger" seeks to assimilate and finds that the dominant society will not let him or her do so? What happens when physical, immutable differences stand in the way of complete acceptance? What happens when one has mastered the communication system only to find that he or she is still forced to stand on the outside looking in?

Simply mastering techniques and forms of communication is not the same as the actual experience of human social interaction. When human beings interact, they do not do so simply as individuals who have mastered certain conversational techniques. They interact as ever-present selves. They interact as two people with motives, historical memory, and powerful prejudices. This is why what assimilationists thought should have happened to African Americans seeking to blend in to the dominant society did not happen. After reaching what seemed to be a plateau of success for African Americans in the corporate world, and with continued devolution of the inner cities, a renewed attack on black intelligence emerged. This attack claimed that because the doors of opportunity had been clearly opened for blacks in education and business, their continued demise in terms of low social achievement reflected a basic, some even claimed inherent, inferiority in which culture and environment were negligible influences.

Falling in line with Binet (1916), Linnaeus (1806), Montagu (1999), and others, in 1994 Herrnstein and Murray introduced their work *The Bell Curve* as evidence for why blacks did not progress to the level of whites with the increase in opportunity. Their thesis regarding race and IQ was given much publicity and was utilized by many to underscore their position that despite affirmative action efforts, blacks simply could not attain the status of white society because they are genetically unable to do so. The conclusion drawn by many is that affirmative action efforts are a waste of time. This is further illustrated in the mission of the Pioneer Fund, the group that sponsored the research presented in Herrnstein and Murray's book. The group is characterized as a "neo-Nazi organization closely integrated with the far right in American politics. The fund's mission is to promote eugenics, a philosophy that maintains that 'genetically unfit' individuals or races are a threat to society" (MacIntyre, 1989, p. 23).

Such anti-black sentiment manifests itself in reaction to affirmative action. As early as 1976, whites began charging that affirmative action efforts in both the private and public sectors resulted in undue advantages given to blacks and other minorities. In that year, a white employee of Kaiser Aluminum and Chemical Corporation objected to the use of quotas to ensure job training for minorities at a plant in Gramercy, Louisiana. A federal judge ruled that the policy discriminated against white employees who had higher seniority and thus violated the Civil Rights Act of 1964. He ordered the practice stopped.[3] Such claims, as well as judicial actions have become commonplace in twenty-first-century America—in the workplace, in higher education, even in professional sporting arenas. Many white Americans, who once invited blacks to be like us, have decided that this is not really what they want.

On the other hand, many blacks began to assert that such attempts at assimilation were not what they really wanted either. During the same period that whites were challenging blacks in their move closer to them in status and achievement, blacks began to see this invited assimilation for what it really was. It was an attempt to erase black culture—to do away with difference and ultimately assimilate into one white country, if not in skin color then at least in culture and practice.

This realization renewed calls for black nationalism, self-love, and self-help. This time blacks asserted not a move back to Africa, as Marcus Garvey and others had attempted, but to build an isolated community within America by black people for black people. New movements and organizations urged blacks toward self-sufficiency—to build their own schools, neighborhoods, and businesses—to carve out a separate and distinct place from whites.

Elijah Muhammed (1965) stated what many people throughout the 1970s and beyond would embrace when he said:

There is no need for us, millions throughout the country, spending our money for the joy and happiness of others. As a result, as soon as we are thrown out of a job, we are back at the doors of white people, begging for bread and soup. How many clothing shops do we operate in the country? Very few. Yet, all of us wear clothes. Who made our clothes for us? Who sold them to us? We have a few grocery stores, but this is not enough to feed 30 million Black people in America. Should we not have clothing factories making clothes for ourselves? Should we not have more stores to sell our people everything that they want or need? (p. 83)[4]

Since the 1970s there has been a dramatic rise in black-owned businesses that cater to the needs of the black community and that predominately employ members of the black community. However, many black-owned businesses have hit a ceiling where they have either extended their market as far as it will go among black consumers or they haven't been able to raise the capital needed to expand and compete with businesses owned by their white counterparts.

The real problem, however, is that corporate isolation in a world of increasing interconnectivity—of integrated capital, communications, human resources, and ideas—will surely lead to failure. However, black-owned businesses have little choice—stay in their isolation, or risk losing their claim of black business, social, and political solidarity.

Earl Graves (2000), publisher of *Black Enterprise* magazine, says:

One of the most important New Economy imperatives cited by our economists is also one of the most intriguing: black entrepreneurs must seek strategic opportunities and alliances with the businesses and industry organizations of other ethnic groups, with the goal of creating what BE economist Margaret Simms of the Joint Center of Political and Economic Studies calls "economic rainbow coalitions." (p. 17)

So, although some blacks have retreated to racial isolation in terms of the marketplace, they still find that it does not produce a fitting outcome or challenge to the dominant system, which they claim has locked them out.

Others espousing isolationist trends have turned to more radical ideological strategies to counter the resistance of whites to their ability to attain some modicum of model success. The New Black Panther Party, "eschewing the health clinics and free breakfast programs of the original Panthers ... have seemed to focus almost exclusively on hate rhetoric about Jews and whites," says a recent *Intelligence Report* by the Southern Poverty Law Center. David Hilliard, a former member of the old Black Panther organization and current director of the Huey P. Newton Foundation, says that the old organization was never separatist. "We worked with all different ethnic groups, especially the white left, to build a coalition," Hilliard (2000) said.

So we see that the desire for adaptation, the move toward maximum assimilation, by African Americans has not resulted in the psychological health or success promised by its theorists. Instead, those who have done all that was seemingly required to meet the new dictates of social and economic standing, have found that the process has been fraught with anger, competing loyalties, and psychological threat. They have found that the dominant society refuses to relinquish the power and control it possesses by being able to define the other and define the criteria for success. The situation for black Americans is like being in a one-hundred-yard dash race with someone else who keeps moving the finish line every time you come within ten yards of it. Is it any wonder why in the past two years two of America's most wealthy men—entertainer Bill Cosby and professional basketball great Michael Jordan—were vehemently blocked in their attempts to purchase a major TV network and major professional basketball franchise (the Charlotte Hornets), respectively (*New York Times*, 1999, May 8, p. D3)?[5]

THE NEW MODEL AND THE CLAIM
TO RACIAL AUTHENTICITY

With the move toward greater isolation among blacks, many African Americans, particularly those in the academy, are seeking to impose their own idea of the model black citizen. Such a model has usually been expressed in aspirations to racial authenticity—the idea that "real" African Americans must share particular loyalties, responsibilities, political agendas, interests, and so on. Such assertions usually are couched in the claim of a magical connection and unity with a common geographical space—the African continent.

Asante (1988) one of the chief proponents of Afrocentrism, claims that "predynastic Egypt ... was inhabited by people no different from the present black population of the United States" (p. 5). As such, he asserts that "Afrocentrism is the belief in the centrality of Africans in postmodern history. It is our history, our mythology, our creative motif, and our ethos exemplifying our collective will. On the basis of our story, we build upon the work of our ancestors who gave signs toward our humanizing function" (Asante, 1985, p. 6).

According to Asante, those who do not hold to this "collective will" have been duped by a white supremacist power structure that has molded one's identity into something that it *should not* be. It is this ideological position that equates Asante's Afrocentrism with Kim's and others' assimilationist theories.

Afrocentrists, such as Akbar (1996), Asante (1988), Jeffries (1999), Karenga (1978), and others, have realized that there is great power in being able to define reality. It is their intent to usurp the power of personal choice, turning toward an ideology that dictates legitimacy and status among members of the black community. They get to say who is black, what counts as appropriate black scholarship, what political, social, and economic actions are relevant and positive for the black community. They have done among the black community what the dominant white power structure has done to the larger American society. They have drawn arbitrary lines of what counts for full citizenship in the black community.

CONCLUSION

The idea of a model minority, in the experience of African Americans, has little meaning. From the era of slavery to the present we have seen that the notion of attaining such a level—reaching an ideal set of values, beliefs, motives, and behaviors by the dominant society—is pointless. The concept of the model minority has created dialectical tensions in the African American community between assimilation and isolation. Whether the dominant society claims at some times assimilation as the ideal situation for blacks or at other times isolation, the fact is that neither provides an attainable goal.

The adaptation theorists have it all wrong. The drive toward adaptation inherently sets up a psychological and practical conflict. Finding that full assimilation is not possible and racial isolation problematic, African Americans are in constant debate within their own psyches, between being members of the dominant society or members of their "own" group. Clarence Thomas finds that he is accepted by the white establishment but eschewed by many blacks for "betraying" his race. Cornel West is accepted by part of the white establishment, highly regarded as a prominent black intellectual, but cannot catch a New York cab and is pulled over and hauled off to jail when he asserts to a policeman that he teaches philosophy at an Ivy League university. In this is embodied the conflict assimilationists and cultural adaptation theorists would simply be content to ignore.

NOTES

1. Because this and all other census information is taken from online sources, it does not include pagination. Therefore, the full citation including the URL is offered. For this information see Black CPS Population and Per Capita Money income: 1967 to 2000, Black Current Population Survey; March, 1998, U.S. Census Bureau "Historical Income Inequality Tables" (Table p-1b), U.S. Census online: http://www.census.gov/hhes/income/histinc/p01b.html.

2. U.S. Census online, Table A-2, "Percent of People 25 Years Old and Over Who Have Completed High School or College by Race, Hispanic Origin and Sex: Selected Years 1940 to 2000." U.S. Census Bureau Internet release date December 19, 2000. Available online at http://www.census.gov/population/socdemo/education/tableA-2.txt.

3. "Reverse Discrimination," in *Business Week,* July 5, 1976, 2103, p. 28.

4. Also see Louis Farrakhan, Final Call Online, April 18, 2000, in "The Key for Success?: Do for Self," *Final Call,* 1 no. 4. Available online at http://finalcall.com/columbus/hem/selfhelp.htm.

5. "Jordan Backs Out of the Hornets Deal." *New York Times,* May 8, 1999, p. D3.

REFERENCES

Akbar, N. (1996). *Breaking the chains of psychological slavery.* Tallahassee, FL: Mind Productions.

Asante, M. K. (1988). *Afrocentricity.* Trenton, NJ: Africa World Press.

Binet, A. (1916). *The development of intelligence in children.* Baltimore: Williams & Wilkins.

Douglass, F. (1845/1968). *Narrative of the life of Frederick Douglass, an American slave, written by himself.* New York: New American Library.

Farley, J. (1999). *Majority-minority relations* (4th ed.). New York: Prentice Hall.

Frazier, E. F. (1957). *The Negro in the United States.* New York: Macmillan.

Frazier, E. F. (1965). *Black bourgeoisie.* New York: Free Press.

Graves, E. (2000, June 2). New economy, new rules. *Black Enterprise, 30,* pp. 11–17.

Gudykunst, W. B., & Kim, Y. Y. (1997). *Communicating with strangers: An approach to intercultural communication* (3rd ed.). New York: McGraw Hill.

Herrnstein, R., & Murray, C. (1994). *The bell curve: Intelligence and class structure in American life.* New York: Free Press.

Hilliard, D. (2000). *Intelligence project.* Southern Poverty Law Center. Available online at http://www.splcenter.org.

Jeffries, L. (1999). The African Americans: Search for truth and knowledge. Available online at http://www.nbufront.org/html/MastersMuseums/LenJeffries/LenJeffriesVMuseum.html.

Karenga, R. (1978). *Essays in struggle.* San Diego: Kawaida.

Linneaus, K. (1806). *A general system of nature through the three grand kingdoms of animals, vegetable, and minerals.* London: Lackington, Allen.

MacIntrye, B.(1989). The new eugenics. *London Sunday Telegraph,* March 13, p. 23.

Montagu, A. (1999). *Race and IQ.* New York: Oxford University Press.

Muhammed, E. (1965). *Message to the black man.* Chicago: Nation of Islam Settlement no. 1.

Newsweek (1996). Relaxing an old taboo. *Newsweek, 128,* July 15, p. 51.

Renolds, F. (1996). *The new American reality.* New York: Russell Sage.

Chapter 7

Being Disabled in Modern Japan:
A Minority Perspective

Miho Iwakuma

He is merely armless and legless, but the rest is fine.

A COMMUNICATION DILEMMA BETWEEN
NONDISABLED PEOPLE AND PEOPLE WITH DISABILITIES

According to the World Health Organization (WHO), approximately 10 percent of the world's population is made up of people with disabilities (Press Release WHO/68, 1999). Humans have always experienced disabilities. Acquiring a disability does not discriminate by age, gender, socioeconomic status, religion, or ethnicity. Indeed, disability is a fact of life, and no one is free from the possibility of becoming disabled.

Despite how pervasive disability is, people with disabilities (PWDs) remain a relatively hidden minority within Japan. Communication with PWDs tends to remain an awkward and anxiety-filled event. Indeed, just as with other minorities, stereotypes and prejudices against PWDs feed communication distortion between the nondisabled and PWDs. As Goffman (1963) and Zola (1991) point out, the core communication problem stems from people's difficulties in talking openly (and listening) about experiences of being disabled. In fact, this researcher has often felt that nondisabled individuals are genuinely curious about the lives of PWDs but that etiquette often precludes them from feeling comfortable discussing the topic. As a result, instead of asking questions directly of individuals with disabilities, the majority of nondisabled persons rely on minority spokespersons to tell them about being disabled, thus generating popular perceptions of the disabled minority.

Such official spokespersons' voices have a great influence in the public sphere. However, according to Zola (1991, p. 159) such minority spokespersons are very often "less representative of the group they are supposed to represent" than is presumed. Ironically, very often individuals attain the position of speaking for the disabled by being the most successfully adapted to the majority culture. In the case of PWDs, the most successful or completely adapted means that spokespersons have achieved a stage of normalcy whereby one "no longer feels disabled."

The question is: How can a person who never had or no longer has a critical awareness of being disabled speak on behalf of PWDs? A similar dilemma often visits other minority groups. Consequently, a vicious circle of miscommunication between the majority and the minority is perpetuated: The majority learns from the limited voices of minority "spokespersons," who share experiences more with the majority than with those they purport to represent. Conversely, the minority feels a need to change "who they really are" and adapt to the majority to be heard.

By using the case of PWDs, this chapter discusses this communication dilemma between the minority and the majority and the paradoxical role of minority spokesperson. I am especially interested in two issues of perception. First, I explore how PWDs come to perceive themselves through the eyes of the mass media, which is basically the point of view of the nondisabled. Second, I briefly investigate how the disabled view spokespersons, who are usually selected by the nondisabled to represent or be the "voice" of all PWDs.

The present research mainly follows the phenomenon of the best-selling book *Gotaifumanzoku* and its author, Hirotada Ototake (2001a). The *Gotaifumanzoku* phenomenon is a good example of this communication dilemma. This case demonstrates why a minority spokesperson is welcomed and needed, how he or she is created, and how other minorities view "their" spokesperson.

PEOPLE WITH DISABILITIES (*SHOGAISHA*) IN JAPAN

According to a Japanese law, *Shogaisha* ("people or person with disabilities") refers to a person "whose daily life or life in society is substantially limited over the long term due to a physical disability, mental retardation, or mental disability" (*Shogaisha kihonho* article 1). The Japanese government estimated that the numbers of Japanese people with physical, intellectual, or psychiatric disabilities were 3,170,000, 413,000, and 2,170,000, respectively (Sori-fu, 1998). Among those with physical disabilities, 1,657,000 (56.5 percent) had disabilities of their limbs, 621,000 (21.2 percent) had internal disabilities (e.g., heart disease), 305,000 (10.4 percent) had visual impairments, and 350,000

(11.9 percent) had hearing impairments. The total population of Japanese with disabilities was about 4.8 percent of the total population of the nation.

As of 1996, in Japan there were 285 institutions that care for persons with physical disabilities, with about 18,000 individuals living in these places (Sori-fu, 1998). Although those institutions are dedicated to the care of those with the most severe disabilities, there are other institutions mainly for rehabilitation. In the latter kind of institution, a person typically stays from a year to five years, usually at a boardinghouse, to (re)learn various life techniques from changing clothes and bathing, to driving a car with hand controls. As of 1997, there were 800 special schools for students with physical disabilities (not including the students with visual or hearing impairments) in the nation, with 75,280 students studying at them. The number of students at special schools tends to decrease, however, because of an integration policy and access improvements at regular schools. Among graduates from junior-high schools for students with disabilities, 89 percent of them continue their education to high school.[1] After high school graduation, about 1 percent of the students go to colleges, 3 percent enter vocational schools, 27 percent get a job, and 54 percent stay at medical/welfare institutions (Sori-fu, 1998).

In terms of getting jobs, because of the decade-long economic recession in Japan, the employment situation surrounding PWDs has been quite pessimistic. Japan employs a quota system to promote hiring PWDs. Currently, the quota requires 1.8 percent of private companies and 2.1 percent of public companies to be employees with disabilities. Nevertheless, due to a lack of understanding and/or access, almost half of the private corporations (49.8 percent) did not exceed the quota (Shimizu, 1998; Sori-fu, 1998). More disturbingly, larger companies tend to employ fewer PWDs than do smaller companies. Though 54 percent of small companies (fewer than 100 employees) kept the quota, only 33 percent of large companies (more than 1,000 employees) did so (Shimizu, 1998). This is because those larger corporations can afford to pay the penalty for not hiring enough PWDs.

As mentioned, 4.8 percent of Japan's total population is made up of persons with disabilities, and this portion is significantly lower than in other developed countries (Heyer, 2000). Despite the fact that the definition of *disabled* in Japan is quite similar to what the United States uses, the U.S. population of people with disabilities is 20 percent (Heyer, 2000). This large discrepancy in numbers indicates that "disability" is not a discrete, objective entity. Rather, disability is an interpretative status based on social convention. Therefore, people have different perceptions toward their fellows with disabilities based on their cultures (Iwakuma & Nussbaum, 2000). In addition to the cross-cultural differences, perception of PWDs within a culture is not fixed but changes over the time. According to Hanada (1999), a historian with a disability, there is an old folk belief in Japan that a baby born with a disability brings bliss to his or her family. Hanada (1999) makes another interesting observation that most of the seven indigenous gods (*Shichifukujin*) are "abnormally" portrayed, and they seem to have such disabilities as a cerebral palsy, obesity, or hydrocephalus. This association of disability with affluence and happiness does not exist in modern Japan. Based on discussions, Japanese perceptions about disability are in constant change, and the birth of *Gotaifumanzoku* has added another dimension to the perceptions of disability by the nondisabled.

GOTAIFUMANZOKU

The book *Gotaifumanzoku* ("born with an imperfect body"; English title: *No One Is Perfect*) was published in 1999 in Japan. It has sold more than 4.6 million copies (see http://www.ototake.net). The book became the second-biggest best-seller in Japan since World War II (Kato, 1999). Ototake, the author, was born with missing limbs and uses an electric wheelchair for transportation. In the book, he talks about his everyday life from his birth to his school life as a "normal" child. His mother was the last person among the family and immediate hospital workers to see the baby because others were concerned how she might react to his appearance. In fact, they waited for thirty days before allowing her to see her son. When finally she met her newborn baby, she did not hesitate to say "what a beautiful baby," which signified that he was accepted and welcomed from birth (Ototake, 2001a, p. 3; translation mine). Because the book is full of humorous episodes and few disability-related stories, toward the end one tends to forget Ototake has such a severe disability.

Due to the success of the book, the author became an overnight celebrity. He was invited to give numerous lectures, he and his book were mentioned in many reviews, he appeared on news programs as a reporter/commentator, and the paparazzi have even chased him for a scoop during a date. Most important, against his will and intention, he came to be regarded as a spokesperson ("the most well-known disabled person in Japan," he said) for people with disabilities. He has repeatedly stated that ironically he hardly remembers or feels that he is disabled in everyday life. Of course one could say that he is not "dis-abled" because he was born the way he is and therefore has never known anything different. Hence, his condition is completely normal to him. Beyond this, he also stresses how the environment treated him like a typical child. Yet what makes his story different, popular, is precisely the obviousness of his condition.

He reports how he went to regular schools all his life, and in his book, no others with disabilities are mentioned. In other words, he never has associated himself with the Japanese disabled community, nor has he expressed much consciousness of being disabled. His self-awareness seems to be the same as that of a nondisabled person.

However, immediately after the mega-success of *Gotaifumanzoku* Ototake became annoyed by the persona that others assumed he must manifest. Often he was described as "a worrier who overcame his disability," "special," and/or "*sawayaka*" ("uplifting" or "refreshing"), and that he had pretended to be someone else to meet their expectations of him (Nakamura, 2000). What became evident was that even though he has accepted his condition as normal, unlike many disabled persons, still the general public did not. Although he was a typical Japanese who loved karaoke and girls, people were shocked when he told them that he had gone to a "love-hotel" with his girlfriend.[2] Ototake seemed to have known this communication gap stemming from stereotypes of "the disabled" prior to his publishing. Otherwise the book would not have occurred to him as such. Yet he seemed surprised by the effect his work had.

In another interview, he was reported in a national newspaper as saying that on the day before the picture shoot for the book cover, he decided to change his dyed blond hair to his original black hair (Nakamura, 2000). As a typical youngster in Japan, Ototake loved fashion, and dyed hair has been very fashionable in recent years. In spite of his fashion preference, he changed his hair color because he had thought his blond hair would not match the nondisabled readers' perceptions of the disabled, which was that the disabled are commendable, serious, and pure.[3] Ototake instinctively knew that to be heard by the majority, he had to adapt to them. The cover shows him sitting in his motorized wheelchair with black hair. His shining smile and his appearance without limbs on the cover generated great attention at bookstores, and it was assumed by the nondisabled public that he is not merely an appropriate but an excellent spokesperson for the disabled in general.

THE DIFFICULTY WITH TELLING AND HEARING ABOUT DISABILITIES

A friend of Ototake commented about him that he "never thinks of himself as 'disabled.' This is why we can be good friends without any conscious effort" (Sasaki, 2000, p. 65; translation mine). In a similar vein, I have also experienced, both in Japan and in the United States, people expressing their feelings that "I never think of you as 'disabled,'" as if that is a compliment or a sign of friendship. Essentially, both Ototake and this researcher have been praised and thereby accepted precisely because they are not like "the disabled," despite the fact that we are. Furthermore, because we are regarded as successful adapters from the point of view of the nondisabled society, we seem normal or to have overcome our disabilities.

But why cannot a person with a disability think, behave, and be perceived as disabled? This is because thinking and talking about one's disability too much is regarded as being preoccupied, obsessed, or too self-absorbed; by doing so, the person with a disability runs the risk of being viewed as defeated by his or her disability. It may also stem from a fear of disability; that the presence of disability reminds nondisabled persons that it could happen to them, too. The public is also enthusiastic about the successful disabled person who has overcome his or her disability, which makes the disability somewhat transparent regardless of its existence. It is a matter of control. The person who is successful, by a nondisabled person's criteria, is seen as someone who has conquered his or her disability, to have tamed or domesticated the wilderness of disease and disability. This may be reassuring to the nondisabled majority who fear disability. Being normal is essential to being acceptable. Zola (1991) contends that "the very process of successful adaptation not only involves divesting ourselves of any identification with being handicapped, but also denying the uncomfortable features of that life. To not do so might have made our success impossible! But this process has a cost. One may accept and forget too much" (p. 162). Zola (1991) further argues that people have difficulty talking (and hearing) about disability on a personal level. This anxiety about disability, which often leads to silence, does not make it go away but merely represses it. This repression constitutes the core of communication discomfort between the nondisabled and people with disabilities. Telling one's disability story is similar to what Coupland, Nussbaum, and Coupland (1991) refer to as "painful self-disclosure" (i.e., talking about one's illness or dying). According to their study, this style of communication (or, perhaps better, communication avoidance) results in an increased communicative distance between interlocutors.[4] In sum, when self-disclosure is painful, the nondisabled are pressured not to argue or disagree with disabled people for fear of appearing unsympathetic and/or lacking empathy—"You can never understand what is like to be ... " Simple conversation may become less anxiety prone but only because it is more superficial in its avoidance of the most salient and obvious issues. By avoiding the obvious, it only becomes more salient as a silent subtext. The silence can be deafening.

Furthermore, Kohama (2000) contends that the majority often put the minority on a pedestal to balance their "superiority" complex in relation to the minority. Because of the superiority complex, the majority feels restrained in communicating with the minority. As already noted, Ototake's friend liked him because the friend did not have to suffer from this complex because Ototake never seemed "disabled." Evidently communication difficulties that surround minorities are the very reasons why minority spokespersons are needed by the majority: to avoid anxiety and interpersonal criticism and to even out the superiority complex the majority may harbor.

Having a spokesperson represent the minority also enables the majority to gain the information they are curious about without having to invest in a face-to-face conversation. What they always want to know but are afraid to ask is: "What is it like to be 'disabled'?" Sympathy, unlike empathy, tends to presuppose a difference in status such that it can foster a sense of superiority, which in current society is regarded as inappropriate. This marks a change in culture not only in Japan but also around the globe. Abject pride in being superior to others has been tempered by modern Western values of propriety.

MINORITY SPOKESPERSON:
A MINORITY'S PERSPECTIVE?

Who needs a spokesperson more, the group they represent or the audience? If the group members already understand what their condition is all about, then it would seem that the out-group audience needs the spokesperson to explain the situation to them. Also the mass media has created a megaphone effect such that only one person at a time can represent an entire group, and by so doing they have the status of "the representative" conferred on them. Because people watch the mass media while their anonymity is preserved, it is much easier for the majority to watch rather than to enter into a difficult conversation personally. All three—the one spokesman per group, the status conferral of media presence, and the anonymity of watching—are modern mass media effects that also function to create diverse "publics" with differing and often competing agendas. In such a communication ecology, each group is presumed to have a spokesperson who articulates the essence of their collective experience and agenda. Otherwise, a group without an acceptable spokesperson (who has a media-friendly face and disposition) is utterly invisible. In the mass media environment, for a group to have an identity, it needs a public-relations front person. But this very process of communicating effectively, efficiently, clearly, and acceptably often narrows the amount of information that can be conveyed about the realities of any group, severely simplifying the true story.

To elucidate this spokesperson function and the resulting distortions in communication, I recorded conversations with many disabled and nondisabled Japanese persons about Ototake and his book. Both groups of people knew about him and his book, and one participant even urged me to read his copy. Not surprisingly, the nondisabled never commented negatively about Ototake. They all expressed how he was active and funny and how they admired his many accomplishments despite his severe disability. They were moved and surprised. The term *sawayaka* ("refreshing" or "uplifting") was often used to describe his personality and appearance. Ototake, indeed, is good-looking. As Kohama (2000) suggests, the book, along with Ototake's *sawayaka* personality (and probably his smart appearance), has helped improve the image of the disabled, which is usually too serious, ugly, frightening, and/or depressing to be widely embraced by a public accustomed to attractive faces and positive attitudes in the media.

Interestingly, people with disabilities regard him quite differently. Although many participants with disabilities in this study felt a shift in public attitudes toward the disabled after the appearance of *Gotaifumanzoku* (not merely the book but the entire media phenomenon), they also noted that the nondisabled referred to the book as an object lesson. Nondisabled people said that the book taught them to better appreciate what they have (for example, mobility) and it inspired them to not forget to count their blessings. A woman with a disability related how she believes the nondisabled interpreted this "inspiring" message, saying, "Even a person like Ototake can do this much. So why can't we [the nondisabled] do better and do more in life?" A man with a visual impairment had a similar experience with a taxi driver who was moved by the book and who told him that "even people like Ototake, with that kind of body, can live such a vital life. We [able-bodied persons], having a perfect body, are inspired to do more."

People without disabilities, however, seem to feel a sense of superiority, even if it is subconscious. The sense of superiority is revealed by comments like *"even* a person with a disability can do such and such." Ototake, who received countless letters from nondisabled fans, was also puzzled by how they often expressed their appreciation for how he had inspired them. They often used such innocent-sounding statements that implicitly expressed an attitude of superiority (Nakamura, 2000). The illegitimacy or even cruelty of this sense of superiority becomes perhaps more obvious if we switch the subject and say, "Even Americans can do many things. We Japanese are inspired by their efforts to do more and better thanks to them." Ototake originally intended to outrun precisely such pitiful sentiments from the nondisabled community (Nakamura, 2000). Ironically his book only provoked more of the same attitude. Ototake's naiveté indicates how he may have been initially deluded by his own celebrity status.

My interviews with PWDs often revealed a sort of critical assessment of Ototake's image, his naive perspective, and his consequent success. For instance, one respondent said, "[Ototake] is in no way a part of the world in which we [the disabled] are living." Some respondents mentioned to the researcher that the nondisabled changed positively after the book. However, when asked about the source of the success of the book, they raised the issue of a "peeping-Tom effect" vis-à-vis the voyeuristic curiosity of the nondisabled public. Some even retorted, "The book is a freak show." According to many interviewees, the public's curiosity came from a desire to see but not to be threatened with or be forced to interact with the disabled and their "exotic" lifestyles. Kato (1999) has made similar findings. According to Kato, a disabled male activist commented that "I can understand very well where Ototake was coming from ... because I used to be just like him" (quoted in Kato, 1999, p. 83; translation mine). The same person added that his disability has "twisted interpersonal relationships" and that "[Ototake] does not understand 'the disabled,' he does not have a clue" (quoted in Kato, 1999, p. 83; translation mine).

Kato (1999) found that communication between PWDs and those who are nondisabled is affected by stereotyping even before the interaction commences. Even prior to interaction, if there is a "depressing and pitiful" perception held by the nondisabled interlocutor toward people with disabilities, this prior condition will affect all subsequent and actual interaction (Kato, 1999). Another male interviewed by Kato retorts that Ototake should not "be so smart" because "in spite of the fact that [Ototake] never has lived as a 'disabled' person, he talks for us as though he knows all about what things are like for them" (Kato, 1999, p. 81; translation mine).

Similar to what I find, Kato (1999) discovered a sharp disparity between the nondisabled and those with disabilities. Not even one person with a disability who was interviewed by Kato reported being moved by the book. He (1999) summarizes:

Most non-disabled were astonished by how Ototake overcame his severe disability [missing limbs], and how he became capable of many things. Also, they assumed that Ototake was trying so hard [to have become what he is now]. On the other hand, individuals with disabilities never thought of Ototake using his short arms and legs as "extraordinary." Instead, they assumed that that was his way of doing things. (p. 84)

Every act, every public appearance Ototake makes is followed by cameras. He has become a sensation. He has visited numerous schools; everywhere he goes, people, including children, are stunned to see him swinging a baseball bat or dribbling a basketball without legs and arms (Ototake, 2001a). A woman who watched him on television for the first time was "astonished" but soon "couldn't help being moved to tears" (Kamisaka, 1999, p. 93). Even such activities as drinking or brushing his teeth were worthy of press attention. Moreover, almost all the articles about him used the terms *sawayaka* and *sugasugasii* ("uplifted" and "refreshing") to describe him. But people felt uplifted or refreshed by Ototake's tricks because their expectation of him was so low. They expected him to be completely dependent.

On the other hand, PWDs perceived him quite differently. For PWDs, living with disabilities is nothing extraordinary but a daily routine; therefore, they were not so mesmerized by his tricks. For example, a quadriplegic man who was interviewed stated that "we [PWDs] think he should be able to look after himself without help from others.[5] *He is merely armless and legless, but the rest is fine* ... [Because the nondisabled did not expect him to do anything], the nondisabled never think he should do more" (translation mine; emphasis added). This statement illustrates the gap between the nondisabled and PWDs in terms of what a disability brings to one's life and what it is like to be a "disabled" person in Japan, and perhaps other places, too.

A COMMUNICATION DILEMMA BETWEEN THE MINORITY AND THE MAJORITY

The discussion so far outlines the phenomenon of *Gotaifumanzoku* and the perceptional gap that exists between the nondisabled and PWDs regarding the role of being a spokesperson. However, the controversy of the disabled spokesperson is not unique to Japan—it has been observed elsewhere.[6] Moreover, several other chapters in this book discuss other social/racial minorities, such as African Americans (Johnson and McIlwain), American Indians (Lujan and Karola), Asian Americans (Min), and Asian Indian Americans (Bhatt), who are in similar predicaments. These social/racial minorities are pressured to conform and adapt to the dominant white Anglo Saxon values in the United States articulated by the ideology of the model minority. Similarly, Tsuda's (1986) research among immigrant workers in Germany found a social/linguistic minorities dilemma. According to Tsuda, an "attempt to acquire the dominant code is not only an expression of deep identification with the dominant class, ... [but] also it is a declaration of dissociation with the dominated class to which their actual 'Me' belongs" (1986, p. 36). Furthermore, minority persons tend to have a greater discrepancy than the majority does between the "I," whom they wish and imagine to be, and the "Me" whom others project them as being (Tsuda, 1986). The case of Ototake falling into this trap is even more complicated.

Prior to the book, Ototake had identified himself as nondisabled; however, the major consequence of his book was to create a perceptual discrepancy between his I and his Me. To make matters worse, the nondisabled, of whom he had thought he was a part, regarded him as a member of and spokesperson for the PWD group (Willems, 2000). Meanwhile, the disabled community in Japan never considered him as such. Similarly, Kato's (2000) analysis found that the Ototake phenomenon was "convenient" for the media and the nondisabled. This is because he does not remind others of the widespread general inaccessibility of the country to PWDs. Ototake also downplays the superiority complex of the nondisabled, making them feel more comfortable with their own dissonance as they shift from pity to feeling superior. There had been a few books by authors with disabilities prior to *Gotaifumanzoku*. However, none were as commercially successful as *Gotaifumanzoku*. Most of them honestly deal with serious and painful disability experiences and also offer arguments against the way the society is unfairly structured. Such books make the nondisabled uncomfortable and sometimes even depressed.

Unlike these disabled authors, Ototake hardly mentions the hardships and inequalities that stem from the social attitudes prevalent in Japan toward disability. In numerous interviews he repeatedly stated that he rarely had complaints or difficulties resulting from living with a disability.[7] However, both rural and urban Japan present a landscape that is exceedingly difficult to inhabit by a person in a wheelchair, for instance. Few buildings have accommodations for such a mode of being in the world. As he spoke, presumably from his own experiences, the nondisabled listened to his stories, assuming that they were generalizable to others with disabilities. He once stated that he had "intended to become only one example of many disabled ... but people now think I am the life of all the disabled, which really scares me" (Aihara, 1999). Ototake probably felt scared by this misperception of him held by the public. He unwittingly gave the public a false impression of what life is like in Japan as a disabled person. His example gave the impression that all PWDs in Japan are just like him, satisfied with the current situation. The problem is that this impression has created a belief that there is no need to change society. Also, PWDs have harshly criticized him because of his appearances in the media.

Surely, people with disabilities have experienced the impact of *Gotaifumanzoku*. Since the publication of the book, the term *barrier-free* has become a buzzword. Nevertheless, Ototake's slogan of having a "barrier-free heart," which refers to removing "the fences around their [the nondisableds'] hearts" to "understand the disabled better" (Willems, 2000, p. 30) has been decoded somewhat differently from his original intention. Ototake (2001a) uses many examples of how his friends and teachers were helpful, enabling him to live an inclusive life, especially in his school days. On the other hand, he never criticized the school board for the fact that his mother had to stay with him through the entire day during his early years in elementary school. Nor has he seriously addressed the fact that the facilities at his school were inaccessible to him. Others may have interpreted these omissions as though such issues are not Ototake's responsibility; that an individual with a disability needs benevolence and goodwill rather than an elevator, a ramp, or a law prohibiting discrimination against persons with disabilities to attend a "regular" school or to obtain a job. Kato (2000) is apprehensive about Ototake, who seems to be used by the media to send his "twisted" messages that are easy on the ears of the nondisabled.

In contrast to the enthusiasm for Ototake from the nondisabled, a male quadriplegic whom this researcher knows once commented that "after *Gotaifumanzoku*, the nondisabled expect the disabled to be just like him, 'happy-go-lucky.'" Many with disabilities who were interviewed even pitied Ototake because he was never regarded as "normal," even though he always emphasized that he was no different from others (Kato, 1999). They saw him as somewhat self-delusional. Most of all, many interviewed PWDs responded that they could not identify with Ototake.

Based on these discussions, it seems that *because* he did not belong to the disabled community in Japan, he could become the spokesperson for the PWDs. This irony is exactly what Zola (1991) and Goffman (1963) refer to as a communication dilemma between the majority and the minority: The minority spokesperson is the most adapted and acceptable to the majority; therefore, they have fewer things in common with the minority.

POST-*GOTAIFUMANZOKU* AND CONCLUDING REMARKS

Ototake himself has been victimized by his own media persona and, most of all, by his own creation, *Gotaifumanzoku*. On his Internet home page (http://www.ototake.net),[8] he bares his heart. After the book was published, Ototake was showered with "a kind and favorable gaze" from others that, nevertheless, is similar to him as the gaze of those "watching little kids on a stage displaying their innocent performances" (Ototake, 2001a, p. 271; translation mine). The look was "never cold, but warm." However, people never saw Ototake as equal. Rather it was a patronizing gaze. They looked on him as if he were a child who was "lovable ... [and] innocent" (translation mine). In addition, since the book, his titles have proliferated, including "the spokesperson of the disabled," "Oto-chan: the fighter," and "ever-smiling [despite his disability]" (translation mine). All are far from the truth about him. The distance between his projected Me and the actual I has grown. As a consequence of the dissonance and stress, he nearly collapsed (Nakamura, 2000; Ototake, 2001b).

Finally, for his own sanity, he decided to reject these titles and to become who he truly wished to be—the "I," regardless of the big "Me." Ototake became a sports writer. He dyed his hair brown again (Nakamura, 2000), and gradually distanced himself from his "haunting" double, *Gotaifumanzoku*. When he was going to graduate from his university, he decided not to be involved with the area of social welfare, which is considered to be closely associated with PWDs. Ototake stopped lecturing on being barrier-free and on the topic of disability. He even stated on a TV program that *Gotaifumanzoku* had become a burden to him. Then, he was flooded with negative letters that accused him of being "deceiving" and "disappointing." The new wave of letters from the majority who had been previously "inspired, [and] saved" by the book (Ototake, 2001a) had a bitter accent. He, however, refused to be convenient any longer.

This chapter outlined a process of how and why a spokesperson for the disabled, Ototake, was selected and how others with disabilities viewed their representative, which was quite different from how the nondisabled perceived him. The phenomenon of *Gotaifumanzoku* seems to capture different worldviews of the nondisabled and of the PWDs with regard to disability. In addition, although these two groups of people regarded the spokesperson phenomenon very differently, this communication dilemma is not unique to the disability community. A similar communication dilemma exists for other minorities. In fact, "interability communication," a word Fox (1999) coins that designates communication between the nondisabled and persons with disability, has many characteristics that are similar to other minority/majority efforts to communicate (i.e., Coleman & DePaulo, 1991 Goffman, 1963). In this chapter, I argue that as seen in the case of Ototake, a "minority" spokesperson is chosen by the majority according to their own criteria rather than by the minority. As a result, he or she represents what the majority wishes the minority to be, which is the very essence of the model minority ideology. Then the real minority is pressured to adapt to the mainstream ideal image of them. Also, I assert that this communication distortion is largely rooted under the name of political correctness or social etiquette. It is here that what is appropriate is defined by the mainstream. This notion of what is appropriate links the group with the individual so that if an individual becomes inconvenient or uncomfortable for the audience, then the source of the problem is personalized. That particular person is deemed unsuitable for the status of spokesperson. Thus a search commences for a new spokesperson who fits the preconceived image held by the majority. Obviously, under such a distorted power relationship, only a certain kind of polite voice is allowed. Thus, communication is "twisted," "distorted," and "prefigured." The alterity of the authentic Other is denied even before it can be expressed. This communication dilemma arises, ironically, from the need for minority spokespersons in the media age. In polite society, such things are not discussed.

NOTES

1. In Japan, the mandatory education level is a junior-high school diploma.

2. In Japan, lovers often go to "love-hotels" for love-making or having affairs. "Love-hotels" differ from other hotels or inns in such a way that for the former, customers sometimes do not have to check in at the front to disguise their identities. Also, "love-hotels" are often built in eye-catching shapes, such as ships and castles.

3. Although the fashion of hair dyeing has increasingly become common in Japan among teenagers, many junior-high and high schools prohibit it as a sign of delinquency. In contrast, Japanese people's perceptions of individuals with disabilities is that they are people who are harmless and never break the rules.

4. Although their work deals specifically with intergenerational communication, it is applicable in this context.

5. Ototake mentions that dressing and toiletry are the few things he cannot do by himself.

6. In the United States, another disabled spokesperson controversy has been observed surrounding the "Superman" actor Christopher Reeve. Since a horseback-riding accident in 1995, Reeve has become not only the most famous person with a spinal cord injury (SCI) in the world but a spokesperson for fund-raising for an SCI cure. Similar to Ototake's case, Reeve has been covered by many magazines and television programs. Nevertheless, the controversy amounts to his appearance in a Superbowl 2000 commercial in which he digitally walked (Fox, 2000). As a consequence, he has been met with severe criticism from the disability community, despite the public's image of Reeve as the spokesperson for the disabled. Ironically, he was viewed by many in the disabled community as a "default" spokesman for disability (Laymon, 1999, quoted in Fox, 2000). This is because Reeve hardly considers himself as being permanently disabled; therefore, he is mainly interested in a cure so that he may return to the able-bodied world. The criticisms from the disability community note that Reeve only emphasizes a negative perception—that acquiring a disability is nothing but tragedy and that leading a satisfying life with a disability is impossible.

7. For instance, I have seen Ototake on a famous daytime talk show in Japan. Toward the end, the hostess of the show asked him about difficulties or inconveniences that he presumably encounters every day. The hostess and the viewers, including myself, must have expected to hear such things as how inaccessible public transportation and buildings are for a person in a wheelchair and how he has suffered unfair treatment. However, Ototake replied, surprisingly, that he hardly felt any inconvenience or unfairness at all. The question was asked of him assuming that he represents others with disabilities.

8. Quotes without page numbers were taken from the cited Web site. These can be found online.

REFERENCES

Aihara, S. (1999). Nichiyobi no hiro [Sunday heros]. Retrieved February 10, 2002. Available online at http://www.nikkansports.com/news/entert/entert-etc3/99/sun990613.html.

Coleman, L. M., & DePaulo, B. M. (1991). Uncovering the human spirit: Moving beyond disability and "missed" communication. In N. Coupland, H. Giles, & J. M. Wiemann (Eds.), *Miscommunication and problematic talk* (pp. 61–84). Newbury Park, CA: Sage.

Coupland, J., Nussbaum, J. F., & N. Coupland. (1991). The reproduction of aging and agism in intergenerational talk. In N. Coupland, H. Giles, & J. M. Wiemann (Eds.), *Miscommunication and problematic talk* (pp. 85–102). Newbury Park, CA: Sage.

Fox, S. A. (2000). *Super-impact: Christopher Reeve and attitudes toward people with disabilities.* Paper presented at the annual conference of the National Communication Conference, Seattle, WA.

Goffman, E. (1963). *Stigma.* Englewood Cliffs, NJ: Prentice Hall.

Hanada, S. (1999). Rekishi ha tsukurareru [A history is made]. In J. Ishikawa & O. Nagase (Eds.), Shogaigaku he no shotai [An introduction to disability studies] (pp. 257–283). Tokyo: Akashi Shoten.

Heyer, K. (2000). From welfare to rights: Japanese disability law. *Asia-Pacific Law and Policy Journal.* Retrieved February 10, 2002. Available online at http://www.hawaii.edu/aplpj.

Iwakuma, M., & Nussbaum, J. F. (2000). Intercultural view of people with disabilities in Asia and Africa. In D. O. Braithwaite & T. Thompson (Eds.), *Handbook of communication and people with disabilities* (pp. 239–255). Mahwah, NJ: Lawrence Erlbaum.

Kamisaka, F. (1999). Kamisaka Fuyuko no "haradachi nikki" [Kamisaka Fuyuko's "Dear Diary"]. *Josei Sebun*, March 11, pp. 92–93. Tokyo: Shogakukan.

Kato, K. (1999). Zureteiku kankei [The widening relational gap]. *We'll, 16* (June), pp. 79–84.

Kohama, I. (2000). *"Jakusha" toha dareka.* Tokyo: PHP Shinso.

Nakamura, S. (2000). Ano "Gotaifumanzoku" no ato nani wo kangaetekimashitaka [After "Gotaifumanzoku," what have you been thinking?]. *Asahi Shinbun*, July 16, p. 35.

Ototake, H. (2001a). *Gotaifumanzoku: Kanzenban* [Born with an imperfect body: The final version]. Tokyo: Kodansha.

Ototake, H. (2001b). Minnakara no meru wo yonde [My response to your mail]. Available online at http://www.ototake.net/mail/back010129.html.

Press Release WHO/68 (1999). International day of disabled persons. Available online at http://www.who.int/inf-pr-1999/en/pr99-68.html.

Sasaki, Y. (2000). Boku niha hito ni makenai mono ga aru soreha teashi ga nai koto [One advantage I have over others is that I have no arms and legs]. *Josei Seven*, December 3, pp. 59–66.

Shimizu, T. (1998). Shogaisha-koyo-sokushin-ho no bappon teki kaisei wo [A need for fundamental changes in Physically Handicapped Persons' Employment Promotion Law]. *Fukusi Rodo*, 81 (winter), pp. 12–26.

Sori-fu (1998). *Shogaishahakusho* [A disability white paper]. Tokyo: Sori-fu.

Tsuda, Y. (1986). *Language inequality and distortions.* Philadelphia: John Benjamin.

Willems, N. (2000). Removing barriers. *Winds,* August, pp. 29–30.

Zola, I. K. (1991). Communication barriers between "the able-bodied" and "the handicapped." In R. P. Marinelli & A. E. Dell Orto (Eds.), *The psychological and social impact of disability* (pp. 157–164). New York: Springer.

Chapter 8

Successful Indians: Benevolent Assimilation and Indian Identity

Karola, and Philip Lujan

You're too successful to be an Indian.

Whether posed by Indian or non-Indian,[1] the topic of success and the Native American always seems to be problematic. There is a nagging suspicion that "success" and "Native American" may not truly belong together, that somehow a successful Indian is endangering his or her authenticity, identity, integrity—his or her Indianness. He or she must do so to be involved in such an inherently assimilative undertaking as success.[2] The dichotomy, however, is illusionary. True, standards of success not gleaned from a Native worldview have been force-fed down Indian throats until we have choked on the message that to be a success one cannot be Indian, or at best, some esoteric Indianness must be held in check or displayed in the most superficial, touristy way—and as Lujan's mother points out, "There's more to being Indian than dancing." Yet whatever their means to achieve it, and even however they define it, successful Indians are Indians; success is part of the Indian experience and always has been. However, the continuous and concerted push to become something other than Indians, and its ruinous consequences, has made it much easier to think in terms of dichotomy, of the Indian world to be embraced and the non-Indian world to be shunned (or vice versa for assimilationists), than it is to think in terms of how these two worlds are really one, coconstituted and integrative. We are all assimilated Indians in one sense or another: Whether we're willing or not, whether it's accurate or not, the non-Indian hegemonic system has made us part of it, and to a certain measure we are all defined by it and partake of it. At the same time, we are all also nonassimilated Indians insofar as we still know ourselves to be Indians. We have been forced to change a great deal, yet we can also master those forces to change as we wish, to hold onto what we find important, to be successful on our own terms, however we choose to define them.

If, as Clifford Geertz (1973) and the many who followed him claim, culture lies more in the intangible and abstract than in the material manifestations of a people, then it is quite reasonable that many Native American cultures are "still around" and members find meaningful existence in belonging to a tribe, clan, and the like. Scholar Paula Gunn Allen, a Laguna Pueblo/Sioux, notes, "You can take the Indian out of Indian country but you can't take the Indian out of the Indian" (Allen, 1986, p. 6). But over the centuries many (including not a few Native Americans) have tried to do just that, and their accomplishment is staggering. Whole ideologies, languages, social structures, and even peoples have been wrenched away, surrendered, forgotten, or transformed into a vague ancestral or cultural heritage.

There has been a persistent inability on the part of non-Indians to let Indians alone. Among all the races encountered by the European, Indians have been continually the most prodded, pushed, and examined. Indeed, the concept of race itself finds its nascence and much of its development in the meeting and mingling of the Old World with the New (Hannaford, 1996), as does the study of ethnology (Bieder, 1986; Pagden, 1982). Lumped together more often than not, independent and disparate Native cultural groups congealed to non-Indians into one homogenous race, patently alien and patently inferior.[3] Top Enlightenment philosophers constructed models of civilizational progress, placing American Indians at the lowest or next to lowest stage, a dubious distinction traded with black Africans, depending on the philosopher (Pearce, 1988). In one of the earliest appearances of the term *civilization* in English (Oz-Salzberger, 1995), Adam Ferguson in his *Essay on the History of Civil Society* notes that "not only the individual advances from infancy to manhood, but the species itself from rudeness to civilization" (Ferguson, 1767/1995, p. 7). To the American "savages" he accords some worthy characteristics, but on the whole finds them wanting even the refinements of "barbarism" (Ferguson, 1767/1995). Georges-Louis Leclerc posits that their "want of civilization in America is owing to the paucity of its inhabitants; for, though each nation had peculiar customs and manners, though some were more savage, cruel, and dastardly than others; yet they were all equally stupid, ignorant, and destitute of arts and of industry" (Leclerc, 1748–1804/1997, pp. 17–18). Immanuel Kant (1764/1997) seems rather more impressed, especially with the Iroquois:

> Among all savages there is no nation that displays so sublime a mental character as those of North America....if a lawgiver arose among the Six Nations, one would see a Spartan republic rise in the New World; for the undertaking of the Argonauts is little different from the war parties of these Indians, and Jason excels Attakakullakulla in nothing but the honor of a Greek name. (p. 56)

Of course, Kant (1764/1997) hardly equated the Indians with Western civilization as it had progressed up to the enlightened eighteenth century; after all, how could they so advance when "these savages have little feeling for the beautiful in moral understanding" (p. 56)?

Branded as ruthless, naked savages (even when including a description of their clothing; see Kupperman, 1997), the inability of Europeans and European Americans to ignore admirable Native traits gave rise to the concurrent image of the noble savage, a guileless child of nature evoking nostalgia for the paradise lost to civilized humans by progress's necessity (Berkhofer, 1979; Kupperman, 1997). Popularized in historical memory by Rousseau's (1755/1992) politically aimed portrait, the noble savage profile, like its dichotomous twin, the bloodthirsty savage, has wandered through non-Indian imaginings since contact and continues to do so. The faceless inhuman hordes leered and murdered their way through settler frontier stories while Natty Bumppo's Mohicans remained ever-popular and sympathetic. Ferocious Indians still make convenient foils in epic Western films, even ones that presume an understanding portrait of Native Americans (O'Connor, 1998). Real-life bloodthirsty Indians no longer seem to have a hold with non-Indians, unless it's as general menaces to society through crime, drunkenness, recalcitrance, and other undesirable hindrances to progress (Allen, 1986). The noble savages persist with their superior "natural" powers. Lujan recalls seeing a documentary on Native American veterans of the Vietnam War in which one soldier's commanding officer continually put him on point based on the apparently sincere belief that an Indian could hear, see, and sense danger better than non-Indians could. To which the Indian soldier replied, "Bullshit." In all, these images of the ignoble/noble savage reveal more about the aspirations and assumptions of the white man than of the red (Berkhofer, 1979; Pearce, 1988).

American Indians occupy the position of ultimate Other to non-Indian American society (Berkhofer, 1979). Although race relations have tended to find their focal point in the "black-white" struggle (e.g., Hughes, 1997; Jordan, 1968), the true enormity of the differentness of the Native position reasserts itself forcefully to any non-Indian attempting to tackle the social and economic concerns of Indian country (e.g., George, 2001). The fact that Indians are the only governmentally defined ethnicity (with a matching federal ID card to boot) and that said ethnicity brings with it a (contested) measure of sovereignty separate from the United States is the tip of the iceberg. The federal government officially recognizes our governments (however truncated),[4] providing a unique U.S.–tribal relationship that is often envied and misunderstood by other minorities. Federal acknowledgment merely attests to the fact that we are not simply another race, ethnicity, or cultural group; we are a different civilization made up of variegated cultures of our own, sharing similar perceptual sensibilities, consciousness structurations, and space-time modalities. Moreover, it would seem that from contact onward, we have been seen as a rival civilization, requiring erasure to justify and glorify European and European American civilization (Pearce, 1988). For that matter, the triumph of Western modalities is most often assumed as a given, with the erasure of Indians posed

as a natural inevitability for a group that can find no place in the civilized or developed world, even as slaves or minimum wage peons (Churchill, 1998; Pearce,
1988). John Smith, for example, rejoiced at the obvious favor the Lord showed
by the decimation of neighboring tribes, which conveniently opened up their
land for proper inhabitation: "God had laid this Country open for us, and slaine
the most part of the inhabitants by civill warres and a mortall disease" that had
bypassed European settlers (quoted in Chaplin, 1997, p. 244). Between destroying the social and economic organization of many tribes and utterly killing off
the populations of others, disease in fact did more to remove the Native presence in the now–U.S. territory than all other contributors combined (Chaplin,
1997; Cronon, 1994; Rountree, 1989).

Despite the ravages of epidemics over the centuries, however, Indians endured,
showing that nature would have to be helped along if they were to make way for
the progress of enlightened civilization. Erasure of the Indian manifested in two
complementary forms: physical extermination/genocide and assimilation. The
threat of the one frequently drove the acceptance of the other, a phenomenon that
worked in both directions (Brown, 1991; Calloway, 1996). Removal, which might
seem to be a third alternative, actually enacted the other two. Various removal
schemes referred to reservations as sort of holding grounds until the Indians'
natural demise (O'Connell, 1992) or training grounds for assimilative projects
(Deloria, 1988; Otis, 1934/1973). Either way, the reservations were often too
small and/or too poor in resources for there to be much choice beyond dependency and a haggard assimilation or slow death (Brown, 1991).

Comments like that of nineteenth-century Colonel John M. Chivington—
"Damn any man who sympathizes with Indians! I have come to kill Indians
and believe it is right and honorable to use any means under God's heaven to
kill Indians" (quoted in Brown, 1991, pp. 86–87)—notwithstanding, assimilation has long been the ostensibly preferred means of dealing with and ultimately erasing Native presence.[5] From the traders' earliest introduction of a
commodity-based economic structure (Cronon, 1994) to the proselytizing of
European Christians horrified at Native heathenism (Diket, 1966), from the establishment of Indian schools in colony charters (Szasz, 1988) to current Bureau of Indian Affairs (BIA) and congressional development schemes for
reservations (Keys, 1997), Indians must surely be the most modeled minority
while easily remaining the last minority espoused as a model. A researcher interested in charting the prevailing hegemonic currents in any particular period
of non-Indian domination need go no further than that period's formal and in-
formal Indian policies. For example, in less secularized times than the present,
the U.S. government doled out various tribes and/or reservations to particular
Christian denominations as their rightful domain (including forced cessions for
establishing churches and clergy residences in tribal territories) and enforced
Christian religious observation in BIA schools as well as mission ones (Berkhofer, 1979; Dawes Act of 1887, 1934/1973; Deloria, 1988). Now the emphasis
on cultural pluralism frees Indians to worship as they please in principle but

not necessarily in practice. Essentially the choice remains an either-or between the priorities of two different civilizations.

For example, in the mid- to late 1980s, a young Cheyenne man made a vow to participate in the Sun Dance, a ceremony once outlawed (Calloway, 1996). This vow represents a commitment not only to dance for the four days of the ritual in a given year but also to dance at subsequent Sun Dances for several years. Additionally, a Sun Dance pledge encompasses a dancer's extended family, who pledge their financial, physical, and emotional support throughout the dancer's commitment. The obligation of attending the ceremony is not analogous to that of attending an important business conference or social gathering. The vow *cannot* be violated. Well aware of his need for time off from his job— a university staff position—to fulfill his promise, the Cheyenne man scheduled his vacation to coincide with the Sun Dance. He was later bumped when a coworker with seniority requested the same dates for his summer vacation. The Cheyenne told his supervisor about his problem. His supervisor informed him that he needed to yield to the greater import (the greater sacredness, if you will) of seniority, and come to work during the days of the Sun Dance. Nothing personal against him; it was simply the price of succeeding at the job. The Cheyenne employee just *could not* have off those dates. Naturally, he left and went to the Sun Dance as promised. He was fired. What should be shocking (but is sadly expectable) is that nothing came of the dismissal in the university community. No one really expressed any outrage except for the few Native American faculty and staff who knew the Cheyenne but could do nothing.

The list of Native civilizational characteristics targeted for assimilation over the years is so seemingly absolute in scope it is numbing: religion, property conceptualizations, moral/legal procedures, language, education, dwelling styles, warfare, clothing, mobility patterns, entertainment, economic structures, marriage and family patterns, social welfare methods, division of labor, gender roles, and government all have been and to a large extent continue to be pressured to fit a supposed norm, which is not Indian in origin but rather the self-effacing transparency that is Western, white civilization's rhetorical modus operandi (Crenshaw, 1998). Because of the ideological presence of the stagal model of civilizational evolution (now focused around development rather than race per se), the worship of productivity, and the exaltation of progress culminating in utilitarianism and pragmatism, proponents of Western civilization could not and very often still cannot conceive of why Indians would not want to follow the "universal" norm (Berkhofer, 1979; Otis, 1934/1973). From such a linear perspective, failure to assimilate must equate to extinction in the face of social Darwinism (Wyss, 1999). As ethnologist Josiah Nott predicted in the mid–nineteenth century, "It is as clear as the sun at noon-day, that in a few generations more the last of these Red men will be numbered with the dead" (Nott, 1854/1969, p. 466). To survive and succeed, Indians must be saved from themselves; to prove their superior successfulness and the validity of their reality sui generis, non-Indian hegemonic adherents must be the saviors.

Although assimilation has taken a variety of forms as dominant social constructions phase in and out, it can roughly be grouped as either benevolent or malevolent assimilation, loosely based on the intents of the given assimilation agents and their conceptualization of the Indian as either the noble, "good" savage or the bloodthirsty, "evil" savage. Both categories overlap and bolster one another: A benevolent assimilation policy, like removing Indians beyond the reach of interfering and unscrupulous white settlers (e.g., Green, 1982), frequently manifests as malevolent, as the Trail of Tears of the Cherokee and numerous tribes attest (e.g., Mankiller & Wallis, 1993).[6]

Benevolent assimilation offers seemingly desirable goals and even sometimes gives what it promises, but its brother, malevolent assimilation, always lurks in the background. Law and economics offer the most striking instances. Indians have had to continually deal with a changing classification in a legal system they neither created nor freely joined (Smith, 1997), one that refuses to allow them to conduct their governments and tribal affairs in a manner in which they see fit (Cornell & Kalt, 1990; Keys, 1997). Interestingly, from about the 1960s to the early 1990s, federal courts were fairly sympathetic to the sovereignty rights of tribal governments in opposition to state legislation as well as chafing BIA (mis)management. Native governments gained greater autonomy over their affairs. Many times non-Indian corporations had to conduct their dealings with Indians in tribal court, rather than state or federal court. However, over the past ten years or so this trend has decidedly declined, and federal court reaction to Indian claimants has been increasingly restrictive in its rulings and hostile to sovereignty. Native Americans' inclusion into a system that is supposed to ensure equality for all actually ensures their continued unfair treatment by its unwillingness to see them as *not* equivalent in legal status to everyone else and to deal with them as nonstandardized, exceptional cases.

Economically, the push to make Indians into model, normative Americans has constantly backfired, frequently because the idealization was completely unrealistic, not to mention inappropriate. A classic example comes from the aftermath of the Dawes Acts (1887, 1891), more popularly known as the General Allotment Acts. Most Indian household heads were to receive 160 acres, the same offered to non-Indians under the various Homestead Acts. Often the allotment agreement included tools and other start-up supplies. Surely this was a benevolent situation offered by the self-styled "friends of the Indian"—except that the Indians themselves usually did not want allotments, were usually unfamiliar with the modern agricultural methods being thrust on them without instruction, and were frequently given tracts of unarable land that a skilled non-Indian farmer would have difficulty cultivating (Elkin, 1940; Otis, 1934/1973). When Indians would try to function in a manner other than assimilated small farmers, such as leasing their lands to sharecroppers or ranchers and attempting to live off the proceeds, they were typically chastised by their local BIA agent, who would then withhold the leasing payments, take over the arrangements ("Interview with Pleasant Porter," 1901), or otherwise thwart the Indians' attempt at economic self-determination (Otis, 1934/1973). One of the methods used was to declare an Indian legally incompetent to handle his or her own affairs. This option persisted in the BIA's administration of many tribes; for example, the allotment policy for the Osage enacted in 1906 as Oklahoma became a state explicitly mentions the Secretary of the Interior's right to decide the competency of adult tribal members (Wilson, 1985). One author's older relatives recall having to take tests up through the late 1950s or early 1960s when they turned eighteen so they could be issued certificates declaring them competent Indians.

The persistent but oh-so-benevolent drive to turn Indians into the founding fathers' ideal vision of the classic yeoman farmer becomes very suspicious when it is considered that the Native land holdings went from 138 million acres in 1887 to 52 million acres in 1914 (Larson, 1997); the drive becomes nearly ludicrous when it is considered that the strongest pushes came at a time when American farming was in an overall slump (Elkin, 1940). Of course, when the benevolent assimilationist tide finally turned to dragging Indians into industrialization in the form of urban relocation throughout the 1950s and 1960s, they fared little better, assimilated into the lowest societal rungs by being assigned housing in low-income neighborhoods and given job opportunities far less illustrious than the benevolent image the BIA relocation agents promised (Burt, 1986; Mankiller & Wallis, 1993; Mucha, 1983; Stull, 1978). Former Cherokee chief Wilma Mankiller was relocated to San Francisco as a youth with the rest of her family. Although the community Indian Center provided her with validation, support, and eventually political mobilization that stayed with her throughout her life, Mankiller notes that the urban setting was hardly benevolent for her or any of the other neighborhood Indians. She writes in her autobiography, "I have met many native [sic] people from different tribes who were relocated from remote tribal communities. They discovered, as we did, that the 'better life' the BIA had promised was, in reality, life in a tough, urban ghetto" (Mankiller & Wallis, 1993, p. 73). To this day, Indian enclaves located in the same poor neighbors persist in many major cities.

Again and again, the assimilationist message resounds: Join the norm, but only on terms not your own; it's the best thing you can do, you must do it or your children will perish, but you can't really join on equal terms because you're just too Indian. Honestly well-intentioned non-Indians have spent their lives trying to take the Indian out of the Indian, so that the final benevolent assimilation into just another anonymous, equal American individual can occur. Given the onus historically placed on being Indian, it is hardly surprising that many Indians indeed have tried and still try to blend unnoticed into non-Indian society. Some manage to do this so well that their descendents have only a vague notion that one of their forebears was Indian. It is also hardly surprising that many more Indians never survived the crushing force of assimilation and died. In a very real sense, one definition of successful Indians is that we have reached this day and age alive, knowing we are Indians.

But this begs the question of what it means to know that one is Indian. Because assimilation pushes so hard, it almost becomes a trick question in which *Indian* is constrained to a particular concept set in opposition against that which is non-Indian or, more specifically, white. Right along with their historic tendency to examine Native Americans according to whatever social constructions are in vogue, non-Indians concerned with Indians have increasingly turned their attention to the question of Indian identity in a postmodern society caught between the isolation of hypertrophy and the awful facelessness of the mass. Native Americans are imagined as remaining authentic in a current world torn by all-consuming simulacra; they are the island of real experience and connection long lost to the white man (Kasdan & Tavernetti, 1998; Riley, 1998; Sandos & Burgess, 1998). But the authentic Indian is a revamped noble savage, a museum piece for a voyeuristic society eager to freeze and exhibit culture (Ikeda & Kramer, 1998; Wyss, 1999). The cultural pluralism guru and ostensive assimilation opponent Horace Kallen (1958), in one of his few writings directly dealing with us, even says as much when he asserts American Indian "authenticity involves some of the traits of Voltaire's 'child of nature' and Fenimore Cooper's 'noble redskin,' with his stoical quiet, his reserve, his decorum, all turning on a basic piety toward personal integrity and tribal ways and works" (p. 470). To be fair, Kallen also totally opposes termination and the attempt to erase Native presence, favors self-determination and self-rule, and praises the National Congress of American Indians by name. Disturbingly though, he credits the twentieth-century turn toward a more "authentic" Native image to "largely the findings of the new generation of ethnologists and cultural anthropologists, whose fertile field for the cultivation of anthropological understanding was the folkways and mores of the tribes, their languages, their creeds and codes and cosmic over-beliefs, their personal relationships, and their arts and crafts" (Kallen, 1958, p. 471).

No wonder the eager anthropologists who nowadays go seeking the "real" Indians to help them share themselves with dominant society are shocked and dismayed when their subjects appear just as embedded in modernity as they are. Especially if his or her lifestyle fits Western civilizational parameters of socioeconomic success, the non-Indian researcher frets that the subject Indian is losing his or her identity and searches for ways in which it is maintained (R. Hassig, personal communication, October 17, 2001). In fact, such delineation of Indian identity as something fragile and elusive, something that can be lost and must be maintained by "real" Indians with the preservation help of their benevolent non-Indian friends, at once grossly over- and understates the core problem presented by the assimilationist complex. Even those who would eschew their existence as Indians cannot escape it; incorporation of elements from another civilization, even incorporation of entire perceptive patternings does not mean leaving original ones behind. Abstract aspects of civilizational modalities are most difficult to dislodge, and these are often the ones conveyed by primary level socialization (Geertz, 1973; Linton, 1940a, 1940b). Undoubtedly life is a process of change and renewal, but also undoubtedly the *esse* imparted to us as Indians from the moment we are born and developed in our raising never leaves—it shades everything we do, whether in the midst of non-Indians or Indians. To portray Native identity as something so easily lost in fact gives into the old construction of the Indian as a creature naturally on its way to extinction and invariably incapable of success, edged out of the competition by the superior demands of Anglo Saxon progress and Manifest Destiny (Horsman, 1981). At the same time, it ignores the very real trauma of having a civilizational encoding that is invalidated at every turn of society. Not just through overt racism and assimilation—though these are bad enough—but through continual, insidious frustration and rejection of ways of perceiving, understanding, and being. Much of Indian civilization is lost, wiped out. Much of what is left is in jeopardy, not in the sense of losing a discrete psychological identity but in the sense of not being respected as present, viable, and vibrant way of successful living.

Still, it is important not to let Indians off the hook in all this concern over identity, success, and what is "real." It is not as if Indians have ever been unaware of the deleterious effects of assimilation on their existential praxis or have not had definite opinions about those who adopted foreign ways. Like all cases of acculturative encounter, some elements and patterns have always been more eagerly blended and accepted than others, especially depending on the degree of shift they represent (Linton, 1940a, 1940b). In the mid–eighteenth century, Canassatego, an Onondaga, told colonial delegates that Iroquois children who had been sent to be educated at the Indian school of the College of William and Mary came back "absolutely good for nothing" that was important to the Iroquois way of life (Szasz, 1988, p. 77).[7] Sometimes Indians who were exposed to intense assimilation efforts like boarding schools transitioned between cultural modalities relatively well (e.g., Simmons, 1976); more often it was a stressful experience that could unsettle an individual for a lifetime (Calloway, 1996). Those who took up assimilative ways were sometimes highly influential in Indian society (e.g., Amos, Coombs, & Attaquin, 1835/1992; Green, 1982; Mankiller & Wallis, 1993; O'Connell, 1992); many, however, were derided as wanna-bes, like the nineteenth-century cut-hairs, breeches men, and hang-around-the-fort Sioux ridiculed by other Sioux still managing to resist reservations and farming (Big Eagle, 1894/1996; Calloway, 1996). In the twentieth century, many traditional structures were eroded as the last few continental states joined the union, and poverty, allotment, and stringent BIA control took their toll. Yet in nearly every tribe, whether they had mostly departed from their once-inveterate ways or managed to cling to them, tension remained between those who espoused things presumed to be Indian and those who (arguably) did not and/or openly pushed assimilation programs. Although it is important not to overstate the situation—after all, many of our families, for example, have some traditional members, some not—the struggle over what-is-Indian is constant and complicated. Vine Deloria Jr. is a good case in point. On one hand, he is quite successful according to the standards of dominant society as a well-respected professor at a major state university. On the other hand, he is an outspoken critic of the assimilationist pressure that threatens to crush Indians, not sparing those Indians whom he feels have given into this pressure and labeling them "Uncle Tomahawks" (Deloria, 1988, p. 181).

One of the most interesting things about the modern intracultural conflict between supposedly nonassimilated traditionals and supposedly assimilated nontraditionals is that it features some oddly assimilative overtones. For one thing, the unease over acting white at the expense of Indian ways has crystallized in some quarters into a "redder-than-thou" attitude (Mihesuah, 1998), which essentially trots out the same museum-atrophied idea of authentic Indian ballyhooed by non-Indians with a few insider modifications (e.g., Wieder & Pratt, 1990). What can be curious about this attitude is that it can overlook as traditional some cultural elements that were obviously imported and condemn as imported some elements that are actually traditional, depending on how everything fits into the picture of authentic Indianness. For example, an Indian on a horse (a creature wonderfully adopted and integrated into Indian life but a European import all the same) is a real Indian; an Indian in a pick-up truck is a cowboy. Tribal governments building casinos are condemned as embracing assimilation, yet many tribes have a rich heritage of gambling on events and their own games of chance (Brown, 1991; Niethammer, 1977).

In all, the attempt to hearken to some mythical Indianness ignores that what demarcates an Indian is not merely material manifestations but also the subtle and often unintentional inculcation of difference from the dominant society that comes from Indian socialization. Something need not be explicitly framed as "this is Indian" to be so; in fact, the case may be that a core Indian attitude may long persist even when cloaked in assimilative garb. One author's mother was raised a southern Baptist in a largely nontraditional family, yet the way she was brought up to believe about God completely reflected the traditional belief structure of a loving life-world, conscious even if inanimate, and alive with spirit(s)—a fact she did not even realize until a recent discussion with some Cherokees about their traditional spirituality sparked a recognition of a similar framework operating in her.

Another assimilative overtone in the traditional–nontraditional debate comes from the specter of impinging white identity being laminated with the culture of poverty, such that any attempt to seek socioeconomic advancement along dominant pathways is immediately suspect. A Delaware woman, home from college for a visit, encountered this attitude when a friend saw her university textbooks and asked, "What, you're trying to be white now? You ashamed of being Indian?" The culture of poverty lens sees attempts at education and even material success in general as selling out, and in fact stifles Indian freedom of destiny just as surely as non-Indians' forcible assimilation or exclusion does (MacDonald, 1995; Mucha, 1984). What is truly sad and insidious about this is that the culture of poverty has been created in the minds of some Native Americans because they have been repeatedly told—now by anthropologists and other dominant voices, now by other Native Americans—that they are diminished, that they are not and will never be the true Native Americans their ancestors were, that they will always lack a pristine Nativeness. Poverty of material condition is thus deserved for those with such poverty of culture; relatedly, poverty becomes the badge of resistance against the oppressor who took away the perfect past (Deloria, 1988).

Yet material success is actually an area of longstanding Indian interest. Like most other peoples in the world, Native Americans historically show no aversion to living well (Cronon, 1994; Rountree, 1989), and contemporary tribal governments are constantly trying to improve the economic and educational lot of their members (e.g., Cornell & Kalt, 1990; George, 2001; Mankiller & Wallis, 1993; Masten, 2001; Ranfranz, 2001). What tends to separate customary Native viewpoints on material success from assimilative ones is the lack of Native emphasis on (or even conceptualization of) a commodity consumptive orientation. Although American Indians are often depicted as traditionally lacking a sense of property in contrast to Europeans' highly developed sense of it, Indian property sensibilities are different, not absent. They hinge on the notion of spiritual- and/or use-value in possessions and property; accumulation of more than what is needed is irrelevant or wasteful, and work solely for profit or the sake of work is bizarre. Sharing abundance, not hoarding it, is the mark of prestige (Cronon, 1994; Larson, 1997; Soldier, 1995). For example, many Indian governmental structures used to be much less formalized and hierarchical than they are now (an assimilationist modification made by colonial and federal officials reluctant to deal with loose authority systems and keen on definite representatives in familiar governmental formats to sign treaties, enforce their provisions, and conduct business; Brown, 1991; Green, 1982; Haines, 1997). One reason chiefs were given honor and influence in many tribes was because they ensured their people's abundance by sharing their own. If the people had to go without, their chiefs certainly did, too (Barsh, 1986; MacDonald, 1995).

Not surprisingly, an outlook so different from that of capital-accumulating and consolidating Western civilization was and is a prime assimilative target. After all, it breaks with the Puritan-inspired and utilitarian-improved ideal of rational maximization of self-interest, work as a calling, adaptation as everyone's duty to the sacred goal of progress, and material wealth as a marker of grace (for supporters of this ideal see, for example, Bentham, 1781/1988 and Spencer, 1877/1970; for critics see, for example, Weber, 1920/1958, and Kramer, 2000). Awaking a desire for the luxuries of modern society and their hegemonic high status is supposed to get the individual Indian to break from the tribal fold, devote his or her life to productive activity, and generally be like all the other useful denizens of the non-Indian world. Nathan C. Meeker, BIA agent for the Utes in the late 1870s, lamented that their lack of greed for consumption prevented them from working hard like whites to accumulate wealth: "Their needs are so few that they do not wish to adopt civilized habits. ... What we call conveniences and comforts are not sufficiently valued by them to cause them to undertake to obtain them by their own efforts ... the great majority look upon the white man's ways with indifference and contempt" (quoted in Brown, 1991, p. 374). The Utes were labeled "actual, practical Communists" by the *Denver Tribune* (Vickers, 1879, as quoted in Brown, 1991, p. 376); an appellation used by Creek chief Pleasant Porter about twenty years later to describe the changes that had taken place in his tribe: "Unconsciously we have passed over from a system of communism to that of individualism" (Porter, 1891, p. 4). Perhaps the most telling remark on the relationship between economic system and assimilation comes from Senator Henry L. Dawes, architect of the most sweeping assimilation project—allotment. The Indians, Dawes claimed, "have got as far as they can go, because they own their land in common ... under that there is no enterprise to make your home any better than that of your neighbors. There is no selfishness, which is at the bottom of civilization" (Dawes, 1885, as quoted in Otis, 1934/1973, p. 10).

To a degree, the push toward commodification and conspicuous consumption worked tremendously. If nothing else, such basic premises as set exchange value or pricing, operation within a market system, and individual economic earning have unavoidably spread throughout Indian country, whether they are welcomed, acknowledged, ignored, or denied. To be sure, the influx of foreign economic structures has cursed us to some extent with the loss that it represents of the lifestyles of the past and with the widespread current corruption in tribal governments that it seems to foster. Still, many Indians enjoy the toys and tools of the industrial, fatted-calf age we are in, just as many have Christianized, moved to urban environments, attended universities, and/or taken up mainstream employment, including with the BIA. Yet most Indians, even if they live materially well and bear all the markers of assimilative success, retain a nonassimilative frame of reference for it all (e.g., Mucha, 1984). For example, a few years ago when a Kiowa man divorced his wife, he drove away from his nice house full of valuable artwork and its eighty-acre lot with horses in a beat-up station wagon with nothing but the clothes he had on and never looked back. He says he didn't leave his possessions out of legal obligation, guilt, or rancor. They just didn't matter to him. Although ownership of it all was legally his as well as hers, he felt that the household rightfully belonged to his ex-wife, reflecting the Kiowa traditional ownership of the home by the woman.

The relatively low emphasis we tend to place on physical objects does not signify a complete disregard for them or an inability to calculate their value. Rather it is part of a larger orientation that is person- and rapport-centered instead of thing- and market-centered. Relationships—with other humans, animals, spirits—are foundational for us. Such a claim should not be mistaken for a restatement of the widespread noble savage image invoked by many non-Indian New Agers as the paradigm of back-to-brotherhood-with-nature mysticism. Much traditional Native spirituality assumes a uniqueness of experience (e.g., the personal nature of visions) and a constant flow of it that cannot be reduced to the prescriptive theological framework often described by non-Indian spiritual chroniclers (Allen, 1986; Barsh, 1986). Second, it assumes a practical edge (e.g., the reverence for animals completely includes the idea of them as food) that spoils the abstract picture of an untouched/untouching Edenic oneness. Relationship-centered living also eludes the cultural studies classification of Native Americans as purely collectivistic. Insofar as we or any other people can be so narrowly described, Native Americans are both collectivistic and individualistic (Barsh, 1986; Miller, 1997). Personal achievement is not at all outside the Indian realm. From the bragging rights of battle warriors who counted coup against the enemy in combat (Calloway, 1996) to the hero status of basketball warriors who bring home a state championship for the reservation high school, individuals who shine are honored. Personal achievement, though, should not be bought at the expense of the family/clan/tribe; it should strengthen and sustain the collective. It is a delicate balance, which is more often than not upset today, especially because charges of buying individual success at the expense of the collective can so easily be leveled at anything smacking of acting white— note that few of the basketball stars take up offers to play for universities after graduation (Donahue, 1997). Of course, personal achievement is personally and interpersonally measured; if, say, a high school basketball star looks back on his career and is content to have not gone further, then that is an achievement, and, provided he is surrounded by loving relationships and does not fall into the chronic despair that haunts reservations, that is a success.

Erich Fromm (1976) contends there are two fundamental human modes of existence: being and having. Being is experiential in orientation, fulfilled by human contact and relationships, concerned about clarity and expansion of perception, and motivated by productive activity. Having is accumulative in orientation, fulfilled by authoritarian contractual obligation, concerned about adaptation to the market and fitting in, and motivated by obsessive busy-ness. Being acknowledges and uses possessions; having craves and exalts them. For the having mode, all life (including and especially people) becomes a thing, with time as its ruler. In contrast, states Fromm (1976), "being is not necessarily outside of time, but time is not the dimension that governs being" (p. 128) and everything becomes alive. Although not mutually exclusive, one modality tends to predominate in societies, reciprocally forming and being formed by socioeconomic structure and normative values.

Despite centuries of pressure to abandon it, the majority of Indians cling fiercely to the being mode of existence. Of course, we participate in the having by necessity, for that is the darling modality of the industrialized modern world; however, most of us do not live according to having's precepts. This is not to say that Native Americans who are more into the having mode are any less Indian, though it is important to remember that Fromm (1955, 1976) felt this modality could be quite injurious to individual happiness and could (or rather, does) produce pathological societies. Certainly Indian societies are far from total happiness and health, but the being mode seems a civilizational value that has persisted strongly over time and is likely to continue doing so.

The reason is fundamental appreciation for being. Skokomish educational consultant Terry Tafoya (1995) puts it nicely: "White culture teaches us to evaluate or judge by *Production*.... But we cannot judge our children's achievement by the number of baskets they make or the salaries they can earn.... White society has always shied away from understanding the purpose of life in terms of the everyday person. The business of life is life" (p. 113). Despite the past, despite the present, despite the losses and heartaches—and maybe also because of them—Native Americans are flexible and strong. We are not too Indian to be successful. Through our being as Indians we will—and do—succeed.

NOTES

1. Typical of the postmodern concern over authenticity in identity that plagues Indian relations, a note on what one is calling the original indigenous peoples of the Americas—in this piece, specifically the inhabitants of what is now the continental United States—is always in order in academic writings. Practically every Indian prefers tribal names: Indians often exchange tribal affiliations on meeting in much the same manner that, say, undergraduates exchange majors on meeting. Beyond that, consensus wanes. Many people (among some tribes, elders in particular) prefer *Indian* or *American Indian* as a collective term (e.g., the National Congress of American Indians, representing 250 tribes to the U.S. government). *Native American* or *Native* is also heard with great frequency (e.g., public radio's weekly program *Native American Call-In*). Some support for terms such as *Indigenous Peoples* or *First Nations* is growing, especially among indigenous social critics, who point to the inherently colonist/hegemonic overtones of *Indian* and *Native Americans*, not to mention their potential for confusion with denizens of India and the popular hegemonic description of anyone born in America as a native. Tribal names are also not without problem, for many are colonizer distortions of traditional names or even disparaging monikers given by enemy tribes. For an interesting discussion of First Native ethnic labels, see Yellow Bird (1999); for the purposes of this piece, the linguistic array and its ever-present snares fall beyond our scope. Hence, tribal names in their most commonly known forms will be used where relevant in individual cases, and *Indian, American Indian, Native American,* and *Native* will be used for general reference. The term *non-Indian* will be used for all other ethnicities, though the historical position of Europeans, European colonists, and European Americans often means that they are the non-Indian ethnicity of note in most situations. Where particularly significant, *European, European American, Anglo Saxon, white, black, black African,* and *colonist* will be used for emphasis.

2. This chapter features a certain looseness in the usage of the term *assimilation*, reflecting its application as a floating signifier in Native parlance to refer to anything and everything taken as non-Indian. Because at its core assimilation denotes total absorption, acculturation is probably the more accurate term. Ralph Linton's discussion of acculturation (1940a, 1940b) at the end of his edited volume on acculturation among seven different tribes, though it is outdated in many respects, nevertheless gives one of the best conceptual breakdowns of the process as it relates to Native Americans.

3. Non-Indians' racialization of Indians overlaps with so-called pan-Indianism among Indians but should not be equated with it. Pan-Indianism describes a general social identity of Native Americans as all belonging to the same broader in-group. Contrary to most accounts that trace pan-Indianism's origins to mid–twentieth century urban relocation enclaves (Mankiller & Wallis, 1993), to the close quarters of removal in Indian Territory (Howard, 1955), or at earliest to the failed efforts of Tecumseh for tribal unification (Sugden, 1986), the sense of shared civilizational psyche connection and deliberate cultural borrowing that pan-Indianism represents have forerunners at least to the colonial period if not to precontact (Green, 1982; Rountree, 1989). As it is experienced today, pan-Indianism does carry the ontological factor of Western racialization; however, the distinction among and respect for individual tribal groupings is preserved by pan-Indianism in a way that it is not by non-Indian ideas of an Indian "race." The cultural blendings enabled and increasingly encouraged by current pan-Indianism do erode particular tribal practices (some more than others), but given the amazing resilience of individual Native nations over the years it should not be assumed that Indians are going to trade tribal identifications for pan-Indianism any time in the foreseeable future.

4. That is to say, the federal government recognizes many tribes but not all. Several of the tribes once federally recognized lost that status during the termination policies of the 1950s and never got it back, whereas others were never quite given the status in the first place.

5. It is important to note that the mere presence of an assimilative policy in no way supplanted outright extermination until quite recently. Extermination often was the driving force behind assimilation. Literally, Indians were offered the choice of assimilate or die, both directly by calling down the massacring force of the cavalry on those wishing to maintain traditional modalities and communal lands and indirectly by withholding treaty-ensured supplies and annuity payments from those who refused to cooperate with assimilation policies, such as sending their children to boarding school (Brown, 1991; Calloway, 1996).

6. Awful as the process of removal was, the Indians did get a bit of a last laugh on the would-be assimilationist policy. In addition to acting as cultural reservoirs and buffers against the negativity of non-Indian society (Calloway, 1996; Tan, Fujioka, & Lucht, 1997), the presence of reservations and communal tribal lands throughout the United States means that many states now have islands of Indian jurisdiction where state power often cannot reach.

7. Interestingly, according to Benjamin Franklin, the Iroquois response also informed the colonists that "if the English Gentlemen would send a dozen or two of their children to Onondago [sic], the great Council would take care of their Education, bring them up in really what was the best manner and make men of them" (quoted by Szasz, 1988, p. 77).

REFERENCES

Allen, P. G. (1986). *The sacred hoop: Recovering the feminine in American Indian traditions.* Boston: Beacon.

Amos, I., Coombs, I., & Attaquin, E. (1835/1992). To the white people of Massachusetts [Reprinted testimonial]. In B. O'Connell (Ed.), *On our own ground: The complete writings of William Apess, a Pequot* (p. 166). Amherst: University of Massachusetts Press.

Barsh, R. L. (1986). The nature and spirit of North American political systems. *American Indian Quarterly, 10,* 181–198.

Bentham, J. (1781/1988). *The principles of morals and legislation.* Amherst, MA: Prometheus Books.

Berkhofer, R. F. (1979). *The white man's Indian: Images of the American Indian from Columbus to the present.* New York: Vintage Books.

Bieder, R. E. (1986). *Science encounters the Indian, 1820–1880: The early years of American ethnology.* Norman: University of Oklahoma Press.

Big Eagle, J. (1894/1996). A Sioux story of the war. In C. G. Calloway (Ed.), *Our hearts fell to the ground: Plains Indian views of how the West was lost* (pp. 91–96). Boston: Bedford/St. Martin's.

Brown, D. (1991). *Bury my heart at Wounded Knee: An Indian history of the American West.* New York: Holt.

Burt, L. W. (1986). Roots of the Native American urban experience: Relocation policy in the 1950s. *American Indian Quarterly, 10,* 85–99.

Calloway, C. G. (Ed.) (1996). *Our hearts fell to the ground: Plains Indian views of how the West was lost.* Boston: Bedford/St. Martin's.

Chaplin, J. E. (1997). Natural philosophy and an early racial idiom in North America: Comparing English and Indian bodies. *William and Mary Quarterly, 53,* 229–252.

Churchill, W. (1998). The tragedy and the travesty: The subversion of indigenous sovereignty in North America. *American Indian Culture and Research Journal, 22,* 1–69.

Cornell, S., & Kalt, J. P. (1990). Pathways from poverty: Economic development and institution-building on American Indian reservations. *American Indian Culture and Research Journal, 14,* 89–125.

Crenshaw, K. (1998). Color blindness, history, and the law. In W. Lubiano (Ed.), *The house that race built* (pp. 280–288). New York: Vintage.

Cronon, W. (1994). *Changes in the wind: Indians, colonists, and the ecology of New England.* New York: Hill and Wang.

Dawes Act of 1887. (1934/1973). Reprinted as Appendix A in D. S. Otis, *The Dawes Act and the allotment of Indian lands* (F. P. Prucha, Ed.) (pp. 177–184). Norman: University of Oklahoma Press.

Dawes Act of 1891. (1934/1973). Reprinted as Appendix B in D. S. Otis, *The Dawes Act and the allotment of Indian lands* (F. P. Prucha, Ed.) (pp. 185–188). Norman: University of Oklahoma Press.

Deloria, V. Jr. (1988). *Custer died for your sins: An Indian manifesto.* Norman: University of Oklahoma Press.

Diket, A. L. (1966). The noble savage convention as epitomized in John Lawson's a new voyage to Carolina. *North Carolina Historical Review, 43,* 413–429.

Donahue, P. (1997). New warriors, new legends: Basketball in three Native American works of fiction. *American Indian Culture and Research Journal, 21,* 43–60.

Elkin, H. (1940). The northern Arapaho of Wyoming. In R. Linton (Ed.), *Acculturation in seven American Indian tribes* (pp. 207–258). New York: D. Appleton-Century.

Ferguson, A. (1767/1995). *An essay on the history of civil society* (F. Oz-Salzberger, Ed.). Cambridge, UK: Cambridge University Press.

Fromm, E. (1955). *The sane society.* New York: Rinehart.

Fromm, E. (1976). *To have or to be?* New York: Harper and Row.

Geertz, C. (1973). *The interpretation of cultures.* New York: Basic Books.

George, K. (2001). Statements. In D. K. Inouye, *Goals and priorities of the member tribes of the National Congress of American Indians and the United South and Eastern Tribes.* Hearing before the Committee on Indian Affairs, U.S. Senate, 107th Cong., 1 (Senate Publication No. S. HRG. 107–35, pp. 23–39). Washington, DC: Government Printing Office.

Green, M. D. (1982). *The politics of Indian removal: Creek government and society in crisis.* Lincoln: University of Nebraska Press.

Haines, R. (1997). U.S. citizenship and tribal membership: A contest for political identity and rights of tribal self-determination in Southern California. *American Indian Culture and Research Journal, 21,* 211–230.

Hannaford, I. (1996). *Race: The history of an idea in the West.* Washington, DC: Woodrow Wilson Center Press.

Horsman, R. (1981). *Race and manifest destiny: The origins of American racial Anglo-Saxonism.* Cambridge, MA: Harvard University Press.

Howard, J. H. (1955). Pan-Indian culture of Oklahoma. *Scientific Monthly, 81* (November), pp. 215–220.

Hughes, M. (1997). Symbolic racism, old-fashioned racism, and whites' opposition to affirmative action. In S. A. Tuch & J. K. Martin (Eds.), *Racial attitudes in the 1990s: Continuity and change* (pp. 45–75). Westport, CT: Praeger.

Ikeda, R. & Kramer, E. (1998). The *Enola Gay*: The transformation of an airplane into an icon and the ownership of history. *Keio Communication Review, 20,* 49–73.

Interview with Pleasant Porter. (1901). *Muskogee Phoenix* (January 17). Typed reprint obtained from the University of Oklahoma Western History Collection, 630. Norman: University of Oklahoma Press.

Jordan, W. D. (1968). *White over black: American attitudes toward the Negro, 1550–1812.* Chapel Hill: University of North Carolina Press.

Kallen, H. M. (1958). On "Americanizing" the American Indian. *Social Research, 25,* 469–473.

Kant, I. (1764/1997). On national characteristics, so far as they depend upon the distinct feeling of the beautiful and sublime. In E. C. Eze (Ed.), *Race and the Enlightenment: A reader* (pp. 49- 57). Cambridge, MA: Blackwell.

Kasdan, M., & Tavernetti, S. (1998). Native Americans in a revisionist western: *Little Big Man* (1970). In P. C. Rollins & J. E. O'Connor (Eds.), *Hollywood's Indian: The portrayal of the Native American in film* (pp. 121–136). Lexington: University Press of Kentucky.

Keys, K. C. (1997). The community development quota program: Inequity and failure in privatization policy. *American Indian Culture and Research Journal, 21,* 31–71.

Kramer, E. (2000). Cultural fusion and the defense of difference. In M. K. Asante & E. Min (Eds.), *Socio-cultural conflict between African American and Korean American* (pp. 183–230). New York: University Press of America.

Kupperman, K. O. (1997). Presentment of civility: English reading of American self-presentation in the early years of colonization. *William and Mary Quarterly, 54,* 193–228.

Larson, S. (1997). Fear and contempt: A European concept of property. *American Indian Quarterly, 21,* 567–577.

Leclerc, G.-L. (1748–1804/1997). From a natural history, general and particular. In E. C. Eze (Ed.), *Race and the Enlightenment: A reader* (pp. 15–28). Cambridge, MA: Blackwell.

Linton, R. (1940a). The distinctive aspects of acculturation. In R. Linton (Ed.), *Acculturation in seven American Indian tribes* (pp. 501–520). New York: D. Appleton-Century.

Linton, R. (1940b). The processes of cultural transfer. In R. Linton (Ed.), *Acculturation in seven American Indian tribes* (pp. 483–500). New York: D. Appleton-Century.

MacDonald, A. L. (1995). Traditional Indian family values. In A. Hirschfelder (Ed.), *Native heritage: Personal accounts by American Indians 1790 to the present* (pp. 16–17). New York: Macmillan.

Mankiller, W., & Wallis, M. (1993). *Mankiller: A chief and her people.* New York: St. Martin's Griffin.

Masten, S. (2001). Statements. In D. K. Inouye, *Goals and priorities of the member tribes of the National Congress of American Indians and the United South and Eastern Tribes.* Hearing before the Committee on Indian Affairs, U.S. Senate, 107th Cong., 1 (Senate Publication No. S. HRG. 107–35, pp. 2–13). Washington, DC: Government Printing Office.

Mihesuah, D. A. (1998). American Indian identities: Issues of individual choices and development. *American Indian Culture and Research Journal, 22,* 193–226.

Miller, B. G. (1997). The individual, the collective, and tribal code. *American Indian Culture and Research Journal, 21,* 107–129.

Mucha, J. (1983). From prairie to the city: Transformation of Chicago's American Indian community. *Urban Anthropology, 12,* 337–371.

Mucha, J. (1984). American Indian success in the urban setting. *Urban Anthropology, 13,* 329–354.

Niethammer, C. (1977). *Daughters of the earth: The lives and legends of American Indian women.* New York: Collier.

Nott, J. (1854/1969). Geographical distribution of animals, and the races of men. In L. Ruchames (Ed.), *Racial thought in America: Vol. 1. From the Puritans to Abraham Lincoln: A documentary history* (pp. 462–469). Amherst: University of Massachusetts Press.

O'Connell, B. (1992). Introduction. In B. O'Connell (Ed.), *On our own ground: The complete writings of William Apess, a Pequot* (pp. xiii–xxvii). Amherst: University of Massachusetts Press.

O'Connor, J. E. (1998). The white man's Indian: An institutional approach. In P. C. Rollins & J. E. O'Connor (Eds.), *Hollywood's Indian: The portrayal of the Native American in film* (pp. 27–38). Lexington: University Press of Kentucky.

Otis, D. S. (1834/1973). *The Dawes Act and the allotment of Indian lands* (F. P. Prucha, Ed.). Norman: University of Oklahoma Press. (Original work published as *History of the allotment policy.*)

Oz-Salzberger, F. (1995). Introduction. In A. Ferguson (Ed.), *An essay on the history of civil society* (pp. vii–xxv). Cambridge: Cambridge University Press.

Pagden, A. (1982). *The fall of natural man: The American Indian and the origins of comparative ethnology.* Cambridge: Cambridge University Press.

Pearce, R. H. (1988). *Savagism and civilization: A study of the Indian and the American mind.* Berkeley: University of California Press.

Porter, P. (1891). Letter of Pleasant Porter to Isparhecher. *Purcell Register* (June 13). Typed reprint obtained from the University of Oklahoma Western History Collection, 630. Norman: University of Oklahoma Press.

Ranfranz, T. T. (2001). Statements. In D. K. Inouye, *Goals and priorities of the member tribes of the National Congress of American Indians and the United South and Eastern tribes.* Hearing before the Committee on Indian Affairs, U.S. Senate, 107th Cong., 1 (Senate Publication No. S. HRG. 107–35, pp. 2–13). Washington, DC: Government Printing Office.

Riley, M. J. (1998). Trapped in the history of film: Racial conflict and allure in the vanishing American. In P. C. Rollins & J. E. O'Connor (Eds.), *Hollywood's Indian: The portrayal of the Native American in film* (pp. 27–38). Lexington: University Press of Kentucky.

Rountree, H. C. (1989). *The Powhatan Indians of Virginia: Their traditional culture.* Norman: University of Oklahoma Press.

Rousseau, J.-J. (1755/1992). *Discourse on the origin of inequality* (D. A. Cress, Trans.). Indianapolis, IN: Hackett.

Sandos, J. A., & Burgess, L. E. (1998). The Hollywood Indian versus Native Americans: Tell them Willie Boy is here (1969). In P. C. Rollins & J. E. O'Connor (Eds.), *Hollywood's Indian: The portrayal of the Native American in film* (pp. 107–120). Lexington: University Press of Kentucky.

Simmons, L. W. (1976). *Sun Chief: The autobiography of a Hopi Indian.* New Haven, CT: Yale University Press.

Smith, M. L. (1997). The INS and the singular status of North American Indians. *American Indian Culture and Research Journal, 21,* 131–154.

Soldier, L. W. (1995). We must encourage the use of our language. In A. Hirschfelder (Ed.), *Native heritage: Personal accounts by American Indians 1790 to the present* (pp. 82–85). New York: Macmillan.

Spencer, H. (1877/1970). *Social statistics: The conditions essential to human happiness specified, and the first of them developed.* New York: Robert Schalkenbach Foundation.

Stull, D. D. (1978). Native American adaptation to an urban environment: The Papago of Tucson, Arizona. *Urban Anthropology, 7,* 117–135.

Sugden, J. (1986). Early pan-Indianism: Tecumseh's tour of the Indian country, 1811–1812. *American Indian Quarterly, 10,* 273–304.

Szasz, M. C. (1988). *Indian education in the American colonies, 1607–1783.* Albuquerque: University of New Mexico Press.

Tafoya, T. (1995). The old ways teach us. In A. Hirschfelder (Ed.), *Native heritage: Personal accounts by American Indians 1790 to the present* (pp. 113–115). New York: Macmillan.

Tan, A., Fujioka, Y., & Lucht, N. (1997). Native American stereotypes, TV portrayals, and personal contact. *Journalism and Mass Communication Quarterly, 74,* 265–284.

Weber, M. (1920/1958). *The Protestant ethic and the spirit of capitalism* (T. Parsons, Trans.). New York: Scribner's.

Wieder, D. L., & Pratt, S. (1990). On being a recognizable Indian among Indians. In D. Carbaugh (Ed.), *Cultural communication and intercultural contact* (pp. 45–64). Hillsdale: Lawrence Erlbaum.

Wilson, T. P. (1985). *The underground reservation: Osage oil.* Lincoln: University of Nebraska Press.

Wyss, H. E. (1999). Captivity and conversion: William Apess, Mary Jemison, and narratives of racial identity. *American Indian Quarterly, 23,* 63–82.

Yellow Bird, M. (1999). What we want to be called. *American Indian Quarterly, 23,*1–21.

Chapter 9

Abandoned People in Japan: The First Generation of Koreans in Japan

Richiko Ikeda

In April 2000, the nationwide long-term care insurance system, *kaigo hoken seido*, started in Japan. It was established to support care of the elderly. Recipients of the service include foreign residents in Japan. This standardized system was based on the basic resident register, which is called *jumin kihon daicho*. According to the *jumin kihon daicho*, foreign residents in Japan are not listed. It is especially problematic that it ignores the first generation of Koreans in Japan (issei) who consists of a substantial number of people over age sixty-five, about half a million (Yun, 2001, p. 77). It seems that the Japanese government anticipates that they would disappear sooner or later and that the problem would simply vanish.

This situation concerning the issei is difficult. Many left without receiving any Japanese social welfare services. The number of participants in the national pension plan is small; thus many issei are struggling in profound poverty. Few of them know that the social welfare system offered by the local government well. This is so because they are left outside the information loop. A relatively high number of issei are illiterate. They read or write in neither Korean nor Japanese. Consequently, they have very limited access to information about government services. Even when they understand that they could receive welfare services, those services are designed for the "Japanese" elderly. Many issei do not feel comfortable receiving benefits from such agencies. To complicate matters, the two major organizations of Koreans in Japan (Mindan and Soren, or Chongryun), have not worked very hard to change this situation and thus improve the quality of issei lives.

Other social issues concerning Koreans in Japan, including suffrage at the local level, have tended to push the most immediate problem of the issei off the public agenda. Members of both Mindan and Soren argue against each other about the suffrage issue. The top personnel of Mindan are busy lobbying Japanese politicians to pass a bill enacting and enforcing suffrage for foreign residents on the local level. The struggle between the Soren and Mindan comes down to this: The Soren do not want suffrage because they believe that gaining political rights will hasten the assimilation of Koreans, making them into Japanese (Kang, 1998, pp. 18–19). In the meantime, while this battle over suffrage rights preoccupies the Korean community leadership, the issei are neglected. The crisis among them is being ignored, and the lives of elderly Koreans in Japan are getting worse. Because of the split between opinions over the issue in the Liberal Democratic Party (LDP), the suffrage bill may not be passed for some time. But the issei do not have the luxury of time.

The issue of the suffrage may be the carrot before the donkey's nose that prevents Koreans in Japan, and their "Japanese" supporters, from tackling the *Issei* issue immediately. The present chapter reveals how the main social discourse surrounding Koreans in Japan tries to conceal the "real" issue, and how it works to keep them in a position of being a "model minority."

THE CREATION OF KOREANS IN JAPAN

The term *issei* here signifies Koreans who were born in Korea, spent their early childhood there, and then moved to Japan sometime before August 15, 1945, remaining there for the rest of their lives (Yun, 2001). The essence of being issei, according to Yun (2001), depends on whether the major part of their socialization process occurred in Korea or Japan. *Korea* in this case means the Korean peninsula. Yun's definition of issei may be debatable because one can become issei-like even if one is raised outside the Korean peninsula, such as in some predominantly Korean residential areas in Japan. Considering the historical reality of the relationship between Korea and Japan, which will be explained later, it seems to be important to follow his definition.

In 1910, Japan annexed Korea to fulfill its wish to join the exclusive global club of colonial empires: to be one of the great powers. After the Meiji Restoration (1868), Japan followed Western countries and aimed for military and economic success in their fashion. One of the ways to materialize this wish was to expand its domination in Asia. As Duus (1995) points out, Japan mimicked Western imperialism. The successes enjoyed in the Sino-Japanese War (1894–1895) and the Russo-Japanese War (1904–1905) enabled Japan to establish its sovereignty over Korea and to extend its imperial power to other regions in Asia.

During Japan's colonization of Korea from 1910 to 1945, a large number of Koreans moved to Japan. This was a direct result of Japan's colonization policy. The number of Koreans in Japan increased from two thousand in 1911, to 2.4 million by 1945, which amounted to about 10 percent of the population of the

Korean peninsula (Yun, 2001, p. 76). Korea was officially annexed in 1910. The imposition of a colonial economy destroyed the traditional Korean agricultural life, and many Koreans chose to move to Japan to make a living. This situation lasted until 1939. From 1939 to 1945, thousands of male Koreans were brought to Japan and forced to work to supplement the labor force during the war. From 1919–1944, the total number of Korean men conscripted was 634,093, including 320,148 who worked in coal mining, 61,409 in metal mining, 129,664 in construction and civil engineering, and 122,872 in manufacturing and machine industries (Kim, 1991, p. 35). They were so severely exploited that many of them were injured (some killed) in accidents and due to malnutrition and maltreatment.

When the war ended, many Koreans in Japan started to go back to Korea. More than 1.3 million returned to Korea. However, the news that their home country had split into a civil conflict along north and south sides and that peoples' lives there were unstable slowed down the number of Koreans returning home. According to Nakatsuka (1991), the immigration back to Korea began to decline in March 1946. Approximately 647,000 stayed in Japan throughout the postwar turmoil.

During the colonial period, Koreans in Japan were categorized as Japanese citizens, although they remained second-class in many respects. To illustrate this ambivalent legal situation, although male Koreans in Japan had the right to vote and be elected to public office, Korean people both in Korea and in Japan were under surveillance by order of various colonial laws. Under this regime, overseas trips made by Koreans were strictly limited. Even travel by Koreans between Korea and Japan was tightly regulated. They had to obtain prior permission from the police. To keep Koreans in Japan as second-class citizens, the *koseki* (household registration) distinguished between "proper Japanese" and Koreans in Japan.

When the war ended, Koreans in Japan were put in an ambivalent legal status. Under the occupation of Allied forces, "the Alien Registration Law of 1947 stipulated that Koreans should be regarded as aliens for the purposes of the application of this law" (Kashiwazaki, 2000, p. 21). At the same time, the Japanese government considered them technically Japanese nationals and tried to deprive them of the rights and benefits that they should have been granted as aliens (Kim, 1991). The Japanese government ordered that the children of Koreans in Japan should go to Japanese schools in 1948, which resulted in depriving them of their tradition, including their parents' original language. The schools built by Koreans in Japan to educate their children after the war were forced to close. Although Koreans in Japan were regarded as aliens, according to the Alien Registration Law of 1947, they were treated as Japanese citizens. In this way, their ethnic identity was denied (Kim, 1991). The Japanese government availed itself of the power to create such an ambiguous identity for Koreans in Japan, claiming that such a process of definition was legitimate because Koreans were "liberated people/aliens."

In 1952, the San Francisco Peace Treaty was made, and it guaranteed Korea independence from Japan. With it, Koreans in Japan were deprived of their Japanese nationality, meaning they lost their rights of political participation, occupational and educational opportunities (including the licensing of certain businesses), and access to national health insurance and social security. "They received a renewable visa-like status and were subjected to tight surveillance, required to be fingerprinted and to carry a registration certificate at all times" (Ryang, 2000, p. 4). The policy of the Japanese government over Koreans in Japan had little to do with securing their rights as foreign residents. Rather, Koreans were the target of control, deportation, and assimilation (Kim, 1991).

Present Situation of the Issei

In 1999, the number of foreign residents from Korea was about 6.36 million, approximately 5.18 million of which came to Japan in the prewar time along with their offspring (Yun, 2001, p. 77). Less than 10 percent of them are considered issei (Yun, 2001, p. 77). The daily lives of most issei are precarious. To be sure, a few are pretty well off due to business successes. However, because the typical Korean in Japan was discriminated against and excluded from mainstream jobs, most of them were not able to work for a company that offered pension insurance. Until 1982, they were also excluded from the national pension plan, which every Japanese national with or without an employee's pension plan must take. In 1982, the Japanese government revised existing laws to comply with the two International Covenants on Human Rights. As a consequence of compliance, the government made public housing and housing loans, child-care allowances, the national pension plan, and the national health care plan available to noncitizens (Ogawa, 1985). However, the government did not take the necessary transitional measures to help people with no national pension plan; as a result, many issei are left without any pension. Survey research in 1994 conducted in Ikuno, Osaka, showed that 3,009 out of 5,067 Koreans (50.4 percent) in the Osaka region have received or will receive no pension (Shoya & Nakayama, 1997, p. 296). To alleviate their hardship, some local governments offer special stipends to them; however, the amount is ¥2,500 to ¥20,000 (about US$20 to US$170) payment per month for the elderly and ¥5,000 to ¥50,000 yen (about US$40 to US$400) for the handicapped. This is not enough to subsist on. The conditions for receipt of these monies is highly restricted. Obviously, this system has offered little help for the financial plight of issei (Shoya & Nakayama, 1997, pp. 301–306). It is merely a token gesture.

The obvious question, then, is how do they survive? Some live with their children. Some receive financial help from their children even though they do not live together. As noted, some receive *seikatsu-hogo*, or income support from the local government. One might wonder why they do not return to Korea. This is not a solution for most of them, for even if they do, they feel uncomfortable because they are often discriminated against there. In Korea, they are sometimes called *pan choppari*, which means "animal toes being spread apart into two." This term is a pejorative phrase in Korean. It has traditionally been used to designate those Koreans who have been Japanized, especially during Japan's occupation of Korea. Because Japanese traditionally wore a form of socks called *tabi*, which by design split the big toe from the rest, the term *pan choppari*, was used to designate Japanized Koreans. Now it is sometimes used to signify Koreans in Japan (Harajiri, 1998, p. 109).

As is evident, many issei are left without much social support in their old age. They find themselves old in a land that never fully reciprocated when they chose to adopt it as their permanent home. A few small, local Korean organizations help them such as Yao Sanporamu and Ikuno Sanporamu in Osaka and Torajikai in Kawasaki, but the larger organizations such as Soren and Mindan do not. Most elderly Koreans in Japan have little to no access to information about welfare programs because many of them are illiterate. Also, very few belong to any Japanese interpersonal circles. Illiterate issei are unable to read written information circulated by local governments, so they have no opportunity to learn about any welfare services unless other family members or friends read for them. Thus, they are isolated. They do not participate in the unofficial communication networks that surround them, the proverbial grapevine.

Survey results collected from 1998–99 in Kawasaki indicate that 72 percent of Korean elderly in Japan (the sample size was fifty-six) have no Japanese friends and that 87 percent of them do not belong to local elderly circles (Ishizaka, 1999, p. 29). The claim that assimilation is tied to "functional fit" or "economic success" is thus rejected (Gudykunst & Kim, 1997). Practically all of these Koreans had a life, had found a "niche" and were "functional," working, raising children, and living in Japan for decades. They participated fully in the local and national economies of Japan up until they were too old to be productive. Then they were disregarded. This indicates that integration is not the same as assimilation and that, as Jean Gebser (1985) notes, integration is not a smooth spiral, "upward and forward," as Gudykunst and Kim (1997, p. 362) claim, but exhibits chunky qualities of fits and starts, of mutation; also there is no guarantee that things cannot slip backward or that a person is integrated in all ways simultaneously or with equal intensity (Gebser, 1985; Kramer, 2000). For instance, many issei may have been satisfied and integral parts of small businesses for many years, valued and reliable employees. But at the same time, they were not integrating on an interpersonal level or socially outside the sphere of work.

The suspicion of officials that many issei harbor keeps them away from welfare services. For a long time after the war, they were the targets of control for illicit liquor making, which was a necessary vice for them to make a living. Generally speaking, prejudice against Koreans among officials used to be strong (Ishizaka, 1999). Issei still remember how harshly officials treated them. Therefore, many of them think official welfare services are the last resort, and they do not actively seek information about such services. Because of these and other reasons already mentioned, many do not understand the long-term care insurance system, which was implemented in April 2000. This system is so complicated that even fully literate Japanese have difficulty understanding it. Moreover, the implementation of the plan was sudden; consequently, some flaws have been revealed only recently. For example, the level of care is arbitrarily decided, and the system does not work well for elderly who suffer from senile dementia. The system is unfriendly to the poor, because the recipients of the care plan must pay 10 percent of the service cost in addition to monthly insurance payments. Such a financial obligation also scares away many impoverished issei.

Furthermore, the system as designed cannot accommodate to the needs of foreign residents, especially issei. The plan was not designed to provide bicultural or at least culturally conscious home helpers. The older issei become, the more they forget Japanese and speak Korean. They prefer Korean to Japanese food. Therefore, less culturally conscious or sensitive home helpers may not satisfy issei needs. Both parties easily become frustrated with each other. This sort of problem was predictable because this care plan was made and standardized based on the basic resident register, which excludes foreign residents. It does not take into consideration the cultural diversity among the elderly at all. The cultural differences between Japanese elderly and issei are not small. What is familiar to Japanese elderly may not be to issei. Popular recreational activities in nursing homes, such as origami (paper folding) and singing Japanese folk songs, exclude many issei.

Overall, the situation surrounding the issei is problematic. The Japanese welfare system tends to exclude them. Government-made plans ignore cultural diversity, which is consistent with the assimilation policy Japan adopted throughout modern history (see Kramer & Ikeda, 1997). However, indifference among other Koreans in Japan to the plight of the issei has made their situation even more miserable.

AN ABANDONED GENERATION

The Korean community in Japan used to keep their own tradition, including Confucian principles, such as filial piety. However, as active members in the society transitioned from the first to the second and third generations, their values and lifestyles became increasingly Japanized, which, ironically, accords with the global standard of modernity. The global standard tells us that the more one consumes, the better one is. Accordingly, the youth of today consume more goods than the older generation. They have become more and more commercialized, transformed into a market. Appealing to this relatively free-spending segment of the economy, commercial interests have transformed popular and normative culture such that youthful preferences have conquered the world. As the global standard of youth culture runs throughout the world, the elderly appear to be obsolete and are reduced to being a mere burden on society and a drag on progress.

Japanese society does not stand apart from this global trend. In fact, it is a leader in such marketing and culture production. Throughout the postwar Westernization process, the elderly lost their respectable status within society. They used to be a repository of wisdom; people asked them what and how to do things, such as raise children, host weddings and funerals, and intermediate quarrels. The elderly were integral to the community; their wisdom was highly respected, essential to the propriety and proper function of citizenship. As Gebser (1985) would say, the elderly are well respected in the mythic world, where communal bond is strong and close interpersonal relationships are highly valued. In traditional societies, because the elderly are the repositories of communal memories, the hub of the communal bonding, people listen to what they have to say and follow them. However, close interpersonal relationships become dissociated in the modern perspectival world (Gebser, 1985). People become "units of the whole" and are forced to work as a part of a larger system, which is beyond local scale. In such a world, the elderly become a burden on society because they are unproductive by the criteria of the new economic system and how it has become so pervasive as to replace culture. According to Ong (1982), as a society shifts from oral history to literacy, the former of which is basically mythic and the latter perspectival, the wisdom of the elderly is replaced with written records. In the perspectival/literal world, one can increase knowledge more efficiently by reading books than by associating with others. This is so because the very concept of what constitutes knowledge changes. It becomes pragmatic, utilitarian in the narrow sense of material production. The global standard values efficiency above all else.

When Japan became a literate, bureaucratic modern nation, the status of the elderly and the repositories of traditional culture shifted. They became the problem, not the solution. They came to be seen through new values as inefficient, hopelessly conservative, and incapable. They became strangers in their homeland—alienated in the most essential sense of the word.

As the second and third generation of Koreans become Japanized, they lost their great respect for the elderly. The following comment made by a welfare commissioner in Ikegami, Kawasaki, substantiates this claim. Concerning the encumbrance of the elderly among Koreans in Japan, she said, "There is no difference between Japanese and Koreans in Japan. Supporting the elderly in a family is difficult for Koreans in Japan. They used to take good care of their parents, but they have become just like Japanese" (cited in Kim & Mikuni, 1999, p. 130).

Issei do not insist that their children take care of them. Interviews with issei in Kawasaki revealed this tendency. When discussing their children's sense of duty, fourteen out of sixteen issei mentioned that they do not want to be a burden to their children (Kim & Mikuni, 1999, p. 129). A seventy-four-year-old female issei said, "We the elderly feel the same. We want to be taken care of by our children. But they have their own lives, which are not so easy. They cannot afford to take care of us" (Kim & Mikuni, 1999, p. 129). This comment shows the struggle between the old Confucian sense of filial piety and the modern sense of independence. Issei want to be taken care of by their children, but they also think they should be independent. This may be related to the ambiguous situation of Koreans in Japan.

Many issei want to keep their tradition and have tried to teach their children to be Korean. However, in practice they gave inconsistent messages to their children. Because they have experienced severe discrimination from Japanese for being Korean and being poor, they wish their children to be free from being bullied and to be successful in Japanese society by *Japanese standards*. For them to protect their children, they taught them to hide their origins and act like Japanese. Many issei themselves tried to assimilate into Japanese society and thus to be successful and survive (Harajiri, 1989). The ambiguous messages that the second generation received mainly worked to keep them away from Korean society in Japan while encouraging them to merge with the mainstream Japanese society. Yet they were also reminded by their parents to be proud of their Koreanness. In reality, many second-generation Koreans moved out of the Korean residential areas to live separately from their parents. This is not exactly what issei wished for their children, but at the same time it seemed the best path. Clearly, there is much dissonance involved in attempting to adapt to a new cultural environment. As a consequence of second-generation Koreans moving out of Korean residential areas, the southern part of Kawasaki lost its younger residents. Korean communities are thus aging very rapidly, with all attendant social problems (Ishizaka, 1999).

The increasing number of Koreans in Japan who have been naturalized may substantiate the tendency of assimilation. Though four to six thousand Koreans in Japan were naturalized per year in the 1980s, more than ten thousand did so in 1995 (Kang, 1998, p. 18; Tei, 1996, p. 77). If this trend of accelerating naturalization continues, there will be no Korean nationals left in Japan by the middle of the twenty-first century (Kobayashi, 1995). Intermarriage between Japanese and Koreans in Japan further facilitates this trend. In 1996, more than 80 percent of Koreans married Japanese, whereas only 16.5 percent of Koreans married other Koreans in Japan (Kang, 1998, p. 18). What this indicates is that assimilation is occurring, but it is not an individual process, as Gudykunst and Kim (1997) maintain. It is not a matter of personal adjustment via cognitive disintegration and reintegration. The original Koreans have not and probably cannot deculturize or unlearn their cultural selves (Gudykunst & Kim, 1997, pp. 335–353). Rather, if it occurs at all, assimilation is a much longer process that is intergenerational. It is much more a sociocultural and historical than a psychological process.

There is an opinion that it is not important to Koreans in Japan for them to obtain suffrage on the local level because many have been and would be naturalized (I. Kim, personal communication, March 8, 2001). Although voting rights continue to have some symbolic meaning, which forces the Japanese government to modify their assimilation policy, it does not contribute to making issei life better.

The Sad Tale and the Myth of Assimilation

The following reasons explain why younger Koreans in Japan have largely chosen to be naturalized. Some chose naturalization to escape from discriminatory treatment by Japanese. In this process many took on Japanese names to hide their heritage. Others had no alternative because they could no longer associate themselves with Korea. There was no going back. As discrimination against Koreans in Japan has attenuated, the latter reason has become the dominant rationale for seeking naturalization. However, even though discrimination against Koreans in Japan has abated somewhat, much of it has merely become covert. Prejudice against Koreans in Japan has not disappeared. Arai Shokei's death reminds us of this fact in a very powerful way.

Arai was a Korean in Japan who won public office and became a prominent politician. One might jump to the conclusion that this proves that assimilation for Koreans in Japan is not only doable but can approach totality. However, Arai committed suicide on February 19, 1998. He was a third-generation "Korean" born in Japan. He obtained his Japanese citizenship at the age of eighteen and strove to be Japanese (Park, 1999). He was, however, forced to remember his place, his origin as a Korean throughout his life. Although he became a member of the House of Councilors in the Japanese Diet as an LDP member, he had many enemies within the LDP. Just before he died, he was cross-examined in the Diet and was about to be arrested for illegal trading violations. Many in the press openly suspected that he had been trapped and used as a scapegoat for a larger crime perpetrated by more powerful LDP members. Arai constantly complained in the media that he had been bullied in the LDP because of his Korean genealogy. It has been said that to be successful in Japanese society, Koreans in Japan have to either hide their ethnic identity or be naturalized. Arai's case, however, shows that to become Japanese legally was not enough to be totally accepted or even survive in Japan.

THE ULTIMATE *KOSEKI* IDENTITY

The official household registration (*Koseki*) functions in part by recording one's genealogical identity, which to this day in Japan remains essential. Every Japanese is recorded in the *Koseki*, which is an officially recognized documentation of one's nationality, name, age, marital status, children, parents, brothers, sisters, and so forth. A newly naturalized Japanese citizen obtains *Koseki*, which includes his or her parents' names, which (in most cases) reveals his or her genealogy. To have this record of one's ethnic identity deleted from *Koseki*, one can either wait until one's children make a new *Koseki*, or one can move one's

Koseki to a different place and replace it with a new one (Harajiri, 1989). In the latter case, however, one may be suspected that the person is trying to hide his or her true (ethnic) identity (Harajiri, 1989). If a deception is revealed, for instance, during preparations for a marriage, it can have devastating results.

The point is that the Japanese legal system works to remind people of their genealogy. The assimilation policy that the government has adopted and maintained in the *Koseki* system has not diminished discrimination against Koreans but facilitated it. Koreans in Japan are Others who were created and are maintained to make "Japanese" feel more Japanese (Kramer & Ikeda, 1997).

Younger generations of Koreans in Japan, however, have not experienced as severe a discrimination as the first and second generations. In this case, discrimination does not motivate them to be naturalized. Many of them obtain Japanese citizenship because they cannot associate themselves with Korea. The following examples substantiate this tendency. A nineteen-year old-woman who is going to be naturalized when she becomes twenty years old said that Korea to her is a foreign country and so she will take Japanese citizenship and live as a Japanese (Terada, 2002). A twenty-five-year-old woman also reported her intention of becoming a Japanese citizen in the near future because she has no desire to live in Korea and thinks having Japanese citizenship is convenient because she lives in Japan (from an interview conducted by Terada, 2002). Most of the third- and fourth-generation Koreans in Japan consider Japan to be their homeland; they do not mind changing their nationality (Kobayashi, 1995). This is partly because they never had an opportunity to go through a rite of passage, which forces a person to wonder who they are (Harajiri, 1989). According to Harajiri (1989), their rite of passage includes discrimination against them, which is powerfully symbolized by being "fingerprinted." However, fingerprinting was abolished for Koreans in Japan in 1992, when the Alien Registration Law was modified.

In each case mentioned, the presumed way to become Japanese is by acquiring Japanese citizenship. Many third- and fourth-generation Koreans wish to abandon the remains of their Korean identities. For those who want to be Japanese, the older generation of Koreans in Japan, especially the issei, are inconvenient reminders. The issei remind them of their Korean identity; they may even consider issei to be a threat to their identity formation. However, one cannot choose his or her identity by him- or herself. In other words, one has little control over one's identity because identity is a social construct. One's identity is constituted through communication. Thus, those who are naturalized and who seek to forget their Korean identity find it impossible to be completely Japanese. In fact, the very process of naturalization underscores their difference. Besides, on a daily basis their ethnic identity remains salient. Even casual relationships often impose reminders.

Sensing this negative feeling of the younger generation toward them, issei tend to suppress their desires to live and have a close relationship with their children and grandchildren. They try to not cause any trouble for their children, so they often express a determination to take care of themselves. Many comments of issei interviewed in Kawasaki, including the seventy-four-year-old woman already cited ("We want to be taken care of by our children.... but they cannot afford to take care of us"), express the stress of ambivalent feelings (Kim & Mikuni, 1999, p. 129). Many issei try to hide their dissatisfaction and loneliness. A seventy-two-year-old female issei said, "Well, even if I want to complain, I swallow it" (Kim & Mikuni, 1999, p. 130). An eighty-seven-year-old female issei who lives with her child's family also mentioned that she swallows her sorrow and complaints because other family members would frown at her if she expresses them.

The communication gap between issei and following generations seems great. Kim and Mikuni (1999) analyzed the generation gap among Koreans in Japan and discovered that it is bigger than that between generations of Japanese. Issei embody substantial Korean cultural heritage. They had little opportunity to go to school. They are less Japanized than their educated children and grandchildren. Instead they began working early and hard throughout their lives. This also factors into understanding the wide gap between issei and the following generations.

Political organizations of Koreans in Japan, such as Mindan and Soren, have shown very little concern about the elderly. They prefer debating over such political issues as local suffrage and the modification of the Nationality Law. The author participated in Mindan's annual gathering on August 15, 2001, in which no leaders mentioned the issue of the elderly. One of the Mindan members told me that top Mindan personnel are eager to associate with Japanese politicians and to try to deal with them on other issues. During their term of office, which usually lasts only a couple of years, they would like to do something to help them stand out in *Japanese* society. They believe that the issue of the elderly is not very dramatic or popular. Because they are seeking a high profile in the eyes of those who constitute the Japanese political establishment, they avoid the issue of the elderly. They actively seek to adapt to the mainstream political culture; to that end they align themselves with topics of interest to Japanese politicians rather than representing the interest of the issei. They are more concerned with what they can do to gain celebrity and attain higher status than what they can do to make the life of their own ethnic group better.

Debating over various issues is not a waste of time, but tackling the issue of the *Issei* is urgent since many don't have much time to waste. The *Issei* issue is a test of the political will and character of the Korean community leadership. It may determine if a genuine Korean-Japanese subculture can survive at all in Japan. If they cannot face this issue, they may be assimilated into mainstream Japan just as the Japanese government wishes. The Japanese government has not taken many measures to help the issei. This became apparent with the introduction of the long-term care insurance mentioned earlier. Theoretically the insurance includes foreign residents, but practically it is ineffective. Not many Koreans in Japan have noticed and spoken out about this absurdity. This indifference is exactly what the Japanese government hoped for. It keeps Koreans in

Japan in a position of being obsequious, which is the essence of model minority behavior and comportment. Expending time and energy on the issue of the local suffrage has diverted attention from the more urgent and costly issei issue. In this sense, as the Koreans become assimilated, they may think that they are finally becoming equals, but in the process they are actually surrendering their very cultural heritage and identity, thus becoming more of a minority until they vanish entirely. In the interim, the generations can communicate with and appreciate each other less.

According to the plan of the majority, to integrate properly, a minority must remain marginal, for that is their desired function within the larger system of relationships. Proper integration, as defined by the majority, means for minorities to know their place and stay there. Thus, to be an ideal minority means for Koreans in Japan to be scapegoats. For them to seek full Japanese identity, to successfully adapt and become one with the majority, which Gudykunst and Kim (1997, p. 365) suggest is the path to mental health and enlightenment, actually reinforces their minority status (model or not). They are following the dictates of the majority's wishes, which are that they disappear. The problem is that although they wish to be Japanese, they cannot. In the scheme of a model minority, being different than Japanese functions negatively. They continue to chase something they cannot attain. The model minority ideal in Japan involves assimilating like a robot, not exercising free will and resisting the normative role they are given, including the dominant expectations that follow from there.

RECONSTRUCTING DIFFERENCES

A model minority that has been forced to assimilate into the dominant society cannot practically assimilate. In theory it sounds nice, perhaps (at least from a right Hegelian perspective), but in reality it does not work. Need for daycare centers, nursing homes, and group homes for issei reveals that they have not adapted to Japanese culture. We can blame the victim for not behaving the way some authorities and social studies writers might claim they should, but this is the proper role of neither social science (which is to describe the world as it is, not how it ought to be) nor democratic polity. Although the number of daycare centers and nursing homes for issei is currently small (there are some in Osaka, Hyogo, Kanagawa, and Tokyo) the number is increasing. This shows how the system, the society at large, can (in fact almost always does to some extent, and if it wishes to be humane should) adapt to the needs of its members, including minority members. One size does not fit all. The immigrant rarely fully adapts to the society into which they have moved.

The author visited some of the nursing homes and daycare centers for issei and witnessed how they enjoy talking with their peers in both Japanese and Korean, eating Korean foods, and singing and dancing to Korean songs. Therefore, adaptation, as it has been theorized by Jourard (1974) and Gudykunst and Kim (1997, p. 362), cannot be attained. According to Gudykunst and Kim (1997) genuine "adaptation" should involve "the very 'disintegration' of the original cultural self to allow for a 'reintegration' of a new self in accord with the cultural requirements of the 'host' environment. Thus, adaptation goes to the core of a psychological restructuration. This amounts to nothing less than the total hegemonic control of identity" (Kramer & Ikeda, 2000, p. 85). Younger Koreans in Japan display a search for identity, which also proves that the theory of intercultural adaptation is wrong, at least in this case (and others as empirically demonstrated by other scholars in this and many other volumes).

Younger "Koreans" born and raised in Japan, many of them third and fourth generation who have never seen Korea, have not assimilated into Japanese society. *Shukan Kinyobi* of August 24, 2001, reported on a panel discussion of three third-generation Koreans in Japan (Kokuseki minzokutte nanda?, 2001). Each of the panel participants identifies him- or herself as positively non-Japanese. Ko Fangi, a twenty-year-old man, has Korean nationality and refuses to carry his Alien Registration card. He thinks that keeping Korean nationality is the only way to prove his ethnicity, because he does not speak Korean or know much about Korean culture. Peck Hyanyi, a twenty-four-year-old woman, has Korean nationality and is familiar with the language and culture because she went to Korean schools in Japan. She expressed how important it is for her to cherish the language and culture, which constitutes her identity. Matsue Tetsuaki, a twenty-four-year-old man, identifies himself as Korean-Japanese. He has Japanese nationality and considers himself to be Japanese with Korean ethnicity. Yet he claims the first half of his hyphenated identity just as much as the last half. Although each has a different way of identifying him- or herself, each shows that he or she is neither Japanese nor Korean. The ambivalence actually empowers them.

Among those who obtain Japanese nationality, some do so to identify themselves as Korean Japanese or Japanese nationals with Korean ethnicity (Kobayashi, 1995; Kokuseki minzokutte nanda?, 2001). Furthermore, after becoming naturalized, some of them register and keep their Korean names (Kobayashi, 1995). This movement demonstrates that naturalization does not mean adaptation or assimilation in the sense described by Gudykunst and Kim (1997).

On the Internet, there is a Web page dedicated to the issue of the Korean minority with Japanese nationality (http://www.asahi-net.or.jp/~en3y-cyn/index.html). According to this source, which is maintained by Korean-Japanese, the number of Korean minority members with Japanese nationality is bigger than Korean nationals in Japan. Naturalized people used to be accused of betraying and discriminated against Korean society in Japan. Thus, they have remained silent until recently. However, today the voices from Korean minority members with Japanese nationality, such as those expressed on this home page, cast a new light on Korean society in Japan. Korean minority members with

Japanese nationality appreciate their differences from both straight Japanese and Korean identities and seek a discursive space for their unique identity.

Young helpers and volunteers in Toraji-kai, a daycare center in Kawasaki, try to learn something important for their lives from the issei they serve. They report appreciating and enjoying the opportunity to associate with issei, which may not last so long. To constitute one's identity, it is precious to understand one's ethnic origin. The issei embody a unique but vanishing identity that has, for no matter how brief a time, added genuine diversity to the Japanese world. Searching for one's identity and appreciating the differences that give one identity makes meaningless the ideal of a single and transcendental set of model minority imperatives.

REFERENCES

Duus, P. (1995). *The abacus and the sword: The Japanese penetration of Korea, 1895–1910*. Berkeley: University of California Press.

Gebser, J. (1985). *The ever-present origin* (N. Barstad & A. Mickunas, Trans.). Athens: Ohio University Press.

Gudykunst W. B., & Kim, Y. Y. (1997). *Communicating with strangers: An approach to intercultural communication* (3rd ed.). New York: McGraw Hill.

Harajiri, H. (1989). *Zainichi chosenjin no seikatsusekai* [The life-world of Koreans in Japan]. Tokyo: Kobundo.

Ishizaka, K. (1999). Kawasaki no zainichi kankoku-chosenjin [Resident Koreans in Kawasaki]. In Research Group of Kawasaki Zainichi Kankoku-Chosenjin no Seikatsu to Koe (Eds.), *Kawasaki: Zainichi kankoku-chosenjin no seikatsu to koe* [Kawasaki: The life and voice of Korean-Japanese] (pp. 7–17). Kawasaki, Japan: Seikyusha.

Jourard, S. (1974). Growing awareness and the awareness of growth. In B. Patton & K. Giffin (Eds.), *Interpersonal communication*. New York: Harper and Row.

Kang, S. (1998). Zainichi korian shakai o henbo saseru "kokuseki," "minzoku kyoiku," "sanseiken" no ryudoka [Change in "nationality," "ethnic education," "suffrage," which may give an impact on Korean society in Japan]. *Sapio* (July 8), 18–19.

Kashiwazaki, C. (2000). The politics of legal status: The equation of nationality with ethnonational identity. In S. Ryang (Ed.), *Koreans in Japan: Critical voices from the margin* (pp. 13–31). New York: Routledge.

Kim, Y. D. (1991). Dainijitaisenchu no chosenjin senjidoin ni tsuite [On wartime mobilization of Koreans during World War II]. In Sengo Hosho Mondai Kenkyukai (Eds.), *Zainichi kankoku-chosenjin no sengohosho* [Postwar welfare for Korean-Japanese]. Tokyo: Akashi Shoten.

Kim, H., & Mikuni, K. (1999). Toraji-kai no genzai to shorai [Present and future of Toraji-kai]. In Research Group of Kawasaki Zainichi Kankoku-Chosenjin no Seikatsu to Koe (Ed.), *Kawasaki: Zainichi kankoku-chosenjin no seikatsu to koe* [The life and voice of Korean-Japanese] (pp. 124–141). Kawasaki, Japan: Seikyusha.

Kobayashi, K. (1995). Kika de yureru minzoku ka riben ka [The issue of naturalization: Ethnicity or convenience]. *Aera,* 24–27.

Kokuseki minzokutte nanda? [What are nationality and ethnicity?]. (2001). *Shukan Kinyobi* (August 24), pp. 34–37.

Kramer, E. (2000). Cultural fusion and the defense of the difference. In M. Asante & J. Min (Eds.), *Sociocultural conflict between African and Korean Americans* (pp. 183–230). New York: University Press of America.

Kramer, E., & Ikeda, R. (1997). What is a Japanese? Diversity, culture, and social harmony. In E. Kramer (Ed.), *Race relations in a postmodern world* (pp. 79–102). Westport, CT: Praeger.

Kramer, E., & Ikeda, R. (2000). The changing faces of reality. *Keio Communication Review, 22,* 79–109.

Nakatsuka, A. (1991). Zainichi chosenjin no rekishiteki keisei [Koreans in Japan created in history]. In T. Yamada & C. M. Pak (Eds.), *Zainichi chosenjin: Rekishi to Genjo* [Korean-Japanese: History and current situation] (pp. 85–115). Tokyo: Akashi Shoten.

Ogawa, M. (1985). Zainichi gaikokujin no shakaihosho hoseijo no jokyo [The legal status of resident aliens in the social security system]. *Horitsu Jiho, 57,* 43–55.

Ong, W. J. (1982). *Orality and literacy: The technologizing of the word.* London: Routledge.

Park, I. (1999). *Zainichi to iu ikikata* [The way how to live as Koreans in Japan]. Tokyo: Kodansha.

Ryang, S. (2000). Introduction: Resident Koreans in Japan. In S. Ryang (Ed.), *Koreans in Japan: Critical voices from the margin* (pp. 1–12). New York: Routledge.

Shoya, R., & Nakayama, T. (1997). *Korei zainichi kankoku-chosenjin* [The elderly Korean in Japan]. Tokyo: Ochanomizu Shobo.

Tei, T. (1996). "Zainichi" no minzoku hiro [Ethnic fatigue of "Koreans in Japan"]. *Chuo Koron* (September), 74–79.

Terada, S. (2002). *Identities of young Korean women in Japan: Hybridity as a challenge to multiple discrimination.* Unpublished master's thesis, International Christian University, Tokyo, Japan.

Yun, K. C. (2001). *"Zainichi" o ikiru towa* [To live as "Koreans in Japan"]. Tokyo: Heibonsha.

Chapter 10

Old and New Worlds

Algis Mickunas

INTRODUCTION

There is a conflation of terminology concerning *immigrants, refugees,* and at times refugees who change to immigrant identity and status. Immigrants are persons who leave a particular country to seek a place regarded as more acceptable or promising. They are usually allowed to come to the new country legally and obtain some modicum of legal protection and, in time, citizenship. This is the case with most of the immigrants from Eastern Europe during late nineteenth and early twentieth centuries. They were coming to the promised land in waves and with few demands, such as legal protection for their universal human rights or clever designs for welfare support. They knew that only hard work for pay awaited them, and they gladly accepted the chance.

Refugees are persons who are thrown out of their homes by wars or persecution for expressing unacceptable views or for some transgression of laws and inevitable punishment. They leave for a temporary duration with a constant search for ways of returning to their homeland. Hence they do not immigrate to another country, but may be accepted for safe keeping until the danger to their lives is over and the door is open for return. In a sense, they do not specifically know where they are going, as long as they escape with their skin: A saying from Eastern Europe goes: "I am running where my eyes lead me." In most cases, they leave everything with the hope that someday on returning all will be regained.

Refugee-immigrants are persons who first are forced to leave by some cataclysm, often a war, and are unable to return to their home country immediately. They will seek legal status as immigrants or other countries that would accept them as legal immigrants. Hence, they cease to be refugees and acquire the status of immigrant. Such groups tend to come in waves and are also grateful for a chance to make a life in a new country, yet they tend to maintain hopes of returning home once the social or political conditions permit. More recently, there is a category that is used to cover a peculiar combination of motives: economic refugees. In their own countries they survive and are not persecuted, nor are they victims of wars, but they regard their means of subsistence as unacceptable and therefore seek a better life elsewhere. They tend to move as families or individuals or small groups and often enter host countries illegally. They tend to regard their countries of origin as their real home and point of self-identity and are in the host country to make a living. Indeed, this living is not just for them but also for their extended families. This category is more current and in part is applicable to recent waves of Eastern Europeans motivated by the collapse of the Soviet Union.

This chapter will consider all three waves and their main attitudes toward the melting pot. It could be stated that the melting pot has not even been a question for most immigrants. They express their belonging, exclusion, or self-exclusion by their actions and commitments, by their words, their pride, dreams, hopes, disappointments, and aspirations.

WAVES FROM THE OLD COUNTRY

The wave of immigrants from Eastern Europe at the end of the nineteenth century and dawn of the twentieth consisted of peoples basically from the land. Poles, Ukrainians, and Bahts hardly knew the wider place of their origin and then only as a story, a mystical place of destination—the land where streets are paved with gold. They might have known their village, or even a provincial town, and perhaps that they were from the Russian empire. Yet such attachments did not constitute for them a nation, or provide a national identity to inspire pride, commitment, patriotism, or sacrifice. They might have fled from twenty-five years of military service in an army whose commands and edicts were in a language they did not understand. But mainly they left places that were replete with degradation, misery, and pain. Day after day, season after season, life returned in cycles of repeated subjection and exploitation by the big *pan* (master), *gospadin* (proprietor), or extended hand of a priest to be kissed while on one's knees. Their reflection on their conditions consisted of the impossibility of being a *pan*, or a *gospadin*, or a "father," because such positions were reserved to those with birthright. The eternal peasant could not even imagine being born into such positions or having concerns about his or her nation. It would be against divine order itself. He or she was born to be a *muzhik*, a serf/peasant whose position was eternally fixed. This suggests that they did not immigrate as economic refugees or those seeking political asylum from oppressive rulers or rulers who denied universal human rights. They were illiterate and hence oblivious to such lofty concepts. Their situation was ontological-essential.

Their reflections from others—the misters and masters, the lords and gods, the czar as father/god—positioned them ontologically to be essentially tied to hard toil, to be illiterate, to live in the same log cabins with straw roofs as their beasts of burden, and at times to be treated as lesser than said beasts. Hence, their migration was not identical with economic refugees seeking more money and a better life but a totalizing move to drop their ontological identities and degraded positions and to be able to be addressed and to address one another in terms of what they only heard reflectively: mister, master of my own domain, and proprietor of my work.

The immigrant from the land had another reflexive awareness. His position on the land was sanctioned by a terminology that constantly appealed to a tradition, to a past: "Through all the ages and their eternity, as it was in the past so shall it be forever." This is an almost Hegelian dialectical process but with a slight modification: "The essence is what has been," and yet the "essence is repeated as the future." For the Eastern European *muzhik* the move to the New World was also a move away from the past and the tradition that inscribed him or her with the indelible ontological mark of restrictions, and the future consisted of the New World, with very different and mainly insecure prospects. Yet precisely such an open future as an aspect of the peasant's awareness comprised a reflexive horizon that revealed the limitations of the Old World as past, as "an essence that has been," a frozen and changeless position without prospects, without being able to be a mister or a missus (a lady). This temporal, and in turn essential, interreflexivity was the constitution of awareness that pitted ontology against its temporal dissolution, and hence toward a radical rearticulation of the peasant who would become a worker for his own living and with prospects to be equal to any other mister, indeed to be a human. After all, the father calls us human from the pulpit—even if we are worse sinners. Yet we live with and as beasts.

This wave of immigrants knew that hard work awaited the illiterate and linguistically mute in the New World. Not only were their old language skills limited to the tasks appropriate for land labor, but the New World's language was also beyond their ken. This aspect compelled these immigrants to form their own linguistic communities, concentrated around centers of production requiring heavy and menial labor. These enclaves created a context for acquiring a national identity that was broader than the village and narrower than a distant empire. They were from other villages and, at times towns, and yet spoke a similar language. This is to say, identity appeared as a reflexively constituted recognition of "us" as distinct from the Americans and from the Russians, the Ukrainians, the Lithuanians, thus positioning "us" as Polish. The same can be said of Ukrainians, Lithuanians, and others. They also acquired reflexive identities and became different from other enclaves. It must be noted that the term *American* was used to designate the others, the "American-speaking" Yankees who were literate, at ease in their world, and even superior. Indeed, they had a different religion and regarded it as enlightened and far above the Catholic and

Orthodox religions of Eastern European immigrants. The latter could hardly count as Christians.

Here, the new immigrant was placed in various ambiguities. She was in America: equal being among all others and yet not an American in contrast to the "real" Americans. She lived in an enclave among her linguistic neighbors and indeed had acquired a national identity that belonged to the Old Country and at the same time defined her community in the New World. She lived in a Polish community or a Lithuanian neighborhood and contributed to the maintenance of that community by donating hard-earned funds to build a parish and even a club. The clergy who came with the waves of immigrants to tend the flock dramatically enhanced the building of ties to the community. The clergy were educated and literate and hence enjoyed a similar status that they had had in the Old Country. As in the Old Country, they commanded respect and exercised authority. Moreover, to the extent that they were literate and could even read American newspapers and documents, the clergy played a mediating role between their ethnic communities and the American world. Hence, they were positioned both as opening the immigrant to the American world and as a barrier that prevented the immigrant from having speedy integration.

From their position, the clergy also provided a powerful reflexive aspect toward establishing national identities among the illiterate immigrants. The latter were told that they are not just from a village or some *gubernija* (governorship) but from a country with borders, usually extended to include the broadest geographic area derivable from historical records. Hence, a Lithuanian from a village of some *gubernija* was aware that he also belonged to the empire of Czar Alexander, but not that he resided in Lithuania. Yet as an immigrant in the New World, he built a community and a church and acquired an identity as Lithuanian through talks with the clergy, who also pointed out that Lithuania once ruled from the Baltic Sea to the Black Sea, and that the czars trembled before Lithuanian rulers. While constituting a national identity in the New World and retroactively acquiring a vague sense of the "nation" left in the Old World, the immigrant tended to regard the latter as past and the New World of America as a place for his future.

Apart from parishes and churches, from which radiated linguistic boundaries, national identity, and acceptance of the immigrant, there were established clubs that were basically pubs with dance floors, with a small band that could play the Old Country tunes and rhythms. At times a kitchen for Old Country foods was also added and thus enhanced one's national identity and also the separation from the American world. The church basement and the club were gathering places that allowed for community organizational work. Such work was specifically concerned with aiding each other in finding jobs, places to live, meeting available marital partners, and mutual support to open ethnic businesses, such as grocery stores, barber shops, shoe repair shops, and even production of ethnic food commodities, such as sausages, breads, and cheeses. No doubt, such an increase in self-sufficiency tended to block integration into mainstream America. Yet it is also no doubt that the new immigrant regarded him- or herself as American, specifically in manners and efforts to speak American (for immigrants, Yankees did not speak English). It must be understood that most jobs were outside of such ethnic communities: steel mills, coal mines, slaughterhouses, doing laundry, and cleaning the homes of the Yankees. Each of these occupations required a specific although very limited American vocabulary.

A vocabulary of American consisted of greetings, calling out names that had been modified or Americanized, and terms required for the performing of jobs: "Au you?" "Purty gut." "Au your missus?" "Vai you standing, no vorkin?" and so on. Yet this vocabulary was immediately brought into the ethnic community and became a common mode of conversation mixed with the immigrant's ethnic language. In many cases American words were given ethnic endings, resulting in a unique language worthy of linguistic studies. For example, *Paidiom stritovat*, "let's go for a walk," uses *street* modified to *stritovat* as a verb. Or, *Gi mi ames*, meaning "give me ham." Such usage was also regarded as a sign of being American.

Other signs of being equal to Americans consisted of attire and addressing others by mister and missus. One bought a suit, a hat, a vest with a watch chain across the midriff, or a dress with somber or flowery patterns and was able to say on Sunday church gatherings, "I am just as good as the boss." He wears a suit, and so do I. The Yankee lady wears a flowery dress and a bonnet, so do I. The boss is mister, and so am I; his wife is missus, and so is mine. The latter case is very pronounced. The men did not speak of wives; they would rather ask "au you missus," and the women would not speak of husbands but ask "au you mister" (How is your missus and how is your mister?). Such designations and attires were not even on the horizon in the Old Country. In this sense, they were becoming Americans, even if symbolically. But the symbolism for them was the reality of being American, wherein the Old Country was sinking into the past and the New World was becoming almost the sole future.

This symbolism became dramatically enhanced when the immigrant went back to the Old Country to visit relatives and former neighbors. In that setting he was an American. He wore his suit, she wore her dress and bonnet, and the whole village would come out to gape at "the Americans." He was now addressed as *pan* or *gospadin*, and even the local priest or landlord would seat them at the table and treat them as equals. In this setting there was no question that they were no longer *muzhiks* but members of another society that was regarded as superior. Being denizens of the New World, they were also higher in rank than what they were when they left. This aspect also comprised a reflexive moment that allowed the immigrants to identify themselves with the New World and on returning to it to be proud of their new identity. They proudly proclaimed to those who just landed on the shores of the New World that "Ya Amerikanets," or "Amerikanski," or "Amerikons." No doubt, despite the backbreaking labor and long hours, they scrounged and acquired homes, became "mister an missus of ous" (mister and missus of the house), and their future appearing in the new generation was radically different from the past of the Old Country. Thus they melted into the melting pot but in quite a unique way. Though constantly reminded of their difference manifest from language through religion, music, and illiteracy, with endurance and patience they strove to surround themselves with paraphernalia of "normal" American life: the Protestant work ethic, frugality, private property, children in schools preparing for good jobs, and, of course, becoming more patriotic than the real Americans. This was indeed in contrast to the reserved Yankees who did not wear patriotism on their sleeves. The pride would increase even more when the clergy would organize parish fund-raising for relief in the Old Country. "We Americans can afford to do the job, while those in the Old Country can't dig themselves out of their holes."

Aspects of this experience that cannot be overlooked include the emergent workers' movements and left-wing politics. Being members of the working class, these immigrants were easy targets not only of left-wing politics but also in many cases of Communist organizations. Leaders of such organizations found fertile ground among these workers and held meetings in ethnic clubs to explain the workers' position in the world of capital. Indeed, although not engaged in radical activities, these working persons, many of whom had become citizens, supported left-wing candidates. They did not regard such activities as un-American, revolutionary, or destructive of America but as a continuation of their hopes and dreams in America. After all, in the Old Country they could not assemble and organize, demand changes, or even help elect representatives. The latter would be empowered to speak with the voice and power of the people and establish laws and programs for them. For example, President Franklin D. Roosevelt established Social Security and other benefits for workers, and he was regarded as the best president there ever was. Reaching retirement years, these immigrants were now secure, and this security was given equally by America to all Americans.

A brief note concerning the tug-of-war to join real Americans comes with the second generation. Although the parishes tended to establish schools and newspapers, they were basically parochial, with an emphasis on maintaining ethnic and religious identities. Outside the parish, enclave public schools were battlegrounds for the second generation. The battle consisted of many levels. The youngsters were made to be ashamed in public schools of being different on the basis of strange names, sometimes their accents, shy and unsure manners, and lesser wealth. Hence, they did their best to become the best they could, Americans. This also created a war at home: The parents were ignorant, did not know how to speak, had no manners, and hence were objects of shame. One could not bring such parents to school. One was ashamed of them and would be exposed to ridicule—even by teachers. At home, the children knew better, and their manners were American in contrast to the moralities that the parents wanted to impose. "Look ma, I can come home anytime I like; this is

America and not the Old Country." When growing up, this second generation of Eastern Europeans tended to Americanize their names by shortening or even completely adopting American names. Thus, from Adamkiewitzch one becomes Adams, from Ivan one becomes John, from Stankevichius one becomes Stankus, and from Stanislav one turns to Stan. In brief, this generation ran from the customs and language of their parents, and indeed from the enclaves to erase their ethnicity and be "normal Americans" without any other trace. It is only by the third or fourth generations that this effort became redundant and one was born American. Names, if they still lingered in some families, no longer signified shame, outsider status, or even being degraded. The immigrant grandparents for the third generation were not objects of shame or avoidance but at most curiosity: "Mom, how come Grandpa talks funny?"

THE WAVES FROM TOWNS

The second wave of Eastern European immigrants stemmed mainly from towns and cities. This wave is a result of World War II. To understand this type of immigrant, a brief context has to be delineated. After gaining independence from the Russian empire and others having established national boundaries, there emerged a sense of national identity among peoples of this region. Whether a peasant or a doctor, one knew that he or she was Polish, Latvian, Czechoslovakian, Estonian, and so on. More important, education was established for all and became extolled as the highest good. One reason for education was the growing industrialization, trade, and a need for various services from teachers through doctors, engineers, and officers. Another reason was a need for an avenue to reduce agrarian populations to avoid the division of land into increasingly smaller lots among children and grandchildren. In accord with the typical practices of inheritance, one son, usually the eldest child, would inherit the land, and perhaps one daughter could be provided with a good dowry for marriage, but others had to go and make their own way in the world through education.

These factors provided a split between town–city as populated by cultured, educated, more prosperous members—the elite—and the agrarian population that although literate were nonetheless not highly educated. High education was prestigious, and those in such positions became cultural and national leaders. Of course, their interests were not only to have such positions but also to ensure their future through the maintenance of national integrity. Although stemming from agrarian backgrounds, the educated looked on agrarian life and people from a psychological and sometimes geographical distance. A hierarchy of well-rewarded professions emerged. People who held such positions were addressed as *pan* and *gospadin*—in short, as mister and sir. Indeed, their spouses were also entitled to the titles: they were Missus Engineer, Missus Doctor, Missus General, Missus Minister, Missus Professor, and so on, and demanded deference from the lower ones, including their servants.

There is no need to speak of various World War II battles or territorial redistributions among the warring powers; what is important is that the Soviet Union was acquiring Eastern Europe. It is also an a priori truth that for the Soviet Union any educated elites were regarded as the most dangerous threat to absolute dictatorship and therefore demanded elimination first. Whether it is the murder of ten thousand Polish officers at Katino or the rounding up of tens of thousands of educated persons—from teachers, doctors, and lawyers to priests and officers during the first Soviet invasion of the Baltic States in 1940—the educated bore the brunt of being transported in cattle cars to the gulag. Hence, the final invasion of Soviet troops on the heels of retreating German armies spelled the death of any educated person who decided to stay in the homeland. Very few chose that fate with the consequence being that many fled en masse toward the West as refugees. Obviously they were not immigrating but simply running toward any safe haven from the red terror. This very designation, which they used to call the advancing Soviet armies, already suggests that they were mostly conservative and that anything resembling Communism under whatever guise would be an enemy. This is not to say that their anti-Communism was entirely unfounded—after all, thousands of their colleagues, friends, and family members had been sent to concentration camps and death. The main populations staying at home were farmers who later also bore the violence of the red terror for owning property (farms), and thus being bourgeois and exploiters of the working class. At any rate, the national elite, the heads of various nations of Eastern Europe, left or were killed.

Most ended up in refugee camps in what then was known as West Germany. Despite hardships, there was no lack of enthusiasm for education. In such camps schools were formed and education of their children, disrupted by war, resumed at all levels. Although the range was from first grade through gymnasium (high school), the teachers included university professors and thus added to the high level of educational preparation for the children of refugees. At the same time they knew and extolled their national identities and knew the enemy in the East that was enslaving their people. The point is that these refugees built up strong immunity against being totally integrated into any "adopted" society (wherever that might be) of their next destination. Their destination was still unknown, and it took a number of years for them to be invited to immigrate to Australia and the Americas. For most, the destination was narrowed down to North America and most preferably to the United States.

The choice of the United States was not random. Eastern European immigrants from the first wave were still alive—even if old and some already retired; hence they were contacted through parishes and were called on to invite relatives—even if remote—to their communities by agreeing to provide contracts of support. The common hope was that such support would be necessary for only a short time and that jobs would be found for the new immigrants through contacts with the old immigrant network and specifically through parishes and organizations. This also located the new immigrants in the enclaves already established by the first wave and, at the very outset, provided a national setting.

The New World offered jobs similar to those occupied by the first wave—menial labor, factory work, as store and restaurant attendants, and as servants. Those who had held elite positions in the Old Country were disqualified for obvious reasons: First, high-level professions, such as law, medicine, diplomacy, and military work required sophisticated language skills. Second, even if one had a strong language background in English, these professions required very different preparation and also legal conditions: One had to engage in a protracted reeducation to pass examinations required by the laws of the New World. Hence an unavoidable dilemma for the mostly middle-aged immigrants with families—they had to work to earn a living for the family, which required that they try to obtain reeducation in the profession acquired in the Old Country. Few made it. Thus, there was an intense concentration on the next generation: Young persons were pushed to go for higher education at any cost. Due to their good educational preparation in the camps, the youth of the new immigrants finished U.S. high schools easily and entered universities in unprecedented numbers. A large majority of these young Eastern Europeans earned university degrees—mainly in practical disciplines, such as business, medicine, engineering, physics, mathematics, and so forth. At the same time, persons of conservative ilk peopled such professions, even among Americans. Very few entered such fields as humanities and liberal arts. Such professions were deemed leftist, intellectual, and suspicious—at least pink if not red.

But what of the heat to melt into the melting pot? The situation is somewhat complex. We must understand the relationship of the new wave with the old one. The latter received the new immigrants from a position of superiority; after all, they were Americans giving aid to those from the Old Country, those who did not understand what it is to be a mister or missus and to speak American. After all, the new immigrants were backward. They were coming from a country the old immigrants had long since left behind and that they regarded as being more or less the same as they remembered. The first-wave immigrants had established their lives in the New World and were proud of being citizens. Meanwhile, the new immigrants regarded themselves as educated, with high positions, the elite of their nation and hence far superior to the old-wave immigrants. The latter were seen as simple though good-hearted and to be tolerated but not taken seriously. After all, they did not realize how much things had changed in the Old World, and hence they were hardly good partners for any intelligent conversation. Moreover, and most important, the old immigrants were a lost cause. They had no nationalistic (apart from being American) passion and could not be counted on to join ranks to help liberate their true homeland in the Old World.

In addition, the old immigrants and even their children were left leaning. As already pointed out, they were working-class people and Roosevelt was the man who provided all sorts of social benefits. If the Old Country is Communist, and if Communists take care of working people, then there was no reason for anyone to leave. Why did these people run away? According to this logic, the best thing for them was to go back, unless they were real enemies of the people. This was a very sore spot between the old and the new immigrants. For the new ones, Roosevelt was the worst thing that happened to Eastern Europe. Hence the positive adoration of this president by the old immigrants was incomprehensible, antinationalistic. It was an attitude and opinion to be rejected. The new immigrants, meanwhile, had been in the New World for only a short duration. They believed that the West, after all, would come to its senses, that people would soon elect leaders who would not tolerate the red terror spreading its enslavement across the world. Indeed, such a threat would be stopped and rolled back. The new wave believed that such a strategic change was just a matter of a few years, and then they could return to a liberated Old World and resume their lives in elite positions as the rightful national leaders of their homelands. This meant that for the new-wave immigrants, there was not even a desire to enter the melting pot. Of course, they believed that they had to work to live and even strive to advance in their careers, but only temporarily.

For the new-wave immigrants, to ensure that they could return as untainted as possible, they immediately formed organizations and took over the schools and mass media that had been previously established by the first-wave immigrant clergy and religious orders. Teachers from the new wave took over instruction in parochial schools and organized language classes to ensure that the children of the new immigrants would be fluent in their ethnic tongue, culture, geography, history, and all the glorious kings, princes, and heroes. At the same time the clubs were expanded—meetings and lectures were organized to solve all sorts of "national" problems and to organize pressure on governments for liberating the home nation. In these organizations the new educated immigrants, while working in factories during the day, called themselves by old titles: Mister Ambassador, Mister Engineer, Mister Doctor, and their ladies, packing cookies in factories during the day, called each other Missus Doctor, Missus Professor, and so on. They carried not only their national identities but also their elite positions within those nations. They expanded and changed the motivation for club membership. The new-wave immigrants set out to socialize the youth in the correct traditions. To that end, they built youth programs with libraries in the mother tongue. They held meetings and balls to which they came dressed as best they could to look regal and extol their old titles. Hardly any of the simple, good-hearted first-wave immigrants were invited.

Meanwhile, the children of the new wave were also organized, nationalized, and positioned to go back to their country and help revive it after the red terror had completely destroyed it. Youth organizations, summer camps, schools for language and history, and even summer courses at the university level for ethnic groups taught by ethnic professors for credit—all were designed to revive, instill, and maintain national identity, pride and separation from the mainstream American culture. As mentioned, the young flocked to universities and were instilled with the notion that they were smarter and of higher culture and class than all other students, including so-called American students. Part-time menial jobs were acceptable only as temporary support for their education. After work and/or school, they gathered in their ethnic clubs, restaurants, and youth buildings to discuss in their ethnic languages all issues; to listen to poets, diplomats, professors; to watch theater and listen to opera—all performed in their languages by ethnic artists. Marriage, too, was expected to be with partners from the same ethnic group. After all, the next generation was expected to continue the national line and return home to take up their rightful place that the parents and even grandparents had occupied. Moreover, it was believed that all the illegal misappropriation of property by Communist governments would be reversed and that "we," the temporary exiles, would reexercise the legal titles to such properties.

In contrast to the first-wave immigrants, who could not join the mainstream host society because of illiteracy and religious and educational barriers but who prided themselves as being Americans, the second wave, due to their higher levels of education and presumption of elite status, overcame such barriers. Nevertheless, the second-wave immigrants closed themselves off from American life because it was to be of short duration. The expectation was that they would soon return home. But the return home began to demand all sorts of activities, chief among them the organized efforts to ensure that the West (and specifically the American government) refuse to recognize the illegal occupation and incorporation of the home nations into the Soviet empire. This meant that participation in American politics was keen and conservative. Roosevelt, the arch-liberal, the red, sold Eastern Europe to Communism. The conservatives regarded Communism as the ultimate enemy. Therefore political organization to support conservative American politicians was central to their efforts to regain their Old World statuses. As already mentioned, this political stance constituted a rift between the old and the new waves of immigrants. The only thing they had in common was religion. Yet even in this arena, the clergy of the new-wave immigrants set a conservative political tone. It is impossible to elucidate all the manifestations that the rift between old and new took, but it may be interesting to point out some aberrations forming among the new immigrants, specifically among intellectuals in the human sciences.

Intellectual groups, formed by academicians in humanities, had a unique position as immigrants. They became more integrated into the American world for a unique reason: liberalism. Liberalism provides arguments for tolerance of ethnic differences and hence for the possibility of maintaining ethnic and national identities in North America. In this sense, such groups seemed to be counter to the conservative majorities, which regarded the liberals as reds. In turn, just as the conservatives called for the liberation of the old nations from the Communist yoke, the liberals argued on the basis of universal rights of nations to self-determination and at the same time of universal rights of members of different societies to political freedoms. But this meant that in principle even Communist views must be tolerated if they are not imposed by force. Hence, "if we go home again, we will have to tolerate people's choices of political parties and governments, even if they choose communists." Such liberal views were branded as unpatriotic, to be stamped out, and not to be allowed "when we get back." Recall that the majority of the second wave associated liberal and democrat with being "red." In a peculiar reversal, the liberals were contributing to the liberation of thought in Eastern Europe by simply being intellectually interested enough to read literature, humanities, and philosophies of the academicians, writers, and poets in their homelands. This led to the establishment of personal contacts and careful dialogues. Western views appeared, even if underground, with increasing frequency and impacted Eastern European intellectual life, helping in its liberalization and at the same time fostering the slow distancing from the Soviet empire, regaining greater national identity. This impact was admitted much later—only after the collapse of the Soviet Union. It is obvious that the conservative majority regarded such intellectual contacts as being worse than sacrilegious: a complete sellout of one's home country to the reds.

AS TIME GOES BY

Though initially unwilling to be Americanized, the new immigrants acquired American ways of practical life: middle-class values, property, and even reputations among the Americans as being equal professionals and solid citizens. Indeed, they were not only good Americans but perhaps even better than the naive and careless locals who did not understand the dangers posed to America by world Communism. Here, their conservatism extended to American patriotism against Communism—specifically in the context of the cold war. America and we Americans stand against Communism. Those who do not stand with us are not worthy Americans. This bifurcation of the world also allowed one to think that, after all, those generations in the Old Country brought up under Communist rule must surely be Communist. As just mentioned, any contact with them was a sellout not only of one's nation but also of America. Eastern European countries are written off and the new aging immigrant becomes a better American than the real Americans. After all, prospects of going home are dimming, the positions one once had are gone and one is also getting too old for any position, apart for retirement and social security provided by America. Although they support and maintain the newspapers, book publishing, radio, and even TV programs (in larger centers), the more interesting and relevant news comes from American media; more interesting programs (including high culture) are better done on American TV, American movies, and American opera. Of course, we still belong to the elite, but we discover that America contains cultural options unavailable anywhere else. Those poor folks at home, under Communism, have nothing cultural in comparison to us Americans. Those admitted for a visit to the Soviet Union and Eastern Europe would point out to their acquaintances in the Old Country what great culture, science, and creativity America possesses, and, of course, "I am American." If you could come and visit, you would not believe your eyes. It became an indirect, reflexive awareness from the Old Country that constituted a moment of practical and psychological immersion into the melting pot. Now their concern with the Old Country shifted toward Westernization and even liberalization through cultural (even if initially narrow) channels. The Old Country has to be Americanized to be able to join civilization someday. This effort was enhanced by the collapse of the Soviet empire.

GOING HOME

This event, the collapse of the Soviet empire, for the now-aged immigrants, was a sign of the correctness of their conservatism that was exhibited by the conservative government in Washington. Moreover, this correctness was also confirmed by their conviction that it is Eastern Europe that finally cracked the iron curtain and forced the collapse of Soviet Union. The most significant demonstration of acceptance of America by the aged immigrants was the refusal to return home. Yet now they returned as American tourists to meet the members of their families who speak with Russian accents and have manners that belong to enslaved people. The time for the Americans has come to undo the damage and to bring back the nationalism they cherished for fifty years of exile. Yet what they brought was and continues to be America. Customs, manners, behavior, political demands, commerce, education, privatization, and even the language are all American. We shall teach them not to look over their shoulder if anyone is watching; we shall show them how to speak freely and without fear in public gatherings—each individual in his or her own name. We shall bring back the true nation that was there before the Soviet empire. Of course, this would mean forgetting that in numerous cases the pre-Soviet governments did not allow free speech without police supervision and did not allow challenges to petty dictators who were continuing their offices for the benefit of the country. This simply suggests that these returning nationalists had been completely integrated into the melting pot, even if they still maintained their enclaves, clubs, and parishes.

This is even more true of the young children of the second wave: well-educated and experienced, they also joined in the Americanization of Eastern European nations. Indeed, the indigenous populations formed an ambivalent attitude toward them. These returning "nationals" were temporary visitors who spoke the local language with an accent but condemned the Russian linguistic acquisitions, accents, and terminological mixtures, and they did their level best to replace such borrowings, yet this time by American terms that were deemed normal. Indeed, such normalizing began to be regarded in the Old Country as Americanization and as in fact leading away from nationalism and toward cosmopolitanism. There are notable shifts in attitudes among the common people (although not among the elite and young educated groups) toward the tourists. The former regard the returning visitors as foreigners, with curious manners and attitudes, indeed unsettling liberalism. The latter are all for becoming Westerners and indeed Americans. Both aspects comprise a reflection on the visiting immigrants and their offspring that they are genuine Americans. This brief sketch suggests that the melting pot does not prohibit the immigrant from forming communities and maintaining Old Country nationality, yet also indicates that enculturation is equally inevitable.

Such nationality, for the first immigrant waves, was basically formed in America—the only national awareness the peasants had was of America. The reflexive forming of the Old Country nation was remote and the experience of it in the past. This is to say, they were American nationals at the present, and their birthplace was not a nation but became one only through their imagination and the claims made by the second-wave elites. But even as such, the sense that the Old Country was a nation in which one had been enfranchised (but not really) was in some imaginary past anyway. Hence it would seem that to be an American national was much easier for the first-wave immigrants. For the second wave, the nation was experienced and maintained in immigration; the problem was that it had vanished into the Soviet empire (or its sphere of dominance without national sovereignty), and hence the second-wave immigrants had to become the sole bearers of these nations as separate and independent entities. This reversal from the first-wave consciousness called on the second wave to maintain the authenticity of their nationalities. This factor added another tension between the returning Americans to visit their old nations (freed from the Soviet empire) and the indigenous populations. The latter, after all, have assumed Soviet nationality, ways of thinking, and ways of speaking through pervasive Russification over five decades. Hence, such a population was tainted, and the returning visitors had no qualms in claiming that they are the true bearers of Old Country nationalities. As already suggested, they were Americans despite themselves, and they brought a nationality from fifty years ago that no longer made much sense in the contemporary setting. Indeed, what they regarded as their separate national identity, brought with them to the New World, became only a memory of comfortable Americans fifty years later.

Yet their Americanism, paraded in the Old Countries, also provided a catalyst for the younger and more daring members to seek the good life in the West. In contrast to the Soviet shabby life, they were offered instant images of material abundance, leisurely life, an unimaginable variety of commodities, and easy money. Coupled with newly elected governments who still operate in the Soviet style—inefficient, completely removed from the daily concerns of citizens, bureaucratic, and dictatorial—the only option was and is to leave. This new, post-Soviet wave consists of educated professionals who have not become nationalistic but who have a view of life as opportunistic. This opportunistic view stems partially from their Soviet education, in which the West was constantly depicted as capitalistic anarchy, where anything goes as long as you make money. If you make money, you will be respected and have a good but alienated and decadent life, and the making of money has no rules. As a result, the current wave does not come to bring its nationality and its preservation but to exploit any opportunity—and in many cases criminally so—to enrich themselves. This does not mean that they are economic refugees whose home life is almost unbearable, almost on the verge of starvation. They want what is paraded from the West in advertisements, in luxuries, fun, and immediate gratifications. Though educated in specific professions, they take any job, or engage in any activity that gives them the good life.

There is one specific conception that is quite complex and quite common. They come to the West, mainly to America, to make money. They know all the latest styles and would be insulted if offered hand-me-downs from previous immigrants. They also know all the legal and social tricks and can immediately find all sorts of loopholes to circumvent legal requirements for their stay. They also claim that apart from making money, life in America is low, mean, brutal, and uncultured; hence, once they enrich themselves, they shall go back home. They follow the Soviet saying that "in America one has everything, but one has no life." On returning, they shall have everything and life.

The reason for this view stems from the inherited attitude toward work during the Soviet period. Most received equal pay, with most other amenities guaranteed, and "work" was very minimal: Do as little as possible, enjoy being with others over a bottle of vodka, and let the government take care of the rest. In short, no hustle, no rush, and no worries. In America, in contrast, there is no time for leisure, for friendly gatherings; one must run from morning until night and become "spiritually" exhausted; at the end of all that, one is given a fare of dull, unintelligent, TV programs. Yet they go home to have immediate gratifications and not to extol their nation. Such dumb gratification seems equally dull in contrast to the fun one could have on the beaches of Florida, gambling casinos in Las Vegas, and jazz in New Orleans.

There is a tension between the second-wave old immigrants and the new opportunists who are not committed to their home nation as nation and who could hardly care less for American liberties and values. The opportunists are thus regarded by both the first- and second-wave immigrants as freed Soviets who think that freedom means "everything goes" and that no civilized or civic rules are to be respected. The difficulty that this immigrant has stems from a lack of identity. He or she has learned not to trust governments, because the Soviet government was a priori oppressive and devious, and hence one had to learn devious ways of circumventing authority. Yet after the breakdown of the Soviet empire, the newly and "freely" elected governments came from the ranks of the former Communist ruling elites; once in power, they behaved in the old ways—with one important exception: The members of governments became unabashedly corrupt and, as the saying goes, they did not establish democracy but kleptocracy. If such governments are representative of the emergent national identities, then there is nothing new from the old system apart from setting an example for how the rest should live. As immigrants, they do not pay attention to legitimate authority, because for them all authority must be corrupt and not heeded. Thus illegal immigration, false visas, and criminal activity are all taken as normal. In principle, for the most part, the post-Soviet wave of immigrants will not be melted into anything, will not be proud of belonging to any specific nationality, and will have no allegiance to any flag or to any specific convictions. It is unabashed self-interest; any means, any country will do as long as it serves as many interests as possible.

It might be the case that this group is in transition and may be regarded as an aspect of globalization. This group is, after all, characterized as abolishing national boundaries, even of identifiable national and powerful entities, such as the United States and nations of Western Europe. Globalism draws into its sphere areas that have hardly begun to form national identities. Such identities are being easily dissolved in the sweep of organizations that respect no borders, including global criminal organizations. If we couple this phenomenon with the immigrants from the newly proclaimed (or recouped) nations of Eastern Europe, we can see that the immigrants might never have experienced their currently emergent nationalities as points of their identity.

The Soviet Union, and by extension its satellites, formed more or less a country wherein these "freed Soviets" were once safe and at home. They could travel (with permission) across vast regions, from the Baltic Sea to the Black Sea; to Irtusk, in the Ural Mountains, to ski; to Kazakhstan, Uzbekistan, and Prague as one continuous nation. Persons brought up in this expanse regarded it as *bolshaya strana* (the grand fatherland) and, apart from Russian linguistic chauvinism (a universally mandatory language) they regarded it as their own. In this sense, although the breakup of the Soviet Union led to an establishment and reestablishment of nationalities, the immediate incursion of the West and globalization offered no window of opportunity to obtain a strong national identity. Apart from opportunism, they may be regarded as nomads without any serious search for and adherence to any national identity. They would melt into the pot if it suited them, but without proclaiming that they are proud to be American. One notable aspect of their psychological attitude is irony, skepticism, and cynicism. Whether this is a passing fad can only be seen with the next generation, both in the Old World and the New. After all, some who come to America only temporarily end up settling down, acquiring property, and raising children who attend American schools, wear the latest teenage styles, and, though well versed in the Old World languages, answer their parents in English while being addressed in their parents' native tongue. If they visit the Old World with their parents, they regard themselves as tourists who must get home before the start of school.

POSTSCRIPT

This chapter makes up a compact disclosure of the essential aspects of awareness of Eastern Europeans in the contexts of their own origins and appearance in America. The essential aspects were explicated in terms of variants of different waves of immigrants to show the ways that these waves coped with their experience, what they brought with them, what they found, and what they retained and discarded.

What appeared across the variants (apart from the latest, post-Soviet wave) is the reflexive positioning of the immigrant as American, despite the efforts to maintain some semblance of former national identity. The reflexive awareness comprised a transcendental condition for the immigrant to see him- or herself in terms of the Other, for example the Other who has become part of the Soviet empire and hence no longer a member of the nation that the immigrant cherished. He or she then became a real American in contrast to a citizen of the Soviet empire and in turn the only one with the right to speak about the rights of self-determination of all peoples. But such rights are, for this immigrant, American. In this sense our offered variations had a focus: In what ways did the immigrants become Americans, despite their psychological, rhetorical, and even political claims?

It is hoped that some light has been shed on how the melting pot functions and the ways that it cannot be avoided. The unavoidable nature of the process for these immigrants is restricted to North America, specifically to the United States. The United States allows one to maintain and even extol one's national identity, and hence this very permission by America and acceptance by the immigrant is being, essentially, American.

Chapter 11

Demythologizing the "Model Minority"

Eungjun Min

> Asian Americans have long been confronted with the glass ceiling. Some
> say the ceiling is actually made of steel, not glass. ... The sad thing is, most
> corporations have preconceived notions of how their Asian American em-
> ployees should behave. We're stereotyped as being dependable and indus-
> trious workers, not effective leaders. (Ng, 2001, p. 8)

In the 1960s, the media promoted a theory of the model minority through
statistics-laden articles (e.g., SAT scores) that depicted Asian Americans as an
exceptionally accomplished and industrious minority group. The media con-
nected African Americans and Latinos with social problems, but Asian Americans represented the hope and possibility of the American dream (Lee, 1996,
p. 5). Initially, Asian Americans enjoyed this bolstering of their image. They
were extolled as a model minority that had overcome racism and had successfully integrated themselves into American society. The model minority theory,
first named by William Petersen (1966), prides Asian Americans on their perse-
verance, hard work, and quiet accommodation. In articles like *Look*'s "Americans
without a Delinquency Problem," *Newsweek*'s "Outwhiting the White," and
U.S. News & World Report's "Success Story of One Minority Group in the
U.S.," claims are made that Chinese Americans no longer occupy a minority status but fully participate in American society with its attendant economic benefits (Chang, 2000, p. 370). Petersen argues that Japanese culture with its family
values and strong work ethic enabled Japanese Americans to overcome prejudice
and to avoid becoming a problem minority (1966, p. 20). He used the term *model*
in two different ways: First, as a way of praising the superior performance of
Japanese Americans, and second, as a way of suggesting that other ethnic groups
should emulate the Japanese American example (Petersen, 1966). The lesson is

that there is something to be learned from the self-reliance of Japanese Americans who work hard instead of relying on welfare. This model minority theory has become a relatively unchallenged assumption about current social reality.

By the late 1960s, however, greater ethnic consciousness and political activism within the Asian community created a backlash against this image. Misinterpreted statistical evidence may underlie the notion that Anglo Saxon values are superior to all others. Often Asian Americans are said to succeed because of their work ethics and because their values are compatible with Anglo Saxon values. At a time when minority groups were participating in civil unrest and mass political protests, the portrayal of Asian Americans as a successful minority served a strategic political need, especially coming as it did during the height of the civil rights movement. The message was clear: Blacks and Latinos should follow the example set by Asian Americans (Chan, 1991; Chang, 2000; Ovando, 2001). This chapter attempts to demythologize the model minority myth that underlies the ideology of model minority discourse and advocacy as well as negative stereotypes. This is accomplished by applying a critical approach including Roland Barthes's theory of semiotics.

MYTH, IDEOLOGY, AND INTERROGATION OF THE OBVIOUS

What is wrong with compliments like *smart* and *successful*? Compared to other minority stereotypes, the model minority seems to be a fine compliment. The problem is the naturalization of difference. If differences among Asian Americans (Chinese American, Korean American, Vietnamese American, and so on) and other races are social, cultural, economic, and political, then they are open to adjustments and change. But if they are natural, such that the implicit or explicit claim is that Asian Americans are inherently smart, hard-working, and unassimilable, then they are permanently hidden and fixed. French semiotician Barthes (1972) defines *myth* as a fictitious, unproven, or illusory thing that circulates in contemporary society, the false representations and erroneous beliefs (109). The magazine articles referenced previously and Petersen's essay share the conviction that what we see as being "natural" is in fact an illusory reality constructed to mask the real structures of power obtaining in society.

When bourgeois ideology becomes omnipresent, its power is self-reinforced by its ubiquitous and unnamed nature. Barthes (1972) contends that "myth is a value" that robs images of their historicity to make them perpetuate dominant bourgeois culture. As Barthes puts it, "The very principle of myth [is to] transform history into nature" (1972, p. 120). Ultimately (because "statistically, myth is on the right") this process showcases and conserves bourgeois culture, framing its transient, historical characteristics as somehow eternal, inevitable, and not to be challenged. Barthes situates myth in the realm of political discourse and argues that myth depoliticizes ideology and thus camouflages present social inequalities (1972, p. 138–141). He begins his investigation into contemporary myths by questioning the ways a variety of cultural forms, including newspapers, films, and art, convince us that the reality they construct is natural. For Barthes, the principle of myth is to transform history into nature: Myth converts historical reality into an illusory image of the world as "nature." Myth deprives the object of all history and prevents us from wondering where it comes from, instead encouraging us to simply enjoy it. For Barthes, myth is also depoliticized speech because it forgets that reality is a product of human activity and struggle. In this sense, the major function of myth is to empty reality by distancing itself from history, thereby serving the maintenance of the dominant ideology by presenting a world of no history and politics and moreover of no contradiction (1972, p. 109–112). In short, Barthes sees myth as a vehicle used by the dominant class to represent, confirm, and preserve its dominant ideology. In this sense, his notion of myth is similar to that of traditional myth in that both types of myth are seen to control the ways of thinking and acting of community members for the sake of status quo. Hence the goal of his study of modern myth is to demythologize the ideology that is constructed and presented through various cultural forms.

Barthes (1972) argues that it is necessary to challenge the innocence and naturalness of cultural texts and practices, which are capable of producing all sorts of supplementary meanings or connotations (pp. 54–56). Every object or gesture is susceptible to the imposition of meaning. Nothing is resistant to this process. Barthes argues that to think is to make explicit the meanings of apparently neutral objects and then move on to consider the social and historical conditions they obscure. Under such critical, reflective conditions, petite bourgeoisie constructs are exposed as arbitrary, and the myths they deploy to discourage resistance and reflective thinking are also exposed. Mythological reality encourages conformity to its own values. We inhabit a world of signs that support existing power structures and purport to be unassailably natural. Barthes interrogates the obvious, taking a closer look at that which gets taken for granted, making explicit what remains implicit. He stops taking things for granted, by bracketing or suspending consideration of their function, and instead concentrates on what they mean and how they function as signs.

Although social practices share certain utilitarian functions, they are not resistant to the imposition of meaning. There is no such thing, for example, as a neutral racial group that is devoid of connotations and resistant to the imposition of meaning. The white majority and Asian Americans share a similar functional goal, the American dream. But no matter how many generations an Asian American person's family has been in the United States, people still ask which country he or she comes from.

DEMYTHOLOGIZING AND DESTEREOTYPING

As mentioned, the model minority theory bolsters the much-celebrated American dream. Defense of the dream is equated with defending the very foundations of democracy and an egalitarian society not only domestically but also internationally. Asian Americans are portrayed as hard-working, intelligent, persistent, diligent, successful, sneaky, obsequious, and eternally evil. They suffer from both positive and negative stereotypes. Even the positive stereotype creates a myth, which then produces debilitating effects like discrimination, alienation, invisible oppression, and unfair pressure on the Asian American population.

The Media Action Network for Asian Americans (MANAA, 2001) has identified a list of restrictive Asian portrayals that manifest stereotypes. First, Asian Americans are viewed as foreigners who cannot be assimilated. This unassimilability is perpetuated by the Orientalist discourse, which argues that there are fundamental differences between East and West (Cheung, 1993). Anything Asian is thus inherently alien to America. An Asian person can never become an American because the United States represents the vanguard of Westernization. According to MANAA, this is reflected in the media by the large number of Asian characters speaking with foreign accents. Even acculturated Asian American personalities have sometimes been portrayed as unassimilated (i.e., the second-generation Japanese American Judge Lance Ito, who was portrayed with a foreign accent in many radio and television shows).

Second, Asian Americans are largely viewed as financial predators. For decades, Americans have viewed Asian immigrants as noncontributors to society. This perception, MANAA argues, was due to early laws making it difficult for Asians to immigrate and impossible for them to become naturalized citizens. Historically, new immigrants faced resentment from those who felt most threatened by their arrival. It was troubling to many how quickly Asian immigrants found their way within America and became economically successful. An example of how media portray Koreans as economic exploiters is evidenced in the film *Falling Down* (1993). In this film Korean Americans are portrayed as ruthless profiteers exploiting the poverty of African Americans. During a radio talk show on WHAT (1340 AM), an AME church minister in Philadelphia categorically condemned Korean merchants as "blood suckers."[1] Many films, such as the Academy Award–winning *Chinatown* (1974), have also portrayed Chinatowns as incomprehensible breeding grounds for corrupt underground economies and criminal activities.

Third, Asian Americans are always trapped in cliché occupations. Despite the fact that Asians and Asian Americans make their livings in a variety of professions, they are often depicted as Chinese restaurant and laundry workers, Japanese businesspeople, Indian cab drivers, Korean grocers, laboratory workers, massage parlor workers, prostitutes, faith healers, or gangsters. This image certainly misrepresents the diversity of the Asian American workforce.

Fourth, Asian racial features, names, accents, and mannerisms are portrayed as inherently comic or sinister, if not just plain strange. For instance, in the Academy Award–winning movie *Fargo* (1996), the only Asian who appears in the film does so for no apparent reason (given the logic of the story) other than to present a very bizarre image of something akin to a mental breakdown mixed with lascivious intentions. Later in the film the heroine discovers that he is an outrageous liar to boot. The Oriental in the film appears not only tangential to the story but is portrayed as less rational than even the murderers. Due to the lack of understanding in the mainstream Anglo American culture, Asian culture in the mainstream media tends to offer characters for quick and easy gags and stunts.

Fifth, Asian Americans are portrayed as people who are comfortable with being limited to supporting roles. Even if a film, or television show, deals with Asian subject matter, the main characters are often non-Asians or non–Asian Americans. Sixth, the sexuality of Asian Americans is portrayed as either overly active or extremely passive. The Asian woman is supposedly sexually active, exotic, and eager to please (for instance *Rush Hour 2*, 2001; *China Dolls*, 2001, and myriad music videos that use female Oriental models for decoration). They are often portrayed as ideal romantic partners for both black and white American men. On the other hand, Asian men are almost never paired with women of any race, including Asian American women. As Cornel West (1993, p. 83) argues, while mainstream America views black sexuality as dirty, disgusting, intriguing, interesting, and even threatening, mainstream media desexualizes the Asian male altogether. Asian men are either evil and greedy gangsters or sexless restaurant workers (for instance "Yellow Uncle Tom") who are good at dying or sacrificing for the lead white characters. The only good Asian is a dead Asian. Asian women are also often portrayed as seductive, backstabbing, and untrustworthy dragon ladies. The dragon lady has the power to hypnotize her male rivals and get rid of them in unexpected ways (Mahdzan & Ziegler, 2001, p. 1).

Responding to these criticisms, some producers have made some efforts to create more positive images for Asian Americans. Asian Americans have indeed played some positive roles in a few films and TV shows. But the overriding image of Asian Americans is as the model minority, depicting them as nerdy if not flawless machine-like workers, patient and overachieving humans with little emotional lives.

Another supposedly positive depiction is the mysterious supernatural power that fixes everything conveniently. Asian cultures are so strange, unknowable, and eternally evil that they can defy the physical realities of Western culture. If Asian characters use magical power, it is usually for demonic purposes. But if the main character learns the power and uses it, it is used in positive ways. As Gilman (1985) argues, the practice of stereotyping seems unavoidable. According to Gilman, when our self-integration is threatened, stereotypes come to fix the instabilities of our perception of the world. Gilman also argues that the creation of stereotype is a necessary concomitant of human development (1985, p. 16–18). This is not to say that it is good, but that stereotyping is necessary for development. At the sociological level, however, stereotyping distorts individual interactions because it encourages identifying people by their group membership rather than by individual salient features. Stereotyping reduces people to a few simple, essential characteristics, which are represented as fixed by nature.

Dyer (1977) identifies three underlying ideologies involved in stereotyping. First, stereotypes manifest a few memorable characteristics about Asian Americans (or any other group), and then reduce, exaggerate, and simplify everything about the group to those traits in a wholesale fashion. Second, stereotyping deploys a strategy of splitting. It constantly divides what is included from what is excluded or the acceptable from the unacceptable. Dyer argues that "a system of social stereotypes refers to what is, as it were, within and beyond the pale of normalcy" (i.e., behavior, which is accepted as normal in any culture) (1977, p. 29). Therefore stereotyping artificially and symbolically sets boundaries and borders. Stereotyping is used to maintain the social and symbolic order of a hegemonic power. It draws the line between insider and outsider, us versus them, normal versus deviant, and acceptable versus unacceptable. Third, Dyer points out that where there are gross inequalities of power the practice of stereotyping goes unchallenged. Power is used against those who are different and therefore who constitute unacceptable people. Said (1978) defines *power* in this sense:

In any society not totalitarian, then, certain cultural forms predominate over others; the form of this cultural leadership is what Gramsci has identified as hegemony, an indispensable concept for any understanding of cultural life in the industrial West. It is hegemony, or rather the result of cultural hegemony at work, that gives Orientalism its durability and its strength ... Orientalism is never far from ... the idea of Europe, a collective notion identifying "us" Europeans as against all "those" non-Europeans, and indeed it can be argued that the major component in European culture is precisely what made that culture hegemonic both in and outside Europe: the idea of European identity as a superior one in comparison with all the non-European peoples and cultures. There is in addition the hegemony of European ideas about the Orient, themselves reiterating European superiority over Oriental backwardness, usually overriding the possibility that a more independent thinker ... may have had different views on the matter. (p. 7)

Power always operates in conditions of unequal relations. It produces new discourses and representations by radiating power downward onto subordinate groups. It's not a conspiracy but a complex physics of domination from above. The images and stereotypes of Asian Americans are only acceptable representations. The stereotyping is invested with power. Sometimes the general idea about who Asian Americans are is not necessarily determined by empirical reality but by a battery of desires, repression, investments, and projections by the dominant group. This general idea is very comforting for the dominant group, a position that the dominant can enjoy forever without being seen. But the dominant group can only see its own creation and nothing more.

But in American society, the fundamental understanding of power and ideology is lacking due to a widespread belief in pluralism. Pluralists interpret the United States as a complex society of interest groups that compete in the political arena. This value-free view makes it difficult to see the real picture. The fundamental reason for the continuity of pluralism is that there exists a broadly based normative consensus on core values. It is further claimed that ideology no longer functions in American society (Bell, 1960). In other words, ideology has come to represent American society's pluralistic nature. In criticizing the theory of pluralism, Hall (1982) argues that although the approach is advanced as being empirically grounded and scientific, it is nevertheless predicated on a very specific set of political and ideological presuppositions. Hall continues:

These presuppositions, however, were not put to the test, within the theory, but framed and underpinned it as a set of unexamined postulates. It should have asked, "does pluralism work?" and "how does pluralism work?" Instead, it asserted "pluralism works"— and then went on to measure, precisely and empirically, just how well it was doing. (1982, p. 59)

For Hall, it is wrong to assume that no structural or class barriers exist in the United States that might obstruct the "process of cultural absorption." The theory rests on "a mixture of prophecy and hope" dressed up as "pure science." The result of these dubious assumptions is that pluralists missed altogether the multitude of unabsorbed elements "still simmering in the American melting pot" (Hall, 1982, pp. 59–60).

Ideology is certainly not a popular term when applied to the United States. This anti-ideology attitude, in my view, is closely related to the broad American hostility to socialism and the lack of left organizations. Bell (1960) declares that "ideology, which was once a road to action, has become a dead end" (p. 370). Bell compares ideology to religion; ideology is religion's successor, appealing to the same sort of faith, passion, and irrationality. Unlike Gramsci, who draws strong parallels between religion and ideology, Bell draws the definitional boundaries of both very tightly, and the validity of his approach depends heavily on a distinction between the decline of ideology and the decline of "old ideologies"—principally Nazism and the former Soviet Communism.

Although his argument about the end of ideology is primarily semantic, I argue that the thesis does contain some substantive assumptions. But his attempt to restrict the concept of ideology and even to eliminate it from Western society is based on questionable premises. According to Bell, ideology is reduced to a mere challenge to totalitarian political thinking. But according to Hannah Arendt (1973), because totalitarian politics became associated in the postwar decades with the Soviet Union, "the end of ideology" thesis often amounts to a thesis about the end of Marxism. As a result, it is ironically an ideological move in current American discourse to claim that ideology is not relevant to advanced industrial societies (Arendt, 1973, p. 471). The other assumption is that it is possible to contrast ideology with science. Science here appeals to empirical observation and a rigid separation of facts from values.

It is difficult to step out of the ideological circle. I do not claim that ideology is the only condition in the production of a product, that we are dupes of ideology. Other conditions, such as the class and/or gender producers, conditions in consumption, and textual forms of representation should also be examined in the production process. What I do suggest is that the theory of the end of ideology is wrong and that the theory of ideological bias may be right for the logics of that moment. Again, there is danger that the latter would neglect the wide range of possibilities in cultural forms (production—text—consumption). It is reductionistic to claim that we need only trace an idea to its source to declare it ideological. Nonetheless, it is necessary to understand ideology before criticizing it and also to adopt a self-reflexive attitude toward its own premises. It is also important to preserve the critical potential of a theory of ideology by linking it with analyses of control and domination. It is thus worthwhile to reconsider the concept.

Barthes obviously uses the myth to mean a prereflexive ideology. His understanding of myth is that it is a socially constructed reality that is passed off as natural. According to myth, the opinions and values of a historically and socially specific class are held up as universal truths. Attempts to challenge this naturalization and universalization of a socially constructed paradigm are dismissed for lacking *bon sens* and therefore excluded from serious consideration. The real power relations in society (between classes, between men and women, etc.) are obscured because references to all tensions and difficulties are blocked out, glossed over; their political threat defused.

There is an example of how the socially constructed model minority, in this case, may have affected the judicial system. Neil Gotanda (2000) documents the case of *The People v. Soonja Du*, a pre-1992, pre–Los Angeles Riot case. He attempts to show how the case was deeply affected by a conflict between the good minority definition (explicit) and the bad minority stereotype. Both are discursive formations that are not explicitly defined and therefore have no relationship to empirical reality but are so implicit in the discourse of this case as to be presumed as a natural, normative truth.

Soonja Du's case heightened the tension between blacks and Koreans before the riot. Du, a fifty-one-year-old Korean immigrant mother and store owner, shot and killed a fifteen-year-old African American girl in a dispute over a bottle of orange drink (Gotanda, 2000, p. 379). The security camera in Du's grocery store showed Latasha Harlins approaching the store counter. Du appeared to shout at Harlins and grabbed her sweater. Harlins punched Du three times about the head. Then Du threw a stool at Harlins. Harlins put the bottle on the counter and walked away. Du pulled a gun from beneath the counter and fired. Du was released on probation with four hundred hours of community service and a $500 fine. She was freed because Du's family had been victimized and terrorized repeatedly by black gang members. Harlins, according to Judge Karlin, provoked the shooting. The following is from Karlin's remarks on the sentencing of Soonja Du that may reflect Judge Karlin's racial stereotypes:

I can't ignore the reason Mrs. Du was working in the store that day. She went to work that Saturday to save her son from having to work. Her son had begged his parents to close the store. He was afraid because he had been the victim of repeated robberies and terrorism in that same store. On the day of the shooting Mrs. Du volunteered to cover for her son to save him one day of fear. (Freer, 1994, p. 10)

This excerpt of Karlin's public statement at the time of Du's sentencing clearly shows sympathy by portraying her as an innocent shopkeeper who cared about her son and who had been repeatedly robbed by gang members. On the other hand, in the judge's colloquy, the victim is portrayed as a criminal and associated with gangs and gang violence (Gotanda, 2000, p. 381). The colloquy, according to Gotanda, is filled with two things: humanizing Du, as a model minority, and demonizing Harlins, as a monitored minority. The model minority theory in this case provides Karlin "an ideological framework both to distance herself from Harlins individually, and to absolve non-blacks generally, especially those in the highest tier of the model minority, of any social responsibility for the effects of racial subordination on African American" (Gotanda, 2000, p. 384).

CONCLUSIONS

Widespread acceptance of the model minority success story hints at discrimination. It is often operative (almost always implicitly) in stereotyping and in excuses not to undertake the difficult task of reforming U.S. schools to help students understand and value the multicultural society in the United States. The attitude that there is no need to worry about the model minorities (Japanese Americans, Chinese Americans, Korean Americans, and so on) because they are doing better than everyone else is divisive and destructive. The reality is that recent immigrants and refugees from Southeast Asia, China, the Philippines, and Pacific Islands require the same special attention as any other minority in America. Additionally, many scholars in Asian studies have argued that the model minority label has obscured the ongoing need for international refugee resettlement, the monitoring of immigrant labor for maltreatment in Chinatowns, and the monitoring of patterns of restricted access to educational and occupational opportunities experienced by Asian Americans (Chan, 1991, p. 171; Chang, 2000; Lee, 1996; Lott, 1998). Furthermore, news media almost never cover problematic aspects of Asian American communities, such as poverty or the problem of youngsters struggling with limited English language proficiency.

Arthur Fletcher, chair of the 1990 Civil Rights Commission on Asians and Pacific Islanders, reported to President George Bush:

Asian Americans suffer widely the pain and humiliation of bigotry and acts of violence. ... They also confront institutional discrimination in numerous domains, such as places of work and schools, in accessing public services, and in the administration of justice. This stereotype leads federal, state, and local agencies to overlook the problems facing

Asian Americans, and it often causes resentment of Asian Americans within the general public. (quoted in Chin, 2001, p. 4)

The model minority myth diverts attention from the problems of many segments of the Asian American community, particularly the Laotians, Hmong, Cambodians, and Vietnamese, who have poverty rates of 29 percent, 55 percent, and 21 percent, respectively. Their rates are much higher than the national poverty level of 12 percent (Chang, 2000, p. 372). According to the 1990 U.S. census, the median family income for Japanese Americans was $51,550. But for the Hmong it was only $14,227 (Chan, 2001, p. 210). Both the 1990 and the 2000 U.S. censuses reported that the median income of Asian Americans was higher than the national average and the white majority's average. But as the old saying goes, when statisticians are done with a landscape once filled with mountains and valleys, all that is left is a flat plane. Statistics conceal as they reveal. Chang argues that the data is misleading because 60 percent of Asian Americans live in three states, California, Hawaii, and New York, where the median income and the cost of living are higher than in other states. It is true that Asian Americans have scored higher on the SAT than any other groups and have had a higher percentage of college graduates. These measures of performance are not, however, exactly translated into higher income. It is no secret that Asian American college graduates do not get the same salaries as their white counterparts. Chang (2000) argues that the model minority myth makes this sort of structural injustice invisible. The invisibility can have harmful effects on those who need to be seen. He also claims that the myth has hurt not only Asian Americans but also other racial minorities and poor whites who are blamed for not being successful, like Asian Americans (Chang, 2000, p. 371–373).

In conclusion, we create images of others and images of ourselves for others. The creation of such finalized images is for art, not for life, as the Russian philosopher Mikhail Bakhtin argues (Morson & Emerson, 1994, p. 180). One cannot even really see one's own exterior and comprehend it as a whole. Our real exterior can be seen and understood only by other people, because they are located outside us in space and because they are Others. Thus, any phenomenon or cultural event requires the perspective of other cultures to develop beyond itself (Bakhtin, 1993, p. 40). Events and artifacts are great in large measure because of potentialities and semantic depths that can be revealed only perspectives, other cultures. For Bakhtin, cultures are never closed semiotic systems. He is not a holistic thinker, for this presumes that a system is totally given in the immediacy of perception and that it is closed. Other cultures provide us the specific ways by which producers orchestrate diverse social voices. The attempt to demythologize the model minority myth is not just to reveal the truth: Asian Americans have problems, just like other racial groups. Instead, this attempt has been an effort to reveal possibilities for Asian Americans to become full participants in American life, working alongside their neighbors toward a more egalitarian society.

NOTE

1. The black minister's radio remarks were related to this author in an interview with the Reverend Woongkyo Park, former associate minister of the Philadelphia Korean United Methodist Church, February 21, 2001.

REFERENCES

Arendt, H. (1973). *The origins of totalitarianism*. New York: Harcourt, Brace, Jovanovich.

Bakhtin, M. (1993). Toward a philosophy of the act (V. Liapunov, Trans., M. Holquist & V. Liapunove, Eds.) Austin: University of Texas Press.

Barthes, R. (1972). *Mythologies*. New York: Hill and Wang.

Bell, D. (1960). *The end of ideology: On the exhaustion of political ideas in the fifties*. New York: Free Press of Glencoe.

Chan, K. (2001). U.S.-born, immigrant, refugee, or indigenous status. In G. Chang (Ed.), *Asian Americans and politics* (pp. 197–229). Washington, DC: Woodrow Wilson Center Press.

Chan, S. (1991). *Asian Americans: An interpretive history*. Boston: Twayne.

Chang, R. (2000). Why we need a critical Asian American legal studies. In J. Wu & M. Song (Eds.), *Asian American studies* (pp. 363–378). New Brunswick, NJ: Rutgers University Press.

Cheung, K. (1993). *Articulate silences: Hisaye Yamamoto, Maxine Hong Kingston, Joy Kogawa*. Ithaca, NY: Cornell University Press.

Chin, A. (2001). *A brief history of the model minority stereotype*. Available online at http://www.modelminority.com/history/primer.htm.

Dyer, R. (Ed.). (1977). *Gay and film*. London: British Film Institute.

Freer, R. (1994). Black-Korean conflict in the LA riot. In M. Baldassare (Ed.), *The Los Angeles riots: Lessons for the urban future* (pp. 175–214). Boulder: Westview Press.

Gilman, S. (1985). *Difference and pathology*. Ithaca, NY: Cornell University Press.

Gotanda, N. (2000). Multiculturalism and racial stratification. In J. Wu & M. Song (Eds.), *Asian American studies: A reader* (pp. 379–390). New Brunswick, NJ: Rutgers University Press.

Hall, S. (1982). The rediscovery of ideology: Return of the repressed in media studies. In M. Gurevitch, T. Bennett, J. Curran, & J. Woollacott (Eds.), *Culture, society and the media* (pp. 56–90). London: Methuen.

Lee, S. (1996). *Unraveling the model minority stereotype*. New York: Teachers College Press.

Lott, J. T. (1998). *Asian Americans: From racial category to multiple identity*. Walnut Creek, CA: Altamira Press.

Mahdzan, F., & Ziegler, N. (2001). *Asian Americans: An analysis of negative stereotypical characters in popular media*. Available online at http://www.modelminority.com/media/stereotypical.htm.

Media Action Network for Asian Americans. (2001). *Restrictive portrayals of Asians in the media and how to balance them*. Available online at http://janet.org/manna/a_stereotypes.html.

Morson, G. S., & Emerson, C. (1994). *Mikhail Bakhtin: Creation of prosaics.* Stanford, CA: Stanford University Press.

Ng, A. (2001). 10 issues commonly faced by Asian American professionals. *Northwest Asian Weekly, 20* (April 20), p. 8.

Ovando, C. (2001). Interrogating stereotypes: The case of the Asian model minority. *Newsletter of the Asian Culture Center,* Indiana University. Available online at http://www.modelminority.com/academia/interrogating.htm.

Petersen, W. (1966). Success story, Japanese American style. *New York Times Magazine,* 6 (January 6).

Said, E. W. (1978). *Orientalism.* New York: Vintage.

West, C. (1993). *Race matters.* Boston: Beacon.

Chapter 12

Asian Indians[1] and the Model Minority Narrative: A Neocolonial System

Archana J. Bhatt

> It is a peculiar sensation, this double-consciousness, this sense of always looking at one's self through the eyes of others, of measuring one's soul by the tape of a world that looks on in amused contempt and pity. One ever feels his two-ness—an American and a Negro; two unreconciled strivings; two warring ideals in one dark body, whose dogged strength alone keeps it from being torn asunder. The history of the American Negro is the history of this strife—this longing to attain self-conscious manhood, to merge his double self into a better and truer self. In this merging he wishes neither of the older selves to be lost. He would not Africanize America, for America has too much to teach the world and Africa. He would not bleach his Negro soul in a flood of white Americanism, for he knows that Negro blood has a message for the world. He simply wishes to make it possible for a man to be both a Negro and an American, without being cursed or spit upon by his fellows, without having the doors of Opportunity closed roughly in his face.
>
> —W. E. B. Du Bois

W. E. B. Du Bois's prophetic insights at the turn of twentieth century reflect the essence of being a person of color in the larger matrix of race politics in the United States. However, within and between communities of color there are important differences in the ways in which these communities negotiate status in relation to the dominant culture. As an Asian Indian/Indian American,[2] my own history and experience as a person of color in the United States is qualitatively different from the experiences of my African American and Latino/a brothers and sisters. For most Asian Americans, our space in the race matrix of the United States is complicated by our positioning as model minorities. Since the 1960s, Asians have been portrayed as a model minority, a phrase originally used to identify individuals of color who conformed to the dominant social system (see *Newsweek*, "Outwhiting the Whites" and *U.S. News & World Report*, 1966, "Success Story of One Minority Group in the U.S."). However, this positioning of Asian Americans as a model minority has been fraught with the political tensions of the day and served to position Asian Americans against African Americans and Latino/as (see Morrison, 1994). Additionally, this notion is measured against an unspoken standard of whiteness. Much work has recently been done on the notion of whiteness (see Frankenberg, 1993; Martin & Nakayama, 2000). Until this recent surge in questioning whiteness, much of our understanding of cultural identity stemmed from the position of that which was unlike the norm. This idea of normal was never explicitly named, though it served as the standard by which all others were measured. This notion of whiteness underscores my discussion of model minorities.[3]

THE MODEL MINORITY
AND CURRENT AMERICAN POLITICS

The term *model minority* is utilized across the U.S. political spectrum in a variety of ways. Both right-wing conservatives and left-wing neoliberals utilize this term specifically in relation to Asian Americans. Though their intent may be distinctly different, the outcome is similarly problematic. Right-wing conservatives present the model minority narrative as an indication of successful assimilation. Model minority groups are seen as capable of making it as Americans in a particular economic, urban, white American way. Neoliberals present the idea of model minority couched in larger terms of multiculturalism, diversity, and cultural tolerance. However, the diversity is measured in quantitative terms, and the multiculturalism often is a vehicle for exoticizing difference. For neoliberals, model minorities represent the best of a multicultural America—community members who serve as a source of learning about the world, ambassadors of America's openness/tolerance of difference, and proof of America's diversity as a community.

Regardless of political leanings, model minority status relegates Asian Americans to being perpetual foreigners desperately striving to distance themselves from their origins while also trying to maintain a Westernized sense of cultural purity. Specifically, the origins we drive to separate ourselves from are rural, communal identities, which are seen as illiterate, backward, and poor. The type of Indianness that is acceptable is a more urban, cosmopolitan, Orientalist image of India—a jewel-in-the-crown type of image.[4]

However, both political ideologies beg the question regarding the actual experiences of these particular groups. As current research indicates (see Bhatt, 2002; Cooks, 2001; Kramer, 2000; Pathak, 1998) assimilation is not a plausible reality for immigrants. Additionally, the assimilationist position presumes the superiority of one culture over another, namely, the superiority of American culture over one's own culture of origin. The neoliberal attitude of diversity and tolerance is also problematic. To begin with, diversity is predominantly a quantitative argument. Statistical balance (see U.S. census for 2000) is seen as equivalent to social acceptance of various groups. Additionally, this reinforces a visiocentric perspective that the diversity we see (such as images of people of color on TV, in advertisements, and in other media) is equivalent to a groundswell of support for these groups (Kramer, 1988, 1993). Or such visible presentations of communities of color indicate that these communities are making it and have earned equal status in the United States. Second, the position of tolerance also presumes the superiority of one group over another. The implicit argument is that the dominant group is benevolent enough to accept difference—a "kind master" positioning. This reinforces the hierarchical positioning of the dominant American culture as normal and everything else as different. Although neoliberalism is much more benevolent in its assessment of difference, it still positions culture in a hierarchy with a particular American culture as the standard of measurement.

These readings of the model minority narrative frame my examination of the model minority experience among Asian Indians in the United States. Earlier essays in this volume thoroughly discuss the model minority experience for African Americans and other specific Asian American groups. My work specifically examines the model minority experience through the frame of the Asian Indian experience in the United States. Focusing on the utilization of the term *model minority* and the application of the model minority narrative by and for the Asian Indian American community, I argue that the model minority narrative in the United States presents a classic neocolonial system that serves the purposes of the growing dominant monoculture—namely, a Western, technological, urban society. This dominant monoculture, epitomized by "America," is encroaching all over the world.[5] However, the perpetuation of this ideology on communities of color in the United States is especially problematic.

The model minority narrative reinforces the ability of a particular ethnic group to maintain a high economic standard, superior academic achievement, low levels of crime and domestic violence, a clear sense of native culture appropriately reflected in specific, controlled ways and healthy, well-developed familial relationships. Furthermore, the narrative tends to perpetuate a certain whitewashing of Indian American society.[6] It rewards behaviors and attitudes that support an elite white minority while using certain minority groups as yardsticks of measure over other minority groups without taking into consideration significantly different immigration histories. This narrative plays out in the Indian American community at various levels. It is both utilized by the community to secure a spot in the race matrix of the United States and abhorred by the community as a repressive tool that limits Indian Americans.

Asian Indian Immigration

To clearly understand the Asian Indian as a model minority, it is important to first examine the immigration history of this community in relation to other

Asian Americans. Like other Asian American immigrants, Asian Indian immigration skyrocketed after 1965, when the 1924 Immigration Act (which banned Asian immigration into the United States) was overturned by the civil rights amendment. However, in particular ways, this group was distinctly different from other Asian immigrants.

First, this group of immigrants came to the United States voluntarily. This notion of voluntarism is based on U.S. Immigration and Naturalization Service's assumptions about what drives populations to leave their native lands and come to the United States. For most post-1965 Indian immigrants, there were no external economic or political forces driving them out of India. These immigrants were not economically, religiously, or politically persecuted. Furthermore, though India is a so-called third world nation and an impoverished land, the post-1965 Indian immigrant was not an impoverished member of Indian society, nor was he a political insurgent seeking protection.

Asian Indian immigrants are in some ways the quintessential immigrants in that they came to the United States to follow the American dream. This dream was an economic dream of their own making. It was a dream of having even more than they already had, a dream of wealth according to Western standards. However, unlike previous immigrants, Indian Americans carried none of the stigma attached to other immigrant groups. They were not the poor, unwanted, unsuccessful members of their own country who were looking for a place to start over. Rather, they were the upper echelon of their own society looking to further improve their lives. These Indians had economic and social security in their own society; however, they immigrated to the United States to further their personal economic strength and gain greater opportunity, educational and otherwise. Asian Indians immigrated so that they could come to America, not so they could leave India.

A second element of Asian Indian immigration into the United States is that most of the post-1965 immigrants had been very much an upper-class, upper-caste population in India. Chandrasekhar (1983) reports that the majority of post-1965 immigrants were either professional, technical, and kindred workers or housewives, children, and others with no occupation reported (p. 90). This further implies that most post-1965 immigrants were white-collar workers who immigrated with entire families. Though the immigration demographics have changed in the past fifteen to twenty years,[7] the post-1965 population that came to the United States included upper-class, well-educated, wealthy citizens with high social status. These individuals were the urban elite of India, members of its upper middle class and upper castes. Their economic status was comparable to the middle class of the United States, and their social class was comparable to the upper class of the United States.

Although Asian Indian immigration has drastically changed over the past twenty years, the primary migrant cohort presents us with a clear picture of the community in general. This migrant cohort is further expanded to include the second-generation children of the post-1965 immigrants, and the newer group of H1B visa holders and their families. (These groups will also be discussed in the context of the model minority narrative.[8]) This immigration from India was a startling and difficult experience for many. Many of the women came over primarily to accompany their husbands and had no specific desire for immigrating to the United States (see Hegde, 1999). Though the language was not as severe a problem for immigrants from India in comparison to other Asian immigrant groups (India has English medium schools and many of the immigrants attended schools where English was a required course), there was some discomfort in using the language with non-Indians. To offset the discomfort, ethnic enclaves provided a comfort zone where one could act as though one were back in India.[9] Additionally, these older immigrants saw themselves as mere sojourners who would return to their home once they had achieved their dreams in the United States.[10]

These initial experiences of immigration were documented in a particular body of literature that emerged in the late 1970s and continued throughout the 1980s. This body of literature serves to present a particularly strong narrative of the model minority. In particular ways, much of the literature about Asian Indians, by Indian Americans and others, serves to perpetuate the narrative in that it presents Asian Indians as a community that has managed to make it in the United States and does not suffer any severe negative repercussions from its migration. This literature clearly shows how Indian Americans have internalized the model minority narrative as a source of power for themselves and their community. Reinforcing a strong sense of hegemony, the narrative positions Indian Americans as "acceptable" others who, if they continue to meet appropriate standards, will receive appropriate rewards. These rewards are then seen by the community as just and acceptable without questioning the cost. Thus, the community itself presents an image, which they believe will strengthen their status and position in the United States (Gramsci, 1972). Furthermore, many of these immigrants have already internalized a sense of urban superiority given their status in India.

The Model Minority Narrative
in Asian Indian Literature

Much of the literature about Indian immigration focuses on the primary differences between Indian and American cultures and how those differences are negotiated. Most of the literature has an anecdotal tone and focuses on a few typical, usually ideal examples of Indian immigrants (Dasgupta, 1989; Helweg & Helweg, 1990; Saran, 1985; Saran & Eames, 1980).

There are several pervasive themes throughout this body of literature that serve to enlighten the reader about what it means for Asian Indians to immigrate to the United States. But it also serves to set a very specific image about the Indian community in general. One such underlying result of the Indian immigrant literature is the perpetuation of the notion of model minority. As explained earlier, this narrative rewards behaviors and attitudes that support an elite white minority while using certain minority groups as yardsticks of measure over other minority groups, without taking into consideration significantly different immigration histories.

The Indian immigrant literature further reinforces a sense of cultural preservation and cultural continuity that is deemed acceptable by the dominant monoculture. This notion of acceptable culture is a primary aspect of the model minority narrative. It serves to set up a colonial reading of Indianness (the exotic) and to set boundaries on the acceptable degree of difference. Saran and Eames (1980) began this wave of literature with their text, *The New Ethnics*. This collection of essays defines the Indian immigrant in the United States. Saran's next work, *The Asian Indian Experience in the United States* (1985), focused on ten case studies of typical Indian families. Another such text is *An Immigrant Success Story* (1990) by Arthur and Usha Helweg. This text followed the process of immigration from the first decision to immigrate to the situation of the immigrated family in today's times. Dasgupta's (1989) *On the Trail of an Uncertain Dream* is also a case study analysis in which she reviews the experiences of several immigrant families.

Much of this literature presents variations of specific themes. To begin with, there is a strong profile of the typical Indian immigrant. Saran provides the description of such a typical immigrant:

It is a relatively young population, the majority of them coming from urban and upper caste backgrounds in India. The average family size is not more than four or five. The most unique characteristic of this population is its high level of educational and professional attainment. Its income is high, more than 50 percent live in their own homes, and they are savings and investment oriented. In terms of their behavior patterns [after immigration to the United States] we find that while they have the potential for acculturation because of their knowledge of and proficiency in English, basically their behavior is more in line with the Indian ethos. (1985, pp. 46–47)

This description provides a sense of where the Indian immigrant fits into the milieu of American society. Furthermore, such a profile establishes a standard by which Indian Americans measure themselves and each other. It sets up its own version of keeping up with the Joneses. Additionally, we see a clear emergence of the dominant monoculture of Western technological urbanization. This particular description of the "typical" Asian Indian immigrant is problematic because it privileges a very particular group of Indians, specifically upper-class, upper-caste Indians from large urban metropolises in India. This particular description disregards many of the lower-class, rural Indians who are also now attempting to immigrate to the United States. It upholds an ideal of small nuclear families that, though able to become American, choose to uphold particular cultural behaviors. It is important to note that this Indian ethos refers to a very particular presentation of the Indian culture. It emphasizes a sense of absolute familial harmony and linguistic fluency perfectly balanced with complete economic success.

In addition to this profile, a central theme for Indian Americans is the importance of culture. Many of the participants cited in the literature discuss the importance of not losing their culture. The quotations revolve around the individuals' needs to show that their culture is the most important part of their identity and that it cannot be compromised regardless of where he or she lives. Additionally, the culture is upheld as the foundational structure on which these families build their lives. In the Indian immigrant literature written by non-Indians, this theme is presented in a positive light, reinforcing the power of the joint family, the amazing level of linguistic retention, and the seemingly smooth obedience of the next generation, regardless of any earlier conflict. In fact, if the conflict between the generations is addressed, the focus is more on the parental concern over the child's success rather than on questions of identity that many second-generation immigrants face. The examination of conflict focuses on the ultimate acquiescence of youth to follow family-set plans. This representation glorifies the strong sense of values, which clearly reflect the family values put forth by political conservatives in the United States.

Regardless of the value of these patterns of behavior, this description does serve a specific political agenda. The value of good placed on the notion of cultural preservation helps separate Indians from mainstream society. This separation serves the model minority narrative in that Indian culture is kept apart from everyday interaction and presented to the white community in very particular ways. However, in seeming contradiction of that separateness, Indians are touted as a model minority because of their economic standing in U.S. society. It is often noted that despite being wealthy and actively participating in American society, these people have managed to keep their culture intact. However, as Dasgupta (1989) notes, this economic standing is exactly the force that allows the Indian American population the freedom from assimilative pressures. By having an already established status in American society (monetary status), Indian Americans do not need to culturally assimilate to show their closeness to mainstream society. Thus, unlike other ethnic groups, there is not as great a pull to "be white." Their difference is seen as acceptable.

This is true for Indian American individuals who came to the United States later in life. However, Indian American youth born and brought up in the United States face a very different experience in regard to their ethnic identity. Indian American youth do often feel that their two worlds (of Indian and American) are extremely far apart and extremely difficult to merge. They see their worlds as two worlds that are separate: Indian at home and American outside the home.

The notion of culture that is touted by Indian Americans is rather unique to the Indian community in the United States.[11] Saran and Eames (1980, p. 178) explain that much of the organization of Indian communities in the United States is based on language and religious affiliation. Dasgupta (1989) indicates that for most Indians, the cultures provide a polarity by which to measure behavior. For most Indians, all things good are Indian. However, this does not necessarily mean all things bad are American. Regarding the prioritizing of values, the literature indicates that many Indians see Americans as lacking morality, specifically in regard to sex. Americans are also seen as being too self-centered and extremist in their behavior. Though there is no need to test or question these values or the hierarchy of these values, this polarity does present a very specific image of Indian Americans and their values.

Dasgupta (1989) refers to this prioritizing of cultural values as cultural selectivity and further indicates that this is a key survival mechanism for Indian Americans. However, this cultural balancing act is not a form of conformist adaptation. Additionally, this value hierarchy reflects something much more than a functional selection of behavior. It serves to reinforce a sense of separateness between "Indian" and "American." This separation in turn helps reinforce one's place in the larger matrix of society. Dasgupta (1989), Saran (1985), and others have all found that most Indians feel that they can act and interact in America without becoming American. Furthermore, rather than facilitating a sense of adaptation, this sense of separateness keeps Indians from viewing themselves as members of American society.

The literature (Dasgupta, 1989; Helweg & Helweg, 1990; Melendy, 1977; Saran, 1985; Saran & Eames, 1980; Takaki, 1989) empirically and consistently demonstrates the intense cultural efforts by Indian Americans to preserve their culture. The literature indicates that most Indian Americans feel that preservation of their culture is of the utmost importance and should be passed on to their children. This is best achieved by joining Indian organizations, participating in religious activities, socializing with other Indians, and traveling to India. Even more moderate Western couples turn to traditional practices with the birth of their children. This cultural preservation is also achieved by marrying only within the Indian community. Though interracial marriages do exist in the Indian American community, they have not been common or easily accepted (see Bhatt, 2002).

Though this may not seem much different from most immigrant communities that have come to the United States, there are certain dynamics to the Asian Indian group that add dimensions to this intense effort at cultural preservation. First and foremost, the economic standing of this community grants its members the freedom to establish cultural centers, interact primarily with other Indians, and afford the requisite travel to India. As mentioned earlier, by having economic status, the Indian-American community is exempt from seeking cultural affiliation with the mainstream. Furthermore, the value hierarchy mentioned earlier reflects a strong political leaning in the United States. In keeping with the notion of family values as presented by Republicans, many Indians find that they fit in both politically and economically.

In the tradition of political and cultural hegemony, Indian Americans, along with other model minority groups, are rewarded for their sense of separateness. They then see this reward as acceptance into the mainstream. As already explicated, the typical post-1965 Indian immigrant fits into the mainstream of

American society in many ways. However, what is often lost is the notion that these individuals are still immigrants, regardless of their economic and educational profiles. What is actually rewarded is the separateness that Indian Americans tend to hold onto. The very fact that the culture is kept within the community creates a sense of Indian Americans knowing their place within the mainstream society.[12] The community thus creates the very environment in which they feel that discrimination hampers their complete success in American society.

As the Indian American community comes of age in the United States, other literature also emerges that reflects the issues of second-generation youth and their struggle for identity. The literature of the early 1990s tends to focus more on the issues of Indian American families and intergenerational questions rather than the history of Indian immigration and lifestyles of Indian Americans. Much of the focus of this literature is on the issues facing Indian parents and their children. The germinal text in this area is Priya Agarwal's (1991) *Post-1965 immigrants into the U.S.* Written from an insider perspective, Agarwal focuses her interviews with her participants solely on questions of negotiating the two cultures. There is much discussion about the negotiation of rules in the family over such issues as food habits (vegetarianism), clothing, hair, friends, dating, marriage, proper respect for elders, attitudes toward gender, and treatment of family members. Though this book illuminates some key problems in the Indian American community, it also serves to polarize the two cultures even further, creating a sense that one can only be Indian or American and that children will be lost unless great care is taken in their upbringing.

Bacon (1996) focuses several of her questions on how culture is preserved and maintained and how it is transmitted to the next generation. Such research carries with it assumptions that inform the results of the study. The primary assumption in this body of literature is the problematizing of identity and the polarizing of the two cultures. The questions are based on the assumptions that families see the cultures as being in conflict and each negotiation results in one winning over the other. This creates the sense of two worlds that are separate and must be carefully managed to avoid the Western culture running rampant over the Indian culture.

Finally, there is a new, growing body of literature that focuses on the sense of hyphenated identity. For example, *Our Feet Walk the Sky, Contours of the Heart*, and *Bolo! Bolo!* are anthologies that focus on the peoples of the South Asian diaspora. There are short stories, essays, poetry, and autobiographical sketches that present the continuing experiences of people who are living in the space of the hyphen. This literature serves to illuminate the purgatory of model minority status for many 1.5- and second-generation Indian Americans.[13] For many Indian American youth, model minority status is problematic in several ways. First and foremost, it perpetuates the narrative that there is minimal struggle between Indian American youth and their elders. This minimization of struggle pushes these youth to mask the tensions that permeate their lives as they struggle to create a sense of space for themselves both in the host culture and at home. Second, much of this literature presents the continual quest to name and claim space in the larger U.S. race matrix. Many of these youth have a strong sense of connection to other communities of color and strive to build coalitions across community lines. However, the model minority narrative as a divisive force pulls Asian Americans away from African Americans and Latino/as. This works against the 1.5- and the second-generation youth in that it keeps them from cohorts who recognize and understand their racialized identities. This is complicated by the lack of understanding the parents have about why their children would want to associate with communities that do not garner respect in the United States.

Though the literature about Indian Americans has evolved to a certain degree, the predominant themes of typical Indian identity and cultural preservation are still the mainstays of the preponderance of literature about Indian Americans. Sheth (1995) provides even more specific information about the typical image and practices of Indian Americans that partially constitute the Indian American stereotype. Sheth points out that according to the 1990 census, Indians are the largest minority group represented in the medical profession. Additionally, many of the Indians who are not in professional occupations are often people with higher degrees who were unable to obtain comparable employment in the United States. He specifically refers to the growing number of Indian Americans who are small business owners, cab drivers, newsstand owners, and members of the hospitality industry. Sheth also notes, however, that New York City and its surrounding areas are the primary location for many of these Indians. The ethnic enclaves in this area are relatively new and represent the newest subgroup of Indian immigrants.

The bias in the literature about Indian Americans was perhaps an attempt on the part of authors to show the success of this immigrant group. However, as future generations of Indian Americans come of age, we begin to see a different image of the Indian American experience. Additionally, this driving need to assure a positive image for the community does not exist in a vacuum. The narrative of success is clearly intertwined with a stronger, more prevalent narrative of model minority identity.

The Model Minority Quest

As already discussed, many Asian Indians immigrated to the United States to follow the quintessential American dream. This quest for the American dream presents its own set of confounding identities within the Indian community. Though many Asian Indians say they are not American and are merely immigrants within this country, there are clear qualitative differences between Asian Indians and other immigrants. Many Asian Indians tend to identify with the wealthy elite in the United States, which also then translates into identifying with whites. Shukla (1997) explains that "class ascendancy has a discursive correlation with whiteness" (p. 311). She continues to explain that Indian Americans "in effect, opt out of racial hierarchy to cash in on their class privilege" (p. 312). Due to the economic privilege of this community as a whole and the native land status of most Indian immigrants, many Indians see themselves as most like the upper-class and conservative communities in the United States. Thus, they tend to identify with and are encouraged to identify with the largely Republican Caucasian community more so than with other immigrant or minority groups (see the works of such authors as Dinesh D'Souza). Yet Indian Americans continue to argue that they are not Americans. Indians feel that their ideology is best reflected by the upper class of the United States and that the Republican party doctrines best serve their needs as a community.[14]

However, in many ways, this could not be further from the truth. In the racial politics of the United States, Indians have been placed in the purgatory of model minority status by the dominant monoculture because of their economic success and their financial contributions to American society. Many Indians see this acceptance as equivalent to parallel social and economic status in the United States. However, this is not as clearly correlated as one might believe. In fact, many Indians do not recognize that in supporting those who are seemingly supporting them they may be digging their own graves. Additionally, Indian Americans also do not recognize that they are conforming to the very system that they claim to dislike so greatly. It is not possible to gain economic status without also gaining the underlying values of that status.

For example, during the 1996 election year, California Governor Pete Wilson made a "sovereign national borders" speech in which he called for the closing of national borders in hopes of retaining national sovereignty. Many of the Indians in California supported Wilson in his speech and his election because they perceived the tone of the speech to be about the influx of Hispanic immigration; what they did not realize was that the closing of borders is not a selective process. By decreasing immigration, Indian immigration is also limited. Additionally, identifying with the Caucasian community in the United States can lead to internalized self-hatred. In many ways, Indian Americans attempt to take on an "American" presentation, which leads them to criticize their own nonverbal presentation.

Another reason that Indians are so liked and have been labeled model minorities is that they are seen as not forcing themselves on American society. They are seen as a quiet, well-mannered group that works to maintain the status quo and achieve a place within that society. This aspect of model minority is further reinforced by a rather nostalgic image of Indianness. Mohanty (1993) discusses this concept in her personal essay about self-definition. "Any purely culturalist or nostalgic/sentimental definition of being 'Indian' or 'South Asian' was inadequate. Such definition fueled the 'model minority' myth. And this subsequently constituted us as 'outsiders/foreigners' or as interest groups who sought or had obtained the American Dream" (p. 354). This idea of model minority is utilized to set up a hierarchy of acceptable behavior among immigrants.

This often serves to pit certain immigrant groups against each other (a classic divide-and-conquer technique). Toni Morrison (1994) discusses the need for many immigrant groups to disassociate from the black American community. For many Indians, like other Asian immigrant groups, there is a powerful need to disassociate from black Americans and Mexican Americans. There is a sense among Asian immigrants that they are more like the upper-class whites in this country than like other immigrant groups, and the Asian immigrant groups work to perpetuate that similarity. In fact, Morrison (1994) argues that racial contempt for African Americans transforms other minorities into whites (p. 97). This similarity to white Americans is fostered by the dominant culture by showing the dissimilarity between Asian immigrants and other minority groups, such as African Americans and Mexican Americans. This need to disassociate is a "need" only from the point of view of the model minority criteria propagated by the mainstream culture. This need (if one wants to be a "success") is further fostered by the model minority system in the United States. What is lost in this disassociation is that the issues of minority rights in this country are not based on which minority one is when laws restricting minorities are passed. They often also affect the Indian American community.

Model Minority Narrative as a Neocolonial System

The model minority discourse in the United States has evolved to such a place that it has moved from singular group analysis to a pervasive inscription of Asian immigration. In many ways model minorities are used as individual agents for transcending oppression, yet they are still marked as different/other. The model minority narrative in the United States is a classic colonial setup. Much like the British raj in India and the slave–master relationship in the pre–Civil War South, Asian Americans are utilized as first-tier minorities to control other minorities. In India, upper-caste, upper-class Indians (predominantly Brahmins and the royal families) were given entry into the British community and then utilized as tools through which to control the masses. In the American South, house slaves were given particular rights and used as markers by which to measure field slaves. It is crucial to understand that by no means am I equating the two experiences here. Rather, the argument is that the colonizer/master had similar intentions and set similar tones, which highlight the similar sensation of these two distinctly different experiences.

It is also important to claim up front that Asian Indians are seen as people of color and suffer oppression in very real ways, as did upper-class/upper-caste Indians in the British raj and house slaves did in the South. Yet both these groups had distinct positions that led to their "status" with their colonizer. For upper-caste, upper-class Indians, aligning with the British helped reinforce the caste system and protect the wealth of the royal families. For the British, the Indian royalty provided financial backing and the Brahmins provided social status and a way through which to approach the masses. The relationship was benevolent yet clearly controlled by the British.[15] For house slaves in the South, their status guaranteed basic needs (housing, food, clothing); for the masters, house slaves became an image to be held up to the field slaves as proof that the other slaves were responsible for their own plight, given that one of their own could succeed. Again, the master was in clear control of the relationship and, unlike the British–Indian relationship, this particular interaction was fraught with tensions and violence.[16] Again, this does not imply that Indian royalty and house slaves did not understand the politics of their positions. Rather, the focus is on how the colonizer/master negotiated the particular issue of status among the colonized/enslaved.

Another important layer in the master-slave relationship was the issue of appearance and cultural acceptability. House slaves were often lighter in color and tended to have more Anglicized features. This was in part because they were often the illegitimate offspring of the master. This made them more palatable to the slave owners and garnered them more access to the master's family. Appearance was also an issue with Indians and the British. The more acceptable Indians were those who had a more urban, educated presentation. In fact, it was Gandhi's insistence of wearing the *dhoti* (a villager's garb) that was often problematic for many British who were forced to deal with him.

The Double Bind

In many ways the current model minority system parallels the two colonial systems. However, there is one crucial difference in this modern system. In very problematic ways, the nature of hegemony differs between minority groups. Because it is predominantly discursive in nature (lacking physical proof of the ideology) the model minority system is presented as apolitical. This empowers the dominant group in that they are taken at face value. Additionally, the model minority ideology is couched in the greater narrative of equality in the United States. This further leads Asian Indians to believe that they have a chance of breaking the racial glass ceiling and achieving dominant culture status. Asian Indians buy into the argument that their group is special, and any questions of identity that occur with second-generation youth are anomalies that can be ultimately discounted. This is then contradicted by the dominant culture's view that individuals have the capacity to transcend the group and succeed.

Thus, a double bind emerges for Indian Americans. If they continue to identify as Indians and members of the group, they maintain a sense of perpetual foreignness; if they do ultimately succeed, they are no longer really Indian. Also, if they cannot resolve questions of identity, they are not part of the group, yet these questions of identity mark their true experience in the United States.

Currently, due to their economic status, model minority groups are touted as being "on the right track" and "like true Americans," creating a sense that mere hard work within the given structure will give them the social status of Caucasians. However, what is not realized is that they will never be mainstream whites, thus, they never receive the rewards of that social status. Regardless, these groups are held up as examples of potential success to other minority groups because they are better off than the average American both economically and educationally. At the same time, this success is being attacked as a form of reverse discrimination. For example, university admissions processes are seen as being overrun by Asians. In fact, given this current uproar, the University of California system has eliminated race as an admissions category.

The argument is made that these model minority groups have been here for far less time than other minorities and have still managed to rise far above those other minorities. Additionally, it is argued that success among model minorities is achieved without any complaint or anger about inequality on the part of the minority. In fact, accepting inequality is seen as proof of one's Americanness. Especially in light of the September 11, 2001, terrorist attacks, many Muslim Americans were told that cooperating with questioning and federal investigations was part of their duty as Americans, regardless of their lost civil rights.

What is not recognized are the historical experiences of these groups. Most model minorities came to the United States after the 1960s and the civil rights movement. They do not share a history of racial inequality and thus buy into the myth that there is no difference between them and the upper-class elite Caucasian community, and thus they face no issues of racism or discrimination.[17] Additionally, model minorities enter the United States with a much more stable economic base than other minorities have had in the past. Thus the comparison between so-called model minorities and other minorities is an inaccurate one. They do not begin at the same starting line. Specifically, for many Asian Indians in the United States, there is also an internalized Britishness that mirrors the fundamental characteristics of the model minority narrative. As already explained, there is an ability to use English, a notion of democratic nation, and a sense of social hierarchy and granted status. This often leads Asian Indians to be more susceptible to the model minority myth.

CONCLUSION

Model minorities are a central part of a much larger race matrix in the United States. They represent the best of America by showing the democratic system as its ideal. But they also represent the worst in that model minority narrative upholds unspoken, powerful racial hierarchies that undergird the American social system. This chapter has served to examine how the model minority narrative in the United States is both utilized by Asian Indians as a tool for social power and for Asian Indians as a tool to control other minority groups. Furthermore, I examined the emerging dominant monoculture that privileges urban, technological wealth over rural, physical, communal bartering systems. In many ways, Asian Americans' fascination with America makes them an ideal tool through which to control and disperse a very specific value system. This fascination with such a growing monoculture is not unique to Asian Americans but in many ways is geared toward them. As Du Bois so profoundly articulated in 1903, the goal of hyphenated identity is not to overpower one culture with another. Rather, it is the recognition of difference as a natural, normal process of society that best serves the larger race matrix in the United States.

NOTES

1. The term *Asian Indian* is utilized by the U.S. Census Bureau to refer to immigrants from South Asia, including India, Pakistan, Sri Lanka, Bangladesh, Nepal, and Bhutan. I utilize both *Asian American* and *Indian American*. The term *Indian American* is often used to refer to the children of Indian immigrants. The term *South Asian* is also gaining strength; however, it refers to a specific political, social, and cultural movement among the second-generation communities and deserves a separate essay.

2. In this chapter, I switch between hyphenating *Indian American* and not hyphenating the term. I posit that the presence of the hyphen is, in a hermeneutic sense, highly contextual. Specifically, I do this to highlight the question of the hyphen in the community. In many ways, the hyphen serves to reinforce a false polarity between the two identities; in other ways, the hyphen simply articulates a polemic of identity that permeates the Indian-American experience. Cultural identity is a much contested issue within the community, which struggles to name an identity that speaks to both their American and Indian worlds.

3. This notion of whiteness is also further problematized by socioeconomic status, education, urbanization, and class. The complex intersection of these issues with whiteness leads to the uprising of a dominant monoculture as posited by the essays collected in this volume.

4. The idea of appropriate Indianness is clearly defined in very particular Western ways. This is what I mean by Westernized sense of cultural purity. This presentation is usually stereotypical, exotic, based on what Edward Said calls an Orientalist gaze (1978).

5. This question of privileging an urban, technological, wealthy society is fast becoming a problematic issue in India as well and deserves attention in a separate essay.

6. Here, I use the term *whitewash* to mean that the cultural difference of a group is glossed over and erased in a manner that serves to homogenize the group so that they seem to be one singular group in the eyes of the dominant society and that one group is fast approaching the status of the dominant culture. This is done to appease the community of color and to keep the dominant group comfortable in their treatment of others; it is never truly possible to become a member of the dominant group in the eyes of the dominant group.

7. The status of these upper-class, upper-caste groups has changed in India as well. However, this change is not one that is familiar or recognizable for many Indian Americans.

8. Current census data indicates that the Asian Indian population has increased 106 percent in ten years (1990–2000). A majority of this increase has been due to the high influx of H1B visa holders and their families. This group adds a unique element to the model minority argument. This will be discussed as a separate issue in the essay.

9. Much of the immigrant group, once in the United States, went to primarily urban areas, such as New York, Chicago, California, New Jersey, and, more recently, Texas. This pattern of migration led to the establishment of Little India consumer hubs in many of these states. It also created strong urban enclaves of Indian communities reinforcing strong ethnic bonds. However, it is important to note that these enclaves are somewhat dissimilar to the previous European enclaves of the 1800s. Little Indias mostly tended to be business centers with large concentrations of merchants providing Indian necessities such as food, clothing, jewelry, media, and services. Even today, Little Indias are not necessarily neighborhoods where only Indians live, as was common with European immigrant communities. However, it is important to note that the Indian community in the United States is rapidly changing. Even as this essay is being written, the community is reshaping itself to fit in with Western society. Though the Indian community has traditionally been a "community in being" (using Goffman's term), there has been a recent rise in more traditional enclaves in the past five to ten years. Areas such as Flushing, New York; Jackson Heights, New York; Bergen County, New Jersey; and Arlington, Texas, are rapidly becoming dominant Indian neighborhoods.

10. See Pathak (1998) for a complete discussion of the "myth of return."

11. There is a good amount of research on Indian immigration into other parts of the world; however, these narrative are distinctly different from the U.S. immigrant narrative. The communities of Indians in England, Africa, the Far East, and the Caribbean are at different points in the cycle of immigration and are somewhat dissimilar to the Indian population in the United States. Much of the literature indicates that U.S. immigration is unlike other Indian immigration, with the exception of perhaps Canada.

12. By the phrase *knowing their place*, I refer to the public and definite sense of the race and ethnic hierarchy in the United States. Though not as blatant as the knowing their place expected of African Americans, there is a specific place for Indian Americans and other Asian Americans.

13. The term *1.5er* is commonly used in Asian American studies to refer to Asian American youth who were born in their parents' country of origin and were then brought to the United States at an early age. Second-generation, then, are Asian American youth who are born in the United States to immigrant parents. The term *1.5er* is used to highlight the differences between the children of immigrants who are born in the same generation.

14. This party affiliation analysis is specific to older Asian Indians, who tend to be high-volume business owners and more socially conservative. Younger Indian Americans are quickly finding their voice in the Democratic party politics as they work to ensure civil rights for South Asians in America.

15. Because this was a colonial system, the Indian groups did recognize the polemic of their interactions with the British. For many, it became a tenuous balancing act between alliance with the colonizer and support of a growing underground freedom movement.

16. This is not to say that there was no violence among the upper-class/upper-caste Indians and the Brits. However, it was much less in the public eye and it was less discussed.

17. Regardless, when discussing issues of race, most Indians clearly state that they prefer doing business with other Indians to ensure fair treatment. It seems to be an issue of the threshold of discrimination. The position is that when comparing themselves to American society in its entirety, Indians are no different from the upper-class whites of this country; however, when compared to the upper-class whites of this country, Indians are somewhat better.

REFERENCES

Agarwal, P. (1991). *Post-1965 immigrants into the U.S.* Palo Alto, CA: Yuvati Press.

Bacon, J. (1996). *Life lines: Community, family, and assimilation among Asian Indian immigrants.* New York: Oxford University Press.

Bhatt, A. J. (2002). Mate selection among Asian Indians living in America: A quest for traditional ritual. In P. Cooper and J. Richard Hoel Jr. (Eds.), *Intercultural communication: A reader.* Boston: Allyn & Bacon.

Chandrasekhar, S. (Ed.). (1983). *From India to America: A brief history of immigration, problems of discrimination admission and assimilation.* La Jolla, CA: Population Review.

Cooks, L. (2001). From distance and uncertainty to research and pedagogy in the borderlands: Implications for the future of intercultural communication. *Communication Theory, 11,* 339–351.

Dasgupta, S. S. (1989). *On the trail of an uncertain dream: Indian immigrant experience in America.* New York: AMS Press.

Du Bois, W. E. B. (1903/1989). *The souls of black folk.* New York: Bantam.

Frankenburg, R. (1993). *White women, race matters: The social construction of whiteness.* Minneapolis: University of Minnesota Press.

Gramsci, A. (1972). *Selections from the prison notebooks of Antonio Gramsci* (Q. Hoare & G. N. Smith, Eds. & Trans.). New York: International.

Hegde, R. S. (1999). Swinging the trapeze: The negotiation of identity among Asian Indian immigrant women in the United States. In D. V. Tanno & A. Gonzalez (Eds.), *Communication and identity: International and intercultural annual.* Thousand Oaks, CA: Sage.

Helweg, A. W., & Helweg, U. M. (1990). *An immigrant success story: East Indians in America.* Philadelphia: University of Pennsylvania Press.

Kramer, E. (1988). *Television criticism and the problem of ground: Interpretation after deconstruction.* Ann Arbor, MI: University Microfilms.

Kramer, E. (1993). Understanding co-constitutional genesis. *Integrative Explorations: Journal of Culture and Consciousness, 1,* 41–47.

Kramer, E. (1997). *Modern/post-modern: Off the beaten path of antimodernism.* Westport, CT: Praeger.

Kramer, E. (2000). Cultural fusion and the defense of difference. In M. Asante & J. Min (Eds.), *Socio-cultural conflict between African and Korean Americans* (pp. 183–230). New York: University Press of America.

Martin, J. N., & Nakayama, T. K. (2000). *Intercultural communication in contexts*, 2d ed. Mountain View, CA: Mayfield Publishers.

Melendy, H. B. (1977). *Asians in America: Filipinos, Koreans, and East Indians*. Boston, MA: Twayne.

Mohanty, C. T. (1993). Defining genealogies: Feminist reflections on being South Asian in North America. In South Asian Descent Collective (Ed.), *Our feet walk the sky: Women of the South Asian diaspora*. Berkeley, CA: Aunt Lute Books.

Morrison, T. (1994). On the backs of blacks. In N. Mills (Ed.), *Arguing immigration: Are new immigrants a wealth of diversity ... or a crushing burden?* New York: Touchstone/Simon and Schuster.

Pathak, A. A. (1998). *To be Indian (hyphen) American: Communicating diaspora, identity and home*. Unpublished dissertation, University of Oklahoma, Norman.

Said, E. W. (1978). *Orientalism*. New York: Vintage.

Saran, P. (1985). *The Asian Indian experience in the United States*. Cambridge, MA: Shenckman Publishing.

Saran, P., & Eames, E. (1980). *The new ethnics: Asian Indians in the United States*. New York: Praeger.

Sheth, M. (1995). Asian Indian Americans. In P. G. Min (Ed.), *Asian Americans: Contemporary trends and issues*. Thousand Oaks, CA: Sage.

Shukla, S. (1997). Building diaspora and nation: The 1991 cultural festival of India. *Cultural Studies, 11*, 296–315.

Takaki, R. (1989). *India in the West: South Asians in America*. New York: Chelsea House.

Chapter 13

A World of Cookie-Cutter Faces

Rachael Rainwater-McClure, Weslynn Reed, and Eric Mark Kramer

Because I didn't like my nose, there was a time when I was young and I used to go to bed every night with the tip of my nose taped up so that it would be shorter and upturned.

—Steven Spielberg

PRESCRIPT

On arrival in the United States, a Japanese foreign exchange student purchased and began to peruse all types of American magazines: fashion, family, and even baby magazines. When questioned by her host family as to what she found so interesting in the magazines she declared, "Americans are so much more beautiful than my people!" (personal experience).

"BEAUTIFUL PEOPLE"

The feelings of this exchange student are not unique. She is not alone in feeling as though her own physical attributes are inferior to those traditionally valued by Westerners. Many go so far as to alter their bodies to look like the "beautiful people" on the glossy pages of Western magazines. Particularly for Asians, cosmetic surgery, colored contact lenses, and hair dyes are popular means of transforming their bodies and faces into the images found in the media (Darling-Wolf, 2000).

Such observations lead one to ask several questions concerning cross-cultural perceptions of beauty. What are the factors influencing individuals to perceive their own bodies as less than adequate? What leads these same people to internalize these perceptions to the extent that they alter their bodies and faces? The theories of W. E. B. Du Bois and Naomi Wolfe can be applied to answer these questions and illuminate this phenomenon.

Double Consciousness

In *The Souls of Black Folk* (1903/1995), W. E. B. Du Bois discusses the experiences of black people in the United States and describes a phenomenon he called double consciousness. This phenomenon, experienced by many ethnic minorities, is the process of internalizing the viewpoint of the dominant culture. One values what is valued by the dominant ethnicity within one's society. In terms of phenotypic aesthetics, that usually means that the facial characteristics most valued are those inherent of the dominant group. The more a minority internalizes the dominant sense of beauty in the process of assimilation, the more such a minority is challenged by a look that they do not possess (Kramer & Ikeda, 2000). Du Bois portrays this sensation as a "sense of always looking at one's self through the eyes of others, of measuring one's soul by the tape of a world that looks on in amused contempt and pity." It is "two warring ideals in one dark body" (Du Bois, 1903/1995, p. 45).

Kramer (2000) introduces the idea of cultural fusion as the combining of elements within two or more cultures to create new cultural forms. But not all fusion leads to peace of mind or so-called psychic equilibrium. The theory of cultural fusion is not prescriptive, as in social engineering. It does not ideologically justify any certain and singular course of action for all people in their efforts to be happy. Rather it is observed that efforts to assimilate can and often do lead to a con-fusion and a chronic sense of alienation. Du Bois's theory also deals with cultural fusion. What he describes is the fusion of consciousness itself. Within a minority person, the identity of the Other is fused with the identity of the dominant group, creating a painful tension, what can be called a chronic sense of cognitive dissonance; in this case about one's very face.

Richard Wright, in *White Man Listen!*, uses Nietzsche's concept of a frog's perspective to describe this phenomenon. It is the perspective of someone looking upward and measuring him- or herself by what is perceived as "above," in psychological distance. "A certain degree of hate combined with love (ambivalence) is always involved in this looking from below upward and the object against which the subject is measuring himself undergoes constant change. He loves the object because he would like to resemble it; he hates the object because his chances of resembling it are remote, slight" (quoted in Gilroy, 1993, p. 161). This is the internalization of what the dominant culture believes one is supposed to be. For black Americans, this is the acceptance of the false notion that "I am supposed to be white," along with the frequently painful realization that "I am not white and cannot be white." The same is true for people of other ethnic minorities or dominated groups who have accepted that there is one standard that is privileged and against which all others are compared (Kramer, 1993).

Standards or ideals of beauty, along with certain behavior patterns that are "normative," seem to reflect this phenomenon of double consciousness. These standards are the most easily replicable distinctions between one race or ethnicity and another, but although one may claim that beauty is only skin deep, the implications of such valuations are quite complex and profound. If one is compelled or inclined to attempt to fit in with white Americans, the first and seemingly most obvious course of action might be to try to conform to Caucasoid physical features before attending to anything else (Eichberg, 1999).

Beauty Myth

The beauty myth is a feminist theory by Naomi Wolfe (1991) that exposes as delusional the claim that one set of characteristics constitutes ideal beauty. She challenges the ideological gambit that claims for itself the mantle of naturalism. In other words, she does not passively accept the idea that certain looks are "naturally," "universally," "objectively" beautiful whereas others are not. Naturalizing (ethnocentric) discourses and beliefs are pragmatically (not merely theoretically) threatening to women's self-esteem, for the ideology suggests that all women must naturally want to look a certain way and that men must want to possess women who embody that look. Wolfe insists that the elevation and privileging of some body images and phenotypes over others is not natural but cultural (contingently within the realm of human free will) and therefore not beyond debate and modification. She argues that naturalized values that are promoted as being obvious and thus hegemonic work as a counterforce against women, keeping them controlled by a white male–dominated society. Bottom line: The more a woman really accepts (internalizes) this version of beauty, consciously or not (mostly unconsciously) the more she really does feel inadequate especially because she must age in the face of an overarching dogma of youthism. Thus, even if she once could and did approximate the ideal, she must suffer the reality of losing her looks. Thus, power relations even among women have changed in the modern world. Instead of looking forward to becoming the matriarch of her family, she fears becoming irrelevant as so defined by the dominant, patriarchal society.

A recent study of young Korean women who were receiving training to enter the workforce revealed the preferences of large (male-dominated) Korean companies for female employees who fit certain physical requirements for height and weight. The requirements were not needed for the actual performance of the job but were to satisfy the companies' definition of beauty (Cho, 2000). Until the mid-1980s, the selection for female clerical employees was based on their school grades, technical qualifications, and potential to fit into their business activities rather than specific physical requirements. But as of the late 1980s, the demand for certain physical requirements has been added to the job criteria. Vocational trainers explained that the trend toward hiring young women who fit the ideal beauty standard was predicted to increase because these women were increasingly hired for positions that dealt directly with the public and that "good looking women handle customers better ... with their nice smile and soft voices ... most complaints are easily resolved or decreased markedly" (Cho, 2000, p. 3). This explanation was given for all positions, even for those that did not deal directly with the public.

Women who accept the beauty myth as truth allow themselves to be manipulated by the forces that impose this value on them. They are the proverbial hamsters in the wheel, forever running to stay in the game and paying any price to retain the veil of beauty. A study done by Larkin and Tayler (1994) of women with eating and weight problems found that the preoccupation with external beauty promotes and upholds the oppression of females who are imprisoned by these values.

The context of Wolfe's theory of beauty is that of male and female relationships, but when extended it can be applied to the larger context of dominant Western culture and other parts of the world with lesser power and influence. The West has embraced the beauty myth and is transmitting it to the rest of the world. It has taken hold in minds within Western culture and today extends far beyond its original borders as a universal standard for many in other rapidly Westernizing cultures (Kramer & Ikeda, 2000). In reality the ideal of aesthetic beauty is a material manifestation of the power of colonization. Thus, an extension of Wolfe's theory of the beauty myth can be applied on a global level. It has intimately real consequences for men and women whose physical characteristics do not match those of the dominant, colonizing powers of the world. Western cultural colonization continues to envelop the globe, which attempts to imitate the criteria of success promulgated by the West. As the non-West embraces the Western ideal that promotes itself as the universal standard of beauty, the non-West proceeds to suffer from wide-scale double consciousness.

The internalization of the beauty myth of Western aesthetics is a form of double consciousness. It is an acceptance of "supposed to be"; supposed to be tall, thin, white, and whatever else is required to fit this mold. Though that attainment of the ideal Western (virtual) beauty is difficult if not impossible for actual Western individuals, for most Africans, Latin Americans, and Asians it is utterly hopeless. They are excluded a priori. If those who cannot possibly compete in this warped beauty contest take this standard to heart, the result can be nothing but a painful longing to be what is unattainable and often hating one's self for being unable, inadequate.

SURGICAL SOLUTIONS

Jewish women demand reductions of their noses to be able to pass as one of their Aryan sisters who form the dominant ethnic group. Adolescent Asian girls bring in pictures of Elizabeth Taylor, and Japanese movie actresses (whose faces have already been reconstructed) demand the Westernizing of their own eyes and the creation of higher noses in hopes of better jobs and marital prospects. Black women buy toxic bleaching agents in hopes of attaining lighter skin. What are being created in all these instances are not simply beautiful bodies and faces but white, Western, Anglo Saxon bodies in a racist, anti-Semitic context (Morgan, 1991, p. 36).

The use of cosmetic surgery to alter one's features to appear Western is evidence of double consciousness and the acceptance of the beauty myth around the world. The historical glorification of the "classical" body (and the denigration of other body types) as a little-questioned assumption has been promoted in the West for centuries. Sander Gilman's (1999) history of aesthetic surgery demonstrates the degree to which Westerners and immigrants to the United States have internalized the notion of northern European classical beauty and the extent to which they have taken drastic surgical action to conform their bodies to fit that ideal. Individuals from ethnic groups whose physical characteristics did not fit the standard often sought the services of aesthetic surgeons who could give them the face they desired. Aesthetic surgeons commonly performed alteration of the "Jewish nose" and the Irish "pug" nose to create new "American noses." In the 1880s John Orlando Roe performed operations in Rochester, New York, to "cure" the pug nose that "plagued" Irish immigrants who could then truly pass as Anglo Saxon. Surrounded by and under the weight of an opposing standard of beauty, these immigrants assumed the consciousness of the host culture. They attempted to meet these standards, in hopes that changing their faces would change their lives (Brubach, 2000). Consonant with the promise that if one disintegrates and reintegrates the psychic self (operationally, functionally, and emotionally) in conformity with mainstream cultural values and expectations then happiness and personal success follow, reconstructing the most prominent aspect of the "behavioral self," the face, has been pursued (Gudykunst & Kim, 1997).

In more recent times, Great Britain has witnessed a startling rise in black and Asian customers for reconstructive cosmetic surgery. Chinese women are also having blepharoplasty (eyelid surgery) to create a Western-style fold. Black women seek liposuction to reduce their fuller figures. Rhinoplasty (nose surgery) is popular with almost all nonwhite groups: South Asians have their stronger noses reduced and tilted at the tip; Afro-Caribbeans have their noses narrowed; and East Asians have implants inserted to give more defined (nose) bridges (Branigan, 2001). The acceptance and internalization of the Western beauty myth, as evidenced through plastic surgeries, is especially visible in Asia and in Asian immigrants to the West.

Asia Looks West

A desire for Western beauty apparently began in Japan in 1868, when Commodore Perry opened the country up to the rest of the world and the Japanese got a glimpse of Western culture and fashion (Darling-Wolf, 2000). In 1896, Japanese surgeon K. Mikamo introduced a nonincision eyelid-altering procedure called the three-stitch technique, whereby the upper eyelids were sutured six to eight millimeters above the eyelash with silk thread, creating a scar line that produced a fold, giving the Japanese patient a desirable Western eyelid. His technique spurred other plastic surgeons to follow his example for the next fifty years (Inoue, 1996).

The demand for eyelid surgery boomed after World War II and "by the 1960s had become an obsession. Fashion-conscious Asian American teens taped their eyelids to emulate their favorite Western film and television stars. Those who could afford the surgery would have it done, to the envy of their pals" (Inoue, 1996, p. 6). In 1963, a Singaporean surgeon, Khoo Boo-Chai, performed his modern nonincision method of Oriental blepharoplasty to create "double eyes" for the purely cosmetic requests of Asian patients. He commented that "our Eastern sisters put on western apparel, use western makeup, see western movies, and read western literature. Nowadays, there even exists a demand for the face and especially the eyes to be westernized" (Inoue, 1996, p. 6; Gilman, 1999, p. 107). In Khoo Boo-Chai's opinion, the three reasons for the surgery are: (1) to be more accepted by Westerners and thus have better socioeconomic status; (2) local beliefs and superstition that Asian eyes were suspicious or "mousy"; and (3) that with altered eyelids a woman had a better chance to snag a husband (Inoue, 1996). For those who chose surgery, the benefits of economic status, marriage, and the avoidance of negative stereotypes outweighed the painful costs of double consciousness (Jay, 2000).

Demands for Cosmetic Surgery Today among Asians and Asian Americans

In the 1990s, people of all ethnic groups were flooding into plastic surgery offices. The American Association of Facial and Reconstructive Surgery indicated that there was a 35 percent rise in cosmetic surgical procedures in the United States since 1990. Asian blepharoplasty is on the rise, especially in California, where both the populations of Asians and plastic surgeons are growing each year (Inoue, 1996). Michael D. Rabkin has practiced cosmetic surgery in San Francisco since 1980 and performs five to seven hundred strictly cosmetic surgeries a year; 30 percent of those are Asian patients. He has seen an increase in cosmetic eyelid surgery in Asian communities, as well as in non-Asian ones. Dr. Andrew K. Choi performed 1,550 surgeries and 300 revisions in Los Angeles from 1989 to 1994 (Inoue, 1996).

In San Jose, the business of eyelid surgery is lucrative. A ninety-minute surgery performed in the office operating room can yield up to $3,500. Some doctors heavily advertise their services to immigrant communities in newspapers, magazines, and billboards. There are hundreds of Web sites for cosmetic surgeons, many of which advertise expertise in Asian blepharoplasty. Timothy

Parsons, a Los Gatos eye physician, runs full-page advertisements in the local Vietnamese monthly, *Thang Mo*. He attributes 5–10 percent of all eyelid surgeries he performs to Asian American teens under eighteen years of age. Dong Chung places advertisements in the Korean fashion magazine *Chubu Saenghwal* promising bigger, fuller eyes for patients as experienced by more than three thousand of his female patients.

It has been estimated that 40 percent of young Korean women undergo this eye surgery. The surgery can cost up to $3,500 in the United States, but only $800 to $1,200 in Seoul. The trend is so popular today that in some parts of Korea one has difficulty finding someone *without* eyelid folds. Im Kwon-Taek, the director of *Sopyonje*, a popular movie set in the 1950s and released in 1993, searched desperately in Seoul for an actress with creaseless eyelids to play one of the major roles, and eventually had to settle on a young woman with no acting experience (Inoue, 1996).

Apparently, many Asians have internalized the idea that beauty is defined in terms of approximation to the Western eyelid; now that modern medicine and technology can provide it, the race is on to acquire the improved look. Young women who might be hesitant about the change or the pain involved in the surgical procedure and subsequent recovery period are often encouraged and sometimes even pressured by older family members to acquire the prettier eyelid. Inoue (1996) interviewed several women who had resolved the dilemma in different ways. He tells of a twenty-two-year-old Korean American named Kimberly who flew to Korea for the surgery when she was just a freshman in high school and for $200 received the palpebral fold across each eyelid. Her aunt had requested that she have the surgery, telling her that she would look much better afterward. Jennifer was afraid to undergo the surgery, but her mother pushed her to have it. Although Jaclyn refused the surgery, pressure began in junior high school when her mother offered to pay for the surgery. "It was a matter of fact that when you get older and graduate from high school, you'll go and have it done. I was led to believe that having it done would make me prettier and more attractive to men, and to find a husband" (Inoue, 1996, p. 4).

Patient Rationale for Aesthetic Surgeries

In the early days of cosmetic surgery, one of the most common reasons patients stated for aesthetic surgery was for the purpose of changing their ethnic features to look more like mainstream Americans. Today, perhaps due to the discourse of multiculturalism and an emphasis on political correctness, more patients deny that assimilation is their objective. They state that the motivation for the surgery is not to look more Western but to look "more beautiful" and to have "more balance to their face." One doctor said, "From having performed surgery since 1981, and teaching the surgical techniques to other doctors for the same period, I honestly believe that most of the Asian patients are not wanting to look like Westerners or their Caucasian friends. Rather, they want to retain their Asian features with the addition of an aesthetically pleasing *Asian* [emphasis mine] eyelid crease" (Chen, 1999). "I think that all females want to look better," explains Jennifer, who immigrated to the United States from Korea at age fourteen. "The main reason people are doing it in Korea is because they want to look pretty" (Inoue, 1996, p. 3). But interestingly, *pretty* in the definition of cosmetic surgeons and their patients is not defined as the ethnic Asian eyelid but as the eyelid characteristic of Westerners. One may argue that people who have rhinoplasty or blepharoplasty are not trying to deny their heritage but are only trying to look better, but that seems to veil the underlying inherent message that Western European standards dominate current thoughts of beauty and that Asians and others around the world are influenced, consciously or unconsciously, by those values (see also Chapter Three of this volume).

ANIME

The Japanese, like many other Asian cultures, seem to be experiencing the effects of double consciousness. Although traditionally they have been racial purists, the Japanese seem to be fervently embracing Western ideals of beauty. Japanese animation, or anime, a uniquely Japanese form of animation, reflects the evolving acceptance and promotion of the Western beauty myth (see Chapter Two about the impact of Twiggy on Japanimation).

Anime represents a pop culture phenomenon around the world (Berman, 2000; Chung, 2000; Corliss, Harbison, & Ressner, 1999; Lefton, 1998; Mallory, 2001). It is in this phenomenon that a reflection of the Western beauty myth is evidenced. This Japanese-originated style of animation is unique in many aspects. Notable for its fast pace and comic book–like action, the characters also remind one of comics—their faces for the most part remain immobile, while the mouth moves (Corliss, et al., 1999). Furthermore, one of its most distinctive characteristics is the Western look of the characters (Cooper-Chin, 1999). Anime points to where the identity-mediating process of double consciousness, the acceptance of the beauty myth, is occurring in Japan. An examination of the physical characteristics of characters in popular programs points to a dependency on perceptions of Western beauty in Japanese culture.

In contrast to the Western standard of beauty, which glorifies a tall, slender frame; big, often light-colored eyes; big breasts; and light skin, the Japanese generally have dark hair; narrower, dark eyes; and smaller stature and slight frames. Most anime, however, points very clearly to Western standards of beauty. *Pokémon, Digimon, Cardcaptors,* and *Sailor Moon,* TV shows that air in the United States, all present characters with notably Anglo features and coloring. The most noticeable and exaggerated are the wide, generally light-colored eyes. These characters are accurately described in *Time* (1999) as "Frisbee-eyed kids." Their eyes are so exaggerated that they often carry a permanent look of surprise. Most also have pale skin coloring as well as brown, blond, or red hair. Sakura, the heroine of the program *Cardcaptors*, is an ideal example of this. She has light brown hair, wide green eyes, and pale skin. The only characters with black or blue-black hair, which might traditionally belong to someone of Japanese origin, also have blue eyes.

Interestingly, cartoons with coloring and features that might be found on a Japanese person are very few; they are usually old or, if young, are male. Brock, for example, one of the main trio of characters in *Pokémon*, has tan skin and slit-like eyes that appear closed at all times. Although his coloring and features do not necessarily look Japanese, neither do they fit the typical appearance of anime characters.

Though it may seem that these trends in children's programming might have been created simply for their Western audiences, they are reflected in more traditional anime film characters as well. There is some intentional cultural editing of the children's shows before they move to the United States from their Asian market. For example, in *Pokémon*, chopsticks are replaced with forks before it reaches the American market (Fulford, 1999). However, the trend of Western phenotypic features was not created to satisfy Western viewers. Even movies produced for Japanese audiences and subtitled in English have the typical big eyes, pale skin, and light hair. One clear example is the popular series of films *Ranma 1/2*. Ranma, the main character, has bright red hair, has blue eyes, and is very busty.

Why are these Anglo features so common in Japanese animation? Anne Cooper-Chin's (1999) analysis of anime heroines, points to the influence of one particular cartoonist, Osamu Tezuka. He discovered that this look—the portrayal of Japanese women as "blondes or red heads with Barbie-doll proportions and large, often blue eyes"—was more appealing to his audience and that bigger eyes could more easily express emotion. This eventually became conventional for the genre and is now common throughout anime but is most pervasive in women's or girls' shows—indeed, it is the standard look.

This offers some (but little) explanation of why big eyes were more popular in the first place (see Chapter Two). It seems to be a reflection of what the Japanese believe to be beautiful, a reflection of an earlier internalized image of Western beauty. For over a century, Japan has received and internalized beauty images from the west. As early as the late nineteenth century, the Japanese had begun to cosmetically alter their features to appear more Western or more white. They underwent various surgical techniques to improve their noses and eyes to enter the modern world (Gilman, 2001). More recently, popular fashion also reflects these attitudes. One trendy Japanese stylist explains that her clients are "usually trying to achieve a unique, but natural hair color like that of westerners" (Klensch, 1996). This acceptance of Western appearances as *the* standard of beauty is quite clearly evidence of double consciousness.

It is possible to see how complete the taking on of Western consciousness has become when one examines the prevailing characteristics of anime more closely. The settings, hairstyles, clothes, and even sometimes the names used in anime programs point to the conclusion that the characters are, in fact, supposed to be Japanese people. Both interior and exterior shots are clearly Japanese settings. Frequently shown in rooms with tatami mats, bamboo screens, and sliding doors, the characters wear kimonos and often-complicated coiffed hair. Although these light-skinned, pale-eyed characters seem culturally Japanese, they manifest a racial ambiguity.

An online magazine about Japanese pop cultural trends, *MyNippon*, has been publishing an ongoing debate about the popular use of cosmetic alteration (makeup, contact lenses, breast augmentation, and hair dye) by Japanese and other Asian women to appear more Western or white. This further implies that the characters represented in anime *are* Japanese. They depict Japanese people who have already taken (increasingly common) steps to beautify themselves in the Western style. They wear colored contact lenses, dye their hair, and augment their breasts.

Rather than exoticizing looks different from their own, the Japanese have normalized them and are now attempting to become "normal," which means Western-looking. This is the epitome of double consciousness. Kramer (1999) explains that this can lead one to hate one's self and one's own traditional values. He describes the fruitless attempts of Japanese after the Meiji Restoration to intermarry and Westernize their race in an effort to "become valuable by being erased." Now, with the ability to alter one's eye and hair color, even change one's facial and body construction, the Japanese have found a new way, bypassing intermarriage, to become valuable by erasing themselves.

This effort is futile. Kramer asks, "How can one conform to a dominating culture that defines you as never being worthy of inclusion?" The obvious answer is that you can't. As pointed out by *MyNippon* (2001), "If continued, Japanese women will compete against the 'stripper' tradition (tall, blonde hair, and large breasts)—a battle they will surely lose."

PASSING

At the beginning of the twentieth century, African Americans were undergoing transformation as they attempted to reidentify themselves in a new social order.

Physically cut off and culturally removed from an African homeland they did not know, and unwanted and derided in the post-slavery West, blacks were a people without a country.... Blackness was a dual-cultural experience—physically they were Africans, but they belonged to the New World.... Self-invention was what being an American was all about, and adopting New World values was tantamount to an application for citizenship. (Arogundade, 2000, 28)

Dominant society derided blackness and demonstrated a bias in favor of the "mulatto aesthetic," therefore, people of color aspired to the beauty values of the dominant class (Arogundade, 2000.) Those African Americans whose physical characteristics did not approximate those of the white majority were encouraged by society and through the media to take the steps necessary to alter their hair and skin to more closely resemble that of the majority (Eichberg, 1999). The black cosmetic industry began in Harlem in the 1890s selling "ethnically altering" skin-lightening and hair-straightening products. Arogundade (2000) notes the revealing nature of some of the names of the skin creams: Black No More, Lucky Brown Bleaching Cream, and Cocotone Skin Whitener. Madame C. J. Walker, daughter of former slaves on a Louisiana cotton plantation, made her fortune as the pioneer of black hair and beauty products. Her invention of the hot comb and hair conditioners were made to "tame" unruly hair, implying that black hair was wild and in need of domestication. According to Arogundade (2000), "Walker's premise—that altering blackness is the starting point for success—has influenced the entire genre of black hair and beauty advertising to the present day. It struck at the heart of black aesthetic insecurity and low self-esteem at a moment when ethnicity was still being systematically degraded throughout popular culture" (p. 28).

The experience of African Americans demonstrates the extent to which beauty values are conditioned by dominant white aesthetic paradigms and the internalization of double consciousness among minorities. The direction of influence in fact helps define the minority from the majority. Although a large majority of African Americans adopted the beauty ideals of the dominant culture, most retained identification with their African American heritage. However, some individuals of mixed African American/white heritage passed as white and changed their social categorization to join the majority. Daniel (1992) stated that attempts to change one's ethnic appearance to fit in was often practiced in the United States by African Americans whose skin was light enough to pass for white so they could gain the privileges afforded to members of the dominant majority. Such acceptance could provide economic stability as well as "the illusion of having escaped the taint of subordinate group status, if not the actual achievement of equality with whites"(Daniel, 1992, p. 92). "Passing is the word used to describe an attempt to achieve acceptability by claiming membership in some desired group while denying other racial elements in oneself thought to be undesirable" (Bradshaw, 1992, p. 79).

Passing Goes Global

In a more global sense, the practice of passing continues today for individuals of other ethnicities who have accepted, as African Americans historically did, the idea that the standard of beauty is established by the dominant group and that to be successful they must fashion their looks to most closely resemble that of the dominant group. Although Adrienne Gosselin (1998) claims that "the idea of passing for White is a uniquely American notion," the trends discussed herein are evidence to the contrary. Alterations made to the body to give the appearance of a more desirable identity continue today, and such practices have expanded across the globe. Worldwide, the use of plastic surgery, hair dyes, and tinted contact lenses are modern forms of passing in which persons attempt to blend in with the dominant ethnic group. The Korean American woman who opts to alter her eyelids to appear more beautiful and the Japanese woman who augments her breasts are making unveiled attempts to pass as Western sophisticates in hopes of receiving the benefits of membership in a privileged class.

These attempts at passing are a result of double consciousness and acceptance of the Western beauty myth. The desire to completely eliminate one's biological characteristics in exchange for a new and improved set of features may seem to result in a kind of fusion, a fusion that is both internal and external, but rather it remains a vicious dualism, which leads to painful cognitive dissonance and self-hate. Double consciousness, the confusion of two identities, manifests itself physically in the manipulation and combination of idealized Western and other traits.

REFERENCES

Arogundade, B. (2000). *Black beauty: A history and a celebration.* New York: Thunder's Mouth Press.

Berman, M. (2000). Japanese invasion. *Media Week, 10* (March 13), pp. 46–48.

Bradshaw, C. (1992). Beauty and the beast: On racial ambiguity. In M. Root (Ed.), *Racially mixed people in America* (pp. 77–88). Newbury Park, CA: Sage.

Branigan, T. (2001). In the eye of the beholder. *Guardian* (October 15). Available online at http://www.education.guardian.co.uk.

Brubach, H. (2000). Beauty under the knife. *Atlantic Monthly* (February). Available online at http://www.theatlantic.com/issues/2000/02/002/brubach.htm.

Chen, W. (1999). *Asian blepharoplasty.* Available online at http://www.asiaeyelid.com/faq.html.

Cho, M. (2000). Bodily regulation and vocational schooling. *Gender and Education, 12,* 149–164.

Chung, W. (2000). Hong Kong. *Billboard, 112,* 53–54.

Cooper-Chin, A. (1999). An animated imbalance: Japan's television heroines in Asia. *Gazette, 61,* 293–310.

Corliss, R., Harbison, G., & Ressner, J. (1999). Amazing anime. *Time, 154,* 94–96.

Daniel, G. (1992). Passers and pluralists: Subverting the racial divide. In M. Root (Ed.), *Racially mixed people in America* (pp. 91–107). Newbury Park, CA: Sage.

Darling-Wolf, F. (2000). Texts in context: Intertextuality, hybridity, and the negotiation of cultural identity in Japan. *Journal of Communication Inquiry, 24,* 134–155.

Du Bois, W. E. B. (1903/1995). *The souls of black folk.* New York: Penguin Putnam.

Eichberg, S. (1999). Bodies of work: Cosmetic surgery and the gendered whitening of America. Unpublished doctoral dissertation, University of Pennsylvania, Philadelphia, PA.

Fulford, B. (1999). Anime opens on Main Street. *Forbes, 164,* 58–59.

Gilman, S. (1999). *Making the body beautiful*. Princeton, NJ: Princeton University Press.

Gilman, S. (2001). Illusions, scalpels, and stereotypes. *UNESCO Courier*, pp. 44–46.

Gilroy, P. (1993). *The black Atlantic*. Cambridge, MA: Harvard University Press.

Gosselin, A. (1998). Racial etiquette and the white plot of passing: (Re)Inscribing "place" in John Stahl's "imitation of life." *Canadian Review of American Studies, 28*, 47–68.

Gudykunst W. B., & Kim Y. Y. (1997). *Communicating with strangers: An approach to intercultural communication* (3rd ed.). New York: McGraw Hill.

Inoue, T. (1996, June 27). Roundabout looks. *Metroactive News & Issues*. Available online at http://www.metroactive.com/papers/metro/06.27.96/asian-eyes-9626.html.

Jay, J. (2000). The valley of the new American. *Demographics, 22*, 58.

Klensch, E. (1996). Japanese comics inspire hair designs. CNN, February 24.

Kramer, E. (1993). Understanding co-constitutional genesis. *Integrative Explorations: Journal of Culture and Consciousness, 1*, 41–47.

Kramer, E. (1999). *Gaiatsu* and cultural Judo. Paper presented at the annual conference of the International Jean Gebser Society, Matteson, Illinois, October.

Kramer, E. (2000). Cultural fusion and the defense of difference. In M. K. Asante & J. E. Min (Eds.), *Socio-cultural conflict between African and Korean Americans* (pp. 182–223). New York: University Press of America.

Kramer, E. & Ikeda, R. (2000). The changing faces of reality. *Keio Communication Review, 22*, 79–109.

Larkin, C., & Tayler, H. (1994). Stories of women, food, and power. *Social Alternatives, 12*, 43-46.

Lefton, J. (1998). Nintendo's Pokémon on the way to block buster status. *Brandweek, 39*, p. 5.

Mallory, M. (2001). Kid's anime hits critical mass. *Los Angeles Times* (October 11), p. 18.

Morgan, K. (1991). Women and the knife: Cosmetic surgery and the colonization of women's bodies. *Hypatia, 6*, 25–53.

MyNippon Team (2001).Un-Japanization of Japan. Available online at http://www.mynippon.com/gainippon/westernization.htm.

Wolfe, N. (1991). *The beauty myth: How images of beauty are used against women*. New York: William Morrow.

Chapter 14

Cosmopoly: Occidentalism and the New World Order

Eric Mark Kramer

Once it is accepted that Western culture is the most advanced culture, all "minor" cultures were inherently un-modern, and every step they took towards Western culture was regarded as progress ... the question whether traditional culture had to be abandoned for the sake of economic progress was the question on the lips of all developing and Third World nations. Japan chose the way of Westernization, cutting itself off from the Edo period and categorizing all of traditional culture as un-modern.... The Position that Japan finds itself in today is clearly a dangerous one, on the very edge of a precipice. Its teacher, the Western world, is engaged in serious self-criticism, and is beginning to identify new goals for itself. This will leave Japan an honors student without a school, and the fact of the matter is that Japan does not know what to do.

—Kisho Kurokawa

A Zen master once said to his disciples as he lay dying, "I have learned only one thing in life: how much is enough."

The First Commandment of market capitalism is: "There is *never* enough ... the market that stops expanding dies."

—Harvey Cox, Harvard theologian

HOW MUCH IS ENOUGH?

This chapter is about communications on a global level, its predominantly one-way flow from a tiny rich and aggressive minority to a vast majority, and its consequences. International communications is made up of any human artifact crossing national boundaries accidentally or deliberately. This includes pollution;

disease; tourism; international student exchanges; military, diplomatic, and religious missions; trade, and mass media messages. Culture is constituted of the values, beliefs, expectations, motivations, and behavior patterns of a people who recognize themselves as a group.

Today, as the human race dramatically increases in numbers, qualitative differences in the form of cultural diversity are rapidly decreasing. The human race is undergoing what has been called a great transformation, not only in behaviors but, more important, in habits of mind, beliefs, expectations, motivations, and values (Gebser, 1985; Greider, 1997; Polyani, 1957). The emerging world culture is not village-like, as the early Marshall McLuhan and some of his not too careful readers (for his later work was not so optimistic) would have us believe, but rather exhibits the qualities of a single global urban culture.[1]

COSMOPOLY

The main thesis of this chapter is that the world is *not* becoming a global village but instead a global city or cosmopolis (Kramer, forthcoming). This is an important difference, for although one constitutes community the other is formed by an aggregate of disinterested if not competing individuals. One is casual, intimate, and spontaneous and the other rushed, impersonal, and rigidly organized. The village offers the security of the clan and the meaning of traditional identity, an identity that is shared (group membership), whereas the city is the place where the stranger is the predominant type of person one encounters. In the cosmopolis, just maintaining contact with one's parents, children, and siblings becomes difficult such that even the traditional respect for and tending of graves is abandoned to indifferent professionals.

The allure of the cosmopolis is rooted in an idealized urban modern lifestyle, a utopian ideology I call cosmopoly. Cosmopoly appeals to the egocentrism that marks Western modernity and perhaps the most base desire of the species. Cosmopoly promises the liberation of the individual from personal obligations and attachments as the very essence of progress, and this spells the end of traditional communities (Lerner, 1958). As cosmopoly moves across the globe, we can trace how many things change. For instance, two things occur. The "primitive" superstitions that articulate a world that is full and alive (full of manna, chi, spirits) and that therefore demands care and obligation for Others, including the environment, gives way to an indifferent universe that is empty and dead (piles of vibrating atoms in utter void). Thus, although a traditional clan may take care to be respectful and perform elaborate and lengthy rituals before cutting a single tree to make a canoe, the modern can cut down an entire forest without hesitation.

A second major change that accompanies modernization is the implosion of the psyche in a way that would have made Ayn Rand proud and that Walter Rostow championed in his anti–*Communist Manifesto* (1952). This implosion amounts to a shrinking and hardening of the ego into a "position," a distillate of personal interests and desires, a singular limited yet arrogant perspective (Gebser, 1985). As cosmopoly spreads we see the village as clan shrink to the extended family, then shrink further still to the nuclear family, and finally that basic unity of society split into monadic individuals immensely selfish of their personal space, time, property, and thoughts. It takes a great concentration of wealth (exploitation of resources) to sustain such happy positivism because competition displaces cooperation.

As nature and culture bifurcate at the level of mythological articulation, the dispersed sacred forces of animism collapse and distantiate into a limited polytheism of anthropomorphic (jealous, emotional) gods that enunciate laws (legality) (Kramer, 1997). The sacred becomes increasingly materialized, spatialized. The divine takes on physical qualities, such as structural ordination, and retreats to distant places like mountain tops. Eventually the articulation of the sacred mirrors the emergence of the modern ego as monotheism comes to dominate, and God exists at an almost infinite distance. Morality and legality become disconnected. Finally, as Friedrich Nietzsche (1886/1973) notes, the sacred and values vanish entirely, leaving only a dead and empty physical (hyletic) substrate governed by deterministic logic.

Cosmopoly is a combination of cosmopolitanism and hegemonic homogenization of world culture, a monopoly of a single set of values, beliefs, motivations, and behaviors. The utopian ideology of cosmopoly is global in reach and claims for itself exclusive validity as to what is positively beautiful, good, (inalienably) right, and true. But such valuations are not honestly presented as judgments, which are contingent, but as transcendental laws of nature codified by scientific notation and verified by scientific observation, which claim to have no perspective. The intense abstraction of late-modern conceptual idealism (formula, for instance) comes to govern the world.

The problem is, *ou topos* literally means "nowhere." In other words, utopias are virtual and not actual phenomena. Therefore, as cosmopoly spreads on the wake of classical European colonialism and exploits new channels of expansion, including telecolonialism (which works its hegemonic magic more on the virtual and ideological level, from the inside out as it were, than classical imperialism that worked more on the level of out-group foreign domination and extraction of physical resources), cosmopoly is erasing the very self-identities of billions of people in the name of its own brand of progress. As the virtual ideal meets the actual limitations of the Earth, we are witnessing an emerging mess made by a very spoiled and childish mentality.

Utopian Modeling

The relationship of virtual to actual in most knowledge systems, including religions, gives ontological priority to the virtual objective ideal over the contingent actual subject (imperfection as the distortion of limitation). Virtual rule and law govern contingent actualities. However, mimetic modeling stresses the priority of the actual such that, for instance, a child will make a plastic small-scale replica of an actual airplane or ship and judge its value by how well it conforms to the proportions of the actual object. Thus, the actual constrains and guides the model. According to mimetic truth, priority goes to the already extant thing. But increasingly this process is being reversed so that the virtual imagination is being liberated from any and all actual constraints. This is what Gebser (1985) has called the will to will in the form of hypertrophic self-expression. Modeling—for instance in the design of cars, buildings, cities, genetics, and so on—is done first on a computer and then made into an actual object. The reduction of the world to building blocks has opened the path to the pure mechanistic might of rearrangement at will and in the service of pure desire. This, as will be discussed, is important to the model minority, for that is a person who by definition should be willing to undergo "psychic disintegration" so that his or her ways of thinking, feeling, and acting can be reorganized in a way that suits the dominant culture's wants and needs, that maintains system stasis (equilibrium) (Gudykunst & Kim, 2003, pp. 367–69). Here we have the flip side of modern hypertrophic individualism, the passivity of modern mass society (Gebser, 1985).

Modernity, for all its claims to emphasize empiricism, manifests the liberation of desire by way of eliminating obligation. It is, as Joseph Campbell (1988) notes, "Libido over credo" (p. 190). If primitivism and savagery are the uncontrolled expression of instinctual drives, the modern West has proven less self-constrained than many traditional cultures. Modernity is the origin of virtual parallel (often mathematical) realities that articulate desires and values, which are then operationalized, thereby claiming the mantle of objective reality. Modern Western magic works with profound impact. Its products are physically demonstrable. They are empirical fact, and so we have the fact-ory. Modernists like to say that the best way to predict the future is to make it. Sometimes vision must wait for engineering to catch up to enable plans to be actualized. Two popular examples are the designs of architect Frank Gehry and President John F. Kennedy's proclamation that the United States would send a man to the moon and return him safely within a decade of the pronouncement. Vision comes before operationalization. Technology and other forms of physical culture manifest desire, ambition, hope, and fear. Waiting for material sciences to make the dream actual involves problem solving and retooling.

This process also applies to model minorities. Minorities are told by dominating Western culture that they must strive to embody the transcendental values and desires of the dominant culture. The tools used to make model minorities were first supplied by eugenics and later by behaviorism (rewards and punishments). The developing world (societies and peoples) is seen as a problem and as a work in progress by the already developed. The progress of minorities can be measured against the presumed ideal that dominates their lives and is imposed from outside their value and belief systems. Across the planet it is presumed that the more Westernized a person or society, the more modern and therefore developed they are. To progress or evolve to a "higher level of self-understanding" the underdeveloped must be willing to "disintegrate" so that they can be reconstituted as moderns in behavior, ways of thinking, and feeling (Gudykunst & Kim, 2003, pp. 379–82). This presumes the modern Western mechanistic metaphysic that twentieth-century physics abandoned, which is ironic for it is from the physical sciences that this metaphysic was originally transferred to the social sciences (Bohm, 1980; Gamow, 1966; Heisenberg, 1958). This metaphysic applied to the self reduces it to a mere resource base that can be fragmented and reorganized at will. This willpower-drive characterizes the modern West and is the origin of its instrumental orientation and definition of the world. It extends even into the biological realm as mere substrate (foundation of building blocks) available for genetic engineering.

Constructing Model Minorities: The Systematic Elimination of Different Selves

Social "science," born of the age of engines, was conceived to engineer a better, more productive human and society, a society that would be an engine of wealth creation. To do this, to achieve optimal competence, a few eggs must be broken. The world is being changed by industrial mass productive and mass consumptive interests, and so nonindustrial ways of being must be transformed. Positivism sees this as growth. Jourard (1974) defines growth this way: "Growth is the disintegration of one way of experiencing the world, followed by a reorganization of this experience ... the disorganization, or even shattering, of one way to experience the world is brought on by new disclosures from the changing being of the world, disclosures that were always being transmitted, but were usually ignored" (p. 456). Since Gudykunst and Kim (2003) argue that culture is "internal to the person" (p. 272), then as people's psyches disintegrate under stress and reintegrate, what is happening is that cultures are disintegrating and reintegrating (developing) as what? People are being encouraged to develop, evolve into what? Western-style moderns.

What is clear here is that Jourard presumes the seventeenth-century mechanical metaphysic that characterizes modernity (Cartesianism). Thus the individual is posited as not being an integral part of the world but instead as being confronted by a world that is "transmitted" to him or her in fragments. Not being part of the dominant world-system, the individual is thus perceived to be a passive target for compliance gaining. The individual is not a part of change but must continually adjust to it. This metaphysical prejudice has been debunked already by many scholars, yet it persists, leading to the variable analytic notion of human behavior.

The variable metaphor of reality suggests that as a person moves toward one end of a line, he or she must move away from the other end with equal and opposite momentum. Thus, as I learn something new, I must unlearn something old as if my mind is a finite container. This version of reality as uncritically applied to human behavior is exemplified by any number of dichotomies, including the popular cultural variable collectivism versus individualism, two cultural orientations that face each other at opposing ends of a presumably single continuum (Parson, 1951). In this case, for instance, as a person moves toward individualism, that person must move away from being collectivisitic. However, observation demonstrates that a person may exhibit both tendencies in differing contexts and even at the same time, as when a teenager resists peer pressure to do something she perceives to be against her personal interest, like smoking, but at the same time will facilitate her cohesion to the group to which she wants to belong. This is cognitive and *affective* dissonance.

In analytic philosophy and the natural sciences, from where the either/or version of analytics was transferred to the social sciences, the scholars are much more careful so that such distinctions are more adequately defined. Thus, in analytical terms one should say up or not up (which is not necessarily the same as down). Or collectivistic, not collectivistic, would be the proper nomenclature in this example, rather than collectivistic versus individualistic. The adjectives *individualistic* and *collectivistic* should not a priori be presumed to be anathema nor even symmetrical phenomena. Each one describes a very complex mode of being.

Similar problems plagued the early cognitivist version of variable analytics, which still holds currency in much social science writing, including Gudykunst and Kim's (2003) description of "growth," which they borrow from Jourard (1974). What they call growth is a process whereby each time something new is learned something old must be "unlearned." But this one-dimensional mechanical version of learning and growth is absurd. In the hermeneutic school of thought, which has had a great impact on learning theory, growth is not a linear zero-sum closed system. Instead it is additive and integrative, so that as a person learns new ways of thinking and behaving, old ones are not necessarily unlearned. Instead the process is more like a musician building his or her repertoire of songs and styles. According to Kramer's (2000a, 2000b) theory of intercultural fusion, this is what occurs when a person such as an immigrant or refugee adopts a new home culture. Learning is not the same thing as unlearning or forgetting, which is the absurd notion put forth in the theory of intercultural adaptation.

For positivists, change, though it is imposed on the individual who is presented as a hapless dissociated monad, is presented as positive-sounding growth. To variable analytic either/or positivists, such forced compliance is even seen as emancipating. According to Gudykunst and Kim (2003), "The process, if successful, means that the individual grows into a new kind of person at a higher level of integration. Even extreme mental illness ... can be viewed as a process of potentially positive disintegration followed by reintegration with new material at a higher level" (p. 381). Notions such as higher and better presume a final goal; otherwise such relative measures are impossible. For

Gudykunst and Kim (2003) the final goal is the evolution of the individual to the point of abandoning the cultured self at the very "limit of humanity itself" per the Buddhist precept of nirvana (p. 385).

Therefore, if global industrialization and cultural extinction are driving people crazy, that is okay because eventually they (at least the ones who keep an optimistic mindset) will conform to the "external system" and be happy with their new lot at a "higher level of self-understanding" (Gudykunst & Kim, 2003, p. 382). The better a person understands the system, which Gudykunst and Kim equate with being satisfied, the better he or she will understand him- or herself and thus become enlightened. Passive conformity, not active integration, is thus defined as a higher level of self-understanding, and as "maturity," and wisdom. People will, if successful, "emancipate themselves from the constraints of various limited, *conventional* perspectives" (Gudykunst & Kim, 2003, p. 382; emphasis added). According to intercultural adaptation theory, conformity is absurdly equated with emancipation, and only the value perspective of Gudykunst and Kim is not conventional.

Another contradiction is Gudykunst and Kim's claim that for people to grow, fit in, be competent, and be psychologically healthy and happy, they must adapt themselves to their host culture as fully as possible. But to achieve ultimate adaptability the person should strive to stop identifying with any culture and evolve to "intercultural personhood" (Gudykunst & Kim, 2003, p. 383). These intercultural experts present two totally contradictory views. On one hand they advise strict nationalism, that a person should strive to unlearn their previous life and assimilate as much as possible. On the other hand they are anticultural, for they also advise that a person should abandon the defilements of culture in general and become somehow transculturally free of all embodied perspectives. Actual cultures, which are not merely conventional but defiled, must be renounced, otherwise the absolute posthuman perfection of cosmopolitan identity cannot be approached (Gudykunst & Kim, 2003, pp. 379–85). This is clearly confusing prescriptive advice, and manifestly Hegelian (except that Hegel was consistent and more plausible in that even the grand idealist himself argued that progress can be manifestly realized only through contingent human history).

According to the advice offered by Gudykunst and Kim (2003) to learn how to fit in and be well adjusted in a new setting, one must forget how one lived before and even how to live in *any* conventional way. According to hermeneutic theory, such prescriptive advice is preposterous. Willful forgetting is impossible, and even if possible unwise because we integrate new information in accord with who we already are. This hatred of being an embodied human, all too human, which is to say hatred of being perspectival, is pure idealism and can only lead to either delusional mysticism or self-hatred.

Another claim of intercultural adaptation theory is that if one successfully abandons one's traditional indigenous culture and language for the new, improved positive intercultural personhood, such a person will become cognitively more complex and achieve "a special kind of personal orientation that promises greater fitness" in the emergent global system, which is apparently not conventional but natural if not supernatural (Gudykunst & Kim, 2003, p. 383).

I argue that it is false to claim that cognitive complexity would increase if it were possible to unlearn entire repertoires of behaviors, attitudes, values, and beliefs. Absurdly, according to Gudykunst and Kim (2003) this reorganization of one's cognitive, emotional, and behavioral self to fit with the requirements of the dominate system equals emancipation. Just as Francis Galton (1904) urged that his solution to the defilements of society be "introduced into that national conscience, like a new religion," so do Gudykunst and Kim (2003) argue that

the educational system has a monumental task of projecting and cultivating a new direction for human character formation. If successful, the educational system can help members of future generations embrace the intercultural world and its diversity and give up outdated national, racial, ethnic, and territorial perspectives. . . . If intercultural personhood is deemed a valid educational goal, and we believe that it is, an extensive search for ways to articulate and implement intercultural human development must be undertaken. The propagation of the goal must go beyond the educational process directly to the political processes and the mass media (pp. 388, 389).

First, this is not a recipe for adaptation to an existing condition but for manufacturing the right kind of condition and person. The educational system itself is to be manipulated to promote a singular perspective, a certain set of beliefs and values. Second, the important question is, if we eliminate outdated perspectives— indeed, pluralistic perspectivism as outdated in general and with it all forms of identity—then what diversity will exist? Their solution to sometimes clumsy multiculturalism is the elimination of cultural differences entirely.

Gudykunst and Kim (2003) have misnamed their ideal model "intercultural personhood," for what they are calling for is the elimination of all differences so that intercultural awareness will become impossible. If they were to be successful, there would be no cultures left for intercultural or interidentity interaction to occur. What they mean is global monoculturalism or cosmotopian personhood. In the interest of system efficiency, the management if not elimination of all potential sources of misunderstanding and conflict is the final solution offered by Gudykunst and Kim (2003). Kramer (2000a) notes that already by 1878 Nietzsche had recognized this dream as a nightmare wherein the ancient mysticism of numerology finally finds its stride. "Here is the 'great liberation' into pure metaphysics—German idealistic philosophizing. This is the realm of the positive scholar who is objective, who sets herself in the position of the interpreter of all our experiences with a knowledge of preconditions and a 'standard of ecumenical goals'" (1878–1880/1996, p. 188).

SOCIAL SCIENCE RHETORIC AS PROPAGANDA

Western social science not only is self-promoting as the positive priesthood that can lead us to salvation but also acts as an ideological apparatus for promoting as not contingent but as absolutely natural, even hereditary, an ideology I call cosmotopianism, which in many ways is bourgeois positivism on a global scale. Quite the opposite of liberating us from conventional perspectives, it claims itself to be the only path to growth, evolution, and happiness. As Gebser (1985) notes, positivism promotes itself as the *non plus ultra* of human development and claims objective (absolute) status for this proclamation. Appreciation for alternative cultures (motives, values, and belief systems) and ways of being is off-limits. Gudykunst and Kim (2003) well exemplify the belief that multiple cultures and identities (in a word, diversity) are the biggest problem facing humanity today because difference causes uncertainty, inefficiency, misunderstandings, and the potential for conflict. We are left to believe that such parochial deviations are quaint echoes of a more primitive, less productive time that might at best function as entertaining caricatures of themselves in the new world order. Otherwise, the elimination of cultural, ethnic, racial, and other identities is the best way to manage conflict.

But there is a problem. Very often people who clearly understand each others' interests are still in conflict because those interests are not identical. To argue that understanding means conformity is false. This is derived from the ancient Aristotelian notion of successful communication defined as perfect reproduction of the sender's intent in the receiver's mind, a model of communication appropriate to machine interaction via passive reception or downloading but not applicable to human communication, which always involves active interpretation. This is clear, as Gudykunst and Kim reiterate the Aristotelian linear model of encoding intent, transmission (sending), and inert channel, which presumes that the act of encoding does not alter in any way intent, reception, and decoding as their communication model. For them language differences, for instance, should make no difference in the meaning of a message. According to Gudykunst and Kim, good communication means identity between encoded intent and decoded message, a model based on the dualistic notion of a correspondence theory of truth proven to be illogical by many scholars, most notably Nietzsche (1882/1974), Gadamer (1960/1975), Heisenberg (1930/1958), and Derrida (1967/1973).

This dream and ambition of perfect fidelity, of disintegration into synchronous cohesion (appropriate fit), leads Gudykunst and Kim (2003) to argue that people should join the same system, think in the same code. But the same can never be proven. In any case, such uniformity in interests, beliefs, and values is a recipe for stagnation and nihilism (Kramer, 2000a).

To be sure, if everyone became identical with everyone else, that would solve the problem of intercultural misunderstanding and conflict, but at what price? There would be nothing left to talk about. The solution to misunderstanding and conflict offered by Gudykunst and Kim (2003) is the elimination of difference, of culture, and identity, and the cessation of communication. Logically they conclude that this will mean the elimination of humanity, of "approaching the limit of humanity itself" (p. 385). Mindless and silent doing (automation) perfect friction-free operation and performance is the definition of the model minority that Gudykunst and Kim (2003) offer. They equate such a state of being with blissful enlightenment. According to their model, equilibrium with the system is anathema to thinking, creativity, deviance, action, and resistance. According to Gudykunst and Kim's model and definitions, such proactivity manifests as nothing but immature, unbalanced, unfit, and mentally ill behavior because such behavior disturbs the zero-energy state of no mind, of utterly silent equilibrium. Just as Ralph Ellison recognized in 1952, the model minority should be invisible, manifesting silent stillness, totally assimilated into the mainstream. According to the theory of intercultural adaptation, the only good minority is a nonexistent one.

Equilibrium is a zero-energy state within a system. Accordingly, the model minority is a person who is ultra-conservative, who works tirelessly to make sure that nothing changes or disturbs the system, and even such effort (if such a word is meaningful in this context) should function at a prereflective, thoughtless level of subconscious behaving in accordance with system requirements, meaning not just scripted behavior but prescribed behavior and thinking. This is why the robot would be, according to Gudykunst and Kim (2003), the ideal model minority and that which all newcomers should strive to emulate (Kramer, 2000a). The model minority is a person who is absolutely compliant, absolutely selfless, not even human anymore.

Perhaps the most troubling aspect of the social scientific description of development is the claim that the less developed are not just economically poorer than the developed but less "cognitively complex" (Gudykunst & Kim, 2003, p. 383). But their mindsets and behavior can be modified, developed, corrected. Their evolution and growth can be properly guided by the values of positive social science. This sounds disturbingly like the nineteenth-century rationale Alfred Binet offered for ranking peoples according to intelligence testing, and Thomas Huxley and Galton's (Darwin's cousin and the inventor of the term *eugenics*) attempt to extend the notion of evolution to character traits and intelligence (Binet & Simon, 1913; Kramer & Johnson, 1997). Gudykunst and Kim (2003) argue that immigrants are "simple minded" and less "cognitively complex" or childlike when they first arrive in an advanced society, but the more they assimilate the smarter they become. "This transformation means their psychic patterns are reorganized on a higher level of cognitive complexity, allowing for a greater capacity to overcome [unlearn their] cultural parochialism [which means to abandon their original cultures and selves in favor of the new, more advanced culture and self]" (Gudykunst & Kim, 2003, p. 383). In short, it is smart to forget who you are, especially if you are an inappropriate primitive.

It is unwarranted to presume that people from "traditional societies" are any less cognitively complex than people from modern urban environments. Such testing itself has problems with cultural variance because it attempts to simplify and reduce intelligence to a contingent set of competencies. Only one culture imposes itself on others this way. As the world shrinks, greater numbers of people are lumped together, and so it is in this context that Lambert A. J. Ouetelet, the first person to apply statistical methods to human beings, became an influence on Galton. During World War I, the U.S. Army began using intelligence testing to sort large numbers of conscripts into job positions even though Wilhelm Stern (who had modified Binet's original instrument in an attempt to measure "mental age") and Binet had both come to doubt the practical value of such tests because they had failed to predict a student's success in school.

Civic Worth and Effective Adaptation

G. W. F. Hegel set the tone for modernity as he understood the emerging relationship between modern authority, morality, organization, and the role of the individual to manifest that order.

For it is the Unity of the Universal, essential Will, with that of the individual; and this is "Morality." The individual living in this Unity has a moral life; possesses a value that consists in this substantiality alone.... It must be understood that all the worth which the human being possesses—all spiritual reality he possesses only through the State ... Then only is he fully conscious; thus only is he a partaker of morality—of a just and moral social and political life. For Truth is the Unity of the Universal ... and the Universal is to be found in the State, in its laws and rational arrangements. (Hegel, 1822/1956, p. 31)

In 2003 Gudykunst and Kim wrote, "Becoming intercultural is a gradual process of liberating ourselves from our limited and exclusive interests and viewpoints and of striving to attain a perspective in which we see ourselves as part of a larger, more inclusive whole" (p. 385). This psychic transformation characteristic of the universal person is "the achievement of an *increasingly inclusive and transcendental perception and awareness*" (p. 385) characterized by a "pattern of perceptual development ... toward greater clarity, depth, scope" (p. 383) like, Gudykunst and Kim (2003) claim, the ancient Chinese sages had (p. 385) and that "upwardly mobile immigrants tend to [have to a greater extent] than those who are less upwardly mobile" (p. 382).

Such a reduction of experience to a single perspective actually contradicts the notion that adaptation leads to an enhanced ability to discern differences (Gudykunst & Kim, 2003, p. 383). Gudykunst and Kim (2003) contradict themselves, arguing that on one hand adaptation leads to greater cognitive complexity, which is the ability to discriminate (p. 383), but that adaptation also leads to liberation from, the dissolution of, the very same distinctions (p. 385).

According to Gudykunst and Kim (2003), successful fit persons have a "higher level of self-understanding" and awareness (p. 382); unlike unsuccessful adapters whose "perception of the environment is simplistic" (p. 362), pliant successful adapters "possess a mental outlook that exhibits greater cognitive differentiation" (p. 384). Fit persons "can and do increase their operational capabilities to enact appropriate and effective technical and social behaviors" (Gudykunst & Kim, 1997, p. 342). This ability is traced by Gudykunst and Kim

(2003) thus, "Along with ethnicity, the *personality* of individual strangers plays an important role in their adaptation" (p. 368), as well as appropriate cognitive and affective orientations (p. 364). Minorities ("strangers") are said to "experience satisfaction" when they "synchronize" their interactions and "achieve a cohesive functional relationship" with mainstream, dominant behavior patterns (Gudykunst & Kim, 2003, p. 364).

In the 1700s Hegel (1770–1831) invented positivism, systems theory, organizational values of operational efficiency and appropriate arrangement, evolution, and the "law of progress," launching the age of ideology. Ideology, as the grand should, is utopian thinking. It is about where we should go as a species, and thus science was transformed into prescriptive engineering, a decapitated philosophy, as Theodore Adorno and Max Horkheimer (1972) put it. The point was no longer to discover and describe the universe but to change it, to improve it, but without honest debate about what would constitute an improvement. Because philosophical debate proved too indecisive, it was discarded for "scientific" improvement in the form of overt social engineering.

Auguste Comte vigorously promoted this mixture of religion, moral imperialism, and the worship of ordination. In 1798 Comte and Auguste St. Simon published *Plan of the Scientific Operations Necessary for the Reorganization of Society*. In the eighteenth century the charge that it is social science's heroic duty to improve the human condition by application of scientific (but actually organizational) principles in the service of moral and functional progress commenced. The duty was to help people understand their place within the system, to help them identify with it and thus achieve better functional fit, improving the system and individual performance, making everything and everyone better and happier. Mental equilibrium and system equilibrium are thus mechanistically perceived to be identical: "A healthy psychological state involves a dynamic fitting of parts of the internal system and external realities, that is, an attainment of internal harmony and a meaningful relationship to the outside world. The psychological health of strangers is associated directly with their ability to communicate and their functional fitness in the new environment" (Gudykunst & Kim, 2003, p. 372). According to intercultural adaptation theory, competent communication ("appropriate techniques") and mental health are synonymous, and all of this is based on a congruence between the individual and the external system. To avoid being disturbed one must get with the mainstream flow by thinking and acting in appropriate, efficient ways in accord with their station. But Gudykunst and Kim (2003) argue that the ability of one to do this is influenced by an individual's "adaptive predisposition" (p. 370). Psychological traits determine a person's "adaptive potential" (p. 370).

According to their eighteenth-century notion of system, dissonant components, by definition, cannot be regarded as parts of the system. The concept of system presumed by Gudykunst and Kim is an outdated version of statics abandoned first by Goethe and Nietzsche and in physics in 1929 when Edwin Hubble and Milton Humason (1929) discovered that the universe is not in a steady state but expanding. More recently, after studying a 12-billion-year-old stream of light, John K. Webb and his colleagues (2001) have discovered that the fine structure constant (in this instance the speed of light) has slowed over the age of the universe. The point is that not even in physics, from where social science borrowed its version of system, are statics relevant. The static notions of certainty and uncertainty, of individual and system, are misleading metaphors for the reality of fusional field dynamics both in natural and social sciences (Kramer, 1997, 2000b).

Happiness for a positivist is constant certainty, and it is the goal of positivists to construct a closed system that will ensure such (nihilistic) constancy. Positivists presume that the happiest minority is the one who knows and accepts his or her inescapable place according to the system. But their version of system is outmoded. According to positive ideology, the more a person identifies with the goals and motives (the logic) of the system, the more he or she will achieve equilibrium with it, which will be manifested by him or her as appropriate and competent behavior (as perceived by others). But the very notion of equilibrium has proven to be pure idealism. No actual system ever realizes equilibrium, except perhaps consciousness after death. The goal of knowing and accepting one's fixed place within a fixed system, according to Gudykunst and Kim (2003), is essential because otherwise the unhappy individual may become hostile and aggressive toward the system, which is, by definition, bad (p. 372). Meanwhile, systemic and constant cultural forces that compel conformity are natural and as such, objectively, factually beyond good and evil, beyond critique. Mental health and evolutionary progress in both the system and the individual are synonymous. On the other hand, if an individual does not identify with the goals and motives of the system, evolutionary progress cannot occur. The system does not comply; the individual must.

The reader should notice this is absurd because change, including progress and evolution, is by definition a form of disequilibrium. No actual system has a zero-energy state and changes always cascade in uncertain ways (Kramer, 1997). Therefore this absurd story of static progress is exposed as an ideological apology and justification for reactionary status quo and as a rhetoric that attempts to discredit proaction as nothing but troublemaking.

IMPROVEMENT EQUALS CONFORMITY

According to the positive-sounding assimilation ideology, the improvement of society depends on the improvement of its individual members. As will be discussed later, this initially meant breeding humans to better fit the needs of the system; later, as this became unpopular, it meant control and guidance of physical behavior by means of operant conditioning and other forms of systematic behavioral modification. Currently, we are on the cusp of a paradigm that combines both approaches to promoting conformity to the dominant val-

ues as personality and physical traits are being modified by both genetic and social engineering techniques.

After being traumatized by the collapse of the monarchical system and the
"chaos" that followed, Comte and St. Simon believed that the discredited ordination that the Catholic Church had instituted had to be replaced by a new religion and that the conflict of revolution had to be stopped. They could not
appreciate that the disturbance of the peace functioned as the protean cradle of
their own vision. Their reaction to the liberation movement was manifested as
an aversion to even the smallest obstacles to smooth political-economic operation. Behavior had to be managed by the priests of the new religion in con-
junction with financial and industrial leaders. It was presumed that markets do
not do well in unstable environments. Political/industrial leaders were envisioned as paternalistic exemplars of appropriate fit and behavior.

Philosophy, which had concerned itself precisely with what constitutes the
good life, was summarily abandoned for not being practically effective enough.
The new charge, as both left and right Hegelians agreed, was to change reality,
not merely describe or debate it. So commenced the new technological enterprise of social engineering presumably without the obstacle of political or
philosophical debate, of openly debating what is good, right, and just. However,
nothing is as political as the claim to be apolitical. Society and its members
would be made better, improved, even though better was never defined except
in terms of military success against other systems and the wealth it ensured.
Such judgments became self-evinced by the European conquests of others
everywhere, proving the doctrine of survival of the fittest.

Science Is Reduced to Quantification and to a Disinterested Handmaiden

In the nineteenth century, so-called positive reason was advanced in the form
of a mathematical approach to social progress (engine-ering), which meant
market expansion. Four Victorian-era members of the Royal Statistical Society
constituted the core trendsetters that became modern (statistical) social science
and the motor for scientific proof of comparative economic performance linked
to hereditary or otherwise internally located (character or personality) traits.
They were Francis Edgeworth, Francis Galton, Karl Pearson, and George Yule.
Edgeworth (1845–1926) was a major influence on Pearson (1857–1936). In
1881, Edgeworth's effort to mathematically study human character (morals)
and conduct appeared as *Mathematical Psychics: An Essay on the Application
of Mathematics to Moral Science.*

In 1870, the codiscoverer of natural selection, Alfred Russell Wallace, published a favorable review of Galton's book *Hereditary Genius: An Inquiry into
its laws and Consequences,* which was one of Galton's many efforts to mathematically demonstrate correlations between hereditary intellect, talent, character, and economic performance. Galton's goal was to promote scientific selection,

to give a scientific basis to the problem of improving the human breed, rather than allowing natural selection to take its course, being random and slow as it is. To this end he invented regression analysis (which he initially called reversion) and formulated the statistical correlation coefficient, which he described in an 1890 paper on kinship. These techniques were expressly devised to enable him and other interested parties to discriminate and evaluate different groups of people. His follower, Pearson, later published an improved technique for deriving the correlation coefficient and also the chi-square test.

From 1893 to 1912, Pearson published eighteen papers in a series titled "Mathematical Contributions to the Theory of Evolution." In 1893, Pearson coined the phrase "standard deviation." For over twenty years (until the mid-1930s), Pearson held the eugenics chair, which was endowed by Galton, at the University College London. In 1925, Pearson founded the journals *Biometrika* (Pearson's choice of a *k* rather than a *c* in the spelling is another story that space does not permit) and *Annals of Eugenics* as outlets for studies establishing classifications and distributions based on anthropometric and psychometric (human measurement) data.

To be practical, to lead to civic worth, everything must have measurable outcomes, and so these journals helped institute one of Galton's dreams, which was the systematic gathering of human measurements in schools (still considered, along with econometrics, to be a major indicator for how well society is doing) and archiving them in huge databases. The effort was to study individual and group variability and to find ways to thwart regression toward mediocrity or worse. Race, of course, is still used today as a popular, defining variable.

Pearson hired Yule (1871–1951), who was interested in agriculture and human demographics and who became an ardent follower of both Galton and Pearson. Up into the 1960s, an introductory statistics textbook for social science written by Yule was considered the standard. Yule's first publication, with Pearson, is "On the Correlation of Total Pauperism with Proportion of Outrelief." Pearson's effort to create a field called biometrics and Yule's work influenced the American racist biologist Charles Davenport. Politically, as one might expect, Galton, Pearson, and Yule often warned against unions and any kind of organized "voice of mediocrity" or resistance to the system.

The point of this summary of the origins of modern (mathematical) social science is to demonstrate its original motive for segregating and comparing groups of people and explaining their economic behavior by correlating it to measures that were salient to the eugenicists and how such learned research was a powerful source of legitimation for Western-style colonialism (including imperial Japan's doctrine of the sphere of coprosperity). They hoped to discover and eliminate the causes of mental deficiency, resistant thinking, and sluggish economic behavior by means of selective human breeding. This synopsis also shows how books like Richard Herrnstein and Charles Murray's (1994) *The Bell Curve* are not aberrations. Instead it and other writings are a consistent extension of the central effort of positive social science to mathematically measure and compare groups of people in the interest of "progress." This synopsis also shows how such arrogance manifests itself in the form of policy suggestions for social engineering, usually on a massive scale in schools and increasingly through the mass media.

Inherent in this process is a rank ordering of comparative human worth, the view that humans should be seen as either assets or liabilities to the system and that they can be measured as such. Everything is reduced to the accounting of a singular value. This ideology sees variance as an obstacle to efficient, competent communication, and it stresses compliance over cooperation. Such measures and comparisons define some groups as being simple minded, retarded in development, as less or underdeveloped. The causes may be hereditary or cultural. Increasingly the two loci of causation are converging as the will to will is taking the form of genetic engineering. The prospects for controlling uncertainty by systematically constructing planned communities and designer people, of cognitively and physically constructing a world entirely in one's own interests and values is becoming realized. The goal of being a self-made man is being operationalized. Thus we have the realization of total assimilation as individuals can be modified to embody and reproduce transcendental system needs, values, and motives. Soon, it will be possible to manufacture embryos with appropriate traits and attributes. The ambition is to create a closed and thus securely predictable system that is self-organizing and self-perpetuating (tautological). Given such a totalistic desire, it is no wonder that even the slightest and "inevitable mosquito bites" of actual existence, as Nietzsche (1882/1974, p. 113) refers to the struggle and uncertainties of life, would be viewed as "shocking," as a "disease for which adaptation is the cure" (Gudykunst & Kim, 2003, p. 379).

In any case, the positive solution to everything is the elimination of undesirable psychological and physical attributes and character flaws. With philosophical inquiry debunked as being too indecisive, positive progress is what the priests of positivism, along with industrial and financial leaders, decree. Philosophy, cut off from any existential import, is reduced to checking the internal consistency of decontextualized propositions. Criteria are presumed without question and are rhetorically naturalized or legitimized as being pragmatic and utilitarian, as though such value judgments are neutral and do not presume interests in contingent goals and contexts. They are, as artificial intelligence experts say, implement-independent (absolute) truths. Validity is thus dissociated from common sense (Gadamer, 1975; Kramer, 2000a). Systems typically inoculate themselves from critique by claiming to be universal and natural. However, a provisional context is presumed, no matter how naturalized it may be.

The new positive social psychological technology set for itself the loftiest of goals, the maximization of human capabilities and efficiencies in the service of civic worth and cooperation in labor. Power flowed from coordinated effort, and so the new technology of social engineering would enhance colonial expansion, thus justifying its own versions of right and valuable from the self-evident fact of might. It was a pragmatic tautology. Those who made the system proved most fit by its (their) own criteria. As the study of philosophy waned, business schools and departments of anthropometry devoted to different regions of human behavior blossomed on university campuses. Galton, Binet, and others began to measure and predict the civic worth of individuals and groups of people. In a Huxley Memorial Lecture, the ambition Galton (1901) had for the social sciences was clearly stated:

To give a scientific [which to his limited thinking simply meant operationalized and measured] basis to the problem of race improvement under the existing conditions of civilisation and sentiment ... Men differ as much as dogs in inborn dispositions and faculties. ... So it is with men in respect to the qualities that go towards forming civic worth, which includes ... a high level of character, intellect, energy, and physique, and this would disqualify the vast majority of persons from that distinction. We may conceive that a committee might be entrusted to select the worthiest of the remaining candidates [for breeding], much as they select for fellowships, honours, or official posts. It is a fair assumption that the different grades of civic worth are distributed in accord with the familiar normal law of frequency. (p. 161)

It is important to separate science from technical engineering as, for example, Einstein sought to understand the universe, not improve it. The use of quantitative methods is not the definition of science.

Galton (1901) continues in his essay "Man" to equate character with moral behavior, which he claims to be highly correlated with "civic worth" as most easily measured by income. He observed, for instance, that "the large body of artisans who earn from 22s to 30s a week exactly occupy the place of mediocrity. ... So far as these represent civic worth they confirm ... a fairly normal distribution" (p. 161). He assessed the relative value of workers in East India Company factories in China (1868), and in his articles "Application of the Method of Percentiles to Mr. Yule's Data on the Distribution of Pauperism" (1896) and "On the Probability of the Extinction of Families" (with Reverend H. W. Watson, 1874), Galton argues that poor families should not be encouraged to have children because they will likely pass on the traits that cause pauperism. He even predicted the civic worth of offspring based on measurable family traits and observable behaviors.

Thus the premise of social science is that through the power of psychometry and anthropometry (statistical measures and tests, such as regression, correlation, and so forth, applied to human behavioral and personality traits) the human breed, its condition, and its prospects could be predicted, controlled, and improved. It amounts to a will to will as those who exhibit the greatest will to survive and propagate across the planet should be explicitly and aggressively cultivated. This new and bold positive ideology legitimized and guided Europe's colonial expansion in the Victorian mode, which in turn proved the worth of the ideology by conquering peoples who were thusly proven to be inferior. Mechanical clock-time became of the essence as European powers raced each other for control of the globe overwhelming other "sluggish" if not flat-out "backward" peoples (witness the cold war). However, it was rather a haphazard effort until a greater precision of measurement and control could be devised.

In response to the protests of many intellectuals, including George Bernard Shaw, H. G. Wells, Friedrich Schiller, and Wolfgang Goethe, Galton (whom many consider the first modern, quantitative social scientist) wrote the article "Why Do We Measure Mankind?" (Galton, 1890). Statistical measures of humans began as an explicit way to categorize and compare groups of people and individuals, to be "a valuable guide to the selection of the occupation for which he is naturally fitted" (Galton, 1890, p. 238). Inspired by Binet's use of human measures in France, Galton proclaimed his "great hope of seeing a system of moderate marks for physical efficiency introduced into the competitive examinations of candidates for employment" (Galton, 1890, pp. 238, 239). A mark meant a grade assigned to a measure of predicted efficiency.

Galton's goal was to collect systematically a large database on individuals and families and categorize them according to what he called "civic usefulness," meaning their relative level of contributions to England's economic worth and might. Using the databases he had, he predicted which families were likely to have children with the desired attributes and to then aggressively select and encourage those families to rear more children. An example is his article "Gregariousness in Cattle and Men" (Galton, 1871). This trait, incidentally, was still being selected for in 2003 by Gudykunst and Kim (2003, p. 369) and other psychologists.

Galton claimed that it was science's duty to "improve and develop the inborn qualities of a race" (Galton, 1904, p. 82). Gudykunst and Kim (2003) claim that "individual traits alone can be used as a good predictor of communication effectiveness" (p. 273), that in the interest of efficiency researchers need to specify "the characteristics of the people who can communicate effectively with strangers (i.e., competence is in the person)" (p. 275). For the sake of "effectiveness" in working with others, they offer advice for how to enhance performance through identifying and encouraging certain psychological attributes while minimizing other undesirable ones. To not "act out" or deviate from appropriate and competent behavior patterns, Gudykunst and Kim (2003) suggest that a person become "mindful," that he or she constantly strive to control his or her emotions in a calculated manner (p. 275).

I want to be clear that I am not claiming that Gudykunst and Kim (1997, 2003) are eugenicists. However, they are presuming that some people are either inherently or culturally unfit (they are ambiguous on this point). In either case the problem is in the individual, not the system. The point of their practical, prescriptive book is to help maladjusted people fit in, which is, I contend, very nationalistic and penultimately ethnocentric. They offer no suggestion for how to change unjust systems but only how to change misfit individuals. For whatever the ethnic environment, they are telling the sojourner that he or she must become a high self-monitor and assimilate or face the threat of being mentally ill (or mental deficiency is the cause of their inability to assimilate; again, they are not clear on the direction of causality perhaps because mental illness and a failure to agree with the system are equated by them).

Because they presume the Aristotelian mimetic model of communication competence, they wrongly believe that understanding is identical with agreeing. They are behaviorists who have misapplied ideas from cognitivism to explain culture and who have uncritically adopted a misapplication of the thermodynamic notion of equilibrium that makes sense only in a closed, zero-sum energy system. They presume that this metaphor accurately describes the human psyche, but it is a misapplication first made by Sigmund Freud and repeated by many psychologists. Human experience is not a closed system.

The point here is to demonstrate that positive social science has consistently, from Hegel and Comte to Galton and Pearson, to Gudykunst and Kim, postulated an ideology that the anthropologist Jules Henry (1963) identified as culture against the individual. The techniques of manipulation go through fashions, but the motives and function of positive social science as a technology for social engineering and a handmaiden to market interests and forced conformity are consistent.

After clearly stating his aim to improve society by improving the behavioral and psychological qualities of the people who constitute it, Galton cannot help himself. He then asks the obvious question, the philosophical question: What is meant by improvement? Claiming scientific disinterest as a refuge from such philosophical nonsense because open reflection on moral and ethical implications obstructs decisive action, he writes, "We must leave morals as far as possible out of the discussion on account of the almost hopeless difficulties they raise as to whether a character as a whole is good or bad" (Galton, 1904, p. 82). But then a line later he defines "better," writing that "all would agree that it was better ... to be well fitted than ill fitted for their part in life" and on their way to a "common civilisation" (Galton, 1904, p. 82).

Why is this better? Because it serves his personal bourgeois values and interests in the hegemony of positivism and its expansion to a single worldwide system, suppressing possible uncertainties and inefficiencies that pluralism in the form of local identities and "cultural parochialism" may threaten. Standardization in all things, including interpretations and predictability, and control (management) are the tools to achieve the goal of smooth economic expansion.

The goal is "for work to be accomplished effectively in the multicultural organization" (Gudykunst & Kim, 2003, p. 4). How do you do this? We are told by Gudykunst and Kim (1997, 2003) that we should do this by minimizing the salience of culture. Cultural distinction and perspectives must be generalized out of existence (which seems to contradict the notion of cognitive complexity), which is dubious advice because without a perspective knowledge and integration are impossible. Insofar as difference can lead to identity, contrariness, and resistance (no matter how minor), it must be managed for the sake of the overarching interest in perpetually increasing efficiency of performance and ever-expanding reproduction of the system. The best way to eliminate cultural differences and the difficulties genuine intercultural interaction always poses is to simply eliminate cultural differences, to "evolve" and progress and become "transcultural" (Gudykunst & Kim, 2003, p. 384). Such growth is not posited by Gudykunst and Kim (2003) as a regression toward a grand average or even as merely mundane progress but as nothing short of "psychic evolution" (p. 384). It is up or out. Gudykunst and Kim's version of evolution (conformity to system's needs and wishes) means to be eliminated.

According to this philosophy (though social engineers deny making value judgments), nonconforming individuals are seen as maladjusted, unfit, incompetent, counterproductive, inefficient, the cause of conflict, and in need of management from a transcending plane with greater understanding, maturity, and moral super-vision. What is moral is given the innocent-sounding monikers "practical" and "reasonable," which only begs the question. Efficiency and competence merge as operational and functional measures and also as the foremost values of the ironically "value-free" priests of the new positive religion (Comte, 1854/1891). This ideology is what Galton (1904) called the new "orthodox religious tenet of the future ... to cooperate with the workings of nature by securing that humanity shall be represented by the fittest races" (p. 82). Of course, such an elitist view is not at all representative but prescriptive.

The bold move from philosophy to practical social engineering supposedly facilitates self-improvement en masse even if improvement comes to mean being practical so that social engineering is self-justifying. Nothing could be better than getting better (improvement), and no one is more heroic than those who engineer improved efficiency. Gudykunst and Kim (1997) recommend their book by extolling what they believe to be its greatest virtue, of being practical, for what is practical is good, meaning "helpful in the performance of their [the readers'] work" no matter what it is (p. xii). This dumb sort of morality of sameness was born of imperial, in this instance British imperial, thinking. Already in 1887, in *The Genealogy of Morals,* Nietzsche (1887/1967) accurately traced its origins thus: "Herbert Spencer espoused that the concept 'good' is essentially identical with the concept 'useful,' 'practical,' so that in the judgments 'good' and 'bad' mankind has summed up and sanctioned ... the 'valuable in itself'" (Nietzsche, 1967, first essay, section 3, p. 27). What is the valuable in itself? The new positive religion answers the new Positive Religion, capitalized because it claims to not be merely a conventional perspective among other perspectives but something that is positively known (substantiated, embodied in appropriate behavior) to be wholly true.

Comte published the book *The Catechism of Positive Religion.* He came to regard himself as the founder of a new religion populated by priests who had a positive knowledge of good and evil and who should judge the abilities and worth of each member of society. Comte's plan for a positive social order would be carried out by such priests, along with the help of leaders in banking and industry. These priests would be the moral guides and censors of society and the definers of community. They would be guided by "spiritual powers," a notion echoed in Gudykunst and Kim (2003) when they evoked Buddhism as the source of their inspiration to "pass beyond the world of opposites, a world built up by intellectual distinctions and emotional defilements ... achieving an absolute point of view," which, as already noted, they call "intercultural personhood" (Suzuki, quoted by Gudykunst & Kim, 2003, p. 385). This is ironic because the previous three hundred pages of their book are dedicated to recounting a plethora of structural functional, cognitive, and behavioral definitions and categorizations.

Assimilation as the Great Leap Forward

Already, in the late 1800s Nietzsche challenged English psychologists (social Darwinists like Spencer) for their hatred of the human world of fallible perspectives and their promotion of a religion of nothing, as "a Buddhism for Europeans" (Nietzsche, 1967, p. 19). The priesthood of social scientists seeks to reduce anxieties by promoting order and stability as ordained by the new "positive truths," the most popular of which is the value of pliant malleability, which generally means being adaptable to the new industrial order. Control must be exercised to make things, especially markets, more stable, more predictable. According to Spencerians, uncertainty is regarded as solely the source of anxiety, which makes sense if you are trying to extract value from labor and the land but which actually leads to an ever-tightening process of command, feedback, and control—hardly flexibility. The bourgeois positivist's desire for steady progress and control leads to greater efforts to measure human beings, their consumption and output, and improve their stock. The goal is to minimize maladjustment to the system and maximize operational fitness. Certain physical and psychological traits—such as "positivity," an "internal locus of control [to blame oneself for system failures], persistence, hardiness, resourcefulness" (Gudykunst & Kim, 2003, p. 369), but most important a willingness to conform—are selected for, promoted for reproduction through either overt breeding or carefully ascertained rewards and punishments (cognitive management, operant conditioning, and psychological reconstruction). The "internal locus of control" is a good example of what Nietzsche meant when he traced the origin of conscience and its usefulness to centralized command and control (Nietzsche, 1967). Nietzsche and Gudykunst and Kim agree that once individuals assimilate (meaning that they have internalized the goals and motives of the system, reaching equilibrium and aligning with it), they are much easier to manage because at that point they self-manage by keeping their behaviors and attitudes within the parameters of system tolerance. Max Weber called this becoming institutionalized (Weber, 1904–1905/1930). The goal according to Gudykunst and Kim (2003) is to promote change "toward *assimilation*," which is accomplished when the individual becomes fully acculturated, identical with the system (p. 360).

In short, here is the great "leap forward," the great *should* (Gudykunst & Kim, 2003, p. 381). Everyone is advised to be flexible and willingly obedient, while the system remains implacably dominant. This, too, is an old value system espoused from the beginning of positivism by Comte and St. Simon in their writings on the industrial system and Spencer's linking of certainty with happiness in his book *Social Statics: The Conditions Essential for Human Happiness* (1850). A dependable person is a good person, just like clockwork (which was the prototype for the interdependent operation of the assembly line). Quality control checks tolerances, including measuring workers' mental and physical performance. It is a stringent, not loose attitude. While Spencer and others were singing the praises of an adaptable workforce, the soft stuff that fills the factory works to make it go, a tune still commonly heard, market laws and mechanisms do not manifest such flexibility or care. The market is a disinterested god. It is the flexible worker, the "just-in-time" permanent temporary worker who has to conform to the transcending rhythms of the market and the pace of industrial manufacture. As the omniscient and omnipotent market dictates, workers must be willing to retool themselves on demand. As Lewis Mumford (1964) observed, in the industrial world contingent individuals are subject to and serve the transcendent machine, not the other way around. Today, industry decries the state of education, demanding smarter labor, but it is a fact that market forces are driving millions to spend great amounts of money and time educating themselves in the hopes that they will be profitable to some corporation in the future. Work has taken over many peoples' lives. People have been very flexible, but there is much evidence that they are being stretched thin. To the market, workers are never pliant enough.

Successful fit involves more than just behavioral assimilation but also an adoption of the appropriate motivations and goals of the dominant system (Gudykunst & Kim, 2003, p. 290). "Competence" includes the adoption of "appropriate motivations" (pp. 275, 276) so that the assimilator will "work effectively with others" (p. 274). "Effectiveness is a function of professional expertise" (p. 274). There is a natural need for predictability, for reliable performance, just like clockwork (p. 276). Gudykunst and Kim (2003) strongly imply that a person who is not satisfied simply does not understand their place within the system (p. 275). Who could believe that being impractical is good? But what is practical to one is not to another because interests conflict. But according to Gudykunst and Kim (2003), those who are dissatisfied with the way a system works either just do not understand or are maladjusted and mentally ill. According to Gudykunst and Kim (2003), such a person is not likely to be effective, which "involves minimizing misunderstanding" and which is practically the same thing as "competence" (p. 271–75).

The bottom line is that only a happy worker can be an effective and competent worker because only he or she will be easily assimilated. But it also seems that happiness is a product of assimilation. In Gudykunst and Kim (2003) the direction of causation is unclear probably because they equate conformity with being well adjusted, with communication competence, with mental health. They also incorrectly equate several other concepts and processes, such as integration, adaptation, growth, learning, assimilation, and evolution. It is a tautological rhetoric, one that is self-contradicting, claiming that to evolve is to adapt to currently dominant conditions. Positivism claims that those who do not have a "positive orientation" (Gudykunst & Kim, 2003, p. 369) will not be good candidates for assimilation, and that those who assimilate have, by definition, a positive orientation. Furthermore, assimilationists claim that if people are not satisfied it is *because* they have not assimilated, meaning that they do not understand themselves and their place vis-à-vis the system. The positivistic evaluation of behavior is tautological, for the evaluation and the behavior are the same thing. To be effective and competent is to behave in effective and competent ways as defined by the priestly judges.

The question remains. Why are some people good, effective, well adjusted, "mature," evolved, and competent, and others are not? Galton's answer is inherent traits. Gudykunst and Kim and other cognitivists say basically the same thing, but not entirely. They claim in part that adaptability is dependent on internal states of mind and personality attributes. The so-called positive thing about this situation is that, either way, efficiencies and incompetencies can be managed and corrected, either through culturally (not naturally, which is far too slow and uncontrolled for Galton's tastes) selective breeding or through operant conditioning with perhaps the aid of pharmacology. But for many, including Gudykunst and Kim, the situation is ambiguous. For they claim that people who behave inappropriately do so because they are incompetent and they are incompetent because they do not possess the correct qualities of character, the correct "personality attributes" such as having a "positive orientation," being "flexible," self-controlling, and beyond this, chronologically young (Gudykunst & Kim, 2003, pp. 272–75, 370). Such characteristics may very well be beyond the control of an individual and may originate in genetic predisposition, which would lead to the solution originally offered by Galton and the other eugenicists like Pearson and Yule.

The best worker is one who has an "unusual degree of integration or stability, and who is socialized on the basis of cultural universals, and a marked telepathic or intuition sensitivity" (Gudykunst & Kim, 2003, p. 273). Such mystical universals are presumably global in application, but actually they smack of a very ethnocentric bias and set of interests. Nevertheless, if things can be corrected through a proper regime of reeducation or resocialization, then the problem of inappropriate and incompetent behavior can be solved by proper parenting. This is exactly the move taken by social engineers, for when human breeding fell out of favor John Watson, Ivan Pavlov, and B. F. Skinner dedicated themselves to the study of child-rearing. The goal of appropriate behavior can be achieved "through the process of enculturation, cultural patterns are etched into our nervous system and become part of our personality and behavior" (Gudykunst & Kim, 2003, p. 376). If we have been "programmed" to think, feel, and behave in unpredictable or "improper, irresponsible, or inferior ways" (p. 376), this can be corrected through reeducation by a process of "psychic disintegration" (also called "deculturation" and "unlearning") toward "greater personality integration and maturity" (pp. 380, 381).

In either case the prediction and modifying control of behavior toward some undebatable good (for that is philosophical nonsense) is the aim of social engineering.

Gudykunst and Kim (1997, 2003) argue that bad mental health, failure to adjust, and being unfit resides in the individual who does not accept the goals and motives of the system. This can be true, but for them this can never be seen as an appropriate response to injustice. Such an individual is defined by Gudykunst and Kim (2003) as "immature" because he or she does not manifest an "internal locus of control" (p. 369). Such a person cannot or will not "reorganize" him- or herself, and therefore they will not achieve the great "leap forward" after the resolution of dialectical stress (p. 381). According to Gudykunst and Kim (2003), to help individuals be more satisfied and the community more stable, the individual must be acculturated into a greater understanding of the system, which insofar as the individual identifies with the system equals greater clarity and depth of self-understanding and self-control. This is pure Hegelianism. Gudykunst and Kim argue that the more a person identifies with the dominant system, the more competent and therefore satisfied they will be and the more they will understand and behave appropriately (fit). Issues of fairness, justice, and the good are never discussed by them, demonstrating that their brand of operational philosophy is not nearly as sophisticated as even the Benthamites, who created the tradition that they unknowingly parrot.

The White Man's Burden and the Victorian Saints

In the nineteenth century Galton and others bombastically abandoned philosophy for objective science, claiming that they made no value judgments, even as they measured social improvement and the "civic worth" of individuals and groups (Galton, 1901). It was falsely assumed that markets could not thrive in the midst of conditions defined by their measures as either inefficient or chaotic (because a polyglot of diverse value and belief systems cannot work together). Assimilation and standardization constitute the recipe for making markets expand. Therefore, for the sake of the market, the values and motives of people must regress toward a common standard culture. The standard culture and universal truth must include committed belief in private property, legal contract, credit financing, profit taking, the virtues of labor, the morality of dependable uniformity, and so forth, all of which are essential to the success of only capitalist market expansion. But notice, market is universalized, as if there have not been for eons other types of economies that functioned successfully—types that were not capitalistic.

Summation

As the once-popular doctrine of human breeding became politically untenable, the effort to modify human character and conduct shifted from controlling hereditary characteristics to controlling cultural causes of outcomes. As noted, this led to efforts to discover the most effective means of behavioral modification with a new focus on child-rearing practices. But as this is terribly complex, another strategy is to promote the elimination of pluralism, of multiculturalism altogether. Progress is thus construed as anticulture, for difference is an obstacle to expansion of the same, of reproduction of the system. With advances in bioengineering, the pendulum is swinging back toward enforcing values, desires, and preferences at the genetic level.

The point here is that although methods change and the locus of cause changes somewhat from heredity to culture, the fundamental motivation for social engineering informed by so-called value-free science remains the same. This shift was overtly manifested in U.S. and British economic policy during the early 1980s, when fashion in economic theory moved away from the Keynesian approach to the economic Darwinian approach of Friedrich von Hayek (von Hayek, 1948). Coincidentally this is the period when intercultural adaptation theory was formulated.

This shift from collective cooperation to comparative competition as the best way to encourage more production and consumption (for profit is realized with each unit sold) is central to understanding the difference between a global village and a global city, in understanding the qualitative global trend toward cosmopoly. In the world of Galton and von Hayek, economic performance is the sole measure of the positive values of "progress," "happiness," "mental health," and "success." This is the worldview being promoted across cultures. Authorities tell those that do not measure up that they must either conform, which became synonymous with being competent and functionally fit, or get out of the way of progress.

GLOBAL CITY

As the world shrinks, intercultural communications is being supplanted by a single emerging world culture that is chasing a dream of greater cosmopolitan sophistication and urban/cosmopolitan escapism from local cultural attachment and identification; what some modern Spencerians call the "incompetence" and "emotional defilement" of cultural identity, and "humanity itself," the corruption of having a sense of place (Gudykunst & Kim, 2003, p. 385). As Nietzsche understood, forced compliance to such a pseudo-religious doctrine of absolute identification (transcendental uniformity) does have actual consequences, though most of the actual consequences do not resemble the ideal at all. Rather than escaping suffering, the cosmopolitan dream, as will be discussed, seems to be causing it. Insofar as this dream of global conformity succeeds in eliminating diversity and thus meaning, it also causes despair. The elimination of difference (universal identification) means no identity and therefore no communication.

As New Age cosmopolitans chant the mantra of holism, confounding boundaries (identities) are indeed being rapidly eliminated. Such sacrifices are seen as a sort of collateral damage that may be unfortunate but necessary for the sake of progress. The fundamental ideological justification behind this assault on local culture and identity was best stated at the height of Victorian colonial expansion by Herbert Spencer in his books *Social Statics* (1851) and *The Factors of Organic Evolution* (1887). It is a combination of Comtean and Hegelian colonial ordination with religious fervor (also see Andreski, 1972). Bourgeois positivism is a self-justifying ideology that offers a utopian vision while refusing to focus on the consequences of global uniformity except in terms of survival of the fittest, efficiency, functionality, and competence in systems operation (profit taking). Bourgeois positivism (including Hegelian historical evolution) forms the core set of ideas in the ideology of cosmopoly.

The cosmopolis is not the same as a physical city. To be sure, it does involve the physical migration and concentration of people into urban centers, but it is also about the idealistic promises that make city life seductive to billions of people (cosmopoly). The cosmopolis is the result of the global diffusion of the ideology of cosmopolitanism, which is a cultural bias and fantasy that originated in wealthy urban centers in the industrialized West.

The global village rhetoric has been an important ideological tool for justifying worldwide Western style urbanization. The village metaphor gives the false impression that the world is becoming less alienating, less stressed, and more stable and equitable. Meanwhile, the cosmopolitan ideology pushes for personal connectivity (which itself indicates fragmentation), social mobility, individualism, and endless economic promise. A major and self-serving aspect of the global village rhetoric and global urbanization is the promotion of competent communication itself as a key to modernity, which is equated with happiness, positive progress, and Westernization.

Yet many assimilationists cannot make up their minds. Do they want global assimilation ("totality"), which involves the elimination of national and cultural identities (transnationalism), or do they want strong assimilation (i.e., a single national language) at the national level?

ABSURD ADVICE

A contradiction emerges in the ideology of social Darwinism generally and intercultural adaptation theory as it is presented by Gudykunst and Kim (2003) specifically. In one hand, the ultimate dream of assimilationists is the elimination of inadequate or defiled cultures and the triumph of a single bourgeois positive culture and "meta-identity" (also called transcultural identity and universal personhood, both of which suggest the end of the possibility of *intercultural* personhood, not its equivalent). On the other hand, the same writers absurdly advise minorities to assimilate as deeply as possible into the dominant local (host) culture (Gudykunst & Kim, 2003). According to nationalists, assimilation is equal to "psychic evolution," "mental health," "functional fitness," "balance," and "maturity" (Bennett, 1993; Buchanan, 2001; Gudykunst & Kim, 2003). In short, if you want to get along, you had better think, feel, and act like the dominant mainstream culture or else you will not survive.

Perhaps the contradiction is only apparent. It may be that Gudykunst and Kim actually promote a linear process of homogenization in hierarchical fashion, such as eventually there should be only one world culture. But they are unclear. But Gudykunst and Kim (2003), also claim that

in becoming intercultural, we rise above the hidden forces of culture and ... in this developmental process we acquire a greater capacity to overcome cultural parochialism and develop *a wider circle of identification*, approaching the limit of many cultures and ultimately of humanity itself. The process of becoming intercultural, then, is like climbing a high mountain. As we reach the mountaintop, we see that all paths below ultimately lead to the same summit. (p. 385; emphasis in original)

It is important to note the singularity of "a circle of identification." Arguing against Gudykunst and Kim, integration does *not* mean total agreement or identification on a global level. This version of happy positivism is just as hopelessly idealistic and potentially dangerous as their mystical notion of escaping the emotional defilements of this world by means of psychic evolution to "realize the spiritual world of non-distinction" (Gudykunst & Kim, 2003, p. 384). By their own definition, their final solution of realizing a world of nondistinction would be the same as death: zero cognitive complexity, absolute equilibrium—no mind. This is why Nietzsche pointed out in 1887 that "pessimistic philosophers," who flee from life and action, instead embrace "administrative nihilism" and place "'adaptation' in the foreground, that is to say, an activity of the second rank, a mere reactivity; indeed, life itself has been defined as a more and more efficient inner adaptation to external conditions (Herbert Spencer)" (Nietzsche, 1967, p. 79).

Recognizing this nihilistic tendency, Nietzsche claims that "actually, what is steaming around all of these positivistic systems is the vapor of a certain pessimistic gloom, something that smells of weariness, fatalism, disappointment, and fear of new disappointments" (Nietzsche, 1974, p. 288, book 5, section 347). Nietzsche suspects Schopenhauer's "Buddhism for Europeans" for its admonition to give up and let go the miserable wheel of life. Insofar as Nietzsche (1974) is correct that "consciousness developed only under the pressure for the need for communication [that] consciousness is really only a net of communication between human beings" (p. 298), we can see how Gudykunst and Kim's solution to intercultural misunderstandings and conflicts, which is the elimination of cultures and the striving for no mind, has a perverse sense to it. The solution to communication, which inevitably includes misunderstanding and conflicts, is to stop communicating altogether. This is accomplished by eliminating all difference.

This is also why such romantic pessimists valorize a "virtuous stupidity," the reduction of the self to a reactionary spectator if not the total elimination of the self. The redemptive goal is the reduction of the self to the impoverished status of an object, a dishonest "it" that claims to be innocently free of all prejudice, all perspective, even while promoting a value-laden ideology (1974, p. 131). Nietzsche notes that the cosmopolitan Roman, who had all the world at her feet, lost her sense of self, of good and evil, that the Roman world became depersonalized, and this was embraced as "redemption and transfiguration as if it were an end in itself" (Nietzsche, 1972, p. 115). It became virtuous to regard oneself as an instrument, as a mirror, that the very notion of knowledge was reduced to a sort of mirroring. The disinterested observer, the "objective man,"

waits until something comes along and then gently spreads himself out, so that not even the lightest footsteps and the fluttering of ghostly beings shall be lost on his surface and skin. Whatever still remains to him of his "own person" seems to him accidental, often capricious, more often disturbing: so completely has he become a passage and reflection of forms and events not his own. (Nietzsche, 1972, p. 115).

Here we have the "sublimest kind of slave," human as formula, as pure form without content, "a delicate, empty, elegant, flexible mold which has first to wait for some content so as 'to form' itself by it—as a rule a man without content is a 'selfless' man," a person who can never "take sides between good and evil" (Nietzsche, 1972, p. 116). Utility transvaluates the just and the unjust. Herein lies the dishonesty of claims to objectively improve society, the rhetorical trick of naturalizing and universalizing contingent interests in an effort to outrun reflection and critique. For what sane person would argue with absolute truth?

A century before the popular theory of cultural adaptation resurfaced with a global focus as *inter*cultural adaptation, Nietzsche offers a compelling explanation of its motives and dubious claim to be value-free and yet redemptive. Here, too, we can see what the virtuous minority, the perfect herd animal should aspire to be—if not a passive instrument of external forces then nothing at all.

To be a "profitable business manager in a multinational company," and to "increase our functional fitness and psychological health," we must follow Gudykunst and Kim's model of human development, which involves grasping the whole or totality (Gudykunst & Kim, 2003, p. 376). But Gebser (1949/1985) reminds us: "It is no accident that the ambivalence inherent in the (Latin) primal word *totus* is evident in the word 'totality.' Although in more recent times the word *totus* has meant 'all' or 'whole,' it would earlier have meant 'nothing.' In any event, the audial similarity between *totus* and [German] *tot*, 'dead,' is readily apparent" (p. 18). As explained, this is precisely the ultimate goal of assimilationism, to achieve nothingness, no mind, the gloomy and ironic consequence of positivism.

OPERATIONALIZING HEGELIAN IDEALISM

Mass communications is an urban phenomenon that promotes the urban perspective. According to this perspective, it should not be surprising that a sure sign of rural inferiority is the lack of print and telecommunication channels available to people. This constitutes the quintessential modern condition, an endless spiral of progress such that the more one is exposed to global media the more one wants to urbanize, which in turn exposes one to more media, ad infinitum (evincing what Rostow in 1952 promoted as the take-off stage in national identity building and economic development). Big cities are where life (news and entertainment) happens. The media plays a cultural binding role, promoting a common national language and set of interests and expectations. Modern ideology teaches that rural people are missing the party both within a nation and among variously urbanized nations. Thus, relative deprivation becomes the source of frustration and conflict. Ghettoization has gone global as information ghettos are popping up around the world. It is the height of arrogance, however, to assume that the information the West has to offer, if unattainable, renders people starved and culturally retarded. How much of their world do we in the urban centers know? Well, that doesn't matter because traditional cultures have nothing worthy of our attention anyway. We know this even though we do not know what we are talking about. According to this view, rural people are at risk of being left behind, of having no future. They are behind Rostow's curve. Thus we have the engineering of dissatisfaction, rising expectations that cannot be met, which leads to rising frustration. With the advent of the Western philosophy of positivism and its linear notion of progress, everywhere else is backward, for the city is forward thinking, the tip of advancing system and developmental evolution.

Model Minority Mind Guards

One important question regards how much we are willing to sacrifice for the sake of progress toward a homogenized global identity. Much has already been sacrificed for Western progress, which ethnocentrically presumes that it is the only kind of progress conceivable (Diamond, 1997; McWhorter, 2002; Zinn, 1980). On the planet there are not only the haves and have-nots but also the dominating and the dominated. Those who strive, who are willing to sacrifice to join the dominant cosmopolitan class are considered by assimilationists to be model minorities. They offer little or no resistance to the inevitable march of progress. Rather than resisting the trajectory toward overwhelming Westernization and modernization and the unprecedented collapse of cultural and therefore biodiversity (for only one version of nature is left when only one culture is left because nature is a cultural invention, and the Western version sees nature as primarily an exploitable base resource), the model minority, working from a Western concept of pure personal interest, fights to fit into the system, to conform for the sake of personal rewards. Model minorities may even become so enamored with belonging that they become what Irving Janis (1982) calls mind guards, or snitches and bullies seeking to curry favor. Though they have little power within the system, as it is given, they become the most fervent defenders of the faith.

Mind guards are self-selecting sycophants who seek to ingratiate themselves with authority by betraying deviants in the hope of personal recognition and reward. With their help everything is more predictable, redundant, and stable. The neo-Hegelian system, which jealously guards its equilibrium with cybernetic channels of feedback (i.e., the KGB in the Soviet system and the SS in the right Hegelian system) always and ethnocentrically defines itself as natural, rational, and good. What is most practical to any centralized command and control system is that which helps perpetuate it. Thus practicality has a perspective and an interest. The minority should never get involved in politics, for that is nonsense, mere subjective valuation and as such irrational. Conformity and certainty are the keys to happiness. Besides, minorities, by definition, don't understand reality. They are still "learning," becoming "civilized," "naturalized."

Only the positivists, the most evolved humans on Comte's hierarchy of knowledge, think right and grasp the Real. Only when minorities become one with the dominant culture, when they think and act like the mainstream, should they venture to participate as politically active members of society.

For assimilationists, conformity equals psychic evolution to higher levels of cognitive complexity and satisfaction. But there is no proof that smarter people experience less anxiety. Experts assure us that certainty and functional fit eliminate anxiety and alienation. But the end of redundancy (certainty and predictability) is boredom, which is highly associated with depression.

Finally, the model minority should unquestioningly accept the world order being handed down; otherwise the system will not reward him or her, the assumption being that he or she is not a part of the system until he or she is identical with it in all aspects of mind and body. Until then it is assumed that his or her presence has no impact on the system. The assumption is that integration means equilibrium. But this is false. Equilibrium means an identification of the part with the whole so that the distinction between the two disappears. But then communication is impossible. Janis (1982) calls this groupthink. Undoubtedly this involves cohesion, but it also results in no independent (critical) thinking. This is precisely why Nietzsche refers to the subjects of assimilationist ideology as herd animals.

Integration is not holistic homogeneity. Integration means that the parts do not dissolve or disintegrate into a uniform whole but rather that they maintain their unique identities so that the parts communicate and the overall system remains dynamic. I argue against Gudykunst and Kim (2003, pp. 383–85), who make an absurd claim that becoming intercultural is the same as becoming transcultural, which means the elimination of all cultural perspectives. I believe that integration does not conclude with equifinality, the ultimate goal of absolute oneness, holistic identity. The Hegelian notion of a final goal of equifinality means that the ideal minority is one who disintegrates and blends into the system, becoming invisible. The system uses the minority individual. According to this philosophy, a minority never brings anything of value or anything new to the community. According to the ethics of assimilation, goodness (value) is only measured by how much the individual fits in (Spencer's survival of the fittest).

Civil and human rights protests, struggles for justice and equity, and resistance can give a person a great sense of purpose, pride, and satisfaction. But for Gudykunst and Kim, no resistance to the system can be seen as valuable, useful, or appropriate. To them, resistance is futile. Resistance to the "hidden forces of culture," the invisible hand, no matter how oppressive, is not appropriate for the model minority, who should instead strive to identify with the system no matter how unjust or oppressive it might be. The only suggestion they offer is to adopt the dominant values and beliefs, even if those values define you as inferior (Du Bois, 1903/1995). Thus the system is self-correcting; the status quo is reproduced with utmost efficiency. There can only be one positive reality. Anticulturalists assure us that we are all the same, but we do not know it until we become mature and "psychically evolved" to the point of no longer being human or cultured. Then we achieve the absurdity of "clarity" (Gudykunst & Kim, 2003, p. 383) without distinction (even though hierarchy, the penultimate Western mode of distinction, is presumed throughout). No wonder Fukuyama (1993) would see fit to announce the end of history and the last Man.

DISENTANGLING EVOLUTION THEORY FROM POSITIVISM

It should be noted that being a natural scientist, Charles Darwin never posited an absolute goal to evolution. Nor did he apply it to human society, like his cousin Galton did. It also should be noted that in systems theory, equilibrium is possible only in a finite system. Therefore if teleology is not presumed, one cannot sensically postulate a hypothetical state of equilibrium. To Darwin, life is not going anywhere. There is no final perfect being, no transcultural meta-identity. Such a notion is, however, common to many ancient teleological systems, engineers, and also to Comte's positive religion, which Darwin wisely avoided. Life's abundance of forms is horizontal rather than vertical. It proliferates in a diversity of forms but with no preestablished final goal-species. Each life form is equally successful as long as it survives. But with the advent of the Enlightenment philosophies, compendia of hierarchical rankings proliferated, beginning with Vico's *Principe de scienza nuova d'intorno alla commune natura delle nazioni* (1725) and continuing through Montesquieu's *Observations on Roman Greatness and Decline* (1734) and Voltaire's *Experiment Concerning the Customs and Spirit of Nations* (1756). Comparisons of groups of people, which led to ever-greater efforts at anthropometry always seemed to prove that Europe was number one (Kramer & Johnson, 1997). As one might guess, Europe always fared well vis-à-vis its own values expressed as standard measures and relative to the primitive savages that populated the rest of the world.

The absolute conceptualization of positive progress to some final goal is a Hegelian invention, anticipated by Lessing's *Education of the Human Race* (1780) and Herder's *Ideas Toward a Philosophy of Human History* (1784). It is no mere coincidence that such ideas proliferated during the height of European colonialism.

Perhaps the first great postcolonial scholar, Gebser (1985), noted in the 1940s that "'progress' is not a positive concept, even when mindlessly construed to be one; progress is also a progression away, a distancing and withdrawal from something" (p. 41). But if that difference, that Other something, is ethnocentrically denigrated as primitive, then progress seems wholly positive. Positivism then presumes a negative critique of the actual in favor of a utopian vision, the future. Vision permits only one perspective; hence, the infinite narrowness of positivism. There can be only one truth, one future.

Make no mistake, whenever a grand *should* is implicated in purpose and goal orientation, when people are sure they are going somewhere, one is dealing with ideology, not science, with social engineering and hypothetical conjecture, not discovery and description. When that goal-oriented reality is absolutely exclusive, even singularly natural, then one is face to face with the dream of totalitarianism, what Greider (1997) calls the manic logic of "one world, ready or not."

Spencer's ideology has come back into fashion in the form of intercultural adaptation theory (Gudykunst & Kim, 2003). But despite this, life has no perspective, and without perspective there can be no backward or upward-forward to evolution. Perspective emerges with the ego, and most powerfully so with the modern I. After reflecting on the fascist (both Left and Right) Hegelian systems that were wreaking havoc in Europe, Gebser recognized the practical implications of this ideology of absolute justifications and historical destiny (fatalism). He observed that

the current situation manifests on the one hand an egocentric individualism exaggerated to extremes and desirous of possessing everything [endless progress], while on the other it manifests an equally extreme collectivism that promises the total fulfillment of man's being [modern mass conformity] ... These two conditions, isolation and aggregation, are in fact a clear indication that individualism and collectivism have now become deficient. (Gebser, 1985, p. 3)

Massification, which marks the modern world, supports status quo, and individual freedom, is also a hallmark of modernity. Individualism, like all -isms, looks astoundingly uniform. Despite private property, all are equal under the touch of Adam Smith's invisible hand, and the coveted property is identically mass-produced, from homes to bumper-sticker philosophies and clothes to furniture, music, and education.

To Gebser, *deficiency* means that a thing or process has qualities and characteristics that may have once been very vital but, in a changing context, are causing it to expire; it is failing to survive. This includes the hypertrophy of egocentrism that was once so vital to Western civilization but increasingly shows indications of hypertrophism and as such is leading to the death of viable community, of reciprocity, and thus of authentic communication and mutual obligation. Most large cities, such as São Paulo, Mexico City, Istanbul, Cairo, Mumbay, and so forth, are barely functional. Such intensification of the modern ego gives rise to alienation in epidemic proportions, a massive experience that has been measured and studied by countless social scientists, urban planners, and human ecologists; a crisis that indeed helped call into existence these very disciplines as evinced in Töennies, Marx, Durkheim, Freud, Mumford, and Weber. Although the West harbors more individuals choosing to live alone because they want total control of everything and cannot tolerate any obstruction to their personal freedom, at the same time those isolated individuals constitute en masse unconscious movements, which are deficient because the participation in them is purely passive, reactionary, and adaptive. They prefer to consume whatever makes its way to their doors and screens but alone, without dialogue. The computer screen with a billion Internet channels is not made for group viewing. There is no need to fight over which channel to watch.

Gebser argues that there is an important qualitative and behavioral difference between community and a massive aggregate of individuals pursuing their disconnected yet standardized personal interests. The bourgeois pursuit of personal happiness has had major costs vis-à-vis community, the person (*anomie*), and the environment. Even morality has become personalized, so that what is good is good for me. But though moderns may try hard to create individual environments ruled by their individual moralities, the global environment remains a shared domain.

ONE UTOPIA FOR ALL

This positivistic notion of progress toward a single world cultural order (for it is impossible to have a totally decultured human being despite the rhetoric) has already demanded great sacrifices from the "primitive," "unenlightened," "less evolved" masses. Hundreds of cultures and linguistic communities have been systematically eliminated, exterminated, by the advance of progress (Diamond, 1993, 1997; Zinn, 1980). As John McWhorter (2002) observes, dying languages leave no fossil trace. Once a language is gone, so is its community. This is especially true for languages that have no written form (which begs the question of the cognitive complexity of traditional oral peoples who must memorize their entire cultural heritage). But even attempts at preservation, which involve the creation of dictionaries, are closer to the function of being a "cultural taxidermist" (Morris, 1969) than an active community member.

Preservation involves a confusion between the actual and the virtual. Although the actual community is disappearing, preservationists rush in to make a record (a fetish) of it. The record is not the same thing as what it mimics. For instance, once dictionaries are compiled, a language is institutionalized; it becomes standardized, encouraging persistence of meaning and usage, what Algis Mickunas (forthcoming) calls permanence enhancement, which means that the vitality characteristic of a living language is lost even as it is preserved (also see Löwith, 1967). Preservation of culture in museums and dictionaries is like saving a bit of something in a jar. It becomes treasured tradition, rather than common practice. It ossifies and becomes quickly antiquated. Once a culture hits a crisis point that demands preservation efforts, it is usually already too weak to save except as a specimen in an archive of extinct worldviews. Within one or two generations its context vanishes and its meaning forgotten. What it meant becomes a synopsis on a card next to its case that encourages rote recitation at best.

To be modern demands the renouncing of local culture and tradition as anything other than antique. This includes the traditional self. One can progress upward-forward only insofar as one moves away from the past, abandoning ("unlearning" and "disintegrating") one's old premodern self and culture (Gudykunst & Kim, 2003, pp. 379–83). The good minority, the model minority, is the one who is defined as being adaptable, which is a euphemism for being eager to disintegrate "cognitively, affectively, operationally," to be willing (for motivation, attitude, and commitment are essential to evolutionary success) to be decultured and psychically reorganized in the mold presented by the dominant culture (Gudykunst & Kim, 2003, pp. 269–73, 360, 369–69). As we have seen more than once in the twentieth century, this line of argument has led to various reeducation programs, such as those in China, Cambodia, the Soviet gulag, and so on, and also the reprogramming efforts of some groups aimed at "deviants" like gays and lesbians (Dittmer, 1974; Koestler, 1946/1984; Lifton, 1999; Lind, 1985; Solzhenitsyn, 1974/1997; Wu-Ming, et al., 1999; Yang, 1986). Ostensibly this effort is for the good of the individual so that they may gain greater mental health, clarity, and self-control, through a "higher level of self-understanding" (Gudykunst & Kim, 1997, pp. 348, 351, 360, 362, 364). In 1807, Hegel made the same suggestions for the accomplishment of greater self-monitoring, adjustment, and evolution in Chapter Four of his *Phenomenology of Mind* (1979), "The Truth of Self-Certainty." Growth, which is "central to Y. Kim's theory of intercultural transformation," is not enrichment through gaining new repertoires of thinking and acting but a zero-sum destruction-reconstruction of the psyche.

This amounts to the absurd equation of learning with forgetting (unlearning), cumulative growth with either/or-ism, which is a vicious trap exemplified by a tiger pacing back and forth in a cage; a dilemma already exposed as such by Kierkegaard in 1843. According to Gudykunst and Kim, growth is *not* cumulative. It is noteworthy that a year later, and some 130 years before Charles Berger and R. Calabrese (1975) invented "uncertainty [and anxiety] reduction theory," Kierkegaard wrote *The Concept of Anxiety*. In this book he demonstrated that the greatest anxiety comes not from uncertainty (for therein lies potential, discovery, and hope), but from the perceived fatalism of certainties, such as original sin, a single positive reality leading to a totally predictable future, death, and (one might add) taxes. Curiously, in the search for the inevitable (absolute certainty), if it were discoverable (which it is not, thankfully), humanity would face a crisis of all tomorrows being as today, a crisis of anxiety and finally nihilistic death. This is why Nietzsche regards positive knowledge (facticity) the height of intolerance and the end of growth/life, true negativism, the "mind of No."

If life accepted the world as it is, *then* evolution would stop. Not accepting the world as it is (positively known) is the source of potential, the birthplace of infinite futures: daybreak. The presence of each organism affects the environment, which in turn offers new opportunities for future forms. Thankfully, nature is not limited to human desires, interests, and imagination.

We must not constrain ourselves to asking only how, which is the mechanical question, but why. Why does the world have to be only this way? Although the mechanical/physical universe is highly uniform and governed by law, the why question is especially important in the human life-world, which exhibits freedom of choice and variance of behavior. Those who work day and night to establish the laws of human behavior, even to reduce culture to physiology, are unwittingly building a cage for themselves. How can such a culture dominate? Like all ideological systems that seek to change the world, it must appeal to base desires. The pseudo-scientific (actually religious) propaganda of positive surety, which claims to know the single best solution to every problem (including life itself), titillates greed and promises to maximize pleasure while minimizing pain. To achieve such salvation, the follower must conform to the creed, the single most efficient way, climbing to the summit where all vistas must converge (hyperperspectivism and ethnocentrism). The positive worldview bribes its adherents with promises of material wealth and happiness if only all variance will obediently converge on the mean, if only all peoples embrace its singular vision of the future. Those who do not will naturally face sanctions.

Following are "facts," but they are provisional, and thus it is hoped that we can yet avert a massive implosion of cultural diversity, drastically shrinking the human mind and life-world. What is offered is in the hope and spirit of the Latin proverb *utinam vates falsus sim*, that I were a false prophet.

URBAN COLONIZATION OF RURAL SURROUNDINGS: THE ABSURDITY OF SALVATION (SAVING) BY CONSUMING

People all over the world are rushing to the cities trying to better their lives and progress in all ways. The romantic dimension of cosmotopian thinking and stimulation, however, quickly wears off once the realities of actual urban life are experienced personally. This occurs when the rural peasant arrives at the great city only to find him- or herself trapped in a squalid slum at the edge of the urban center, like the *callampas* in Chile or the *favelas* in Brazil. The city cultivates tremendous gaps between the haves and the have-nots, which do not reflect traditional village life. Neither the existence of mobility nor the presence of a between or middle class eliminates the gap but only partially fills it. So the existence of an economic middle class and limited mobility is not a solution to the gap itself but merely makes it more tolerable and therefore more resistant to challenge. The existence of limited mobility and a middle class shifts responsibility for one's condition from the context to the self, and thus individualism is stressed in the urban world.

No city is self-sufficient, so all cities must colonize the surrounding territories to survive. Consequently, all cities are essentially imperialistic. Also, all cities consist of complex divisions of people and labor, from the first city of Ur in Asia Minor to the first great imperial metropolis of Rome (Morris, 1969; Mumford, 1961, 1964). Such divisions become institutionalized and normalized; with this process coalesce distinctive status differences and levels of participatory power and privilege. To integrate in the highly hierarchical modern society means to accept one's niche as though it is natural and logical and separate from the one who fills it (see Chapter One on the ideology of nichism).

As the planet urbanizes, such gaps are materializing on a global level. Increasingly, the well-educated and wealthy urban elite in countries like Pakistan and Russia share more in common with each other than they do with their poor countrymen just down the road. This is a common pattern around the world not only of wealth distribution but also of mental perspective.

For instance, in Africa's largest city, Cairo, hundreds of thousands of people live in the tombs of the notorious city of the dead, a huge cemetery on the edge of the city. They do so because they were attracted by a romantic vision of the urban lifestyle, but the reality is that the city does not offer them affordable housing, basic sanitation, educational opportunities, or livable wages. Meanwhile the urban elite, only a few miles away in the city center, live in a different world of transnational values, experiences, opportunities, and behaviors. The same gap can be observed all over the world, from Rio de Janeiro to New Delhi, Shanghai to Mexico City, and Istanbul to Manila.

Cosmopolitanism is an ethnocentric ideology that legitimates the growth of the global city. It is a cultural perspective and set of values that originated in the life experiences of a small minority of urbane and wealthy European elite. Today however, this ideology has spread worldwide as the wealthy elite of other countries seek to mimic their European and American role models. In turn they convey this cultural perspective through various means, including domestic mass media, which confers further status unto their image, to their poorer countrymen, thus creating a rising tide of unrealistic and frustrated expectations (Baudrillard, 1968). As rural populations are also striving to become cosmopolitan, the entire globe is urbanizing and becoming no longer self-sufficient. The problem is that unlike a typical city, the global city has no territories external to the earth itself to colonize and exploit to maintain this ideal lifestyle. Instead, humans are taxing the ability of the planet to sustain the lifestyle of the global cosmopolis. Humanity is testing the carrying capacity of our world.

WORLD CULTURE AND THE END OF FRONTIERS

The Western philosophy of positivism claims that every problem has just one best solution. As may be expected, positivists claim that the one best and most true, rational, and even natural solution to human social organization is positivism itself. The primary value of European bourgeois culture is the unending accumulation of wealth. Bourgeois positivists believe that greed is the most natural of all human instincts. This is an extremely ethnocentric prejudice but a widely and rapidly spreading one nonetheless. Many (if not most) cultures have not promoted the belief that greed is good or natural. For instance, the cultures of Japanese Bushido and the ancient Greek Spartans held other values, such as honor and courage, above being wealthy and even took pride in not needing much material luxury to be satisfied. Their ideals were simplicity, fraternity, honesty, and valor. Most traditional cultures, like the Spartans, are collectivistic, meaning that they devalue the importance of the individual. By contrast, modern bourgeois positivism values individualism and the accumulation of privacy in wealth, time, space. Only in the urban world does austerity become poverty and a shame, even a potential threat to the mass production/consumption system. New markets must be continually opened (as evinced by the histories of India, Japan, and China, even up to today).

When bourgeois positivists impose their cultural values and beliefs on other ways of organizing society as criteria for determining the best solution to the problem of human organization, it is not surprising that they conclude that positivism is the most natural, rational, and best solution. But of course this is a self-serving and a self-fulfilling prophecy. Nevertheless, the predominantly commercial mass media are very persuasive in spreading the values and beliefs of bourgeois positivism around the world. As the world embraces positivistic bourgeois culture, its values, and way of living, it is leading to what Paul Feyerbend (1987) has called world culture. Reflecting on this new, world culture, Feyerbend observes: "By now Western forms of life are found in the most remote corners of the world and have changed the habits of people who only a few decades ago were unaware of their existence. Cultural differences disappear, indigenous crafts, customs, and institutions are being replaced by Western objects, customs, organizational forms" (Feyerbend, 1987, pp. 2–3). Standardized modern artifacts and culture are replacing handcrafted local products and cultures. Local cultural products and arts are being replaced by cheap reproductions of the great masters who hail from the traditions of the G7 nations. Miniaturized recordings of mass-marketed Western rhythms and instrumental sounds are displacing folk music. Indigenous craftsmanship is also disappearing as mass-produced modern plastic imitations of more expensive goods take their place. Why make music when you can buy "better" modern electronic music made by entertainment superstars? Art has become an industry. Likewise, counterfeiting high-priced designer products is a major industry in the third world.

Ironically, just as they are being driven into extinction, genuine folk arts (like sacred masks from Africa and ceremonial jewelry from Indonesia) are being commodified by collectors in the industrial centers of the new world order. Because the traditional ceremonies for which such art forms were produced are disappearing, such artifacts are increasingly being sold on the world market as investments. Meanwhile, "folklore societies have been rapidly formed to bewail and reverse this trend, but the damage has already been done. At best, all they can achieve is to act as folk-culture taxidermists" (Morris, 1969, p. 67).

Similarly, Diamond (1993) tells us that in 1979, when he worked on New Guinea's Rouffaer River, missionaries had found a tribe of four hundred nomads. In Brazil and Peru previously unknown small bands had also turned up in remote areas. He estimates that "at some point within the last decade of the twentieth century, we can expect the last first contacts, and the end of the last separate experiment at designing human society" (Diamond, 1993, p. 234). According to Diamond, this will mark the "end of a long phase of human history" when societies yet existed totally unaware of other humans in the world (p. 223). He observes, "While the last first contact won't mean the end of human cultural diversity ... it certainly does mean a drastic reduction" (Diamond, 1993, p. 234).

I call the situation of the last first contact the end of the concept of frontier. This is impacting the psyches of both colonized and colonizer. When all is explored and known, the wonder of adventure and the meaning of life are diminished. In the interest of positive efficiency, literally thousands of languages are becoming extinct in the wink of a historical eye; what is left is increasingly being reduced to an index of acronyms and logos. The last first contact represents a plunge in cultural diversity worldwide. This means a fantastic and abrupt decline of the semantic wealth bequeathed to us by our predecessors.

Though they were few, our ancestors, whom we like to see as hopelessly dim-witted, invented innumerable social experiments and ideologies, including bourgeois positivism itself. Meanwhile, our current modern culture is proving to be far more destructive than our ancestors ever were. In its totalitarian arrogance, it may be that modern positivistic culture cannot imagine any possible world beyond itself worthy of existing. According to positivism, there is only one best answer to each question, and positivism is it. Our medieval ancestors may have given birth to a sterile world that sees no need to give them grandchildren. Progress in the one modality has become absurd, for it has become an absolute virtue. Progress has become a permanent and the only conceivable pursuit.

Citing the introduction of mass media, trade, and tourism to every remote corner of the world and missions in the service of religious conversion and military operations, Diamond (1993) recounts a case of postcontact cultural homogenization: "When I visited an isolated tribelet of 578 people in Bomai [New

Guinea] in 1965, the missionary controlling the only store had just manipulated the people into burning all their art. Centuries of unique cultural development ("heathen artifacts," as the missionary put it) had thus been destroyed in one morning" (p. 231). The nihilistic trend toward global monoculture involves the extinction of "separate experiments at designing human society." Armand Mattelart reminds us that, already in 1874, Nietzsche had recognized that "beneath the grand celebration of universalisms [lurks] the morbidity of the European expansionist instinct" (Mattelart, 1994, 29). Exhibiting a profound understanding of the modern megacity and its first example in imperial Rome, Nietzsche warns that even the initial kaleidoscope of novelty that characterizes nascent cosmopolitanism can lead to a decline in the veracity of identity and the consequent collapse of the will due to a lack of meaning. The thrill of conquest soon leads to boredom as novelty is domesticated and made a commodity or eliminated altogether through the process of cultural streamlining, which constricts heterogeneity by creating a common symbolic environment by means of repetitive patterns of mass-produced images and products (Gerbner, 1990). What happens when we finally achieve the mountaintop from which we see with clarity is "that all paths below ultimately lead to the same summit" (Gudykunst & Kim, 1997, p. 366)? Nietzsche notes that the novelty of overstimulation followed by extermination of diversity, and therefore meaning, affects the colonizer as much as or even more than the colonized:

The Roman of the Empire ceased to be a Roman through the contemplation of the world that lay at his feet; he lost himself in the crowd of foreigners that streamed into Rome, and degenerated amid the cosmopolitan carnival of arts, worships and moralities. It is the same with the modern man, who is continually having a world-panorama unrolled before his eyes by his historical artists. He is turned into a restless, dilettante spectator, and arrives at a condition when even great wars and revolutions cannot affect him beyond the moment. (Nietzsche, 1874/1984, p. 73)

In modern mass media studies this is called becoming overstimulated and desensitized. Other cultures come to be seen as either obstacles to economic growth and expansion or as merely entertainment to be consumed. This is the "tourist gaze" (Kramer, 1997). The world becomes either a toy or something in need of discipline.

THE URBAN WORLD

Not only is the world's population growing at an explosive rate, but at the same time people are being lured off the land and into urban centers by this cosmopolitan ego-hypertrophy by which the individual is "desirous of possessing everything" and presumes to be permitted everything, in the course of the fantasy of modernism and development (Gebser, 1985, p. 3). The force of this shift in worldview is impacting millions at the very basic level of personal identity. Mass communications has disseminated urban values to rural populations, convincing them that their modes of living are antiquated and deficient and enticing them to move to cities where true satisfaction and enrichment supposedly await them.

Meanwhile, assimilation leads to standardized uniformity, the general-issue human and urban landscape. All cities increasingly look alike, indicating the emergence of a single urban culture that is displacing local identities and our sense of place and belonging, leading to a relentless search for home that is increasingly reflected in the arts of the global nomad such that "airport departure lounges and hotel rooms are the settings in more and more novels" (Iyer, 2000, p. 167). Some writers refer to this as the postmodern condition. It means that increasingly, no matter where one goes, everyone and everything is the same, including forms of social relations, from the family to the corporate structure. Families are becoming nuclear everywhere, dating is becoming common as a courtship ritual, and the same divisions of labor and job titles exist everywhere. Everyone attends educational institutions that are Western in style; everyone wears Western-style clothes, like blue jeans, T-shirts, and suits and ties. They all carry cell phones and briefcases, use electricity and internal combustion engines, wear wristwatches, eat hamburgers and French fries, listen to rock and roll and jazz. They drink cognac, soft drinks, and designer coffee and smoke cigarettes. They live in practically identical concrete and glass high-rises, litigate their disputes in courtrooms, and dream of becoming independently wealthy and famous. In short, to be cosmopolitan is to be urbanized in the Western cultural fashion. The very concepts of wealth and fame are urban inventions. If individuals infected by these foreign dreams are not already doing these things, they are striving to.

Three measures indicate rate of urbanization. A country becomes more urbanized as (1) the number of cities grows, (2) the size of the cities continually increases, and (3) the proportion of the country's population living in urban areas increases. This can be said of the planet as a whole. The entire human species is rapidly urbanizing. This involves a global homogenization of cultural norms, mores, and values. This homogenization process does not mean, as some writers claim, that people are transcending culture. That is quite impossible, and such a claim could only be made from a very idealistic perspective (Kramer, 2000a). Rather, it means that one form of urban culture is taking over and displacing all other kinds. This form is basically modern Western capitalism. It is a new monotheism marked by the invisible hand of market forces that are omniscient and inescapable in their logic of rewards and punishments. With its mystical, transcendental imperatives, this new monoculture is displacing the plurality of local cultures. I call it *cosmotopia*, which means that the cosmopolis is held up as a utopian ideal for which it is worth abandoning one's very self-identity.

Increasingly we see the emergence of megacities of 10 million people or more, most in poor countries that cannot support them. The city itself symbolizes wealth and power. Not surprisingly, the wealthiest countries are the most urbanized. Industrialized transportation and communications have enabled urban sprawl, which spreads to connect once-separate cities into megacities of hundreds of miles of continuous urban landscape. Examples include the Tokyo–Yokohama–Kawasaki region in Japan, the Randstadt in The Netherlands, the Boston–New York–Washington, D.C. eastern corridor in the United States, and the Ruhr Valley in Germany.

Poor nations are attempting to mimic the city as a sign of economic wealth and cultural maturity—in a word, *development*. In fact, they are told that such development is evolutionary, meaning that it is to be expected (even inevitable) and that it should follow a systematic process of progress toward a fixed goal, not revolutionary, which is unpredictable and disruptive of markets.

Either way, being relatively poor, the results of urbanization in most countries, as will be discussed in further detail, are not what the development dream promised. Development means that the world's poor should strive to develop into Western-style consumers, for herein lies salvation. But mass consumption leads to many problems. The greatest issue facing the developing world today is whether or not an economy based on mass production and mass consumption is environmentally sustainable and even desirable in the long run.

As might be expected, the rate of urban population growth has leveled off in the most developed nations. Consequently, at the turn of the millennium, the greatest rates of urban growth are to be found in developing countries. For instance, the most urbanized country on Earth is The Netherlands, where 90 percent of the population lives in urban density, whereas only 13 percent of Ethiopians currently live in an urban center, although they are rushing to get there. According to the United Nations, the top ten countries in terms of rate of urbanization in descending order are: Liberia (ranked number one) followed by Rwanda, Afghanistan, Burundi, Botswana, Oman, Yemen, Laos, Nepal, and Bhutan. Meanwhile, out of 185 nations, Japan ranks 170th, the United Kingdom 178th, and the United States 147th. In 1900, 1 in 10 humans lived in population centers of 1,500 people or more. By 2000, half of all the people in the world lived in urban centers. It is estimated that by 2025, two-thirds of all people will live in cities.

This means that as the human population explodes, it is also imploding into increasingly concentrated centers of population density and homogenizing into a singular urban, modern, largely Westernized consumer culture. Before 1800, cities of over a million people were rare. In 1900, there were thirteen cities with populations of over a million. By 1968, there were sixty-eight such urban centers. By 2000, the number of cities of more than a million people was 255. Most are in Asia, specifically in India and China. By 2020, many large cities, like Bogotá, Buenos Aires, and Rio de Janeiro, are expected to exceed 20 million people.

THE FALSE URBAN UTOPIA

Such urban agglomerates create huge problems of air, noise, and water pollution. Transportation congestion is rising rapidly as the numbers of automobiles is increasing exponentially, while the production of food crops has declined due to the corrosive effects of acid rain produced by sulfur dioxide and nitrogen oxide exhausts from automobiles and coal- and oil-fired power plants that service the electric cities. For instance, Mexico City today suffers from severe housing shortages and transportation problems. Fully one-quarter of the 17.9 million inhabitants of Mexico City do not have access to running water. The air pollution in the valley where the city is situated is so bad that the city center is periodically closed to traffic. Acid rain and chemical runoff from highways, runways, and farms, combined with leakage from storage tanks and pipelines, are ruining both surface waters and subterranean aquifers.

Worldwide, the scarcity of potable water is becoming a major source of concern and increasingly international conflict. According to several organizations, currently more than 1 billion people lack access to safe drinking water and about 80 percent of the earth's urban dwellers do not have adequate supplies of potable water. However, most fresh water is not used for domestic consumption. About 70 percent of it goes to agriculture, with 23 percent used by industry and only 8 percent for domestic consumption. Demand for water is rapidly rising everywhere as efforts to expand agriculture through massive irrigation are increasing along with general industrialization. To make matters worse, chemicals used on crops, such as fertilizers, herbicides, and pesticides, often contaminate water used for irrigation.

Meanwhile, in an all-out effort to boost yields, farms increasingly use subterranean water to irrigate lands that otherwise could not sustain agriculture. It has been discovered that nature replenishes aquifers much more slowly than humans are using up the underground water supplies. Furthermore, it is virtually impossible to clean it once leaching chemicals pollute aquifers and salt water fills the void where fresh water has been pumped out of the ground. For instance, in many metropolitan places like Jakarta, Indonesia, and Lima, Peru, sea water has rushed into aquifers to take the place of fresh water that has been pumped to the surface, thus contaminating what is left. Beyond this, 95 percent of human waste water in the developing world is discharged untreated into nearby rivers, killing fish, causing deleterious algae blooms in the oceans where the rivers empty out, and creating health problems by causing waterborne infectious diseases.

WHY ARE MILLIONS MOVING TO THE CITY?

So why are people rushing to the cities? Why is endless growth equated with progress and heralded as always good, especially in markets? The romantic or positive dream that is characteristic of the global cosmopolitan culture is the key. Over the twentieth century, global channels of mass communications purveyed values, expectations, motivations, and behaviors that originated from the urban centers of wealthy, industrial countries. These images and values have changed the expectations about the future for much of the world's inhabitants.

As we shall see, the difference between a global village and a global city has many profound implications.

A traditional village population is small and culturally and ethnically very homogeneous, but a city is where most people are strangers to each other; physical, economic, and social mobility are encouraged; diversity is common; and trust and obligation are supplanted by competition and the more abstract rule of law. In the city, happiness is believed to come from material accumulation as a never-ending progressive process, whereas in traditional societies, status and value are marked more by one's role within family and the extended collective community.

Global Growth and Migration

Because this chapter sets out to discuss the role of global urban communications in the production of the current global condition, it is imperative that this condition be briefly outlined.

Around the beginning of the Common Era, it is estimated that there were about 200 million humans on the planet. This number was sustained for nearly two thousand years. It took the human race until around 1850 to reach the 1 billion population mark. In just eighty more years, another billion was added—by 1930, the population doubled to 2 billion. By 1975, it doubled again to 4 billion. According to the U.N. Population Fund, on October 12, 1999, the 6 billionth person was born somewhere in India.[2] On that Tuesday about 370,000 children were born, fully half in Asia. Thus, in the last 150 years the world's population has grown sixfold. The rate of growth is compounding. Currently about 90 million people are born every year and rising. That is the equivalent of adding another Germany to the world every twelve months. In 1950 the population was only 2.5 billion. It took only twelve years to add the last billion to the current total. The next billion will be added in about nine years. Every ninety-six hours another million people join the population.

Most of the growth has been in the poorest countries. In 1960, Europe had twice as many people as Africa. According to U.N. estimates, by 2050 there will be three times as many Africans as Europeans. Ninety percent of the increase in global population is occurring in the poorest countries, where already 80 percent of the world's population resides. For instance, countries like Mozambique and Nepal, which have 4 percent growth rates, will double their populations in about 17.5 years, whereas in France and Japan it will take about two hundred years with their current growth rates. In the next fifty years Pakistan and Nigeria will double and Ethiopia will triple, that is, unless the AIDS epidemic does not slow the growth.[3] Furthermore, despite family planning and human rights advances (especially for women), which have lowered the average global birthrate, the peak has not yet been reached because the poorer populations are also the youngest. In countries like Uganda and Niger, the median age is fifteen. There are a billion teenagers living today mostly in the third world. Thus, fertility rates, though falling, will not offset the simple fact that so many people have not yet reached reproductive maturity.

In Africa, where many women still have six or seven children, half the population is under fifteen years of age. Meanwhile the median age in Italy and Japan is forty and the United Nations projects that by 2050 fully one-quarter of the developed world will be over age sixty-five. Ironically, given the global conditions, experts like Stephen Moore refer to Europe as a "demographic catastrophe" (quoted in Crenson, 1999). But what they really mean is that it is an economic problem. Simon and Moore decry the decrease in fertility for economic reasons, arguing that at current rates of decline, in five hundred years there will be eight Italians and three Irish left on the face of the Earth.[4]

This explosion in population is directly linked to the dissemination of ideas, notably medical knowledge and practices that have lengthened life spans and radically reduced infant mortality rates. But as it became increasingly evident that the world population was growing faster than our ability to feed, clothe, and shelter ourselves, the mass media was then recruited to spread family planning information and new agricultural techniques to boost crop yields (i.e., the infamous Green Revolution). Although some claim that new biotechnologies like genetically engineered crops will keep up with the growth, the fact is that yields have leveled off and even declined some since 1983 (U.N. Population Information Network at http://www.undp.org). Furthermore, although many of the crops engineered for the Green Revolution produced high yields, they required liberal amounts of petrochemicals. This has made many developing countries vulnerable to volatile petroleum prices. Countries that were once self-sustaining are now incurring great debt because they must borrow money to buy the chemicals necessary for their hybrid crops to produce. Furthermore, with increased exploitation and pollution of ground water faster than nature can replenish it, continued high yields look increasingly dubious.

Global Communication, Networking, and Positive Consumerism

The world is expanding quantitatively but shrinking qualitatively. By almost all measures, there are more people today, and they are living longer than ever before. They are also consuming more natural resources and creating more pollution than ever before, and these increases are accelerating. Meanwhile, biodiversity is shrinking. So, too, is cultural diversity. All of these massive and rapid changes can be linked to mobility.

Transportation moves people and things, including diseases. Communication moves ideas. Transportation and communication began to accelerate in unprecedented ways only about two hundred years ago, and the rate of acceleration continues to increase. Concurrent with this increase in the speed and scope of transportation and communication is an explosive growth in human population, resource consumption, and pollution.

The causes of European power and wealth were not due to inherent intellectual or physical superiority over all the rest of the world's inhabitants but rather to their coordinated and aggressive pursuit of exploitable resources. In a word, unbridled greed was their great motivator, and often relatively passive indigenous peoples were met with force of arms. As Diamond (1997) has argued, the aggressive use of steel, gunpowder, and germs conquered the world.[5] Of course, history demonstrates that for many people, like the native peoples of the Americas, European progress meant not happiness for them but instead the destruction of their cultures and lands. European progress (wealth and happiness) came at great costs to others, including the abduction and slavery of thousands of black Africans and indentured servitude for thousands more Irish and Chinese.

Industrialization began in Europe and America with the application of scientific rationality to the extraction of raw materials, labor management, and the mass production of goods, which created enormous wealth for industrialists. There was one problem, however. Mass production requires mass consumption. Profit is realized only when sales occur. As a solution, mass media were developed as channels of advertising to generate a sense of inadequacy in people's minds and a demand for the new industrial products. Thus was born the commodity, which was a mass-produced object specifically manufactured for sale and the human as consumer. The mass media is largely a network for commercial enterprise. Initially it was developed to serve two basic purposes: (1) as a means to keep investors informed of various market conditions and (2) to advertise consumer products. *Consumerism* is the term used to describe this overall system of production and consumption.

Before this, most things that people made were not for sale but were created for immediate use in farming, hunting, or personal adornment. For example, if a farmer made a plow, it was for his own use and not as a commodity to be sold to another farmer. Prior to the Enlightenment most economic transactions were by barter, for money was not widely used among most of the world's inhabitants. Even where it would come to be, as in the United States prior to the 1860s, money was so easily counterfeited that it was practically worthless. But with growing urbanization, which means the migration of farmers to large towns and cities, the economy became more abstract and standardized, and people began to trade actual products for capital currency. This became the new norm.

The Cold War

The most vigorous development of global communications after World War II, which also marks the beginning of the greatest migratory wave of urbanization on the planet, cannot be understood outside the context of the cold war. The cold war was an ideological struggle between Soviet-style state-controlled economy and the private capitalist economies of the Western industrial powers. Capital economy is not a rural village type of phenomenon but a new urban form of exchange. In many ways, Soviet-style socialism presumed a sort of mutual obligation typical of collectivistic rural societies. By contrast, the intensely individualistic tendencies of Western-style capitalism are essential qualities of modernism (both recent and ancient as in republican Rome). Neither is more natural or universal than the other. Both are cultural artifacts or organized modes of behavior. The Soviet system was in many ways "state capitalism" as it, too, sought to make a return on investment and colonial expansion to a global level.

Just like mechanical clock time, which synchronizes the movements of huge masses of people and is more standardized than natural time, capital is a form of minimalism. Minimalism simplifies things to formal rules. It ignores heterogeneous complexities as unimportant contingencies. This means that capital economies are much more formal, abstract, and standardized than are barter economies. Every yen is identical in value to every other yen, and it can be exchanged for an endless list of commodities, services, and even other currencies.

Capital, like clock time, is a scale of measurement that is widely generalized. Such massifying scalar phenomena are the products of a prejudice that favors simplicity and efficiency (standardization, including standard time zones) over complexity and variance.

A truly globalizing, universally generalizing mentality started to emerge during World War I. But even before that, in 1864, the first modern international organization, the International Telegraph Union (ITU; today the International Telecommunications Union) was formed with the expressed goal of standardizing electronic communications technologies around the world. This involved transcending national sovereignty to establish global standards and doing so even before the concept of nationhood itself existed for many of the world's inhabitants. In fact, during the 1950s and 1960s, domestic mass communications were widely used in many postcolonial, newly independent countries to help foster a sense of national identity among the people living within newly drawn borders. The irony is that even before nationalism had completely solidified in the minds of most humans, transnationalism was already being promoted by Western powers. Corporate globalism used the rhetoric of transnationalism to circumvent national sovereignty issues. Commercial interests want direct access to the people in every land.

Globalism means the establishment of international governing bodies that surpass and subsume national governments in regulatory reach. Thus, concerns about communications led the way in expressing the first sense of international and transnational, global thinking, governance, and uniformity.

The objective of the ITU is expressed in their official charter thus:

The objectives of the ITU are to maintain and extend international cooperation for the improvement and rational use of telecommunications of all kinds; to promote the development and efficient operation of technical facilities in order to improve telecommunication services, increase their usefulness, and make them generally available to the public; and to coordinate the actions of nations so they may attain these goals.[6]

Thus, the longest continually operating extragovernmental regulatory agency, the ITU, was expressly formed to organize and manage technical standards around the world, in effect transcending local governments and their sovereign rights to self-determination and regulation.

This change in thinking from local to global purview is paralleled in transportation. Initially the United States had over eighty time zones. Each little town administered and regulated its own time. Consequently, it was possible to take a train and arrive somewhere before you left. Train schedules were in chaos. So a system of just four time zones was initiated by the transportation industry and became the norm for the entire United States (Mattelart, 1991/1994).

Global thinking became galvanized as the predominant perspective of political and economic leaders between the "world" wars. The idea of global markets became not only thinkable but the major motive for big business. After World War II, a concerted effort was made to create a global communications system that would promote and support mass production/mass consumption industrialism. Growth and expansion are the most essential of all positive postulates. Colonialism is not only good but also divinely mandated as manifest destiny. The linear direction of positive growth is singularly exclusive of all alternative futures.

In 1952, Rostow explained in a book subtitled *A Non-Communist Manifesto* how electronic mass media should be used as a proselytizing tool in poor countries to introduce and foster the adoption of a consumer culture. The most positive use of mass communications was said to be in creating orderly and ever-expanding commodity markets. Later, in 1958, in his famous book *The Passing of Traditional Society*, Daniel Lerner, an expert in psychological warfare and the author of an earlier book entitled *Sykewar: Psychological Warfare against Germany*, explained how the mass media should be used to promote modern Western concepts of happiness, satisfaction, dissatisfaction, and desire based on relative material consumption.

The theory of development communications postulated that advertising, radio and TV shows, and movies depicting wealthy people being happy would create demand and increase expectations among poor populations. To be smart came to be equated with being materially wealthy, and so to learn, to evolve means to become an ever more mature and developed consumer. Consumption became equated with human progress and human progress became unquestionably positive (good). Years before Baudrillard made similar claims, the anthropologist Jules Henry (1963) referred to the modern world as an obsessively acquisitive civilization that proclaimed that truth is what sells. Rostow and Lerner equated modernization with development, which in turn meant capitalist forms of mass production and consumption. This was legitimized by Spencerian social Darwinists as a natural evolution in human development. It was held up as the normal way to live, as the model all should strive to mimic. Manufactured dissatisfaction would then motivate the world's poor to begin to develop, evolve, and modernize into normal mass consumers for Western-made products. This is how markets and consumers are created. They are not naturally occurring phenomena, even though many positivists claim that mass marketing is the most natural of all laws of human nature. Very few cultures exhibit this mode of economic organization.

Thus, mass economies could be developed by creating dissatisfaction, heightened expectations (or positivistic optimism), and demand for greater material accumulation. Rural countries, rich in natural resources but poor in capital currencies, were encouraged—sometimes violently, as in South Africa, Chile, China, India, Venezuela, Liberia, and Nigeria—to efficiently exploit their natural treasures on an industrial scale for sale to industrial powers. The development of poor countries' natural resources would thus enable them to begin to accumulate Western-style hard currency and credit (and debt, of course) for the purchase of imported Western products like TVs and radios that would in turn purvey even more images that would manufacture greater discontent and demand for modernization, defined as the accumulation of material wealth and massive exploitation of natural resources.

Following Lerner's lead, several writers actively promoted the use of mass media as catalysts for capitalistic economic and political development around the world. They include David McLellan, who wrote two influential books in the early 1960s, *The Achieving Society* (1961) and *Communications and Political Development* (1963), and Wilbur Schramm, who wrote *Mass Media and National Development* in 1964. Everett Rogers became famous promoting Rostow's ideas and traveling the world teaching his own theory of the diffusion of innovations.[7]

Rogers's diffusion of innovations basically meant that poor countries should first develop communication infrastructures that then could be used to diffuse modern, rational ideas and ways of thinking. This Rogers and others have called development communications. To be rational means to establish a network for systematically propagating bourgeois values as progressive.

Big-City Lights

The primary assumption behind development communications is that the rural hamlet or village is backward, underdeveloped, and deficient. Wealth is not a natural resource but must be created in an orderly fashion beginning with the refining of natural resources. The manipulation of basically worthless resources, making them into consumable products, is a process economists call value-added operations. Mass marketing, as developed by the new science of psychology, is crucial to the creation of demand. According to this way of thinking, wheat is worthless until it is turned into bread, forests are worthless until they are timbered, diamonds are worthless until they are mined, and so on. This is, however, an ethnocentric and species-centric way of thinking. It means that value is defined on how exploitable and profitable somebody or something is to somebody else. In other words, nothing has value unless it lends itself to exploitation and profit taking.

The coordination of large-scale extraction takes place not in rural agricultural villages but in urban centers, which cannot support themselves. Great cities can survive only by constantly importing vast quantities of basic needs, such as food, fuel, and water from rural areas. Thus the ideology, in fact the new morality of interdependence among component parts, was promoted to supplant the ancient ideal of self-sufficiency and primitive socialism as it exists among highly homogeneous organic collectives. Subsistence farming came to be seen as practically a degenerate if not evil mode of life. But the feudal farmer and the Mesolithic-style hamlet had survived for millennia. Such socioeconomic arrangements do not need the city. Rather, the city needs them. The positive-sounding ideology of interdependence is actually an expression of urban need.

Cities are concentrations of culture, which is in many ways the antithesis of nature. Cities are the origins of modern mass-mediated dreams and aspirations. They are the cores of exploitation and therefore value. Although the concept of diffusion itself was spread through Western educational materials as a panacea for world poverty, vast numbers of the world's inhabitants began to long for a better life, for mobility, growth, and progress. They began to look for ways to be exploited. They moved to the cities looking for work. The rural poor became convinced that material accumulation was more important and practical than traditional indigenous lifestyles. But as Baudrillard wrote already in 1969 about fantasies of consumption and the "revolution of rising frustrations," it was becoming clear to more observers that unrealistic expectations of endless progress and democracy-by-consumption would lead to a global crisis, not a content little global village.

TWIN CRISES AND THE NEW MONOTHEISM

The global expansion of positivism has brought with it two crises. One is environmental. The other is cultural. As mentioned, both biodiversity and cultural diversity are being drastically reduced in the interest of efficient profit taking. According to the ideology of social Darwinism, if a cultural or biological form cannot adapt to the emergent global city and its definition of valuable—meaning exploitable, functional—then it deserves to disappear. This is cast in the rhetoric of both fatalism and minimalism. The success or failure of a cultural form is based on the simple laws of the market.

"The market" has become the new god. It has a life of its own that dictates how the rest of us live. It is transcendental and impersonal, indeed Olympian. It is a pure logic that sees all and knows all. It has forces. Sometimes it is said to be fickle, nervous, jittery, weak, strong, even relieved. One can fool the market only so long before its imperatives deflate all fantasies or bubbles. One should have no false gods before the market. A bubble economy is a false market. If someone or something breaks its laws, they are punished without mercy. This is what the economist Adam Smith called the invisible hand of the market, an idea later taken up from the "spirit of ages" by Hegel and Thomas Malthus.

Thus we have the unseen guiding force applied as both an explanation and a justification of economic development, population control, and evolution. The message is simple and religious in conviction: The rules are supply and demand, those who conform are rewarded, those sinners who do not conform die. The market is simple yet shrouded in mystery, and so priestly well-paid experts and soothsayers abound. As Karl Polanyi in his classic work *The Great Transformation* noted, the market has risen to be the first and final cause over all other value systems only in the last two hundred years. Thus we speak of "market forces," and the "will of the market." This new system with iron-clad rules has convinced the world's countries that they must conform or be ostracized and left behind. Thus the world is taught a new global religion, and we are taught that it is inescapable.[8] The only path to happiness is to conform. All resistance indicates irrationality if not outright mental illness.

To convince people that the current trend is good, positive ideology has dubbed the emerging system a global village. But the Mesolithic hamlet, which still exists in rural parts of the world, is self-sustaining and in equilibrium with its surrounding physical environment and also acts as a stable place where identities and other cultural forms have endured for countless generations. By contrast, the modern city is very much out of balance with its physical environment and not at all self-sustaining; its overriding drive for capital gains either co-opts traditional cultural forms like Christmas for exploitation or eliminates traditional cultural forms as worthless if they do not lend themselves to exploitation.

THE GLOBAL VILLAGE?

The positive-sounding global village, popularized by McLuhan, is a misnomer. It is a myth propagated to promote the information age as a millenarian promise of salvation. As Mumford noted in 1964, "What McLuhan understands has long been familiar to students of technics: it is his singular gift for *mis*understanding both technology and man that marks his truly original contributions" (p. 456).

So what did McLuhan claim? According to McLuhan, the world is becoming a global village. Beyond the fact that he lifted this phrase from Wyndham Lewis's 1948 book *America and Cosmic Man*, in which Lewis writes, "The earth has become one big village, with telephones laid on from one end to the other, and air transport, both speedy and safe," it is wrong (p. 21). But before we rush on, we must pause to also note that McLuhan liberally borrowed the sense of the emerging telesphere from Pierre Teilhard de Chardin's (1955/1965) concept of the noosphere and practically all else of any explanatory value, from

Sigfried Giedion (1955) (one of Gebser's students), to Mumford (1934) and Harold Innis (1950).

According to J. Carey and J. Quirk (1970), a clear expression of the redemptive promise of communication had already been promoted in *The Silent Revolution* by Michel Angelo Garvey (published in 1852), which was criticized by Thoreau in 1854 as he commented on the first transatlantic cable carrying information of dubious value about the queen of England's colic to titillate and divert Americans from other immediate pursuits. Included in the millenarian promise of communication is the assurance of a new social harmony that should be created, thanks to "a perfect network of electric filaments" (quoted in Carey & Quirk, 1970, p. 227). For others, like Thoreau, social harmony is in no way dependent on technology and social engineering. In fact, many, like Emerson, agree with Thoreau on this matter.

However, the basis of this technotronic dream, with its promise of being a source of profits, was identified by Charles Cooley in his book *Social Organization* (1901), which had been inspired by Saint-Simon's 1821 book *Le systeme industriel* (The industrial system). According to Cooley, the utopian hope for global communication is found in its "enlargement of mental perspective," "mental animation" resulting from "frequent exposure to novelty" (p. 63).

But Cooley failed to understand that what was driving the attainment of technologies that would defeat location (space) and duration (time) was colonial conquest and the extermination of novelty. Comte had plainly and repeatedly argued in his various works, such as his *Catechisme positiviste* (*The Catechism of Positive Religion*), that "progress is the development of order," and that this is the greatest mission of civilization in its attempt to help peoples not yet capable of governing themselves. Positivism is said to be synonymous with civilization, and in *A General View of Positivism* (1848), Comte sought nothing less than the reorganization of production and the moral order of society on a global level.

COMTE'S DREAM COME TRUE: COSMOTOPIA AND THE REORGANIZATION OF MINDS AND SOCIETIES

"Village" is a reassuring bit of rhetoric, but it is a very misleading metaphor, one that belies what is occurring on the globe today. Today vast migrations of our species are moving from an agrarian lifestyle that has sustained the human race for millennia to an industrially inspired cosmopolitan way of being. The process of cosmopoly leads from urban center to empire, and on to regional convergences of interests, as in interimperial allegiances like the European Union, and finally on to global government (Zolo et al., 1997; Toulmin, 1992, 1998). Today, our cities are growing at alarming rates, and they are increasingly alike. A migration of the human herd from the land to an urban centralized environment in the hope of gaining modern forms of wealth and status is under way. This is an expression of what has been called Westernaholism. It has been resisted in few places.

The consequences have been profound. Population density is rising at the same time that the sheer number of humans is exploding. Cities are witness to an urban implosion of masses of people. Infrastructures are being sorely over-taxed. The entire migration is fueled by emotional desires for happiness in the form of more wealth and power, phenomena often confused with freedom. In fact, the most successful capitalist economies, like Singapore, Communist China, South Korea, South Africa, and Taiwan, range from starkly repressive to only marginally democratic, especially in terms of free union activities and en-vironmental protection (Greider, 1997). Thus the claim that capitalism and pos-itive economic structures are inherently democratic is false. What we are witness to at the turn of the twenty-first century is the instituting of a whole new way of interacting: cybernetics. We live, as Zbigniew Brzezinski (1970) ar-gues, not in a global village but a global *city* (Kramer, 1997, 2000a, 2000b).

So what is the difference? The modern systemized urban milieu is very dif-ferent from the Mesolithic hamlet (Mumford, 1961). We must hasten to re-mind ourselves that much of humanity still lives such a premodern lifestyle, but it is vanishing before our eyes. Extending the work of Patrick Geddes and Mumford, Brzezinski's description of our technotronic society is more correct than McLuhan's (1967) erroneous claim that the world is retribalizing.

The technotronic society is characterized by technocracy (expert knowledge), fragmentation, isolation, ego-hypertrophy, competition, and other qualities that remind one of Töennies's (1887/1957) conceptualization of instrumental *Gesellschaft* culture, not organic *Gemeinschaft* culture. The older *Gemein-schaft* culture emerges out of common needs, not competing interests. Brzezin-ski's work, when combined with Mumford (1934), Chardin (1955/1965), and Gebser (1949/1985), goes far in explaining the qualitative difference between living in a village among intimate acquaintances (probably kin) and living in a modern city. The latter is characterized by the existence of the stranger. The city is a high-density settlement with vast populations of people one sees every day who are complete strangers or even more dissociated, disembodied neti-zens.

With the city comes dissociation, abstraction, and alienation. The stranger is a consequence of cosmopoly; that is, the superordination of masses of city dwellers. Several scholars, including Mumford (1961, 1964) and Morris (1969), note that the extreme super-status differentials that are conveniently natural-ized by central urban authorities do not exist among hunter-gatherers or among the inhabitants of the Mesolithic hamlet. Huge inequalities in status do not emerge until the Other is a stranger. Then and only then do super–high-and-mighty divine rulers and super–low-and-weak slaves appear. This occurs only with the emergence of the city as centralized imperial authority. It is only with the rise of the first true metropolises like ancient Rome that labor becomes fragmented and specialized, as do markets. Here we find the inception of the human as commodity. Slave markets are organized. To be sure, capturing one's enemies is an ancient practice. But typically captives became integrated eventually into the community. But with the formation of systematic slave markets and permanent caste systems, slave status plummets below human status. Slaves are not seen as human.

True to the cosmopolitan tendency to have huge discrepancies in wealth and power, today the digital divide, or information gap, is growing. Nearly a billion people in the world are illiterate, two-thirds of them women. It has been repeatedly demonstrated that as educational opportunities become available to women, birth rates decline and standards of living increase.

Only 17 percent of homes in the developing world have a phone. Ninety percent in the wealthy industrial nations have a phone. The gap is even wider for Internet access. The United States has the greatest number of Internet users, at around 76 million. Second place is Japan, which is not even close, with 10 million users. In the United States, one in four has access to the Internet; in China, for instance, one in eight hundred and in India one in twenty-one hundred have access. In Africa, access to the Internet is only one in every four thousand people.

CONCLUDING REMARKS

Currently, about 1.3 billion people are impoverished, living on the equivalent of less than US$1 a day, and the gap between rich and poor is increasing. About 60 percent of the 4.8 billion living in developing countries lack basic sanitation, and nearly one-third have no access to clean water. People are becoming more concentrated in urban areas. The number of cities with more than a million inhabitants will increase to about 370 by 2010, up from 173 in 1990. In 1960, only two cities had more than 10 million people, New York and Tokyo. By 2015 there will be at least twenty-six such megacities, twenty-two of them in less developed areas. According to the United Nations, in 2000, some 841 million people were "chronically malnourished," and there were 88 "food-deficit" countries. *Food deficit* means they can neither feed themselves nor afford the imports they need.

Meanwhile, population distribution and migration trends are clear and becoming more solidified with each passing year. The rural world of the village and hamlet, which concerns itself with agriculture and animal husbandry, is becoming devalued as backward, while the urban world with its capital economy is seen as progressive and modern. Thus billions are abandoning the village lifestyle and migrating to urban centers creating ever-greater population densities with all the attendant problems.

Culture is a qualitative phenomenon. Culture may be defined as the values, expectations, motivations, beliefs, and behavior patterns of a group of people. The number of cultures in the world is declining at the same time that human population, migration, and international and intercultural communication are increasing. The number of cultures, cultural diversity or life-worlds, or semantic systems is shrinking. The vast diversity of different kinds of cultural manifolds, different kinds of time and space, is collapsing at an astounding rate as Western-style mechanical clock time and digital measurement are displacing traditional ways of making sense of the world.

The quality of life is changing. Around the world people are rapidly (by historical standards almost instantaneously) abandoning rural ways of living to adopt urban, mostly Western forms of culture. Why and how this is happening is complex. This change is largely self-legitimizing and self-promoted. Western European civilization, beginning with Christopher Columbus and the age of European colonialism and greatly accelerating after the end of World War I, is conquering the globe. It is the major issue of international communication, and it increasingly impacts intercultural communication because it promotes intercultural exchange while making it increasingly impossible because of cultural homogenization around the world.

The nihilistic tendency of monoculture is real and problematic. Because positivistic modernism leads people to believe that each problem has only one correct answer it tends to lead people to ask what may be the wrong question. They ask what is the meaning of life, rather than how to make life meaningful. The first question belies a Western goal-oriented bias that presumes just one correct answer. The second, perhaps more interesting question exhibits a presumption that the value of life is in the living and that there are many ways (perhaps, as Nietzsche suggests, an infinite number of ways) to live. If just one drives all others into extinction, then the world is much impoverished, and human freedom is greatly constricted.

NOTES

1. Which is to say that late in his career McLuhan came to agree with the likes of Lewis Mumford and to be less and less optimistic about the effects of world communications patterns on social and individual happiness.

2. This was as much a public relations stunt by the U.N. Population Fund to raise public pressure to force its member signatories to pay their allotted dues as anything else. Meanwhile the U.S. Census Bureau calculated that the 6 billionth person had already been born about three months earlier, on July 19. But the point is not lost that in any case, sometime during 1999, somewhere on earth the 6 billion population mark was passed.

3. Currently, in some sub-Saharan countries, one in four adults is infected with HIV (Worldwatch Institute).

4. As quoted by Matt Crenson of the Associated Press in his article, "Six Billion Strong," found at http://www.ABCNEWS.com.

5. Also see Diamond's 1994 book *The Third Chimpanzee*, which chronicles the extinction of most of the world's languages before the linguistic steamroller of English.

6. International Telecommunication Union Web site, online at http://www.itu.int/home/index.html.

7. It is important to note that belatedly, but in response to critiques in the third world and critical theorists in the first world, Rogers proposed to abandon this highly ethnocentric perspective in the late 1970s.

8. See the wonderful article by Cox (1999).

REFERENCES

Adorno, T. W., & Horkheimer, M. (1972). *Dialectic of enlightenment.* New York: Herder and Herder.

Andreski, S. (1972). *Herbert Spencer: Structure, function and evolution.* London: Methuen.

Baudrillard, J. (1968/1992). *La morale des objets.* Paris: Gallimard.

Bennett, W. (1993). *The de-valuing of America: The fight for our culture and our children.* New York: Touchstone.

Berger, C., & Calalabrese, R. (1975). Some explorations in initial interaction and beyond. *Human Communication Research, 1,* 99–112.

Binet, A., & Simon, T. (1913). *A method of measuring the development of the intelligence of young children.* Lincoln, IL: Courier.

Bohm, D. (1980). *Wholeness and the implicate order.* London: Routledge and Kegan Paul.

Brzezinski, Z. (1970). *Between two ages: America's role in the technotronic era.* New York: Viking Press.

Buchanan, P. (2001). *The death of the West: How dying population and immigrant invasion imperial our country and civilization.* Fairfax, VA: Dunne Books.

Campbell, J., & B. Moyers. (1988). *The power of myth.* New York: Doubleday.

Carey, J. W., & J. J. Quirk. (1970). The mythos of the electronic revolution. *American Scholar (39) 2,* 219–241 and *(39) 3,* 395–424.

Chardin, T. (1955/1965). *The phenomenon of man.* New York: Harper & Row.

Cooley, C. (1901). *Social organization.* New York: Scribner's.

Cox, H. (1999). The market as god. *Atlantic Monthly* (March 1999), pp. 19–23.

Crenson, M. (1999). Six billion strong: World population growing astronomically. Associated Press/ABC News Online, October 6.

Derrida, J. (1967/1973). *Speech and phenomena* (D. Allison, Trans.). Evanston, IL: Northwestern University Press.

Diamond, J. (1993). *The third chimpanzee.* New York: HarperCollins.

———. (1997). *Guns, Germs, and Steel.* New York: Norton.

Dittmer, L. (1974). *Liu Shao Chi and the Chinese cultural revolution: The politics of mass criticism.* Berkeley: University of California Press.

Du Bois, W. E. B. (1903/1995). *The souls of black folk.* New York: Penguin Putnam.

Ellison, R. (1952/1995). *Invisible man.* New York: Vintage.

Feyerbend, P. (1987). *Farewell to reason.* London: Verso.

Fukuyama, F. (1993). *The end of history and the last man.* New York: Avon.

Gadamer, H.-G. (1960/1975). *Truth and method.* New York: Seabury Press.

Galton, F. (1871). Gregariousness in cattle and in men. *MacMillan's Magazine, 23* (136), 353–357.

————. (1890a). Kinship and correlation. *North American Review, 150,* 419–431.

————. (1890b). Why do we measure mankind. *Lippincott's Monthly Magazine,* 236–241.

————. (1896). Application of the method of percentiles to Mr. Yule's data on the distribution of pauperism. *Journal of the Royal Statistical Society,* 392–396.

————. (1901). Man: The possible improvement of the human breed under existing conditions of law and sentiment. *Smithsonian Institute Report, 132,* 161–164.

Galton, F., with H. W Watson. (1874). On the probability of the extinction of families. *Journal of the Anthropological Institute, 4,* 138–144.

Gamow, G. (1966). *Thirty years that shook physics.* New York: Dover.

Gebser, J. (1949/1985). *The ever-present origin* (N. Barstad & A. Mickunas, Trans.). Athens, OH: Ohio University Press.

Gerbner, G. (1990). Advancing on the path of righteousness (maybe). In N. Signorielli & M. Morgan (Eds.), *Cultivation analysis: New directions in media effects research.* Newbury Park, CA: Sage.

Giedion, S. (1955). *Mechanization takes command.* New York: Norton.

Greider, W. (1997). *One world ready or not: The manic logic of global capitalism.* New York: Touchstone.

Gudykunst, W., & Y. Kim. (1997). *Communicating with strangers: An approach to intercultural communication,* 3d ed. New York: McGraw Hill.

————. (2003). *Communicating with strangers,* 4th ed. Boston: McGraw Hill.

Hegel, G. W. (1956). *Philosophy of history* (J. Sibree, Trans.). London: Dover.

————. (1979). *Phenomenology of mind* (J. N. Findlay, Trans.). Oxford: Oxford University Press.

Heisenberg, W. (1930/1958). *Physics and philosophy.* New York: Harper & Row.

Henry, J. (1963). *Culture against man.* New York: Random House.

Heyak, F. (1948). *Individualism and economic order.* Chicago: University of Chicago Press.

Hubble, E. (1929). A relation between distance and radial velocity among extra-galactic nebulae. *Proceedings of the National Academy of Sciences, 15* (3).

Humason, M. (1929). The large radial velocity of N. G. C. 7619. *Proceedings of the National Academy of Sciences, 15* (3).

Innis, H. (1950). *Empire and communication.* Toronto: University of Toronto Press.

Iyer, P. (2000). *The global soul: Jet lag, shopping malls, and the search for home.* New York: Knopf.

Janis, I. (1982). *Groupthink: Psychological studies of policy decisions and fiascoes.* Boston: Houghton Mifflin.

Jourard, S. (1974). Growing awareness and the awareness of growth. In B. Patton & K. Giffin (Eds.), *Interpersonal communication.* New York: Harper and Row.

Koestler, A. (1946/1984). *Darkness at noon.* New York: Bantam.

Kramer, E. (1997). *Modern/postmodern: Off the beaten path of antimodernism.* Westport, CT: Praeger.

————. (2000a). *Contemptus mundi:* Reality as disease. In V. Berdayes & J. Murphy (Eds.), *Computers, human interaction, and organization: Critical issues* (pp. 31–53). Westport, CT: Praeger.

————. (2000b). Cultural fusion and the defense of difference. In M. Asante & J. Min (Eds.), *Socio-cultural conflict between African and Korean Americans* (pp. 183–230). New York: University Press of America.

Kramer, E., & Johnson, L. Jr. (1997). The articulation of race: Eugenics, and the ideology of intelligence. In E. Kramer (Ed.), *Postmodernism and Race* (pp. 31–50). Westport, CT: Praeger.

Kurokawa, K. (1994). *The philosophy of symbiosis.* London: Academy Editions.

Lerner, D. (1958). *The passing of traditional society.* New York: Macmillan.

Lewis, W. (1948). *America and cosmic Man.* London: Nicholson and Watson.

Lifton, R. J. (1999). *Destroying the world to save it.* New York: Holt.

Lind, P. (Ed.). (1985). *Stubborn weeds: Popular and controversial Chinese literature after the cultural revolution.* Bloomington: Indiana University Press.

Löwith, K. (1967). *From Hegel to Nietzsche.* New York: Anchor.

Mattelart, A. (1994). *Mapping world communication.* Minneapolis: University of Minnesota Press.

McLuhan, M. (1967). *The medium is the massage.* With Quentin Fiore. New York: Bantam.

McWhorter, J. (2002). *The power of Babel.* New York: Freeman.

Morris, D. (1969). *The human zoo.* New York: Delta.

Mumford, L. (1934). *Technics and civilization.* New York: Harcourt Brace & World.

———. (1961). *The city in history.* New York: Harcourt Brace.

———. (1964). *The myth of the machine.* New York: Harcourt Brace.

Nietzsche, F. (1874/1984). *Untimely meditations* (R. J. Hollingdale, Trans.). London: Cambridge University Press.

———. (1878–1880/1996). *Human all too human.* (R. J. Hollingdale, Trans). Cambridge: Cambridge University Press.

———. (1882/1974). *The gay science.* (W. Kaufmann, Trans.) New York: Vintage.

———. (1886/1972). *Beyond good and evil* (R. J. Hollingdale, Trans.). New York: Vintage.

———. (1887/1967). *On the genealogy of morals* (W. Kaufmann, Trans.). New York: Vintage.

Polyani, K. (1957). *The great transformation.* Boston: Beacon Press.

Rostow, W. (1952). *The process of economic growth: A non-Communist Manifesto.* New York: Norton.

Solzhenitsyn, A. (1974/1997). *Gulag archipelago* (Vol. 1) (W. Thomas, Trans.). Boulder, CO: Westview Press.

Töennies, F. (1957). *Community and society* (C. P. Loomis, Trans.). East Lansing: Michigan State University Press.

Toulmin, S. (1992). *Cosmopolis: The hidden agenda of modernity.* Chicago: University of Chicago Press.

———. (1998). *Utopia and cosmopolis: Globalization in the era of american literary realism (New Americanists).* Durham, NC: Duke University Press.

Webb, J., Murphy, M., Flambaum, V., Dzuba, A., Barrow, J., Churchill, C., Prochaska, J., Wolfe, A. (2001). Further evidence for cosmological evolution of the fine structure constant. *Physics Review Letters, 87,* 091301.

Weber, M. (1930). *The Protestant work ethic and the spirit of capitalism.* (T. Parsons, Trans.). New York: Routledge.

Wu, M.-S., Ning, P., & Pu, N. (1999). *Flower terror.* New York: Homa & Sekey.

Yang, C. (1986). *Six chapter of life in a cadre school: Memories from China's cultural revolution.* Boulder, CO: Westview Press.

Zinn, H. (1980). *The people's history of the United States: 1492–present*. New York: HarperCollins.

Zolo, D., et al. (1997). *Cosmopolis: Prospects for world government*. New York: Polity Press.

APPENDIX

For the most up-to-date demographic and development data available online see:

- http://www.odci.gov/cia/publications/factbook (U.S. Central Intelligence Agency fact books)
- http://www.itu.int/home (International Telecommunication Union)
- http://www.iwmi.org (International Water Management Institute)
- http://www.prb.org (Population Reference Bureau)
- http://www.unfpa.org (UN Population Fund)
- http://www.undp.org (UN Population Information Network)
- http://www.worldbank.org (World Bank Regional and National Development Information)
- http://www2.wcmc.org.uk (World Conservation Monitoring Centre)

Selected Bibliography

Abe, J., & Zane, N. (1990). Psychological maladjustment among Asian and white American college students. *Journal of Counseling Psychology, 37,* 437–444.

Adler, P. (1987). Beyond cultural identity: Reflections on cultural and multicultural man. In L. Samovar & R. Porter (Eds.). *Intercultural communication: A reader* (4th ed.) (pp. 362–380). Belmont, CA: Wadsworth.

Agarwal, P. (1991). *Post-1965 immigrants into the U.S.* Palo Alto, CA: Yuvati Press.

Aihara, S. (1999). Nichiyobi no hiro [Sunday heroes]. Retrieved February 10, 2002, from http://www.nikkansports.com/news/entert/entert-etc3/99/sun990613.html.

Ainu Museum. (1993). *Ainu bunka no kiso chishiki* [Basic knowledge of Ainu culture]. Tokyo: Sofukan.

Akbar, N. (1996). *Breaking the chains of psychological slavery.* Tallahassee, FL: Mind Productions.

Allen, P. G. (1986). *The sacred hoop: Recovering the feminine in American Indian traditions.* Boston: Beacon Press.

Amos, I., Coombs, I., & Attaquin, E. (1835/1992). To the white people of Massachusetts [Reprinted testimonial]. In B. O'Connell (Ed.), *On our own ground: The complete writings of William Apess, a Pequot* (p. 166). Amherst: University of Massachusetts Press.

Anderson, B. (1983). *Imagined communities: Reflections on the origins and spread of nationalism.* London: Verso.

Arendt, H. (1973). *The origins of totalitarianism.* New York: Harcourt, Brace, Jovanovich.

Arogundade, B. (2000). *Black beauty: A history and a celebration.* New York: Thunder's Mouth Press.

Asahi Shimbun. (1999). *Japan almanac 2000.* Tokyo: Asahi Shimbun.

Asante, M. K. (1988). *Afrocentricity.* Trenton, NJ: Africa World Press.

Bacon, J. (1996). *Life lines: Community, family, and assimilation among Asian Indian immigrants.* New York: Oxford University Press.

Bakhtin, M (1993). *Toward a philosophy of the act* (V. Liapunov, Trans., M. Holquist & V. Liapunove, Eds.) Austin: University of Texas Press.

Barsh, R. L. (1986). The nature and spirit of North American political systems. *American Indian Quarterly, 10,* 181–198.

Barthes, R. (1973). *Mythologies* (A. Lavers, Trans.) New York: Noonday Press.

Baudrillard, J. (1983). *In the shadow of the silent majorities.* New York: Semiotext(e).

Bell, D. (1960). *The end of ideology: On the exhaustion of political ideas in the fifties.* New York: Free Press of Glencoe.

Bennett, W. (1992). *The de-valuing of America: The fight for our culture and our children.* New York: Summit Books.

Bentham, J. (1781/1988). *The principles of morals and legislation.* Amherst, MA: Prometheus Books.

Berkhofer, R. F. (1979). *The white man's Indian: Images of the American Indian from Columbus to the present.* New York: Vintage Books.

Berman, M. (2000). Japanese invasion. *Media Week, 10* (March 13), pp. 46–48.

Berry, J. W., & Kim, U. (1988). Acculturation and mental health. In P. R. Dasen, J. W. Berry, & N. Sartorius (Eds.), *Health and cross-cultural psychology: Toward applications* (pp. 207–236). Newbury Park, CA: Sage.

Bieder, R. E. (1986). *Science encounters the Indian, 1820–1880: The early years of American ethnology.* Norman: University of Oklahoma Press.

Big Eagle, J. (1894/1996). A Sioux story of the war. In C. G. Calloway. (Ed.), *Our hearts fell to the ground: Plains Indian views of how the West was lost* (pp. 91–96). Boston: Bedford/St. Martin's.

Binet, A. (1916). *The development of intelligence in children.* Baltimore: Williams and Wilkins.

Bloom, A. (1987). *The closing of the American mind.* New York: Simon and Schuster.

Bornoff, N. (1991). *The pink samurai: Love, marriage, and sex in contemporary Japan.* New York: Pocket Books.

Bradshaw, C. (1992). Beauty and the beast: On racial ambiguity. In M. Root (Ed.), *Racially mixed people in America* (pp. 77–88). Newbury Park, CA: Sage.

Branigan, T. (2001). In the eye of the beholder. *Guardian* (October 15). Retrieved from http://www.education.guardian.co.uk.

Brown, D. (1991). *Bury my heart at Wounded Knee: An Indian history of the American West.* New York: Holt.

Brubach, H. (2000). Beauty under the knife. *Atlantic Monthly* (February). Retrieved from http://www.theatlantic.com/issues/2000/02/002/brubach.htm.

Buchanan, P. (2001). *The death of the West: How dying population and immigrant invasion imperial our country and civilization.* Fairfax, VA: Dunne Books.

Burger, J. (1987). *Report from the frontier: The state of the world's indigenous peoples.* New Jersey: Zed.

Burnam, M. A., Hough, R., Karno, M., Escobar, J., & Telles, C. (1987). Acculturation and lifetime prevalence of psychiatric disorders among Mexican Americans in Los Angeles. *Journal of Health and Social Behavior, 28,* 89–102.

Burt, L. W. (1986). Roots of the Native American urban experience: Relocation policy in the 1950s. *American Indian Quarterly, 10,* 85–99.

Calloway, C. G. (Ed.) (1996). *Our hearts fell to the ground: Plains Indian views of how the West was lost.* Boston: Bedford/St. Martin's.

Cash, T. F. (1981). Physical attractiveness: An annotated bibliography of theory and research in the behavioral sciences. *JSAS Catalogue of Selected Documents in Psychology, 11*, 85.

Cash, T. F., Rossi, J., & Chapman, R. (1985). Not just another pretty face: Sex roles, locus of control, and cosmetics use. *Personality and Social Psychology Bulletin, 11*, 246–257.

Cash, T. F., & Wunderle, J. M. (1987). Self-monitoring and cosmetics use among college women. *Journal of Social Psychology, 129*, 349–355.

Cash, T. F., Dawson, K., Davis, P., Brown, M., & Galumbeck, C. (1988). *The effects of cosmetics use on the physical attractiveness and body image of college women.* Unpublished manuscript.

Chan, K. (2001). U.S.-born, immigrant, refugee, or indigenous status. In G. Chang (Ed.), *Asian Americans and politics* (pp. 197–229). Washington, DC: Woodrow Wilson Center Press.

Chan, S. (1991). *Asian Americans: An interpretive history.* Boston: Twayne.

Chandrasekhar, S. (Ed.). (1983). *From India to America: A brief history of immigration, problems of discrimination admission and assimilation.* La Jolla, CA: Population Review.

Chang, R. (2000). Why we need a critical Asian American legal studies. In J. Wu & M. Song (Eds.), *Asian American studies* (pp. 363–378). New Brunswick, NJ: Rutgers University Press.

Chaplin, J. E. (1997). Natural philosophy and an early racial idiom in North America: Comparing English and Indian bodies. *William and Mary Quarterly, 53*, 229–252.

Chen, W. (1999). *Asian blepharoplasty.* Retrieved from http://www.asiaeyelid.com/faq.html.

Cheung, K. (1993). *Articulate silences: Hisaye Yamamoto, Maxine Hong Kingston, Joy Kogawa.* Ithaca, NY: Cornell University Press.

Chin, A. (2001). *A brief history of the model minority stereotype.* Retrieved from http://www.modelminority.com/history/primer.htm.

Cho, M. (2000). Bodily regulation and vocational schooling. *Gender and Education, 12*, 149–164.

Choi, J. M., Callaghan, K. A., & Murphy, J. W. (1995). *The politics of culture: Race, violence, and democracy.* Westport, CT: Praeger.

Chung, W. (2000). Hong Kong. *Billboard, 112*, 53–54.

Churchill, W. (1998). The tragedy and the travesty: The subversion of indigenous sovereignty in North America. *American Indian Culture and Research Journal, 22*, 1–69.

Coleman, L. M., & DePaulo, B. M. (1991). Uncovering the human spirit: Moving beyond disability and "missed" communication. In N. Coupland, H. Giles, & J. M. Wiemann (Eds.), *"Miscommunication" and problematic talk* (pp. 61–84). Newbury Park, CA: Sage.

Cooks, L. (2001). From distance and uncertainty to research and pedagogy in the borderlands: Implications for the future of intercultural communication. *Communication Theory, 11*, 339–351.

Cooper-Chin, A. (1999). An animated imbalance: Japan's television heroines in Asia. *Gazette, 61*, 293–310.

Corliss, R., Harbison, G., & Ressner, J. (1999). Amazing anime. *Time, 154,* 94–96.

Cornell, S., & Kalt, J. P. (1990). Pathways from poverty: Economic development and institution-building on American Indian reservations. *American Indian Culture and Research Journal, 14,* 89–125.

Coupland, J., Nussbaum, J. F., & Coupland, N. (1991). The reproduction of aging and agism in intergenerational talk. In N. Coupland, H. Giles, & J. M. Wiemann (Eds.), *"Miscommunication" and problematic talk* (pp. 85–102). Newbury Park, CA: Sage.

Cox, C. L., & Glick, W. H. (1986). Resume evaluations and cosmetics use: When more is not better. *Sex Roles, 14,* 51–58.

Cronon, W. (1994). *Changes in the wind: Indians, colonists, and the ecology of New England.* New York: Hill and Wang.

Dale, P. (1986). *The myth of Japanese uniqueness.* New York: St. Martin's Press.

Daniel, G. (1992). Passers and pluralists: Subverting the racial divide. In M. Root (Ed.), *Racially mixed people in America* (pp. 91–107). Newbury Park, CA: Sage.

Darling-Wolf, F. (2000). Texts in context: Intertextuality, hybridity, and the negotiation of cultural identity in Japan. *Journal of Communication Inquiry, 24,* 134–155.

Dasgupta, S. S. (1989). *On the trail of an uncertain dream: Indian immigrant experience in America.* New York: AMS Press.

Davis, C. (1992). *Criticism and culture.* Harlow: Longman.

Dawes Act of 1887. (1934/1973). Reprinted as Appendix A in D. S. Otis, *The Dawes Act and the allotment of Indian lands* (F. P. Prucha, Ed.) (pp. 177–184). Norman: University of Oklahoma Press. (Original work published as *History of the allotment policy.*)

Dawes Act of 1891. (1934/1973). Reprinted as Appendix B in D. S. Otis, *The Dawes Act and the allotment of Indian lands* (F. P. Prucha, Ed.) (pp. 185–188). Norman: University of Oklahoma Press. (Original work published as *History of the allotment policy.*)

Deloria, V. Jr. (1988). *Custer died for your sins: An Indian manifesto.* Norman: University of Oklahoma Press.

Derrida, J. (1978). *Writing and difference.* Chicago: University of Chicago Press.

Diamond, J. (1993). *The third chimpanzee.* New York: HarperCollins.

Diket, A. L. (1966). The noble savage convention as epitomized in John Lawson's a new voyage to Carolina. *The Carolina Historical Review, 43,* 413–429.

Dion, K., Berscheid, E., & Walter, E. (1972). What is beautiful is good. *Journal of Personality and Social Psychology, 24,* 285–290.

Diop, C. A. (1974). *The African origin of civilization.* New York: Lawrence Hill.

Donahue, P. (1997). New warriors, new legends: Basketball in three Native American works of fiction. *American Indian Culture and Research Journal, 21,* 43–60.

Douglass, F. (1968). *Narrative of the life of Frederick Douglass, an American slave, written by himself.* New York: New American Library.

Du Bois, W. E. B. (1903/1995). *The souls of black folk.* New York: Penguin Putnam.

Duus, P. (1995). *The abacus and the sword: The Japanese penetration of Korea, 1895–1910.* Berkeley: University of California Press.

Dyer, R. (Ed.). (1977). *Gay and film.* London: British Film Institute.

Eichberg, S. (1999). *Bodies of work: Cosmetic surgery and the gendered whitening of America.* Unpublished doctoral dissertation, University of Pennsylvania, Philadelphia, PA.

Eliade, M. (1998). *Myth and reality.* Prospect Heights, IL: Waveland Press.

Elkin, H. (1940). The northern Arapaho of Wyoming. In R. Linton (Ed.), *Acculturation in seven American Indian tribes* (pp. 207–258). New York: D. Appleton-Century.

Ewen S., & Ewen, E. (1992). *Channels of desire: Mass images and the shaping of American consciousness.* Minneapolis: University of Minnesota Press.

Fabriga, H., & Wallace, C. A. (1971). Acculturation and psychiatric treatment: A study involving Mexican Americans. *British Journal of Social Psychiatry and Community Health, 4,* 124–136.

Fanon, F. (1991). *The wretched of the earth.* New York: Grove Weidenfeld.

Ferguson, A. (1767/1995). *An essay on the history of civil society* (F. Oz-Salzberger, Ed.). Cambridge: Cambridge University Press.

Fernandez, M., & Liu, W. T. (1986). Asian Indians in the United States: Economic, educational, and family profiles from the 1980 census. *Studies in Third World Societies, 38,* 149–177.

Festinger, L. (1957). *A theory of cognitive dissonance.* Stanford, CA: Stanford University Press.

Fish, S. (1989). *Doing what comes naturally.* Durham, NC: Duke University Press.

Fisher, A. (1980). *Small group decision making: Communication and the group process.* New York: McGraw Hill.

Fisher, M. P. (1980). *The Indians of New York City: A study of immigrants from India.* Columbia, MO: South Asia Books.

Fitzhgh, W. (1999). Ainu ethnicity: A history. In W. W. Fitzhugh & C. O. Dubreuil (Eds.), *Ainu: Spirit of a northern people* (pp. 9–27). Seattle: University of Washington Press.

Flaskerud, J., & Hu, L. (1992). Relationship of ethnicity to psychiatric diagnosis. *Journal of Nervous and Mental Disease, 180,* 296–303.

Foucault, M. (1989). *The archaeology of knowledge.* London: Routledge.

Foundation for Research and Promotion of Ainu Culture. (2000). *To understand the Ainu.* Sapporo, Japan: Foundation for Research and Promotion of Ainu Culture.

Fox, S. A. (2000). *Super-impact: Christopher Reeve and attitudes toward people with disabilities.* Paper presented at the annual conference of the National Communication Association, Seattle, WA.

Frazier, E. F. (1957). *The Negro in the United States.* New York: Macmillan.

Frazier, E. F. (1965). *Black bourgeoisie.* New York: Free Press.

Freer, R. (1994). Black-Korean conflict in the LA riot. In M. Baldassare (Ed.), *The Los Angeles riots: Lessons for the urban future* (pp. 175–214). Boulder, CO: Westview.

Fromm, E. (1955). *The sane society.* New York: Rinehart.

Fromm, E. (1958). *Man for himself.* New York: Rinehart.

Fromm, E. (1976). *To have or to be?* New York: Harper and Row.

Fukuyama, F. (1993). *The end of history and the last man.* New York: Avon.

Fulford, B. (1999). Anime opens on Main Street. *Forbes, 164,* 58–59.

Gadamer, H.-G. (1975). *Truth and method.* New York: Seabury Press.

Gebser, J. (1985). *The ever-present origin* (N. Barstad & A. Mickunas, Trans.). Athens: Ohio University Press.

Geertz, C. (1973). *The interpretation of cultures.* New York: Basic Books.

Gellner, E. (1983). *Nations and nationalism.* Oxford: Basil Blackwell.

George, K. (2001). Statements. In D. K. Inouye, *Goals and priorities of the member tribes of the National Congress of American Indians and the United South and*

Eastern Tribes. Hearing before the Committee on Indian Affairs, U.S. Senate, 107th Congress, first session (Senate Publication No. S. HRG. 107–35, pp. 23–39) (April 5). Washington, DC: Government Printing Office.

Gilman, S. (1985). *Difference and pathology.* Ithaca, NY: Cornell University Press.

Gilman, S. (1999). *Making the body beautiful.* Princeton, NJ: Princeton University Press.

Gilman, S. (2001). Illusions, scalpels and stereotypes. *UNESCO Courier,* pp. 44–46.

Gilroy, P. (1987). *There ain't no black in the Union Jack.* London: Routledge.

Gilroy, P. (1993). *The black Atlantic.* Cambridge, MA: Harvard University Press.

Gilroy, P. (1993). *The black Atlantic.* London: Verso.

Goffman, E. (1963). *Stigma.* Englewood Cliffs, NJ: Prentice Hall.

Gosselin, A. (1998). Racial etiquette and the white plot of passing: (Re)Inscribing "place" in John Stahl's "imitation of life." *Canadian Review of American Studies, 28,* 47–68.

Gotanda, N. (2000). Multiculturalism and racial stratification. In J. Wu & M. Song (Eds.), *Asian American studies: A reader* (pp. 379–390). New Brunswick, NJ: Rutgers University Press.

Gramsci, A. (1972). *Selections from the prison notebooks of Antonio Gramsci* (Q. Hoare & G. N. Smith, Eds. and Trans.). New York: International.

Graves, E. (2000). New economy, new rules. *Black Enterprise, 30* (June 2), pp. 11–17.

Green, M. D. (1982). *The politics of Indian removal: Creek government and society in crisis.* Lincoln: University of Nebraska Press.

Greider, W. (1997). *One world ready or not: The manic logic of global capitalism.* New York: Touchstone.

Gudykunst W. B., & Kim Y. Y. (1997). *Communicating with strangers: An approach to intercultural communication* (3rd ed.). New York: McGraw Hill.

Haines, R. (1997). U.S. citizenship and tribal membership: A contest for political identity and rights of tribal self-determination in Southern California. *American Indian Culture and Research Journal, 21,* 211–230.

Hall, S. (1982). The rediscovery of ideology: Return of the repressed in media studies. In M. Gurevitch, T. Bennett, J. Curran, & J. Woollacott. (Eds.), *Culture, society and the media* (pp. 56–90). London: Methuen.

Hanada, S. (1999). Rekishi ha tsukurareru [A history is made]. In J. Ishikawa, & O. Nagase (Eds.), *Shogaigaku he no shotai* [An introduction to disability studies] (pp. 257–283). Tokyo: Akashi Shoten.

Hannaford, I. (1996). *Race: The history of an idea in the West.* Washington, DC: Woodrow Wilson Center Press.

Harajiri, H. (1989). *Zainichi chosenjin no seikatsusekai* [The lifeworld of Koreans in Japan]. Tokyo: Kobundo.

Hegde, R. S. (1999). Swinging the trapeze: The negotiation of identity among Asian Indian immigrant women in the United States. In D. V. Tanno & A. Gonzalez (Eds.), *Communication and identity: International and intercultural annual.* Thousand Oaks, CA: Sage.

Hegel, G. (1979). *Phenomenology of mind* (J. N. Findlay, Trans.). Oxford University Press.

Helweg, A. W., & Helweg, U. M. (1990). *An immigrant success story: East Indians in America.* Philadelphia: University of Pennsylvania Press.

Herrnstein, R., & Murray, C. (1994). *The bell curve: Intelligence and class structure in American life.* New York: Free Press.

Herskovitz, J. (1997). Shiseido makes over the way it sees international markets. *Advertising-Age, 68* (October 27), 3.

Heyer, K. (2000). From welfare to rights: Japanese disability law. *Asia-Pacific Law and Policy Journal.* Retrieved February 10, 2002, from http://www.hawaii.edu/aplpj.

Hobsbawn, E., & Ranger, T. (Eds.). (1983). *The invention of tradition.* Cambridge: Cambridge University Press.

hooks, b.(1990). *Yearning.* Boston, MA: South End Press.

hooks, b.(1995). *Killing rage.* New York: Holt.

Horsman, R. (1981). *Race and manifest destiny: The origins of American racial Anglo-Saxonism.* Cambridge, MA: Harvard University Press.

Howard, J. H. (1955). Pan-Indian culture of Oklahoma. *Scientific Monthly, 81* (November), pp. 215–220.

Hughes, M. (1997). Symbolic racism, old-fashioned racism, and whites' opposition to affirmative action. In S. A. Tuch & J. K. Martin (Eds.), *Racial attitudes in the 1990s: Continuity and change* (pp. 45–75). Westport, CT: Praeger.

Ikeda, R., & Kramer, E. (1998). The *Enola Gay*: The transformation of an airplane into an icon and the ownership of history. *Keio Communication Review, 20,* 49–73.

Ikeda, R., & Kramer, E. (2002). *Ibunka komyunikeshon nyumon* (2nd ed.) [Introduction to intercultural communication]. Tokyo: Yuhikaku Press.

Imanishi, H. (2000). *Kokuminkokka to mainoritei* [Nation state and minority]. Tokyo: Nihon Keizai Hyoronsha.

Inoue, T. (1996). Roundabout looks. *Metroactive News & Issues* (June 27). Retrieved from http://www.metroactive.com/papers/metro/06.27.96/asian-eyes-9626.html.

Interview with Pleasant Porter. (1901, January 17). *Muskogee Phoenix.* (Typed reprint available from the University of Oklahoma Western History Collection.)

Ishizaka, K. (1999). Kawasaki no zainichi kankoku-chosenjin [Resident Koreans in Kawasaki]. In Research Group of Kawasaki Zainichi Kankoku-Chosenjin no Seikatsu to Koe (Eds.), *Kawasaki: Zainichi kankoku-chosenjin no seikatsu to koe* [Kawasaki: The life and voice of Korean-Japanese] (pp. 7–17). Kawasaki, Japan: Seikyusha.

Iwakuma, M., & Nussbaum, J. F. (2000). Intercultural view of people with disabilities in Asia and Africa. In D. O. Braithwaite & T. Thompson (Eds.), *Handbook of communication and people with disabilities* (pp. 239–255). Mahwah, NJ: Lawrence Erlbaum.

Janis, I. (1982). *Groupthink: Psychological studies of policy decisions and fiascoes.* Boston: Houghton Mifflin.

Jay, J. (2000). The valley of the new American. *Demographics, 22,* 58.

Jeffries, L. (1999). The African Americans: Search for truth and knowledge. Retrieved from http://www.nbufront.org/html/MastersMuseums/LenJeffries/LenJeffriesVMuseum.html.

Jensen, J. M. (1988). *Passage from India: Asian Indian immigrants in North America.* New Haven, CT: Yale University Press.

Jordan, W. D. (1968). *White over black: American attitudes toward the Negro, 1550–1812.* Chapel Hill: University of North Carolina Press.

Jourard, S. (1974). Growing awareness and the awareness of growth. In B. Patton & K. Giffin (Eds.), *Interpersonal communication.* New York: Harper and Row.

Jung, C. (1981). *The archetypes and the collective unconscious* (collected works of C. G. Jung vol. 9, part 1) (H. Read, Ed.). Princeton, NJ: Princeton University Press.

Kallen, H. M. (1958). On "Americanizing" the American Indian. *Social Research, 25,* 469–473.

Kamisaka, F. (1999,). Kamisaka Fuyuko no haradachi nikki [Kamisaka Fuyuko's diary]. *Josei Sebun,* pp. 92–93. Tokyo: Shogakukan.

Kang, S. (1998). Zainichi korian shakai o henbo saseru "kokuseki," "minzoku kyoiku," "sanseiken" no ryudoka [Change in "nationality," "ethnic education," "suffrage," which may give an impact on Korean society in Japan]. *Sapio* (July 8), 18–19.

Kant, I. (1764/1997). On national characteristics, so far as they depend upon the distinct feeling of the beautiful and sublime. In E. C. Eze (Ed.), *Race and the Enlightenment: A reader* (pp. 49–57). Cambridge, MA: Blackwell.

Karenga, R. (1978). *Essays in struggle.* San Diego: Kawaida.

Kasdan, M., & Tavernetti, S. (1998). Native Americans in a revisionist western: *Little Big Man* (1970). In P. C. Rollins & J. E. O'Connor (Eds.), *Hollywood's Indian: The portrayal of the Native American in film* (pp. 121–136). Lexington: University Press of Kentucky.

Kashiwazaki, C. (2000). The politics of legal status: The equation of nationality with ethnonational identity. In S. Ryang (Ed.), *Koreans in Japan: Critical voices from the margin* (pp. 13–31). New York: Routledge.

Kato, K. (1999). Zureteiku kankei [The widening relational gap]. *We'll, 16* (June), 79–84.

Kayano, S. (1999). The weight of word: History and culture of the Ainu. In Y. Ishii & M. Yamauchi (Eds.), *Nihonjin to tabunkashugi* [Japanese and multiculturalism] (pp. 36–50). Tokyo: Yamakawa.

Keys, K. C. (1997). The community development quota program: Inequity and failure in privatization policy. *American Indian Culture and Research Journal, 21,* 31–71.

Kida, S. (1926). Tohoku minzoku kenkyu joron [An introduction to research on ethnic group in Tohoku]. In S. Kida & S. Kida (Eds.), *Chosakushu 9* [Collected papers of Sadakichi Kida 9]. Tokyo: Heibonsha.

Kierkegaard, S. (1983). *The sickness unto death: Kierkegaard's writings* (vol. 19) (H. Hong & E. Hong, Trans.). Princeton, NJ: Princeton University Press.

Kierkegaard, S. (1992). *The concept of irony/Schelling lecture notes: Kierkegaard's writings* (vol. 2) (H. Hong & E. Hong, Trans.). Princeton, NJ: Princeton University Press.

Kikuchi, I. (1994). *Ainu minzoku to nihonjin* [The Ainu and the Japanese]. Tokyo: Asahi Shimbunsha.

Kim, H., & Mikuni, K. (1999). Toraji-kai no genzai to shorai [Present and future of Toraji-kai]. In Research Group of Kawasaki Zainichi Kankoku-Chosenjin no Seikatsu to Koe (Ed.), *Kawasaki: Zainichi kankoku-chosenjin no seikatsu to koe* [The life and voice of Korean-Japanese] (pp. 124–141). Kawasaki, Japan: Seikyusha.

Kim, Y. D. (1991). Dainijitaisenchu no chosenjin senjidoin ni tsuite [On wartime mobilization of Koreans during World War II]. In Sengo Hosho Mondai Kenkyukai (Eds.), *Zainichi kankoku-chosenjin no sengohosho* [Post-war welfare for Korean-Japanese]. Tokyo: Akashi Shoten.

Kobayashi, K. (1995). Kika de yureru minzoku ka riben ka [The issue of naturalization: Ethnicity or convenience]. *Aera,* 24–27.

Koestler, A. (1967). *The ghost in the machine.* New York: Macmillan.

Koestler, A. (1946/1984). *Darkness at noon.* New York: Bantam.

Kohama, I. (2000). *Jakusha toha dareka* [Who are the powerless?]. Tokyo: PHP Shinso.

Kokuseki minzokutte nanda? [What are nationality and ethnicity?]. (2001). *Shukan Kinyobi* (August 24), 34–37.

Kono, M. (1998). Ainu [the Ainu]. In H. Harajiri (Ed.), *Sekai no minzoku* [Ethnic groups in a world] (pp. 33–53). Tokyo: Hoso Daigaku.

Kramer, E. (1992). *Consciousness and culture: An introduction to the thought of Jean Gebser.* Westport, CT: Greenwood.

Kramer, E. (1993a). The origin of television as civilizational expression. In K. Haworth, J. Deely, & T. Prewitt (Eds.), *Semiotics 1990. Sources in Semiotics* (vol. 11) (pp. 28–37). New York: University Press of America.

Kramer, E. (1993b). Understanding co-constitutional genesis. *Integrative explorations: Journal of Culture and Consciousness, 1,* 41–47.

Kramer, E. (1994). Making love alone: Videocentrism and the case of modern pornography. In K. A. Callihan (Ed.), *Ideals of feminine beauty: Philosophical, social, and cultural dimensions* (pp. 78–98). Westport, CT: Greenwood.

Kramer, E. (1995). A brief hermeneutic of the co-constitution of nature and culture in the West including some contemporary consequences. *History of European Ideas, 20,* 649–659.

Kramer, E. (1997). *Modern/post-modern: Off the beaten path of antimodernism.* Westport, CT: Praeger.

Kramer, E. (1999). *Gaiatsu and cultural judo.* Paper presented at the annual conference of the International Jean Gebser Society, Matteson, Illinois.

Kramer, E. (2000a). *Contemptus mundi:* Reality as disease. In V. Berdayes & J. Murphy (Eds.), *Computers, human interaction, and organization: Critical issues* (pp. 31–53). Westport, CT: Praeger.

Kramer, E. (2000b). Cultural fusion and the defense of difference. In M. Asante & J. Min (Eds.). *Socio-cultural conflict between African and Korean Americans* (pp. 183–230). New York: University Press of America.

Kramer, E., & Ikeda, R. (1997). What is a Japanese?: Diversity, culture, and social harmony. In E. Kramer (Ed.), *Race relations in a postmodern world* (pp. 79–102). Westport, CT: Praeger.

Kramer, E., & Ikeda, R. (2000). The changing faces of reality. *Keio Communication Review, 22,* 79–109.

Kramer, E., & Johnson, L. Jr. (1997). The articulation of race: Eugenics, and the ideology of intelligence. In E. Kramer (Ed.), *Postmodernism and Race* (pp. 31–50). Westport, CT: Praeger.

Kuki, S. (1930). *The structure of Iki* (M. Otake, Trans.). Unpublished doctoral dissertation, Syracuse University, Syracuse, NY.

Kuo, W. (1984). Prevalence of depression among Asian Americans. *Journal of Nervous and Mental Disease, 172,* 449–457.

Kupperman, K. O. (1997). Presentment of civility: English reading of American self-presentation in the early years of colonization. *William and Mary Quarterly, 54,* 193–228.

Kurian, G., & Srivastava, R. P. (1983). *Overseas Indians: A study in adaptation.* Delhi, India: Vikas Publishing House.

Kurokawa, K. (1994). *The philosophy of symbiosis.* London: Academy Editions.

Lacan, J. (1982). *Ecrits* (A. Sheridan, Trans.). New York: Norton.

Laing, R. D. (1967). *The politics of experience.* New York: Pantheon.

Lang, J. G., Munoz, R. F., Bernal, G., & Sorenson, J. L. (1982). Quality of life and psychological well-being in a bi-cultural Latino community. *Hispanic Journal of Behavioral Sciences, 4,* 433–450.

Larkin, C., & Tayler, H. (1994). Stories of women, food, and power. *Social Alternatives,* 12, 43–46.

Larson, S. (1997). Fear and contempt: A European concept of property. *American Indian Quarterly, 21,* 567–577.

Leclerc, G.-L. (1748–1804/1997). From a natural history, general and particular. In E. C. Eze (Ed.), *Race and the Enlightenment: A reader* (pp. 15–28). Cambridge, MA: Blackwell.

Lee, E., & Lu, F. (1989). Assessment and treatment of Asian-American survivors of mass violence. *Journal of Traumatic Stress, 2,* 93–120.

Lee, S. (1996). *Unraveling the model minority stereotype.* New York: Teachers College Press.

Lefton, J. (1998). Nintendo's Pokémon on the way to block buster status. *Brandweek, 39,* 5.

Lewin, K. (1948). *Resolving social conflicts: Selected papers on group dynamics.* New York: Harper and Row.

Lifton, R. J. (1999). *Destroying the world to save it.* New York: Holt.

Lin, K. (1986). Psychopathology and social disruption in refugees. In C. Williams & J. Westermeyers (Eds.), *Refugee mental health in resettlement countries* (pp. 610–673). Washington, DC: Hemisphere Publishing.

Linton, R. (1940a). The distinctive aspects of acculturation. In R. Linton (Ed.), *Acculturation in seven American Indian tribes* (pp. 501–520). New York: D. Appleton-Century.

Linton, R. (1940b). The processes of cultural transfer. In R. Linton (Ed.), *Acculturation in seven American Indian tribes* (pp. 483–500). New York: D. Appleton-Century.

Lott, J. T. (1998). *Asian Americans: From racial category to multiple identity.* Walnut Creek, CA: Altamira Press.

Luhmann, N. (1982). *The differentiation of society.* New York: Columbia University Press.

Lyotard, J.-F. (1984) *The postmodern condition.* Minneapolis: University of Minnesota Press.

MacDonald, A. L. (1995). Traditional Indian family values. In A. Hirschfelder (Ed.), *Native heritage: Personal accounts by American Indians 1790 to the present* (pp. 16–17). New York: Macmillan.

MacIntyre, B. (1989). The new eugenics. *London Sunday Telegraph* (March 13), 23.

Mahdzan, F., & Ziegler, N. (2001, July 4). *Asian Americans: An analysis of negative stereotypical characters in popular media.* Retrieved from http://www.modelminority.com/media/stereotypical.htm.

Mallory, M. (2001). Kid's anime hits critical mass. *Los Angeles Times* (October 11), 18.

Mankiller, W., & Wallis, M. (1993). *Mankiller: A chief and her people.* New York: St. Martin's Griffin.

Marcuse, H. (1964). *One-dimensional man.* Boston: Beacon Press.

Martin, W. C. L. (1841). *A general introduction to the natural history of mammiferous animals, with a particular view of the physical history of man, and the more closely allied genera of the order quadrumana, or monkeys.* London: Wright.

Masten, S. (2001). Statements. In D. K. Inouye, *Goals and priorities of the member tribes of the National Congress of American Indians and the United South and East-*

ern Tribes: Hearing before the Committee on Indian Affairs, U.S. Senate, 107th Congress, First Session (Senate Publication No. S. HRG. 107–35, pp. 2–13) (March 22). Washington, DC: Government Printing Office.

McLuhan, M. (2001). *The medium is the massage.* Corte Madera, CA: Gingko Press.

Media Action Network for Asian Americans. (2001). *Restrictive portrayals of Asians in the media and how to balance them.* Retrieved from http://janet.org/manna/a_stereotypes.html.

Mihesuah, D. A. (1998). American Indian identities: Issues of individual choices and development. *American Indian Culture and Research Journal, 22,* 193–226.

Millar, F. E., & Rogers, L. E. (1987). Relational dimensions of interpersonal dynamics. In M. Roloff & G. Miller (Eds.), *Interpersonal processes: New directions in communication research* (pp. 117–139). Newbury Park, CA: Sage.

Miller, B. G. (1997). The individual, the collective, and tribal code. *American Indian Culture and Research Journal, 21,* 107–129.

Miller, L. C., & Cox, C. L. (1982). For appearances' sake: Public self-consciousness and make up use. *Personal and Social Psychology Bulletin, 8,* 748–751.

Miller, R. A. (1978). The spirit of the Japanese language. *Journal of Japanese Studies, 3,* 251–98.

Mizuo, J. (1998). *Keshouhin no brando shi* [A history of brand of cosmetics]. Tokyo: Chuo-kouronsha.

Mohanty, C. T. (1993). Defining genealogies: Feminist reflections on being South Asian in North America. In South Asian Descent Collective (Ed.), *Our feet walk the sky: Women of the South Asian diaspora.* Berkeley, CA: Aunt Lute Books.

Montagu, A. (1999). *Race and IQ.* New York: Oxford University Press.

Morgan, K. (1991). Women and the knife: Cosmetic surgery and the colonization of women's bodies. *Hypatia, 6,* 25–53.

Morrison, T. (1994). On the backs of blacks. In N. Mills (Ed.), *Arguing immigration: Are new immigrants a wealth of diversity … or a crushing burden?* New York: Touchstone/Simon and Schuster.

Morson, G. S., & Emerson, C. (1994). *Mikhail Bakhtin: Creation of prosaics.* Stanford, CA: Stanford University Press.

Mucha, J. (1983). From prairie to the city: Transformation of Chicago's American Indian community. *Urban Anthropology, 12,* 337–371.

Mucha, J. (1984). American Indian success in the urban setting. *Urban Anthropology, 13,* 329–354.

Muhhamad, E. (1965). *Message to the black man.* Chicago: Nation of Islam Settlement no. 1.

Mumford, L. (1966). *The myth of the machine: Technics and human development.* New York: Harcourt, Brace and World.

Munoz, F. U. (1979). Pacific islanders: An overview. In U.S. Commission on Civil Rights Conference (Ed.), *Civil rights issues of Asian and Pacific Americans: Myths and realities* (pp. 342–348). Washington, DC: Government Printing Office.

Murasawa, H. (1987). *Bijin shinkaron* [The theory of evolution of beautiful women]. Tokyo: Tokyo-Shoseki.

Murphy, J. W., & Choi, J. M. (1997). *Postmodernism, unraveling racism, and democratic institutions.* Westport, CT: Praeger.

MyNippon Team (2001). Un-Japanization of Japan. Retrieved from http://www.mynippon.com/gainippon/westernization.htm.

Nakamura, S. (2000). Ano "Gotaifumanzoku" no ato nani wo angaetekimashitaka [After "Gotaifumanzoku," what have you thinking?]. *Asahi Shimbun* (July 16), 35.

Nakatsuka, A. (1991). Zainichi chosenjin no rekishiteki keisei [Koreans in Japan created in history]. In T. Yamada & C. M. Pak (Eds.), *Zainichi chosenjin: Rekishi to Genjo* [Korean-Japanese: History and current situation] (pp. 85–115). Tokyo: Akashi Shoten.

Newsweek (1996). Relaxing an old taboo. *Newsweek, 128* (July 15), 5.

Ng, A. (2001). 10 issues commonly faced by Asian American professionals. *Northwest Asian Weekly, 20* (April 20), 8.

Niethammer, C. (1977). *Daughters of the earth: The lives and legends of American Indian women.* New York: Collier Books.

Nietzsche, F. (1886/1972). *Beyond good and evil.* New York: Vintage.

Nietzsche, F. (1882/1974). *The gay science.* New York: Vintage.

Nishide, K. (1986). Amerika gasshukokushi to senju minzoku [History of the United States of America and indigenous people]. In Department of Human Sciences, Sapporo Gakuin University (Ed.), *Hokkaido to shosu minzoku: Hokkaido bunkaron* [Hokkaido and minority ethnic groups: Culture of Hokkaido] (pp. 1–59). Sapporo, Japan: Sapporo Gakuin University Cooperation.

Noelle-Neumann, E. (1984). *The spiral of silence: Public opinion—our social skin.* Chicago: University of Chicago Press.

Nott, J. (1854/1969). Geographical distribution of animals, and the races of men. In L. Ruchames (Ed.), *Racial thought in America: Vol. 1. From the Puritans to Abraham Lincoln: A documentary history* (pp. 462–469). Amherst: University of Massachusetts Press.

O'Connell, B. (1992). Introduction. In B. O'Connell (Ed.), *On our own ground: The complete writings of William Apess, a Pequot* (pp. xiii–xxvii). Amherst: University of Massachusetts Press.

O'Connor, J. E. (1998). The white man's Indian: An institutional approach. In P. C. Rollins & J. E. O'Connor (Eds.), *Hollywood's Indian: The portrayal of the Native American in film* (pp. 27–38). Lexington: University Press of Kentucky.

Ogasawara, N. (1997). *Ainu sabetsu mondai dokuhon* [Readings in Ainu discrimination problems]. Tokyo: Ryokufu.

Ogawa, M. (1985). Zainichi gaikokujin no shakaihosho hoseijo no jokyo [The legal status of resident aliens in the social security system]. *Horitsu Jiho, 57,* 43–55.

Oguma, E. (1998). *Nihonjin no kyokai* [The boundaries of the Japanese]. Tokyo: Shinyosha.

Ong, W. J. (1982). *Orality and literacy: The technologizing of the word.* London: Routledge.

Onoda, L. (1973). Neurotic-stable tendencies among Japanese American Senseis and Caucasian students. *Journal of Non-White Concerns, 5,* 180–185.

Ortiz, V., & Arce, C. (1984). Language orientation and mental health status among persons of Mexican descent. *Hispanic Journal of Behavioral Sciences, 6,* 127–143.

Otis, D. S. (1934/1973). *The Dawes Act and the allotment of Indian lands* (F. P. Prucha, Ed.). Norman: University of Oklahoma Press. (Original work published as *History of the allotment policy.*)

Ototake, H. (2001a). *Gotaifumanzoku: Kanzenban* [Born with an imperfect body: The final version]. Tokyo: Kodansha.

Ototake, H. (2001b). *Minnakara no meru wo yonde* [My response to your mail]. Retrieved from http://www.ototake.net/mail/back010129.html.

Ovando, C. (2001). Interrogating stereotypes: The case of the Asian model minority. *Newsletter of the Asian Culture Center* (Fall), Indiana University. Retrieved from http://www.modelminority.com/academia/interrogating.htm.

Oz-Salzberger, F. (1995). Introduction. In A. Ferguson (Ed.), *An essay on the history of civil society* (F. Oz-Salzberger, Ed., pp. vii–xxv). Cambridge: Cambridge University Press.

Pagden, A. (1982). *The fall of natural man: The American Indian and the origins of comparative ethnology.* Cambridge, UK: Cambridge University Press.

Park, I. (1999). *Zainichi to iu ikikata* [The way how to live as Koreans in Japan]. Tokyo: Kodansha.

Pearce, R. H. (1988). *Savagism and civilization: A study of the Indian and the American mind.* Berkeley: University of California Press.

Petersen, W. (1966). Success story, Japanese American style. *New York Times Magazine,* 6 (January 6).

Phinney, J. S., & Chavira, V. (1995). Parental ethnic socialization and adolescent coping with problems related to ethnicity. *Journal of Research on Adolescence, 5,* 31–53.

Phinney, J. S. (1996). When we talk about American ethnic groups, what do we mean? *American Psychologist, 51,* 918- 927.

Porter, P. (1891). Letter of Pleasant Porter to Isparhecher. *Purcell Register* (June 13). (Typed reprint available from the University of Oklahoma Western History Collection)

Posey, D. (1999). Introduction: Culture and nature—the inextricable link. In U.N. Evironment Programme (UNEP) (D. A. Posey, Ed.), *Cultural and spiritual values of biodiversity.* London: Intermediate Technology.

Prashad, V. (2000). *The karma of brown folk.* Minneapolis: University of Minnesota Press.

Press Release WHO/68 (1999). International day of disabled persons. Retrieved from http://www.who.int/inf-pr-1999/en/pr99-68.html.

Radhakrishnan, R. (1996). *Diasporic mediations.* Carbondale: Southern Illinois University Press.

Ranfranz, T. T. (2001). Statements. In D. K. Inouye (Vice Chair), *Goals and priorities of the member tribes of the National Congress of American Indians and the United South and Eastern tribes.* Hearing before the Committee on Indian Affairs, U.S. Senate, 107th Congress, First session (Senate Publication No. S. HRG. 107–35, pp. 13–20) (March 22). Washington, DC: Government Printing Office.

Renolds, F. (1996). *The new American reality:* New York: Russell Sage.

Riley, M. J. (1998). Trapped in the history of film: Racial conflict and allure in the vanishing American. In P. C. Rollins & J. E. O'Connor (Eds.), *Hollywood's Indian: The portrayal of the Native American in film* (pp. 27–38). Lexington: University Press of Kentucky.

Root, D. L., & L. M. Root. (1993). New perspective on the Asian cosmetic market. *Drug and Cosmetic Industry, 153,* 28–35.

Rountree, H. C. (1989). *The Powhatan Indians of Virginia: Their traditional culture.* Norman: University of Oklahoma Press.

Rousseau, J.-J. (1755/1992). *Discourse on the origin of inequality* (D. A. Cress, Trans.). Indianapolis, IN: Hackett.

Ryang, S. (2000). Introduction: Resident Koreans in Japan. In S. Ryang (Ed.), *Koreans in Japan: Critical voices from the margin* (pp. 1–12). New York: Routledge.

Said, E. W. (1978). *Orientalism.* New York: Vintage Press.

Sandos, J. A., & Burgess, L. E. (1998). The Hollywood Indian versus Native Americans: Tell them Willie Boy is here (1969). In P. C. Rollins & J. E. O'Connor (Eds.), *Hollywood's Indian: The portrayal of the Native American in film* (pp. 107–120). Lexington: University Press of Kentucky.

Saran, P. (1985). *The Asian Indian experience in the United States.* Cambridge, MA: Shenckman.

Saran, P., & Eames, E. (1980). *The new ethnics: Asian Indians in the United States.* New York: Praeger.

Sartre, J.-P. (1948). *Anti-semite and Jew.* New York: Schocken Books.

Sasaki, Y. (2000). Boku niha hito ni makenai mono ga aru soreha teashi ga nai koto [One advantage I have over others is that I have no arms and legs]. *Josei Seven* (December 3), 59–66.

Schlesinger, A. (1992). *The disuniting of America.* New York: Norton.

Shimamori, M. (1998). *Koukoku no hirointachi* [Heroines of advertisements]. Tokyo: Iwanami.

Shimizu, T. (1998). Shogaisha-koyo-sokushin-ho no bappon teki kaisei wo [A need for fundamental changes in Physically Handicapped Persons' Employment Promotion Law]. *Fukusi Rodo, 81,* 12–26.

Shoya, R., & Nakayama, T. (1997). *Korei zainichi kankoku-chosenjin* [The elderly Korean in Japan]. Tokyo: Ochanomizu Shobo.

Shukla, S. (1997). Building diaspora and nation: The 1991 cultural festival of India. *Cultural Studies, 11,* 296–315.

Siddle, R. (1999). Ainu history: An overview. In W. W. Fitzhugh & C. O. Dubreuil (Eds.), *Ainu: Spirit of a northern people* (pp. 67–73). Seattle: University of Washington Press.

Simmons, L. W. (1976). *Sun Chief: The autobiography of a Hopi Indian.* New Haven, CT: Yale University Press.

Smith, A. (1986). *The ethnic origin of nations.* Oxford: Basil Blackwell.

Smith, E. M. (1985). Ethnic minorities: Life stress, social support, and mental health issues. *Counseling Psychologist, 13,* 537–579.

Smith, M. L. (1997). The INS and the singular status of North American Indians. *American Indian Culture and Research Journal, 21,* 131–154.

Smith, P. (1997). *Japan: A reinterpretation.* New York: Random House.

Soldier, L. W. (1995). We must encourage the use of our language. In A. Hirschfelder (Ed.), *Native heritage: Personal accounts by American Indians 1790 to the present* (pp. 82–85). New York: Macmillan.

Solzhenitsyn, A. (1973/1997). *Gulag archipelago* (vol. 1) (W. Thomas, Trans.). Boulder, CO: Westview Press.

Sori-fu (1998). *Shogaishahakusho* [A disability white paper]. Tokyo: Sori-fu.

Spencer, H. (1877/1970). *Social statistics: The conditions essential to human happiness specified, and the first of them developed.* New York: Robert Schalkenbach Foundation.

Stark, W. (1963). *The fundamental forms of social thought.* New York: Fordham University Press.

Stull, D. D. (1978). Native American adaptation to an urban environment: The Papago of Tucson, Arizona. *Urban Anthropology, 7,* 117–135.

Sue, D. W., & Kirk, B. (1973). Differential characteristics of Japanese-American and Chinese-American college students. *Journal of Counseling Psychology, 20,* 142–148.

Sue, S. (1977). Community mental health services to minority groups: Some optimism, some pessimism. *American Psychologist, 32*, 616–624.

Sue, S., & Chin, R. (1983). The mental health of Chinese-American children: Stressors and resources. In G. Powell (Ed.), *The psychosocial development of minority group children* (pp. 385–397). New York: Brunner/Mazel.

Sue, S., Fujino, D., Hu, L., Takeuchi, D., & Zane, N. (1991). Community mental health services for ethnic minority groups: A test of the cultural responsiveness hypothesis. *Journal of Consulting and Clinical Psychology, 59*, 533–540.

Sugden, J. (1986). Early pan-Indianism: Tecumseh's tour of the Indian country, 1811–1812. *American Indian Quarterly, 10*, 273–304.

Szasz, M. C. (1988). *Indian education in the American colonies, 1607–1783*. Albuquerque: University of New Mexico Press.

Tafoya, T. (1995). The old ways teach us. In A. Hirschfelder (Ed.), *Native heritage: Personal accounts by American Indians 1790 to the present* (pp. 113–115). New York: Macmillan.

Tajfel, H. (1978). Intergroup behaviour: Group perspectives. In H. Tajfel & C. Fraser (Eds.), *Introducing social psychology: An analysis of individual reaction and response* (pp. 423–446). Middlesex, England: Penguin Books.

Takagi, H. (1994). Ainu minzoku he no dokaseisaku no seiritsu [Formation of assimilation policy onto the Ainu]. In R. Kenkyukai (Ed.), *Kokumin kokka wo tou* [Questioning nation state] (pp. 166–183). Tokyo: Aoki Shoten.

Takaki, R. (1989). *India in the West: South Asians in America*. New York: Chelsea House.

Takakura, S. (1939). *Ainu no tochi mondai* [Land issues of the Ainu]. Shakai seisaku jihou 230. Tokyo: Kyouhoukai.

Tamura, S. (1999). Ainu language: Features and relationships. In W. W. Fitzhugh & C. O. Dubreuil (Eds.), *Ainu: Spirit of a northern people* (pp. 57–65). Seattle: University of Washington Press.

Tan, A., Fujioka, Y., & Lucht, N. (1997). Native American stereotypes, TV portrayals, and personal contact. *Journalism and Mass Communication Quarterly, 74*, 265–284.

Tei, T. (1996, September). "Zainichi" no minzoku hiro [Ethnic fatigue of "Koreans in Japan"]. *Chuo Koron*, pp. 74–79.

Terada, S. (2002). *Identities of young Korean women in Japan: Hybridity as a challenge to multiple discrimination*. Unpublished master's thesis, International Christian University, Tokyo, Japan.

Töennies, F. (1957). *Community and society* (C. P. Loomis, Trans.). East Lansing: Michigan State University Press.

Tomita, T. (1989). *Hokkaido kyudojin ho to dozu ho: Hikakushiteki kokoromi* [The Hokkaido former aborigines protection act and the Dawes Act: A comparative historical perspective]. *Sapporo Gakuin Daigaku Jinbun Gakkai Kiyou, 45*, 5–21.

Tsuda, Y. (1986). *Language inequality and distortions*. Philadelphia: John Benjamin.

Tsunemoto, T. (1999). The Ainu sinpo: A new beginning. In W. W. Fitzhugh & C. O. Dubreuil (Eds.), *Ainu: Spirit of a northern people* (pp. 366–368). Seattle: University of Washington Press.

Uemura, H. (1992). *Sekai to Nippon no senjuminzoku* [World and Japanese indigenous people] (Iwanami Booklet 281). Tokyo: Iwanami.

Vega, W. A., Warheit, G., & Meinhardt, K. (1984). Marital disruption and the prevalence of depressive symptomatology among Anglos and Mexican Americans. *Journal of Marriage and Family, 46*, 817–824.

Wagatsuma, H., & Yoneyama, T. (1967). *Henkenn no kouzou* [Structures of prejudice]. Tokyo: Nihon Housou Kyoukai.

Watanabe, S. (1974). *Bunka no jidai* [Age of culture]. Tokyo: Bunshun Bunko.

Weber, M. (1920/1958). *The Protestant ethic and the spirit of capitalism* (T. Parsons, Trans.). New York: Scribner's.

West, C. (1993). *Race matters.* Boston: Beacon Press.

Wieder, D. L., & Pratt, S. (1990). On being a recognizable Indian among Indians. In D. Carbaugh (Ed.), *Cultural communication and intercultural contact* (pp. 45–64). Hillsdale: Lawrence Erlbaum.

Willems, N. (2000). Removing barriers. *Winds* (August), 29–30.

Williamson, J. (1994). *Decoding advertisements: Ideology and meaning in advertisements.* New York: Marion Boyars.

Wilson, T. P. (1985). *The underground reservation: Osage oil.* Lincoln: University of Nebraska Press.

Wittgenstein, L. (1953/2002). *Philosophical Investigations.* Cambridge, England: Blackwell.

Wolf, N. (1991). *The beauty myth: How images of beauty are used against women.* New York: William Morrow.

Wyss, H. E. (1999). Captivity and conversion: William Apess, Mary Jemison, and narratives of racial identity. *American Indian Quarterly, 23,* 63–82.

Yellow Bird, M. (1999). What we want to be called. *American Indian Quarterly, 23,* 1–21.

Ying, Y. (1995). Cultural orientation and psychological well-being in Chinese Americans. *American Journal of Community Psychology, 23,* 893–911.

Yoshino, K. (1992). *Cultural nationalism in contemporary Japan: A sociological enquiry.* London: Routledge.

Yoshino, K. (1997). *Bunka nashinarizumu no shakaigaku: Gendai nihon no aidentetei no yukue* [A sociology of cultural nationalism: Where modern Japanese identity goes]. Nagoya, Japan: Nagoya University Press.

Yu, K. & Kim, L. (1983). The growth and development of Korean-American children. In G. Powell (Ed.), *The psychosocial development of minority group children* (pp. 147–158). New York: Brunner/Mazel.

Yun, K. C. (2001). *"Zainichi" o ikiru towa* [To live as "Koreans in Japan"]. Tokyo: Heibonsha.

Zimmerman, M. E. (1996). The death of god at Auschwitz. In A. Milchman & A. Rosenberg (Eds.), *Martin Heidegger and the Holocaust* (pp. 246–260). New Jersey: Humanities Press.

Zola, I. K. (1991). Communication barriers between the able-bodied and the handicapped. In R. P. Marinelli & A. E. Dell Orto (Eds.), *The psychological and social impact of disability.* New York: Springer.

Name Index

Subject Index

Contributors

ARCHANA J. BHATT is Assistant Professor of Communication and Culture in the Rhetoric and Communication Studies Department at the University of Richmond. She has taught in India and in the Asian American Studies and Speech Communication Departments of California State University, Fullerton. Her areas of research interests are intercultural communication, gender and feminist studies, and interpersonal communication. Specifically she has been investigating diasporic phenomena, especially those pertaining to South Asian populations throughout the United States and Canada. After the terrorist bombings of the World Trade Center towers on September 11, 2001, she was drafted by several community-based organizations in the Los Angeles area to speak about cultural diversity and multiculturalism and the need for calm and acceptance of minority groups living in the United States. She is currently the second vice chair and program planner for the Feminist and Women's Studies Division and the third vice chair of the Asian/Pacific American Studies Division of the National Communication Association.

JUNG MIN CHOI is Associate Professor of Sociology at Barry University in Miami Shores, Florida. His areas of interest are race relations and postmodern theory. He has published numerous articles and book chapters and has coauthored several books on race relations.

CHI-AH CHUN is an Assistant Professor in the Department of Psychology at California State University, Long Beach. She received her doctorate degree in Clinical Psychology at UCLA and her postdoctoral training in health services research at the VA Palo Alto Health Care System and Stanford University

School of Medicine. Her research focuses on identifying the extent of cultural influences on several components of the stress process in Asian Americans: (1) coping with stress, (2) manifestations of psychological distress, and (3) mental health treatment and services. Currently, she is a principal investigator on a psychiatric epidemiological study of Cambodian refugees funded by the National Institute of Mental Health and conducted by the RAND Corporation.

LUIGI ESPOSITO is Assistant Professor of Sociology at Barry University, Miami Shores, Florida. His main areas of interest are sociological theory and race relations. His most recent work is related to the development of a global ethic in terms of the globalization process.

RICHIKO IKEDA is Associate Professor at the International Christian University, Tokyo, and Ombudsman for Mitaka City. She is coeditor of the *Journal of Intercultural Communication* and Deputy Director of Academic Affairs of the Communication Association of Japan. She is coauthor of *Ibunka Komyunikeshon Nyumon* [Introduction to intercultural communication] and coauthor of *Sekushuaru Harasumento* [Sexual harassment, new edition] as well as numerous articles and essays in Japanese and English.

MASAKO ISA is Associate Professor of the Communication and Director of the International Communications Program at the University of Okinawa. Her most recent works include *Josei no kikoku tekiou mondai no kenkyu* [A study of the social-cultural reintegration of women] and *Tabunka shakai to ibunka komyunike-shon* [Multicultural society and intercultural communication]. The high quality of her research has been recognized and supported by the Ministry of Education in Japan.

MIHO IWAKUMA researches intercultural communication, communication and people with disabilities, and health communication. Her articles have appeared in both Japanese and English journals.

LONNIE JOHNSON JR. teaches in the Department of Communication at Langston University. He is currently working on his doctorate at the University of Oklahoma. His research includes intercultural communication with an emphasis on race relations and cross-cultural comparison.

ERIC MARK KRAMER is Associate Professor of Communication at the University of Oklahoma. He is a member of editorial boards for many journals and has written several books and articles, including *Modern/Postmodern: Off the Beaten Path of Antimodernism* and *Postmodernism and Race*. He regularly lectures at institutions and universities around the world, including in Germany, England, Taiwan, Bulgaria, Japan, Belgium, Canada, and so on. His primary areas of research interests are intercultural, mass, and international communications. He is coauthor of a best-selling intercultural textbook in Japan and has team-taught seminars with such luminaries as Maya Angelou, Erwin Knoll, and Kurt Vonnegut.

PHILIP LUJAN is Associate Professor in the Department of Communications and has been Director of Native American Studies at the University of Oklahoma for over three decades. He is also Chief District Judge for the Court of Indian Offenses, Western Oklahoma, as well as Chief District Judge for the Cheyenne, Arapaho, Fox, and Potawatomie Nations. He is a Kiowa/Taos, enrolled Kiowa.

CHARLTON D. McILWAIN is Assistant Professor/Faculty Fellow in the Department of Culture and Communication at New York University. His research interests include African American culture, intercultural communication, and philosophy of communication.

MASAZUMI MARUYAMA is Associate Professor of International Communication at the Faculty of Economics, Nagasaki University, Japan. He earned a doctoral degree in communication from the University of Oklahoma in 1998 with majors in intercultural and international communication. His major publications include "Ibunka komyunikeshon wo saikou suru" [Rethinking intercultural communication studies: beyond "cultural nationalism"], "External Variable and Systems Approaches in Nonverbal Communication Studies: Comparisons," and "How Is Society Possible? Two Approaches: Functional-Structural Approach and Ethnomethodology."

ALGIS MICKUNAS is Professor Emeritus of Philosophy at Ohio University. He is author of over one hundred articles and book chapters and over twenty books. His primary areas of interest include contemporary European (East and West) philosophy, phenomenology, semiotics, and comparative civilizations. He is a member of the board of directors of the Center for Advanced Research in Phenomenology, founder of the International Circle of Husserl Scholars, founder of the International Circle of Merleau-Ponty Scholars, founder of West-Japan phenomenology cooperation, and founder of the International Center for Studies in Globalization. He is also coeditor of the *Encyclopedia of Phenomenology*. Since 1990, he has been a regular lecturer in Lithuania at the Universities of Vilnius, Kaunas, and Klaipeda on topics of political philosophy, nationalisms, semiotics, and methods of comparative studies of civilizations.

EUNGJUN MIN is Associate Professor of Communication at Rhode Island College. He is President of the Korean American Communication Association. He has published numerous articles and books on cultural approaches to studying media representations, their construction, and their impact on culture. He has a book forthcoming about Korean cinema.

JOHN W. MURPHY is Professor of Sociology at the University of Miami, Coral Gables, Florida. He is author of more than a dozen books on symbolic violence and democracy and over fifty journal articles. His interests are sociological theory, social philosophy, and globalization. His most recent work relates to unraveling the negative effects of the market on Central America.

RACHAEL RAINWATER-McCLURE is a doctoral student in communication at the University of Oklahoma. She received her bachelor's and master's degrees from Abilene Christian University, Abilene, Texas. Her interest in intercultural communication was developed during the eight years she lived and worked among the people of Brazil. Her travels and experiences with various ethnic groups have taught her to value the unique contributions each group and each individual have to offer our world.

WESLYNN REED is a minority woman and graduate student in communication at the University of Oklahoma. Her interests are gender studies and intercultural communication.

KAROLA [M. SCHWARTZ] is currently a doctoral student at the University of Oklahoma. She has degrees from Northwestern University and the University of Texas and has published numerous book chapters and articles. She is a member of the Osage Nation. Her primary research area is in intercultural communication, with a particular interest in Native American studies. Her other areas of scholarship include interpersonal communication, social theory, film studies, technology and human society, political rhetoric, and small group communication.

CPSIA information can be obtained
at www.ICGtesting.com
Printed in the USA
LVOW09*1105250317
528383LV00024B/168/P